T0392250

Your Money
Is
Your Business!

By
Stephen Freeman

authorHOUSE

AuthorHouse™
1663 Liberty Drive
Bloomington, IN 47403
www.authorhouse.com
Phone: 1 (800) 839-8640

Published by AuthorHouse 08/21/2017

ISBN: 978-1-5246-6916-4 (sc)
ISBN: 978-1-5246-6915-7 (e)

Library of Congress Control Number: 2017901907

Print information available on the last page.

This book is printed on acid-free paper.

Because of the dynamic nature of the Internet, any web addresses or links contained in this book may have changed
since publication and may no longer be valid. The views expressed in this work are solely those of the author and
do not necessarily reflect the views of the publisher, and the publisher hereby disclaims any responsibility for them.

(www.ymiyb.com)

The website for this book at (www.ymiyb.com) contains formats you can use to begin preparing a current financial
statement, personal business plan, and a projected financial statement budget. You will be reading about these
financial management tools in Chapter 4. The website also contains other information you might find useful.

Dedication

To my father Stanley Whitman Freeman, Jr., for the gift of books.

To my mother Lyllian Freeman, for the gift of words.

To my sister Judith Freeman McSweeney DeVan, may her eternal light shine from Monarch Bay.

To my sister Barbara Freeman Zimmerman, for the gift of her love at work in the world.

Table of Contents

Chapter 1. Why you should read this book

5 Good reasons to read this book

1. Many ideas to think about and suggestions to consider that might help you:
- Increase your income.
- Reduce your spending.
- Increase your savings.
- Improve your investment management.
- Focus your thinking on how to live a satisfying life in pursuit of your dreams.

2. It is an introduction to the universe of financial literacy resources that are available to you – advisors, classes, books, the internet, etc. If you were to read no other book, I would urge you to read *The Way to Wealth* written by Benjamin Franklin in 1757 – for my money, the granddaddy of all personal financial management self-help books. It is staggering how much wise advice Franklin crammed into so few pages in such an entertaining and understandable way. Financial advisors today still preach most of what Franklin wrote all those years go.

3. It's honest.
- The book doesn't dodge the fact that improving the way you manage the money in your life is likely to require you to change some of your behavior - and changing behavioral habits can be tough. Think about all the New Years' resolutions that are made in December and broken in January.
- It doesn't try to sell a quick and easy "miracle" way to wealth. There is no miracle way.

4. It can be used as a tool that might help make it easier to talk with your family members about money.
- Many people find it tough to talk with family members about money, especially when they think family members are having a negative impact on their money.
- Having a non-family member like me raise money management issues that lots of other families are also confronting can take some of the sting out of you raising these potentially touchy issues.
- Consider asking family members to read the book and then have a family meeting to discuss those parts that you think are relevant to your family.
- If you are finding it particularly tough to talk with a family member about a specific issue, consider reading relevant pages together as a means to help stimulate a healthy conversation and keep the conversation from seeming threatening or annoying.

5. It's likely to be one of the easiest to understand books about money management that you will be able to find. I tried to write as if I were talking to family and friends.

DISCLAIMER: the only professional license I hold is that of a property and casualty insurance agent. I am NOT certified or licensed as a personal financial planning professional or life coach. I am NOT certified or licensed to offer you advice as to how to manage your money, your career, or your life. Discuss the ideas and suggestions in this book with appropriately licensed professionals in the fields of study we touch upon, such as financial planning, career management, accounting, law, and family counseling. *Question everything said in this book.* Think for yourself. Make well-informed and well-reasoned decisions about what is best for you to do in your life based upon all the unique circumstances of your life. *Pay close attention to Chapters 7and 8 regarding decision making and gathering decision making information.*

Reasons I wrote the book

Encourage readers to help themselves improve the way they manage their money by:
- Managing their money as if it was a business.
- Preparing written business plans and projected financial statement budgets.
- Developing and using a formal decision making process.
- Learning and adopting the best practices of successful business managers.
- Heeding the consensus financial management advice of the financial service industries.
- Understanding that the amount of money in their lives is mostly a function of lifestyle choices they make.
- Realizing that if they feel they are drowning in financial despair there are professional financial lifeguards who would jump in to help save them if they just called out for help.

My hope is that you will be able to use the book to help improve the way you manage your money.

My dream is that enough people use the book to help improve the way they manage their money that their actions combine to make a noticeable contribution to managing the serious financial challenges we all face together as a nation. Our financial challenges include:

1. *Too many people are suffering through financial crises* such as:
- Buried under a mountain of debt and distraught about their ability to dig out from under.
- Out of work and having a real hard time finding a new job.
- Trying to figure out how to pay big medical bills.
- Getting closer and closer to retirement age and thinking that they haven't saved enough money to afford a comfortable retirement.

2. *Even more people are worried enough about money that their worry is affecting their health.*

3. <u>*Many more voters need a more functional knowledge of the fundamentals of prudent financial management if we are to avert a national financial catastrophe that hurts us all*</u>. A number of pressing issues will require financially savvy government leadership and mind-boggling amounts of money in order to deal with them effectively. The greater the contribution that each of us as a financially savvy voter makes toward dealing with these massively expensive issues, the better the quality of life each of us will have in the future. These issues include:
- Developing an economically sustainable plan to finance programs such as Social Security, Medicare and Medicaid far out into the future.
- National security in this new era of physical and cyber terrorism.
- Infrastructure maintenance and improvements: aging roads and bridges (how quickly we forget after a bridge collapses or a section of elevated highway drops); mass transit systems; water and sewer treatment plants; electricity grid; etc. *Research the trillions of dollars that the American Society of Civil Engineers says we should be budgeting to spend on infrastructure, and the far too little money we are actually budgeting to spend.*
- Escalating rate of global economic competition that requires us to develop a viable plan for retaining our current jobs and creating new jobs (e.g. globally competitive tax code).
- Education and training of the American workforce for the type of well-paying jobs (along with the childcare and transportation services that many people who want to work will need in order to get to work) that enable the financially secure population we need in order to (a) maintain a healthy economy in which we each can maximize our prosperity,

and (b) avert social unrest caused by too many people feeling there is too much income inequality and too little opportunity for them to get well-paying jobs.

- *Availability of fresh water*: increasing demand from an increasing population for predictably available fresh water. Learn about depletion of major underground aquifers, impact of droughts, disputes among states over use of water from rivers and lakes, and costs of desalinization plants (e.g. acquiring sites for plants, construction costs).
- Paying the costs of environmental degradation: pollution of air, water and land resources; destruction of life sustaining forests; loss of biodiversity; impact on the ocean biosphere of global fishery depletion, acidification, and accumulating masses of plastic trash.
- Managing economic risks of climate change, e.g. drought, severe storms, rising sea level.
- Developing environmentally sustainable and affordable alternative energy sources as fossil fuel supplies are being depleted and global demand for fossil fuel is accelerating.

Write a book that readers will actually USE to help themselves improve the way they manage the money in their lives. Books being available and books being used effectively are two entirely different things. Many, many books on the market offer prudent advice about how to manage our personal financial affairs. But not nearly enough people are reading those books and using that advice. As the saying goes, "you can lead a horse to water but you can't make him drink". This is my shot at motivating people to seek out and use the good advice offered to us by financial service professionals in those books (and websites, podcasts, blogs, etc.).

Please don't be intimidated by the length of the book. I tried to lay out my thoughts and suggestions in 18 chapters that flow together as smoothly as I could link them, while also enabling you to read one chapter, one section within a chapter, or one individual page and get something useful out of it. Think of the book as a soup to nuts buffet of suggestions regarding money management. You can try little tastes of a few buffet items, and if you like those tastes, come back again as often as your heart desires to find more suggestions you would like to try.

Promote universal financial literacy classes in our schools.
- The business of governing ourselves requires tax dollars to pay for the government services we collectively decide we want. *The greater the financial literacy of voters and elected representative alike, the better the decisions we can make about the government services we want and about how we will pay for the services we want*.
- As the industrial revolution has evolved into the technology revolution, the United States has come to realize the economic value of universal education for training our country's human resources (learn about the history of public education).
- The time has come for every publicly funded high school to require a class in the fundamentals of personal financial management to supplement the other life skill classes we think are important to teach - reading, writing, and arithmetic, etc.
- The time has also come for every publicly funded college to require that all students - not just business majors – take a follow-up class on the prudent financial management of government (local, state and federal) that enables students to become financially savvy voters who elect financially savvy government officials who make financially savvy decisions that provide a vibrant economy in which we can all prosper far into the future.
- If you agree that school age people should have the benefit of a good education in the fundamentals of personal financial management, please use this book as a conversation starter with your local school leaders and your elected government representatives about requiring mandatory financial literacy classes in the schools you fund with your tax dollars.

What's in it for you?

The book offers you:
- *The idea* that treating your money as a business is likely to help you improve your financial management performance.
- *A framework* upon which you can build a personal business plan and a projected financial statement budget that help guide you toward making your dreams come true.
- *An introduction* to a broad range of subjects about which you should learn at least a little if you want to become the best money manager you have the capability to become.

The book is meant to be:
- <u>*A financial literacy primer that motivates you to embark on a lifelong journey of continuous continuing education*</u> - a "McGuffey's Reader" of business and finance that leads you into a progressively deeper study of business and financial management.
- <u>*A reference book that you can use over and over again*</u> <u>as you would use a dictionary</u>. It is not meant to be read once and then put back on a shelf to gather dust.
    - o It's organized to be a useful learning tool. You can use it like a textbook.
    - o You might skim it and zero in on specific topics that grab your interest.
    - o Or, you might read it from cover to cover to get an overview of the breadth and depth of the subject of financial management, and then come back to re-read a specific paragraph, section, or chapter when you think it would be useful.
    - o <u>The expanded outline format is intended to emphasize key ideas the first time you read the book, and make it easy for you to find those ideas when you come back to re-read it</u>. The outline format also fits in with my concept of pitching you a business proposal.
    - o Chapters are organized by functional utility.
    - o **Bold** and *italic* letters and <u>underlines</u> are used to help you spot key points.
- A conversation starter you can share with your family, friends, elected government representatives, and local school leaders in order to help stimulate a national discussion about how we can improve the level of financial literacy in our country.

The book is NOT:
- A comprehensive guide for managing your money successfully. No book could, or should even try to, provide such a comprehensive guide.
- *A "one size fits all" set of specific instructions* to follow step by step. It simply offers ideas to consider and discuss with appropriate professional service providers.

Condensed compilation of:
- *Best practices* of successful business people I have known. Most successful business people say and do most of the things compiled here.
- *Generally accepted advice* offered by the financial service industries and business consultants. Most of the ideas are so commonly held by so many people that I can't remember when, where, or from whom I heard them first.
- *Common threads that run though most prudent business and personal financial management books*: there isn't much new that prudent authors can say – the same things tend to be said, just in different ways.
- *Folk wisdom* in the form of adages, axioms, and proverbs that have been passed down from generation to generation by parents, community elders, religious leaders, and old books of wisdom. I tried to put "quotation marks" around this folk wisdom.
- Ideas that stuck in my brain after years of taking classes, attending seminars, and reading.

The book:
- Condenses as much information as I thought most readers could digest in one book.
- Compiles that information in chapters that flow together as smoothly as I could make them flow.

Personal interpretations of business terms, principles, and theories that I have studied in school or otherwise learned about. My interpretations have worked for me in my business; however, *the further I stray from textbook text, the greater the risk of my misinterpretation or error. I encourage constructive critique* to help me revise future editions of this book.

Some ideas are my own - I think - at least I don't recall seeing or hearing them anywhere else. However, most "new", original ideas aren't really all that new. They are built upon a foundation of the ideas of other people. Our brains absorb the ideas of others that we read and hear, and then rework or synthesize those ideas into our own "new" ideas. This book gave me the opportunity to write down how my brain has reworked and synthesized other people's ideas that I have come to know.

Language that is as plain and simple as I could make it.
- I tried to use plain and simple "layman's" language to explain business and financial management terms, principles, and theories.
- My mother used to say "eschew obfuscation" - avoid confusing people by obscuring what you are saying with fancy jargon and extra words. I hope Mom would say I did.
- Most of the fundamentals of business management and financial management are pretty easy to understand. They are rooted in common sense and the ways people have learned to live with each other and do business with each other through the ages. I tried to reflect this idea in my writing.

Lots of sports analogies because:
- There are so many commonalities in the fundamentals of sports and business - well thought game plans, dedication to practice, rules of good conduct, teamwork, etc.
- Sports analogies tie in with my belief that sports and business are just two of the many smaller games we play during the grand game of life.

The book is as gender neutral as I could make it. The women in my life have given me an appreciation for how male oriented so much of the business and financial worlds remain today. With that in mind, and the fact that money doesn't know male from female, the chapters alternate between using the masculine words he and his and the feminine words she and her (Chapter 1 uses "she and her", Chapter 2 uses "he and his", and so forth).

Repetition: many ideas are repeated in different places for two reasons:
- Repetition helps us humans learn new things and remember what we have learned.
- Many ideas are inextricably linked to many subjects – they couldn't be restricted to just one place in the book, e.g. using common sense and controlling emotions apply to just about every aspect of business and financial management. Therefore we talk about common sense and controlling emotions in many places throughout the book.

<u>Key point "take aways"</u>

Choosing a few key points that I hope you take away from this book is like picking a favorite child. There are so many important and inter-related factors that contribute to successful money management that it is hard to pick just a few points to highlight as "key". *Like each child in a family, each point is special in its own way, and the family of financial management wouldn't be the same without it.*

That said, here are a few key points I think are especially important for you to take away and use:
- *Don't try to use every single suggestion in this book.* Let the unique circumstances of your life, and your satisfaction with your management of your money, guide you toward the suggestions you decide to try. Don't micro-manage your life.
- Accept responsibility for your financial well-being.
- Take charge of your financial destiny by thinking of yourself as the president of your own financial management company and managing your money as a business.
- Use a business planning and projected financial statement budgeting process.
- Use a formal decision making process to make well-informed, well-reasoned decisions.
- Surround yourself with good people who are good influences on you and your money.
- There is more to life than money.
- Plan a career path that leads you toward doing what you love to do.
- Get happy and stay happy.
- Be a nice, civil person. Treat everyone with dignity, respect, and fairness.
- Don't fight change. Anticipate it, adapt to it, and seek opportunities in it.
- "Take the high road" when making decisions. Seek win/win decisions. Share the wealth.
- Develop a reputation for being trustworthy and honest.
- Save up cash reserves that are prudent for your unique situation in life.
- Avoid as much debt as possible.
- Buy best value not lowest price.
- Follow consensus advice offered by the financial service industries.
- Hire professional financial management help.
- Have a Plan B.
- Make a lifelong commitment to continuous continuing education.
- Learn how professional financial service providers advise us to:
  o Manage a bank checking account; reconcile a checkbook with the monthly statements provided by banks; use the online financial management tools provided by banks.
  o Manage a credit card account; reconcile personal records of purchases with the purchases listed on monthly credit card statements; use the online financial management tools provided by credit card issuers.
- *Adopt a scientific approach to gathering and evaluating the information upon which you base your decisions - especially decisions that might have significant impact on your life or your money (see Chapter 8).*
  o *Question the validity of all the information, ideas, suggestions, and advice you gather – including everything written in this book.*
  o *Test the validity of information by seeking confirmation from multiple sources, e.g. other experts in the field of study, people you know who you think are well-informed about the matter at hand, the internet.*
  o *Don't blindly accept everything you are told as being the gospel truth. Think for yourself.*

So, what qualifies me to write this book?

A career in the surety bond industry spanning more than 40 years:
- Learning from some of the best business minds in the country in real life situations: company presidents, financial officers, bankers, financial advisors, CPA's, attorneys, consultants, colleagues, and other people who are really good at what they do.
- Gaining continuous continuing education through analyzing and evaluating the financial positions and management practices of many, many companies and company owners.
- Explaining to clients, in terms they understand, how surety company underwriters evaluate the credit worthiness of their companies.
- Explaining to surety company underwriters, in terms they understand, why my clients deserve surety credit.
- Offering observations, opinions, and surety advice to clients.

Experience in varied work and volunteer positions enabled me to learn about business and financial management from different perspectives:
- *Military*: officer in the United States Army.
- *Non-profit organization employee*: district executive of the Boy Scouts of America.
- *Non-profit organization volunteer*: officer and director positions in a number of trade associations; church board of trustees; officer of homeowners' associations; coach of recreation league and youth sports teams.
- *Business*: surety bond underwriter; surety company branch manager; partner in an insurance agency; officer of M&T Insurance Agency, a subsidiary of M&T Bank.

Experience as a parent helped me learn and re-learn valuable money management lessons. Explaining the fundamentals of business and financial management to my children helped me learn to talk about business and financial matters in terms they understood.

Experience as a teacher: teachers have the opportunity to learn a lot from preparing lesson plans and class presentations, students' comments on class material, information students share in class that they have learned from their life experiences, and trying to answer students' insightful questions. I have taught classes such as:
- Junior Achievement classes at the middle school and high school levels.
- Career related classes and seminars on business management and business finance.

Experience as a mentor in the Microenterprise Mentoring Program of Community Ministries of Montgomery County, Maryland.

Lessons learned from my mistakes, and mistakes I have seen other people make: there is a pretty good chance that I have either made most of the financial management mistakes you could make or observed other people make those mistakes.

Formal education
- Bachelor of Science, Business Administration, University of New Hampshire
- Master of Science, University of Baltimore
- United States Army: Infantry Officers Basic Class and Psychological Operations School
- Boy Scouts of America: District Executive Training School
- Aetna Casualty and Surety Company: Bond Trainee Program
- Continuous continuing education classes and seminars

Chapter 2. Your Money Is Your Business!

Your money is your business!

Your money is your b-u-s-i-n-e-s-s.

"Your business" has two meanings in this book - a "double entendre".
- Meaning 1: you have the right to decide what you do or don't do about the money in your life, and the responsibility to live with the outcome of your decisions. It's your business what you do with your money.
- Meaning 2: manage your money as if you were the owner and president of your own personal financial management company.

Your money is yours:

- *To take care of and grow*; or

- *To NOT take care of, and quite likely lose* - your choice.

Your money does NOT belong to:
- Your bank.
- The financial institutions managing your investment and retirement savings accounts.
- A smooth talking brother-in-law, an all knowing Uncle Harry, or any other family member who seems to think your money is just an extension of his money and that he can tell you what do with your money.
- A pushy neighbor who tries to make you think that your money should be pooled in with his money to be invested in his get-rich-quick scheme.

Treating your money as a business will help you:

- Earn as much money as you have the determination and time to earn.

- Save as much money as you have the desire and self-discipline to save.

- Maximize the wealth you amass over the course of your life.

- Minimize your risk of losing any of your money.

- Make your dreams come true by using a practical "eyes on the sky, feet on the ground" approach to life in general and to money management in particular.

<u>Why your money IS your business</u>

You already ARE in business, even if you don't yet think you are.

Business is the just the name we give to the everyday behavior of exchanging our money for the goods and services of other people (and companies) so that each person gets something that he wants from the other person.

You are in business every time you:
- Go to work and sell your services to your employer.
- Buy something from a store.
- Pay a bill for electricity, gas, water, or telecom services supplied to you.
- "Lend" a dollar to a bank by depositing that dollar into a savings account and the bank pays you interest income in return for the right to re-lend your money to someone else for a higher interest rate.
- Contribute a dollar to a religious or charitable organization to help fund its business operations, and they supply you the satisfaction of doing good for others.
- Contribute a dollar to a political candidate in return for his campaign promise to supply you with the government services you want at a tax "price" you are willing to pay.
- Invest a dollar in your retirement account and the financial institution managing your account charges you a fee for their services.

People are continuously attempting to do business with you in order to get some of your money.
- People set up business organizations staffed by skilled workers and marketing professionals for the purpose of attracting your business.
- Think about all the advertising you see and the solicitations you receive for financial contributions.
- All sorts of people compete with each other each day to get you to spend some of your money with them.

The <u>capitalist</u> <u>democracy</u> in which you live is based upon self-reliance, private ownership of property (money), and people using their money to buy things they don't make or do for themselves.
- The founders of the United States intended for men (inequality goes way back) to be self-reliant – to take care of themselves and provide for their families' financial well-being.
- Learn what the leaders of the English colonies in America thought about self-reliance:
    - o John Smith is said to have told the colonists of Jamestown to heed a passage from the Biblical book Thessalonians 3:10 "… if any would not work, neither should he eat".
    - o Plymouth Colony's Mayflower Compact: the colonists switched from the communal farming model they had initially adopted to a self-reliance model that required each family to grow its own food on its own farming plot because some people had been 'slacking off" and "not pulling their own weight".
    - o Puritan work ethic.

Our <u>capitalist</u> economy provides each of us:
- The right to earn as much money as he can earn legally; and
- the right to spend his money any way he wants; and
- the right to amass as much wealth as he desires;

- with the minimum amount of government involvement needed to protect his rights;
- and the responsibility to live with the consequences of his decisions.

Our <u>democracy</u> provides each of us:

- The right to do whatever we want to do so long as what we don't infringe upon the rights of others.
- The right to elect fellow citizens as our representatives to manage the business of governing ourselves.
- The responsibility to live with the laws and tax codes put in place by our fellow citizens who we elect as our government representatives.

Laws have been established to make clear that you own your money and that you are responsible for managing your money.

- *Laws protect everyone's rights to*:
  - o Own private property, and to protect ourselves if anyone should try to take any of our property away from us without our consent.
  - o Buy any asset we so desire, in any location, from any vendor.
  - o Invest our money in any way we so desire.
- Laws protect your money from illegal and negligent activity on the part of financial service professionals to whom you cede care, custody and control of your money in service agreements or contracts, but NOT from:
  - o Losing money because of risks inherent in the work typically done by a professional in his industry.
  - o The actions of financial service professionals that turn out to have been just plain dumb, ill-informed, or overly aggressive - but not to the point of being negligent.
- Laws say you are responsible for making prudent decisions about the people to whom you cede care, custody and control of your money in service agreements or contracts.

Nobody has a legal obligation to manage your money for you until you cede care, custody and control of your money in a service agreement or contract.

You were destined to become president of your business the day you were born in a capitalist democracy (or became a naturalized citizen).

<u>Why your money SHOULD BE your business</u>

Treating your money as a business will provide you:
- *A business mindset* that:
    - Enables you to organize in your mind all the assets that you own, all the money that you owe to others, all of your income each year, and all of your expenses as components of one manageable entity - your company.
    - Focuses your mind on proactive management of your money.
    - Provides an inner sense of personal empowerment to control your destiny.
    - Helps cement in your conscious mind the ownership of, and responsibility for, your money.
- *A business framework for*:
    - Thinking of your money as being a financial management company.
    - Managing the money connected to the different parts of your lifestyle along the same lines as presidents of other companies manage the different divisions, departments, and work groups within their companies.
    - Considering the people with whom you have close relationships to be your personal business team.
    - Adopting "best practices" of successful business managers and money managers.
    - Using the principles and theories of business management and financial management that have helped countless business people succeed.

"Owning responsibility" for any part of his life that a person wants to improve is a common thread that runs through virtually all self-improvement programs, books, and counseling.
- You must "own" up to the idea that you are responsible for whatever you have been choosing to do or not do with the money in your life.
- You must "own" up to the idea that you are the only person who can improve your money management behavior. Nobody can do it for you.

Money management is just one of the many threads that must be woven into the fabric of the lifestyles we choose. Just as the threads of healthy nutrition habits and healthy exercise habits must be woven into the fabric of our lifestyles if we are to attain and maintain the best possible physical health, so too healthy money management habits must be woven into the fabric of our lifestyles if we are to attain and maintain the best possible fiscal health (fiscal being a synonym for the word financial in the business world). Consider the following:
- *A majority of nutrition professionals* agree on the basics of food and drink that we should blend into a healthy, sustainable diet lifestyle, e.g. vegetables, fruits, whole grains, beans, lean meat, fish, plenty of water. A healthy diet is not just a miracle new diet system or new food supplement that is tried for a few weeks and then abandoned.
- *A majority of medical professionals* agree on the basics of exercise that we should blend into a healthy, sustainable exercise lifestyle, e.g. aerobic training for cardio-vascular efficiency, weight resistance exercises for muscle strength and bone density, stretching for flexibility, exercises that help us with our balance, and getting enough sleep. A healthy exercise regimen is not just a miracle new piece of exercise equipment that gets used a few times and is then relegated to a closet or basement to gather dust.
- *A majority of financial planning professionals* agree on the basics of money management that we should blend into a healthy, sustainable fiscal lifestyle, e.g. preparing financial plans and budgets, living below our means, maximizing savings as early as possible in life in order to harness the power of compounding, diversification of investments. A healthy fiscal management lifestyle is neither making a New Year's resolution each

December to spend less and save more (which is then forgotten by the end of each January) nor a new miracle system being hyped by some financial guru.

Lifestyle threads that influence how much money you bring into your life include:
- The schools you have attended and the things you learned while in school.
- The geographic location in which you live and the vibrancy of the economy in that location.
- The job you have chosen, or resigned yourself to accept for the time being.
- The people with whom you work and the quality of their work (people whose work impacts your work, which in turn influences your pay raises and promotions).

Lifestyle threads that influence how much money you spend include:
- Family members living with you who directly influence your food, housing, clothing, and education expenses.
- The lifestyle to which you grew accustomed to living while you were growing up.
- The economic cost of living where you live influences your cost of housing and the prices of the things that you buy locally in your community.
- Type and size of your home influence your heating, cooling, lighting, maintenance and repair, furnishings, and other household expenses.
- Friends who influence the amount of money you spend buying things like they buy and doing things that they do (especially if you get caught up in the game of "trying to keep up with the Joneses").
- Marketing and advertising to which you expose yourself in what you choose to read, watch, and do.

Nobody can be as motivated to take care of your money as you should be motivated to take care of it.
- It's human nature for each of us to think of ourselves first. That makes each person Number 1 to himself. You're Number 2 to everybody else.
- Each of us has an internal survival instinct that can and should drive us to take good care of ourselves and take good care of the money we need to finance taking good care of ourselves. No financial advisor, no banker, no stockbroker, no life insurance agent, nobody, can have the same internal drive that you have - because your life is not their life, and your money is not their money.
- No financial service professional is as dependent on your money for <u>his</u> future financial security as you are dependent on your money for <u>your</u> future financial security. Financial professionals spread their financial risk by having many clients. You only have you.

Nobody can know as much about you, and what you really want in life, as you know.
- *It's tough for each of us to be honest with ourselves about money* – what we truly think and feel about money, our real financial objectives, and the risk we are actually willing to accept in investing our money. *It's even tougher for us to open up and tell other people the whole truth about what we actually think and feel about money.* Financial advisors I know tell me that many of their clients don't reveal all their assets and/or other information about themselves and their lives that would have a bearing on the advice those financial advisors provide to their clients.
- *It is virtually impossible for even the most skilled and experienced financial advisor to get inside a client's head to know everything the client is really thinking and feeling.* Even the best financial advisor who is part psychologist, part mind reader, and part

Sherlock Holmes sifting through clues you provide to him, could not know as much about you as you know.

- You only have one person to get to know down deep, to keep track of, and to take care of – you. Financial advisors have a number of clients that they must get to know, keep track of, and take care of. You are just one of many clients.
- There are too many different factors that come into play in your unique lifestyle for any other person to have as good an awareness and understanding of all those factors as you can have: your objectives, intensity of family or peer pressure, your feelings about spending today versus saving for tomorrow, your risk tolerance, your knowledge of all the assets you own, your potential future income, and on and on.

It makes good common sense to proactively manage and protect your money in our imperfect world.
- Everybody makes mistakes, and other peoples' mistakes can hurt your pocketbook.
- People don't always do what they are supposed to do, nor do what they say they will do.
- With most other people thinking about themselves first, they may not be thinking as much as they should about how their actions might cause you financial harm.
- Some people are just plain crooked and out to get your money.
- Unexpected stuff can happen pretty quickly – employers can go out of business overnight, recessions can seem to come out of nowhere (especially to the unobservant), and investment bubbles burst.

The "Great Recession" of the late 2000's gave us classic examples of why we each should do all that we can do to protect our own money.
- Corporate managers who thought more about how to increase their own compensation than they thought about the best interests of their customers and investors (you and me).
- Boards of directors who didn't provide the management oversight that they should have.
- Regulators who didn't regulate as they should have.
- Relatively new financial products were created that not enough people fully understood.
- Too many of us went along for the joy ride without asking enough questions about what was supporting a financial house of cards.

"There are no free rides". If we want to achieve a significant measure of financial well-being we need to take control of our money and proactively work to achieve that financial well-being.

Capitalist democracy governments and charitable organizations are service businesses.
- Capitalist democracy governments are in the business of maintaining social order among their citizens and providing for protection of the lives and private property of citizens.
- Charitable organizations are in the business of providing help to people who need help.
- Being service businesses, capitalist democracy governments and charitable organizations must generate enough revenue (money) from some people in order to pay the expenses of providing financial assistance services to other people - for each person who receives financial assistance other people must part with some of their money to pay for that assistance.
- It is impossible for government and charitable organizations to pay for all the financial needs of all the people in a capitalist democracy.
- Learn about various financial assistance programs that are available to people where you live, why those programs came into being, and what they are designed to do. Also learn about well-informed, well-reasoned critiques of those programs.

As a friend quoted her mother "the best place to find a helping hand is at the end of your arm".

You put in all the time and hard work that was needed to earn your money. It's only fair that you should get to manage your money any way you choose.

And maybe most important of all, it is likely to make you feel good to think about yourself as president of your own business, and to know that you are working toward making your dreams come true.

Chapter 3. Create Your Own Business School

Create your own business school - in your head. Give it a name you will enjoy visualizing.
- As president of your personal financial management company, send yourself to business school to learn all you can about how to manage your business - your money.
- This chapter suggests some introductory classes to include in your business school curriculum, and a few key topics to study in each class. You can decide what subjects to study and when to study them.
- *Become a career student.* Take class after class without ever graduating. Nobody has the brain power to cram all the potentially useful information that is available into one semester, or four years, or any other artificial time constraint – too much to learn, and too little time to learn it. Seek to learn something new every day.
- *Have fun.* Let the joy of learning guide you from subject to subject, from formal class to self-study, from one-on-one conversations with smart people to the vast learning resources of the internet. After you learn something, let that new knowledge lead you to learn about something else that grabs your interest, which in turn leads you to learn about something else, and on, and on. *The more fun you have learning, the more motivated you are likely to be to keep on learning more and more things.*
- *Practice integrative education*: look for ways that one lesson or new piece of information can have a cross-over application to multiple fields of study, e.g. psychology to marketing, English to resume writing, history to management, mathematics to finance.
- *Use this book as one of your textbooks.*

"Liberal arts" classes are included in the suggested curriculum because a well-rounded liberal arts education is an invaluable business asset.
- The more you know about the more things, the better informed your decisions will be and the better equipped you will be to achieve your business plan and projected financial statement budget objectives.
- Your brain operates like a computer. The more data that you store in your brain, the more data your brain can crunch to make decisions – to identify decision options from which you might choose, to evaluate the most likely outcome of each option, and to choose the optimal decision option.

The physical campus of your business school can be wherever you would like it to be:
- Local schools and colleges: take classes and participate in continuing education programs in subjects that interest you
- Local library(s): become a friend of the librarians. They can help you find books and other resources on subjects that interest you.
- Bookstores: ask for recommendations of books about subjects that interest you.
- Coffee shop: equivalent of a college's student union building for conversations with people whose brains you want pick.
- Your workplace: consider it a work/study program such as many business schools offer.
- Computer: to connect you with the global campus of internet educational resources.

If you are a high school or college student, use this chapter:
- As suggestions of information to seek in your required classes – information that is likely to have high use potential in your working career and in managing your money (see Chapter 8).
- To help guide your choices of elective classes.

Business Management 101

Business is the specialized behavior of people exchanging products and services so that each person gets something that she needs or wants. It is just one of the many different ways we humans interact with each other.
- Think of people first and business is likely to fall into place pretty naturally for you.
- Think in terms of business <u>relationships</u> as much as you do business <u>transactions</u>.

Management is a pro-actively planned and coordinated process that seeks to influence the behavior of people and the course of events for the purpose of achieving an objective (as opposed to a series of "one-off" spur-of-the-moment actions and reactions to events).

Companies are groups of people, not things. People organize themselves into companies for many reasons, including:
- The security of earning a living with the help of a group of other people.
- Pool their individual time, talents and resources so that each person can achieve her individual objectives by means of helping their company achieve its objectives.
- Capitalize on the special skills and abilities that each person brings to the group effort - "specialization of labor".
- Make it easier to raise the money (capital) needed to finance their pooled efforts.
- Create a legal entity that shields each individual person from personal legal liability in the event that a lawsuit was to arise from their business activities.

Companies are not nameless, faceless, soulless things.
- Each company is the sum of its people, with all of their collective human strengths and weaknesses.
- People create the business plans and make decisions that determine what companies do.
- People do the work of the company: make and sell the company's products, program and run the company's computers, maintain the company's property and equipment, etc.
- Companies change as new employees are hired and as old employees depart or retire.

Part science, part art
- Business management is <u>part well researched, proven science</u>, and <u>part creative, intuitive art</u>.
- In a perfectly predictable world in which perfect people did exactly what they said they would do without making mistakes, and perfectly educated people had the perfect knowledge needed to make perfect decisions, and principles and theories could be used to make perfectly accurate predictions, the science part might be all we would need.
- But the world isn't perfect, and people aren't perfect. Predictions of decision outcomes, future events, and human behavior don't always play out the way principles and theories say they should. Dealing with our imperfect world is where the art part comes in to play.

The science part of business management is based upon such things as:
- Logical, analytical, "left brain" thinking (some researchers now think left brain versus right brain is an anatomical myth; but it can still be a descriptive term for our use).
- Mathematical models, hard facts, and statistical analyses.
- Principles and theories that help explain and predict the behavior of individual people, companies, and entire economies. Some of these principles and theories can sound confusing at first. Rest easy. Most of these principles and theories are fairly easy to

understand after technical jargon is translated into plain English. If people use words and terms you don't understand, ask them to explain in plain English the words and terms you don't understand.

The accumulated body of knowledge of business management science has been organized into fields of study such as:
- Accounting
- Economics and behavioral economics
- Finance and behavioral finance
- Statistical analysis
- Marketing and advertising

The science part can be learned through formal schooling, self-study, and on-the-job training.

The art part of business management is based upon such things as:
- Creative, intuitive, "right brain" thinking (again, even if the old idea of left brain versus right brain thinking is an anatomical myth, the terms can still help us differentiate between logical, analytical thinking and creative, intuitive thinking).
- Personal interpretation of the facts at hand in specific situations.
- Common sense ability to reason (as mothers have so often said "the good common sense you were born with").
- "Street smarts" that each person acquires through her unique life experiences.
- Hunches and gut instinct. Be careful about trusting your hunches and gut instinct. The more that your hunches have turned out to be correct in the past, the more you can "trust your gut" in the future.
- Inherited (genetic) physical talents, capabilities and appearance:
    o Mental acuity, e.g. IQ, memory - ability to remember facts, figures, faces.
    o Physical bearing, e.g. height, body type, strength of voice.
- Each person's unique personality.
- The way that each person perceives that people react to her appearance and personality (how she thinks people see her). Think about the way that the thinking and behavior of high school students can be shaped by the stereotype personality categories into which students tend to place each other (e.g. jock, cheerleader, nerd).
- Passion to succeed (drive, desire, motivation): as with all the other arts, the degree of passion a person brings to the art part of business management is a major determinant of the quality of business art each person produces.

It is art the way that each person:
- Deals with unique situations or circumstances for which there are no exact historical precedents; irrational human emotions; unforeseeable events; discoveries and inventions; natural disasters; departures and deaths of key people; etc.
- Makes decisions based upon her unique combination of skills, abilities, experience in life, and knowledge.

Two examples of the art of business:
- Newspapers sometimes contain two separate articles, each written by a well-respected economist who makes a prediction about the economy based upon the same set of recently released statistics. One economist says the economy will get better over the next year and the second economist says the economy will get worse.

- If two CPA's were given exactly the same set of year end accounting records, it is likely that each CPA would compute a slightly different income tax due.

Experience and practice are:
- The best ways to learn the art part of business management.
- The best guides to use in blending the science and art parts together.

The best people typically deliver the best performance.
- The most successful companies typically have assembled the best teams of people in their industries.
- In some types of work one top flight employee may be able to do the same amount of work as two average employees, and do that work with higher quality and less supervision.

"Pay for performance."
- The most successful companies typically offer the best compensation packages in order to attract and retain the best people.
- The best employees typically are smart enough to know the value of their services relative to the value of their job seeking competitors' services, and they seek compensation commensurate with the best value they know they provide to an employer.

Good personal behavior habits are good business management habits. Remember the lessons your parents, teachers and coaches taught you about how to get along with people and how to be successful in school and in sports. Go back over your mental notes and reflect on how all those lessons apply to business: civility, trustworthiness, concern for the well-being of others, doing the right thing without having to be told to do it, studying, practicing hard, etc.

Study the wisdom passed down from generation to generation by our ancestors in books, folk tales, adages, and the like. These time-tested lessons about how to lead a successful life are also good lessons in business management. *Aesop's Fables* and the *Book of Proverbs* are examples of ancient wisdom books that are excellent management texts. *Aesop's Fables* in particular should be on the required reading list in your business school. Every student of business should understand the lessons taught by fables such as:
- Ants and the Grasshopper: ants worked all summer gathering food to eat during the winter while the grasshopper spent his whole summer singing and playing. Come winter, the ants had plenty to eat, but the grasshopper did not. Business lesson: work hard and save money to use in the future rather than spending it all as soon as it is earned.
- Hare and the Tortoise: slow and steady wins the race. Business lesson: wealth accumulation is usually achieved in a long marathon run rather than in a short sprint.
- Fox and the Stork: help others succeed and they will help you succeed. Business lesson: seek win/win outcomes.

Leadership - motivating people to do what you would like them to do. There are a number of ways to lead people:
- *Example*: setting a good example is perhaps the most effective way to lead.
- *Reason*: explaining the reasons why it makes good sense to do what the leader wants done; and when applicable, explaining how the person can help achieve her own objectives by helping the leader achieve his objectives ("here's what's in it for you").
- *Education*: teaching people how the leader would like things done. After people learn how the leader would like things to be done, they can do those things the leader's way

with a lot less of the leader's time and effort being spent on supervision. Well trained, competent people can just about lead themselves.

- *Reward*: the promise and delivery of a reward helps motivate people to do things the leader wants done the way the leader wants them done. Different people are motivated to differing degrees by different rewards: job satisfaction (creating jobs people enjoy doing); recognition (a heartfelt thank you or pat on the back for a job well done); money (often the least effective motivator of good people). "A carrot is better than a stick". "You can attract more flies with honey than with vinegar."
- *Authority of position*: a leader who occupies a superior position in a relationship is vested with authority to tell "subordinates" what to do – the position confers authority to give orders, e.g. "Do it because I said so." But typically giving orders is not a good way to lead. People don't like to be ordered. They sometimes rebel against orders and react in less than optimum ways. It is best to use the authority that a position confers in the form of a suggestion or a request – smart "subordinates" typically "get the message" to do it.
- *Power*: threatening people with some type of harm – financial, physical, or other – "do it or else." Threats should be used only as a last resort. Threats typically raise emotions, and a leader can never be sure exactly how an emotionally charged person will react – it might just be a nasty reaction that hurts the leader badly – people might quit in the middle of a job, or seek revenge by intentionally botching a job, or a lot worse.
- *Situational leadership*: in specific situations it is sometimes best to pass the baton of leadership to a person who has more expertise or experience in the specific matter at hand.

Good "lines of communication" are critical for good leadership. People being led must understand what their leader wants them to do if they are to do what the leader wants done. Learn all you can about oral and written communication skills, listening skills, and body language communication (both what your body language communicates to others and reading other people's body language).

Ask, don't tell. Observation of many good leaders over many years has taught me that:
- *Asking for help* is more effective than giving orders.
- *Politely suggesting a course of action* is more effective than rudely telling people "do it".

Employee motivation: study the psychology of human motivation. Learn what various people have to say about what motivates us do what we do. You might start with:
- Abraham Mazlow's theory of a hierarchy of need satisfaction - Mazlow proposed that our needs are arranged in a hierarchical order, and that we are motivated to satisfy each need in serial order before moving on to satisfy the next need. This hierarchy of needs is typically illustrated as a pyramid.
  - o Basic life needs at the base of the pyramid: air, food, drink, shelter, sleep …
  - o On the next level are safety needs: protection, security, law, order …
  - o Then love and belonging needs: family, friendships, work groups …
  - o Then esteem needs: reputation, status, responsibilities …
  - o Lastly, self-actualization needs at the peak of the pyramid, e.g. self-fulfillment, creativity, problem solving.
- Frederick Herzberg's Two Factor Theory (Motivator-Hygiene Theory) which organizes multiple factors in two groups:
  - o Motivator (intrinsic) factors that create motivation when present - recognition, satisfying work, responsibility, growth potential, etc.
  - o Hygiene (extrinsic) factors that reduce motivation when absent - money,

employee benefits, job security, etc.
- Four quadrants of motivation / leadership

Trust in each other is critical for people to live together in a society and for people to do business with each other. We wouldn't do business together if buyers didn't trust sellers to provide what they say they will provide and sellers didn't trust buyers to pay all the money they say they will pay; we wouldn't buy cars if we didn't trust carmakers to make safe and reliable cars; and we wouldn't get married if we didn't trust our marriage partners.

That said about trust, "behavior control systems" are needed because people don't always behave the way we expect them to behave (in the business world behavior control systems are called "internal controls", with internal meaning within the organization):
- E-v-e-r-y-b-o-d-y has human weaknesses. As managers we need an internal control system to help us manage human weaknesses such as greed, fear, panic, forgetfulness, self-delusion about what we really can do, and dishonesty.
- We all make mistakes. Even the people who have the best expertise and experience, and the best intentions, can fall victim to "slip-ups" as the result of mental and physical fatigue from trying too hard for too long.
- Personal problems (e.g. addiction to alcohol, gambling losses) can lead good people to behave in ways they wouldn't normally behave.

Internal controls serve two critical functions:
- *Keep good people on the "straight and narrow path" doing what they know they should do, and not doing what they would later regret having done.*
- *Prevent people with proclivities to do bad things from doing those bad things.*

A system of checks and balances encourages everybody in an organization to do the right thing by splitting up job duties among different work groups and different people:
- *Checks*: each person knows that other people are observing her performance – "checking" on what she does or doesn't do.
- *Balances*: spreading out (balancing out) work among different people or work groups so that no single person or work group does every aspect of every job within an organization helps minimize the risk that any single person or work group could cause the organization serious harm.

Examples of checks and balances systems:
1. Government of the United States: the founders planned for the dangers of unchecked power by:
- Splitting duties among three branches of government - executive, legislative and judicial.
- Establishing staggered term limits for elected federal officials – 2 years for congressional representatives, 4 years for president, 6 years for senators.
- Centralizing some powers in the federal government and decentralizing other powers to state governments.
- Providing citizens with "board of directors" power to hire and fire by means of voting.
2. Publicly traded corporations
- Management duties split among multiple officers.
- Board of directors that has "independent" directors (directors who are not employees).
- Independent external auditors (CPA's).
- Government regulators.
3. News media (the "fourth estate") that checks on the behavior of governments, companies,

individuals, etc., and critiques their public statements to give us a balanced perspective.

Employee training (education) programs help bring out the best in good people. Smart employers understand the benefits they gain from providing employees with educational opportunities:
- Employee training programs help create a "culture of excellence" within a company – a culture of doing work the best that it can be done - which helps workers maximize their productivity and generate repeat business sales.
- Initial training of new employees provides them with the knowledge and skills needed to do their jobs, and teaches them "the company way" to do things.
- Apprenticeship, mentoring, and other on-the-job training programs in which employees help each other learn job skills, improve job performance, and achieve peak productivity.
- Seminars and classes provide opportunities to refine old skills and learn new skills.
- Education expense reimbursement programs also encourage employees to refine old skills and learn new skills.
- Trade association meetings and conferences help employees keep abreast of new developments in their industry, new technologies, and new methods of doing work.
- Employee training programs also help develop a stream of "home grown" talent that a company can use to grow its business "organically" (by using its own proven human capital resources rather than hiring unproven "outsiders" or buying other companies).

The Peter Principle: Dr. Laurence J. Peter and Raymond Hull provided classic management advice in their book *The Peter Principle: Why Things Always Go Wrong* (William Morrow and Company, 1969), *"In a hierarchy every employee tends to rise to his level of incompetence"*. Think about that. People tend to be promoted to successively higher and higher positions in an organization until they reach a level of incompetence. Countless people have risen to a position at which they do not have all the skills and abilities that a person in that position should have. The Peter Principle proved itself so useful in the years after the book was published that it became ingrained as a term in the business vernacular; regrettably it seems to have faded out of the vernacular. This book should be on the required reading list in your business school.

The Flow Down Principle (a term I use - I haven't been able to determine if the term has already been coined): the thinking and behavior of the people in an organization tend to flow down from the president through the organization to the lowest positions in an organization's hierarchy.
- It is said that "a fish rots from the head". So too, companies tend to prosper, or rot, from the president on down.
- *Over time the people in an organization tend to think and act in much the same way that the president thinks and acts.* The president tends to hire senior managers who reflect his core values, objectives, strategies, and business practices. Those senior managers in turn tend to hire and promote lower level managers who think and act like themselves, and so on from top to bottom throughout the organization's hierarchy (managers who disagree with the president's strategies, business practices, etc. tend to get weeded out).

Street smarts are learned through life experiences "out on the street" in the "real world" managing real world situations and observing how other people managed situations they were in.
- Street smarts help people figure out what to do when events in their lives aren't playing out the way the textbooks say that those events should be playing out.
- Street smarts are like a sixth sense that helps guide managers' decisions and actions.

Psychology and Sports Psychology

Psychology is the study of how and why we humans think and behave in the ways that we do.
- Whereas business is the specialized behavior of people exchanging goods and services, the more that we learn about psychology the better equipped we become to:
  - o Influence the behavior of people through leadership and negotiation.
  - o Recognize how other people may be trying to influence our behavior.
  - o Evaluate the likely outcome of decision options that involve human behavior.
- Psychology is an integral part of other subjects that business managers should study, including social psychology, economics, behavioral economics, behavioral finance, marketing, advertising, the art of negotiation, and human resource management.

Sports psychology zeroes in on how to use our minds to help improve our performance in sports. The more we learn about sports psychology, the better equipped we become to improve our performance in managing our money.

Two levels of thinking in our brains:
- *Conscious mind*: thoughts we are aware we are thinking
- *Subconscious mind*: thoughts we are not aware we are thinking; thoughts that just come to us passively when we aren't proactively trying to think them – when we are asleep dreaming, jogging, letting our minds wander aimlessly as we lay in the grass on a spring day watching the clouds, meditating, etc.

Stages of life: we tend to think differently about life and money at different stages of the aging process; an 18 year old student typically thinks differently than a 40 year old parent; a 40 year old entering her prime earning years tends to think differently than a 65 year old who is planning for the next chapter in her life. Learn how your thinking is likely to evolve as you age.

Learn how the physical development of our brains, and the ways we exercise and train our brains, affect the way we think.
- *Neuroplasticity*: learn how the electrical connections in our brains develop, wire and re-wire themselves as we age.
- *Maturation process*: learn about the interplay of hormones, emotions, and rational thinking during various life stages as we mature from babies to old age.

Motivation: why we do what we do. Learn about factors that motivate people, such as:
- *Seek pleasure and avoid pain*; we seek to do things we enjoy doing, and avoid doing things we don't like to do.
  - o If we make business and financial management as enjoyable as possible, we are more likely to achieve the best possible human performance.
  - o Learn what psychologists (and others who focus on human performance) think about the importance of happiness, and what they think makes people happy.
- Self-actualization: gaining satisfaction from becoming what we desire to be.
- Altruism: desire to do good things for others.
- Recognition: thank you's, pats on the back, and compliments, etc.
- Social pressure: feelings of pressure from people to do things – family pressure from parents or spouses, peer pressure from friends or co-workers, etc.
- Money.

Cooperation and competition: learn why we cooperate with each other in certain circumstances and compete against each other in other circumstances.

Cognitive behavioral therapy: *changing our thinking can help us change behavior we want to change – changing the way we think about money management can help us change our money management habits, i.e. thinking that your money is your business may well help you.*

Cognitive dissonance: we don't always act the way we think we should act. When looking back on their lives in retrospect, many people wish they hadn't done things that they "knew better" than to do. Two examples:
- Investors who tell themselves they are too smart to follow the herd of investors who are rushing to buy real estate when the real estate market is skyrocketing into a potential bubble, but they go out and buy property anyway.
- People who cheat on their diets with "just this one little exception" while they are telling themselves they are doing a good job of sticking to their diets.

Cognitive distortion: our minds play tricks on us; our perception of what we think is happening does not accurately reflect what is actually happening.

Personality types: learn about personality assessment tools that some employers use to evaluate personality types of current employees and prospective new hires in order to match employee personality types with certain types of jobs, such as:
- Meyers-Briggs Personality Type Indicator: seeks to assess personality type based upon four aspects of personality: thinking or feeling; extraversion or introversion; sensing or intuition; judging or perception.
- DISC (Dominance, Influence, Steadiness, Conscientiousness [or compliance]): seeks to assess personality type based upon these four aspects of personality.

Also learn about Type A and Type B personalities. From what I can gather, Type A and Type B personality types were first identified by medical doctors to help identify people who might be more prone to heart disease. Apparently professionals in the field of psychology don't give much credence to these personality types because they are too broad, and trying to sort people into just two personality types doesn't allow for the wide variety in peoples' personalities. However, the business world uses these terms to describe the following tendencies in people:
- Type A: dominating, "controlling" personality; compete aggressively to win.
- Type B: more laid back people; more comfortable "going with the flow".

Importance of sleep to clear thinking: especially important for students and workaholics.

Pre-programmed perceptions of reality: *we tend to "see what we want to see, and hear what we want to hear"*. Learn about the craft of sleight-of-hand magicians.

Mindfulness and self-fulfilling prophesies: what we think and feel will happen tend to actually happen - eventually. Our mindsets guide our behavior and our awareness of the world around us. Learn about "mindfulness", and how psychologist Ellen Langer and mindfulness coaches such as George Mumford (*The Mindful Athlete: Secrets to Pure Performance*) say we can use mindfulness. Mindfulness can help us think positively, and positive thinking can help create self-fulfilling prophesies of good by:
- Helping us do our best at whatever we set our minds to doing.
- Helping us recognize the opportunities presented by the world around us.

Sociology and Social Psychology

Sociology is the study of how we live together in social groups such as families, companies, communities, and countries.

Social Psychology is the study of how our thinking and actions are influenced by the people in the social groups to which we belong. It links sociology and psychology in the study of "group dynamics".

Rules of acceptable social behavior govern how we live in community with each other and do business with each other. Learn how and why two types of rules develop:
- *Norms*: rules of acceptable behavior (norm-al behavior) that groups of people have developed over time because these norms facilitate the ability of group members to live in harmony and to predict each other's behavior (think about what your family, school, and community life would be like if there were no generally accepted norms of proper behavior to expect).
- *Laws*: certain norms are considered so important to the functioning of a society that they are institutionalized as laws with penalties (sanctions) for breaking those laws.

Most of the norms that govern good social and business behavior carry over from culture to culture, but some cultures may have slightly different takes on some of the rules of good behavior (particularly in the area of politeness – what is polite behavior in one society might be seen as impolite in another society).

Formal groups are consciously (formally) planned, and organized with a structured leadership hierarchy, e.g. companies, governments, social clubs, sports teams, and religious institutions.

Informal groups just "kind of happen" without formal planning (think of cliques).
- Members of virtually every formal group organize themselves into informal subgroups based upon factors such as friendship, common interests, same age, same sex, same lunch time, and physical proximity in school or the workplace.
- Informal groups develop their own rules of acceptable behavior for group members and they develop their own internal pecking order hierarchies.
- *Informal group leaders* "emerge from the crowd" based upon factors such as personality, the way they interact with other group members, expertise, and physical bearing.

Learning about informal group dynamics can be a huge help in maximizing success in the workplace because virtually every job in every employer's organization is linked in some way through inter-dependent work. That makes the success of each individual employee dependent to some extent upon the work of her co-workers in both the formal and informal work groups of which she is a member. Developing good working relationships with members of the informal groups to which you belong, or groups with which you must coordinate your work, will help you optimize teamwork, thereby optimizing the prospects for you to achieve your objectives. Conversely, informal group relationships that go bad can hurt your efforts to succeed.

Managing informal group relationships involves:
- Identifying informal groups of co-workers who influence your job performance. Informal groups don't hang out signs saying "here we are". Identifying informal groups requires observing and listening to what's going on around us.
- Analyzing the "power structure" of each informal group; identifying the leaders (movers,

shakers, and decision makers) and the followers (people who go along for the ride; people who tend to say "I don't care, whatever you want to do").
- Gaining acceptance by the leaders and influential members of those informal groups (e.g. having them think and say "she's OK").
- Motivating group members to support your work efforts - being nice, cooperative, and trying to help them are some of the best ways to motivate them.

Generational groups: understanding differences in social behavior patterns of people born in different generations is an important factor in personnel management, e.g. The Greatest Generation (Radio Generation), born 1928-1945; Baby Boom, born 1946-1964; Gen X, born 1965-1980; Gen Y (Millennials), born 1981-1992; and Generation Z (Post-Millennial or the iGeneration), born after 1993 (years delineating generations are approximate).

Three types of group behavior are important to understand:
- *Herd behavior* – "going along with the crowd": many people tend to follow along with whatever they perceive the majority of other people are doing. People with a "herd mentality" seem to think "*if everybody else is doing it, it must be the right thing to do*".
- *"Group think" behavior*: people who join groups in which members share certain strong beliefs tend to reinforce the strength of each other's beliefs. This can result in the thinking of each individual member falling into a lockstep "group think" agreement with the thinking of other members - *they all think pretty much the same way, and behave the way they think group members expect them to behave*. They can convince themselves that their way of thinking and behaving is the "right" way, and that everyone else's way is the "wrong" way. Group members' minds become calcified in dogma. An extreme example might be Hitler's Nazi Party in Germany during World War II.
- *Mob behavior*: people in a crowd can get emotionally lathered up and do things "in the heat of the moment" as a "mob" that they would never have thought about doing as individuals on their own.

"Nature and nurture." Social behavior is influenced by both nature and the nurturing we get.
- *Nature* = our genetic inheritance at birth; human instinct (e.g. survival instinct).
- *Nurture* = what we are taught as members of families, communities, and other social groups, and the way we were treated (nurtured) as we grew up. "It takes a village."

Game theory
- Win-win: each party in a transaction thinks she won – that she received fair value; "my success is your success"; co-operative nature. Seek win-win.
- Win-lose: one party's gain is the other party's loss; worst case is one party tries to get the better of the other party; competitive nature. Avoid win-lose.

Sports analogies abound in business because human behavior in games of sport is so closely related to behavior in the game of business. In both sports and business:
- People interact with each other in social groups to accomplish specific objectives.
- Specific rules of social behavior govern play.
- Outcomes are tough to predict because of all the human behavior variables that can affect outcomes. In sports, experts who closely study players and teams are frequently wrong when they try to predict winners and losers; if business behavior was easy to predict, we'd all be rich.

Philosophy

Philosophy is a freedom machine for your mind. The study of philosophy is not just for egghead intellectuals. Studying philosophy should be a personal adventure in which you ask yourself the big picture questions about life, what you believe and why, and then search for the answers that make the most sense to you for your life.

Studying philosophy will guide your thinking about objectives and strategies to include in your personal business plan. Ask yourself questions such as:
- What is the purpose of life in general, and my life in particular?
- What do I value most in my life? What roles should money and wealth play in my life?
- What is a "good" life? A life well lived? How should I live my life?
- What is right? What is wrong? What should be legally right and wrong?
- What is ethical behavior? What might be legal behavior but unethical behavior?
- What is civil behavior among people in families, communities, companies, countries, global economy? Is civil behavior a shade of gray, not black or white, good or bad?
- What roles should cooperation and competition play in a civil society in order to foster a vibrant economy? Supportive cooperation? Every person for himself competition?
- How much uncivil behavior can a civilization tolerate and still continue to function?
- How should people govern themselves? Is a capitalist democracy the best way?
- How self-sufficient should each person seek to become?
- What should we do for each other as a group in the form of government services?
- What rights and responsibilities do citizens have? Do I have a social responsibility to spend some of my time and money to help fellow citizens (e.g. contribute to religious and community service organizations; pay taxes that fund social safety net programs)? Why?

Question dogma. *Doubt, and the questioning of dogma, play a central role in intellectual life.* Question what people tell you to believe. Free your mind to objectively evaluate the pros and cons of the different answers that different people and different cultures have had for the big questions about life. Open your mind to the possibility of changing your mind about what you think and what you believe. What do you think makes the most sense? What do you believe?

Two suggestions for starting your study of philosophy:
- Take a class with a teacher and classmates. They can help open your mind to be as objective as you can be in your intellectual pursuits. Their questions, thoughts, opinions, and observations can help stimulate your thinking and free your mind of preconceived ideas you might have brought into class. Plus, a class provides a safe, secure academic environment in which you can practice questioning how and why people think and believe the way they do.
- Ask your local librarian for recommendations of introductory level books written by authors such as Will Durant who present the key ideas of the great philosophers in language that is relatively easy to understand. After you get your feet wet with an introductory book or two, work your way into reading more about those philosophers and their ideas that spark your interest. You might even try reading the original works of the philosophers whose ideas spark your greatest interest so that you can interpret for yourself what each philosopher meant. But be aware that the original works of many (most?) philosophers can be really tough to read and understand (it seems to me that the intended audience of most philosophers is other philosophers and serious students of philosophy who are conversant in each other's "philosopher's jargon"). An interesting sidebar might be to learn what texts "well educated" people have read over the centuries.

English

Language evolved so that people could communicate their needs, wants, and thoughts to each other. The better your English language skills, the more effectively you can communicate your needs, wants, and thoughts to people with whom you do business (to be precise, those people who also use English as their primary language).

You have a vested interest in the English language skills of everyone around you. The better their oral and written language skills, the more likely they will understand what you intend to communicate to them, and the more effectively they can communicate their thoughts back to you.

Languages evolve as the societies that use the languages evolve.
- New words are created to describe new discoveries and new ideas. Conversely, as old technologies and ideas fade away into obsolescence, the words and figures of speech used to talk about them also tend to fade away.
- Over the past few years, the business world has experienced significant evolution in communication technology and tools, and the language we use with them. For example:
  o During the 1970's, 80's and 90's the old business language of "shorthand" (a form of speed writing) faded into near extinction. Hardly anyone in today's business world uses shorthand.
  o As shorthand was fading out, the new language of "text messaging" (including emoji) was evolving to accommodate the emerging mobile device technology.
- Different generations tend to use different words and phrases, sometimes so much so that they can almost seem like different languages to the different generations. When you are communicating across generations try to use language the other person will understand.

Words are the building blocks with which our minds construct our ideas and communicate them. New words are created by people who need those new words to describe new ideas, new things, and new ways that people are thinking or acting (think about how many new words come into being through pop culture and sports, not to mention science and other creative endeavors). New words allow us to think and communicate thoughts that we couldn't think or communicate before the words came into existence.

Slang / vernacular / trade jargon: special words and acronyms used by members of sub-groups of people within a larger group of people who speak the same language.
- Learn the trade jargon of the people with whom you do business and the "generational jargon" and "cultural references" that people of different generations commonly use.
- Avoid using the jargon of your company and industry with "outsiders" who may not understand those special words and acronyms.

Vocabulary is the total number of words you know in a language - and know how to use properly. The more words you know (the broader your vocabulary) the more detailed and complex the thoughts you can string together in your mind, and the better your ability to communicate exactly what you intend to communicate.
- I have heard that indigenous people in the Amazon use many different words to communicate different shades of meaning for the animal identified by the one English word "parrot".
- Likewise I understand that the Greek language has at least four words to convey different shades of meaning for the single English word "love": *storge*, love of family; *philia*, love of a friend; *eros*, sensual love; *agape*, spiritual love.

- Consider differences in how we use the words nude and naked; nude is used to mean naturally unclothed, as in art; naked is used to mean harshly stripped, and coldly alone.

Good business people choose their words wisely. They use only words that they are sure they know how to use properly. Try not to show off by using big words that you don't really know how to use properly. It could make you appear less smart to people who know their English.

Grammar is the set of rules that governs the use of vocabulary. The Greatest Generation (born before 1945) and Baby Boom Generation were schooled in a culture that stressed the use of proper grammar. History teachers were known to evaluate grammar as well as content when grading essays. English classes taught students how to diagram sentences in order to learn proper sentence structure. If you don't know how to diagram a sentence, learn how – it's a fascinating game. *Apology to English teachers and other grammarians - I take poetic license with grammar throughout this book in in an effort to make my writing more accessibly colloquial.*

Rhetoric is the art of using words to communicate effectively. Study rhetoric to help you string together the words in your vocabulary in such a way that listeners and readers:
- Understand what you are saying in the way you intend them to understand you.
- Are influenced to think or act the way you would like them to think or act.

The best business people I know can talk with the guys on a company's loading dock as easily and effectively as they talk with the company's president.

Debate involves presenting well-reasoned arguments that defend or refute the issue to be debated – pro or con. Debaters typically prepare for a debate by researching both sides of the issue so that they can present well-reasoned arguments on both the pro and the con side of the issue. That enables them to present the best arguments for their side and counter what the other side might say. Debating skill is a valuable business skill.

Public speaking: learning to make an effective oral presentation to a group can provide a valuable business skill. However, many of us must learn to overcome a fear of public speaking. Suggestions to help overcome that fear include:
- Start speaking up in group meetings by asking questions and offering comments.
- Joining a local Toastmasters group to learn and practice public speaking skills.
- Just be yourself and speak from the heart. Don't get hung up on thinking that people expect you to put on a show as though you were a master emcee.
- Classic advice to shake a case of nerves - picture the audience sitting in their underwear.

Effective business communication is clear and concise. Keep it "short and sweet". "Cut to the chase." A famous acronym says it well - *KISS "keep it simple, stupid"*. Effective business communication is neither poetry nor creative writing. It is much closer to Ernest Hemingway's stripped down, simple writing style than it is to Dostoyevsky's complex style. A business writing class can be a valuable investment.

Learn at least one other language. The process of learning another language can help you improve your English skills, and provide insight into subtle differences in the way people communicate in different languages. I have heard that having a second language stored in your brain helps improve the brain's functioning because the brain gets good exercise by thinking consciously and unconsciously in both languages.

History

History offers valuable lessons to business managers - successes to emulate, mistakes to avoid. *Become a history detective.* Use historical events and the behavior of historical figures as clues to help project how current events are likely to play out in the future. Learn about:
- What successful people did in order to become successful?
- How some people used change to prosper (from scientific discoveries, inventions, etc.), and how other people suffered from change because they failed to see how the world was changing around them or they failed to adapt to change that they knew was happening.
- How quests for financial gain alone have caused misery and wars throughout history.
- Trends and cycles: learn to identify trends and cycles, and how to use them to *see the future through the past*; the more you learn about the history of developing trends, and about historical economic and business cycles, the better you will be able to:
  - o Project how those trends and cycles are likely to play out in the future.
  - o Use that knowledge to help predict the most likely outcomes of the decision options from which you have to choose when making your decisions.
- Reasons for the rise and fall of companies, industries, countries and their economies.

"History tends to repeat itself, unless we learn from it."
- People from generation to generation have been making the same types of mistakes for thousands of years. The more you learn about mistakes people made in the past, the better prepared you will be to avoid making the same mistakes yourself.
- *"Youth is wasted on the young."* Learn why this adage has been passed down from generation to generation. One reason is that younger people do not yet have the benefit of valuable life lessons that older people have had the opportunity to learn. Talk to older folks. Ask them to share things they have learned about life and money management that they wish they had known when they were young.

Biographies: *individual people haven't changed much over the past few thousand years.* We still think and act in pretty much the same ways that our ancestors did when they first began to leave us written records. Read some ancient Greek and Roman histories, plays, poetry, and philosophy … an eye-opener as to just how similar we are to our ancestors.

Biographies offer lessons on what successful people did right, and did wrong, on their way to achieving success, e.g. Benjamin Franklin (printing), George Washington (real estate), Cornelius Vanderbilt (railroads), Andrew Carnegie (steel), J.P. Morgan (banking), Henry Ford (automobiles and innovation of the assembly line), John D. Rockefeller (oil), Thomas Edison (electronics), Warren Buffett (investing) Bill Gates (computer software), and Steve Jobs (computer hardware).

History of societies: individual people may not have changed much over the years in the ways we think and act, but *societies and their economies have experienced continuous evolutionary change* as successive generations have benefited from the accumulation of knowledge and wealth passed down to them by prior generations.
- New ideas, new discoveries, new inventions, and new technologies typically are rooted in the ideas and the work of people who came before.
- Improvements in transportation and communication technologies (the ability to transmit knowledge from person to person and generation to generation) have been increasing the quantity and quality of information that successive generations have had available to use.
- Advances in medicine have been progressively improving the quality of life of successive generations, and increasing the average life span that people have had in

which to learn, discover, and create new things.

- Learn how the pace of change has been accelerating, and how change occasionally has been spiked along by a revolutionary innovation, e.g. fire, domestication of animals, agriculture, the wheel, writing, metallurgy (bronze, iron, steel), the printing press, industrial revolution of machines and methods of manufacturing, and now computers.

Don't get hung up on memorizing exact dates and specific facts - although memorizing certain dates and facts typically is required for students to pass history tests in school.

- For business purposes, seek the "back story" of historical events - the why and the how events happened - rather than just trying to memorize a few specific details of the story. Learn to see "the forest (the grand sweep of historical events) for the trees (dates and facts)" - to hear the symphony of the era, rather than just a bunch of unconnected notes sounded by exact dates and specific facts.
- Focus on how people dealt with the circumstances they faced in their times.

Study American history to learn:

- Business reasons why European royalty and wealthy merchants financed establishment of colonies in the New World (the Americas) – primarily to seek riches of natural resources, such as silver, gold, furs, tobacco, and cotton. Seek lessons as to how different methods of "harvesting" natural resources today are likely to play out in your future.
- How Europeans appropriated land from the indigenous people in the New World; how they justified their "land grabs"; and how these land grabs serve as examples of land grabs that happened around the world throughout history, continue to happen today, and will continue to happen in the future unless we learn how to prevent them.
- Economic drivers of life in the English colonies: colonists seeking a better life than they had in the "old country"; obligations to repay the investors who financed the colonies (e.g. The Virginia Company, Plymouth Company, and Massachusetts Bay Company); Mayflower Compact; Puritan work ethic. Also learn about economic drivers of life in the Spanish, French, and Dutch colonies.
- Reasons for and the results of significant social dissent at various points in time, such as:
  - Movement to oppose British taxes (and The Intolerable Acts) in mid-1700's as a primary driver of the Revolutionary War.
  - Abolitionist (anti-slavery) movement during the 1840's -1860's.
  - Civil rights and anti-war movements during the 1960's and 1970's.
- How the Revolutionary War was financed: lack of authority for the colonies to tax themselves; use of Robert Morris' personal wealth; why and how European countries provided financial and military assistance.
- Why founders chose a capitalist democracy government (many people wanted George Washington to be a king); what influenced their thinking, e.g. ancient Roman government, ideas of John Locke, Thomas Paine's essay *Common Sense*, etc.
- Constitution and Bill of Rights: citizens' rights and duties in a self-governing society; belief that individual citizens should be self-sufficient. Historical influences?
- Why systems of checks and balances are needed in our capitalist democracy - i.e. the dangers of money and power – examples such as "Boss" Tweed's Tammany Hall political "machine", Teapot Dome scandal, "robber baron" business moguls, rise of labor unions to secure safer working conditions and counter abusive management practices, financial institution crisis during the late 2000's.
- Evolution of a system of public and private schools and colleges, and legislated mandates for universal education in our capitalist democracy.
- Evolution of women's rights and roles in the economy, e.g. voting, education, jobs.

- Evolution of the middle class.
- Why and how economic depressions developed, and how the economy recovered: 1819, 1837, 1857, 1873, 1893, 1907, 1929 - and the Great Recession of 2008.
- How Americans handled past financial challenges such as fighting World War II: re-purposing factories to manufacture weapons and ammunition; recruiting women into the work force to replace men gone to fight; rationing food, fuel and other resources at home in order to feed, clothe, and supply fighting forces.
- When and why government departments and agencies were created to manage government operations, collect taxes, regulate business and enforce regulations. Learn the history of US Government departments and agencies such as Office of Management and Budget, Congressional Budget Office, Treasury, Inspector General, Attorney General, IRS, SEC, ICC, FCC, and ATF.
- How "social safety nets" developed, who provided them, and at what cost to whom, e.g. fraternal organizations, social welfare (utopian) societies, government programs such as Social Security and Medicare.

Study the economic history of at least one other country to gain a broader perspective on the evolution of the American economy, and where our economy may be headed in the future.
- Trace the geographic, political, and economic development of a modern country back through its history. When, why, and how did it become the country we know it as today?
- How was the country governed: interrelationship of government, religious institutions, and business; roles of slavery / abusive labor practices, intolerance of dissent?
- Role of warfare; ways in which defeated peoples were managed, e.g. slaughtered, subjugated, offered citizenship?
- Disparities in lifestyles between rich ruling classes and poor working classes. Has a middle class developed in the country today?
- Roles of kings, warlords, chiefs, and religious leaders (and their governance mistakes).
- Roles of land, natural resources, fresh water, and access to rivers (as transportation highways) and ocean ports, in the evolution of the country and its economy.
- Why and how wars were fought as a means of economic and political competition.
- How have the economy and political governance of the country (or predecessor geographic area) evolved? How has its economic and political position in the world evolved? If at one time the country was a major economic power, but is no longer, why? How did the country lose its economic competitive edge?

Suggestions:
- England: perhaps the British Empire Era and the Industrial Revolution.
- France: perhaps causes of social unrest that led to the French Revolution.
- Germany: perhaps evolution to military and manufacturing powerhouse in 1900's.
- Japan: perhaps evolution to manufacturing powerhouse in 1900's.
- Russia: from monarchy to the Union of Soviet Socialist Republics back to Russia.
- China: from regional power, to colony, to global power.
- India: from regional power, to colony, to emerging global power.
- Greece: Alexander the Great's Macedonia, and the city states of Athens and Sparta that preceded the country of Greece.
- Italy: Rome, Florence and other city states that preceded the country of Italy.
- Spain, Portugal, or Holland, perhaps in the Age of Discovery spawned by sailing ships.
- Egyptian, Persian, or Ottoman Empire.
- Aztec, Incan, or Mayan Empire.

Geography

Geography is becoming increasingly important to business people because money is flowing through an increasingly intricate global web of economic supply and demand. Virtually every country depends upon other countries to supply at least some of the things that its citizens need or want. Learn which national economies are linked with which other national economies by ties of supply and demand for natural resources, manufactured products, and food.

Geography is not just the study of maps. While a significant part of geography today is indeed knowing the location of places on Planet Earth, geography also involves how the location of things influences the lifestyles we live, economics, demography, politics, etc.

Studying geography will help you gather "market intelligence" about supply and demand factors at work in the planet Earth marketplace. Learn about the locations of:
- *Land* available on which to live, work, and grow food (continents, countries, states, cities, and islands).
- *Fresh water* in rivers, streams, lakes, and underground aquifers that we need to drink and to use for all sorts of agricultural and industrial purposes.
- *Salt water* in oceans, seas, bays, estuaries that we use for transportation and to harvest seafood; and learn about the economic impact of rising sea levels in coastal areas.
- *Natural resources* needed to manufacture the things you buy.
- *People*: distributions of populations in the global marketplace – your colleagues and competitors in the game of business. Learn about the "*demographics*" of various geographic regions and countries, e.g. number of people in various age groups; male and female; average income and wealth.

A few questions to get you started in your study:
- *Job availability and pay*: How far could you, and would you, commute to get a job? What type jobs in what companies are available within an acceptable commuting distance? What do jobs in other geographic areas pay in comparison to your pay in your job in your geographic area (your financial compensation is impacted by how much other people are paid)?
- *Your competition for jobs*: what jobs are moving to which states and countries? Why? Competitor country demographics: numbers of people; age; average wages v US wages; education v US (e.g. number of engineering students v US engineering students)?
- *Fresh water availability and cost*: what are the sources of the water that comes out of your faucets: rivers, streams, lakes, underground aquifers? Who else uses water from those same sources? How fast is demand for that water growing? Will supply be able to satisfy growing demand in 10 years? In 20 years? In 50 years?
- *Food availability and cost*: where does your food come from today (grains, vegetables, fruit, fish, meat)? Where will your food come from tomorrow? How much does it cost to transport food from its source to you? How fast is demand growing in the world's rapidly growing economies for the limited supply of the world's food resources?
- *Air quality and weather*: learn what roles forested land plays in the quality of air you breathe and in the weather systems in your geographic area. Learn how much of the world's "disappearing" tropical rain forests have been cut down over the past 50 years for economic development projects, and how the continuing loss of forest will affect your life and your money.

Accounting

Accounting is the financial records keeping part of business. *Understanding a few accounting fundamentals is essential for financial planning, budgeting, and successful money management.*

Financial statements are reports of historical financial management performance. Two key parts to understand in a financial statement:
- Balance sheet
- Statement of income and expenses

Balance sheet - a snapshot of a person's financial position as of one particular day.
- Three main parts: *assets* (list of what you own); *liabilities* (list of what you owe); and *net worth* (money remaining after subtracting liabilities from assets).
- A balance sheet tells the story of: (a) amount of savings (net worth) you have accumulated in life up to the date of the balance sheet; (b) how those savings have been invested (assets); (c) how much money is owed to others, and deferred income tax that will become payable in the future (liabilities).

Assets = things you <u>own</u>
- Current / liquid assets: cash and other "liquid" assets that could be converted into cash in a short period of time, e.g. certificates of deposit, treasury bills, stock, bonds.
- Non-current / fixed / capital assets: property and equipment intended to be owned for a relatively long period of time, e.g. real estate, cars, boats.
- Other assets: collectibles (e.g. art, antiques, stamps), notes receivable, etc.

Liabilities (debt) = money you <u>owe</u>
- Current liabilities: money that must be paid within one year, e.g. credit card balances, payments due on loans such as car loans and mortgages over the next 12 months.
- Long term liabilities: money owed more than one year in the future, e.g. amount of long term loans minus the current portion of those loans.
- *Deferred tax*: estimate of income tax expenses that will become payable in a future year when income is recognized from sources such as the sale of appreciated stock or withdrawals from a tax deferred retirement account such as an IRA or 401(k).

Net worth ("stockholders equity" on balance sheets of businesses): assets remaining after all liabilities have been paid - assets you would own after you repaid all the debt you owed.

A balance sheet is called a balance sheet because:
- Assets are listed in one column - typically on the left side of the page.
- Liabilities and net worth are listed in a second column - typically on the right side.
- The bottom line totals in each column should be the exact same amounts. In other words, the <u>total of the assets</u> column on the left side <u>should equal or "balance"</u> the <u>total of liabilities plus net worth</u> column on the right side (<u>picture the two totals being weighed on an old fashioned, see-saw type of scale - like the proverbial scales of justice</u>).

A balance sheet is an especially useful financial management tool for people who have difficulty grasping the fact that they don't yet fully own assets that they purchased with borrowed money. An asset purchased with a loan serves as security for the lender, so that if the borrower defaults on repaying the loan, that asset can be "repossessed" (taken away from the borrower) by the lender. *A borrower doesn't "own" anything until she finishes repaying all that she "owes".*

Statement of income and expenses - tells the story of how money flowed through a person's life during a specific period of time, such as one month, a calendar quarter, year to date, or one full year (not precisely the term that accountants use for this report, but I think this term better describes the information presented; the terms *"income statement"* and *"profit and loss statement" are also used*).

The main parts of an income statement are revenue, expenses, and net profit. Organize your income statement in a way that works best for you to help you manage your revenue and expenses. Below is a suggested format you might consider:

- *Revenue (called income by most non-accountants, and called gross income on income tax forms)*: "top line" on an income statement; includes total of all sources of money received during the reporting period, such as salaries, wages, bonuses, dividends, interest, etc.
- *Direct expenses*: expenses connected directly with generating revenue - expenses you must incur in order to work at your job - such as child care, commuting, work clothes. Expenses you would not incur if you were not generating that revenue.
- *Gross profit*: revenue minus direct expenses (computing gross profit can help you evaluate if a job is financially worth the time you invest in it).
- *General and administrative expenses* (also called G&A, or overhead): money you <u>need</u> to spend in order to stay alive and maintain your current lifestyle, e.g. food, clothing, housing, water, heat, light. For companies, these are expenses that must be incurred in order to remain in business ("to keep the doors open") even if no revenue is being generated.
- *Discretionary expenses*: money you <u>want</u> to spend but don't need to spend, e.g. entertainment, vacations, luxury items (<u>that part of the cost of a Rolex that is in excess of the cost of a Timex</u>).
- *Tax expenses,* such as:
   - o   Federal, state, and local income taxes. Learn about the differences between:
      - ▪   Ordinary income tax rates.
      - ▪   Dividend and capital gains tax rates.
   - o   Real estate taxes.
- *Net profit (income / savings)*: "bottom line" on the income statement; revenue minus all expenses; net profit is carried over to the balance sheet and added to net worth.

Bank statements and credit card statements - reports everyone should learn how to use.
- Online reports and tools offered by the financial institutions with which you do business.
- *Checkbook register*: to track deposits, checks written, cash withdrawals, and cash remaining.
- *Maintain a running total list of credit card purchases each month* (keep copies of your credit card receipts) on paper or on an electronic device, or monitor daily credit card purchases listed on your credit issuer's of website. This running total list will help you (a) keep track of how your actual spending is tracking with your spending budget each month, (b) and plan to have enough cash available when your statement arrives each month to pay the total balance due.
- Learn how to <u>reconcile</u> the accounting records you keep with the monthly statements you receive. "Reconcile" means to make sure your accounting records match up with their accounting records.

Finance

Finance is the study of financial planning, budgeting, and money management.

Three ways to finance your life:
- *Cash flow financing*: using revenue received on a regular basis (cash flow) to pay for expenses, a/k/a *"pay as you go"*. Common sources of personal cash flow are paychecks, interest, dividends, pensions, and social security. *Cash flow financing typically requires developing a predictable stream of revenue.*
- *Equity financing*: saving up money to build cash "equity" reserves that you can use to buy relatively expensive "big ticket" items that cash flow alone can't cover, and pay for unplanned expenses, e.g. uninsured medical emergency or home repair.
- *Debt financing*: borrowing money to pay expenses that cash flow financing plus equity financing can't cover, e.g. education, car, home, emergency healthcare.

"Cash is king" is a commonly used adage in finance for many reasons.
- Cash can grant financial freedom. The more cash you have, the more financial freedom you have to do what whatever you want to do.
- Cash is the "universal" asset. You can use it to buy any other asset or service you want.
- Cash flow financing and equity financing are the lowest risk ways to finance life.
- Cash provides negotiating leverage to secure the best terms from lenders when you decide that debt financing is prudent. It is said that a lender's favorite type of borrower is a person who has plenty of cash reserves and doesn't need a loan, but wants to borrow money for prudent financial planning reasons, i.e. *the easiest time to borrow is when a person least needs a loan.*

Debt financing is an inherently risky way to finance life.
- An inability to repay borrowed money has hurt countless people.
- All sorts of stuff can happen to interrupt cash flow or use up cash reserves that people had planned to use to repay loans, e.g. loss of a job, fixed income drops when interest rates drop, medical emergencies.
- Debt can be a good financial management tool when used prudently by people who know how to use it safely and effectively, but, but, BUT, borrowed debt can be extremely dangerous for people who don't know how to use it prudently.
- *Learn all you can about debt financing BEFORE you borrow money.*

Financial reserves should be considered in two ways while planning to finance your life.
- *Working capital* (liquidity) = current assets (cash and assets you could convert to cash quickly) minus current liabilities. Uses of working capital include:
  - Equity financing - to pay cash for big ticket purchases.
  - Contingency reserve "security blanket" - to supplement cash flow in the event of:
    - Loss of job or interruption of income from other sources of income.
    - A large unplanned expense
- *Net worth* (equity) = total assets minus total liabilities. A primary use of net worth is to provide financial freedom – the greater a person's net worth, the greater the financial freedom she would have to do whatever she dreamed of doing.

Time value of money
- Present value of a dollar today versus estimated value of that same dollar in the future
  - Factors to consider in estimating present value include: immediate utility of a

dollar (what you could buy with that dollar today versus what you might be able to buy with it in the future); investment income potential (how much money you could earn if you invested that dollar); future tax rates; inflation.
   o "A bird in the hand is worth two in the bush".
- *Compound earnings – your money making more money for you over time.*
   o Interest and dividend income that is paid to you on interest and dividend income that you reinvest.
   o The fuel of compound earnings can power all kinds of financial strategy engines.

Investment management
- *Get investment advice and investment management help from a professional financial advisor* (perhaps a mutual fund company – see Chapters 9 and 15).
- Do enough research on investment management to get a general idea of the breadth and depth of the subject and an understanding of basic investment industry terminology.
- Diversification: investing in different classes and types of assets can help you "spread the risk" of losing money and accomplish three different financial planning objectives:
   o Preserve capital (protect against loss in value).
   o Appreciate (increase) in price.
   o Generate income (your money making more money for you).

Return on equity
- Return on investment equity: the percentage increase in dollar (economic) value of an investment portfolio from the beginning of the year until the end of the year.
- Return on "sweat" equity: the return (joy, satisfaction, money) received on the time and effort (sweat) you invest in a job.

Credit score management: a credit score is a measure of a person's ability to repay a loan as determined by an independent credit reporting company.
- Each person has a credit score that is computed by each of three national consumer reporting companies (Experian, TransUnion, and Equifax),
- Each of the three companies also prepares a credit report on each person that they can sell to lenders (creditors) who use those credit reports as a part of their loan prequalification process.

Typically, the more debt a person has and the worse a person's debt repayment history:
- The lower a person's credit score and the greater the risk a creditor might think the person poses to default on a loan.
- The tougher it will be to get a loan.
- The higher the interest rate and the tougher the terms of any loan that might be offered.

Learn about the Fair Credit Reporting Act (FRCA), credit reports, how a person's credit score is computed, and how to manage your credit score.
- Factors that impact each person's credit score include: types of credit used (credit cards, car loan, student loan, mortgage), debt repayment history, current amount of debt, length of debt management track record, number of credit facilities recently opened).
- FRCA entitles you to a free copy of the credit report issued each year by each of the three credit reporting agencies at (annualcreditreport.com).

Budgets are such essential financial management tools that we cover budget management in five chapters, Chapters 11-15.

Economics

Economics is the study of the rules that govern how we do business with each other, why things have value, and why and how money moves within a population.
- The study of economics is rooted in common sense and pretty simple logic.
- Wikipedia says *our English word "economics" is derived from two Greek words meaning "rules of the household"*. This derivation points out that modern economic theory is rooted in the ways that people have learned to live together in families and communities over thousands of years.

Supply and Demand
- "Supply" - the amount of a particular thing that is available to a particular population at a particular time.
- "Demand" - a measure of how much that population desires it and is willing to pay for it.

Scarce resources: there is a limited supply of every single physical thing on our planet Earth. Given the finite amount of space on Earth there isn't room for an infinite supply of any one thing, let alone everything. Even if at any particular time, in any particular place, it might seem like there is an unlimited supply of something available to all people, there is NOT an unlimited supply. There is a limited supply of ALL physical things. Play a mind game. Try to think of just one material thing that is available at all times in all places to all people in unlimited supply.
- Good clean air to breathe? Think about the air pollution and smog in so many places, and the relatively thin layer of life sustaining atmosphere that surrounds Planet Earth.
- Fresh water for drinking and farming? Think about nature's cycle of droughts, depletion of underground aquifers by cities and farms, and the increasing use of water resources by expanding global populations.
- Good farming land? Think about erosion, soil nutrient depletion, conversion of arable land to housing for an ever expanding population of people.

Trade is another name for doing business - the activity of people exchanging (trading) money, goods, or services when each person has something that the other person wants.

Price is the amount of money that a buyer is willing to pay, and a seller is willing to accept, in exchange for a product or service. *Price is a function of supply and demand.* Typically:
- As the supply of comparable products or services increases, and demand remains relatively constant, price decreases.
- As demand for a product or service increases, and supply of comparable products or services remains relatively constant, price increases.

Price elasticity: Wikipedia says "elasticity is the measurement of how changing one economic variable affects others." Elasticity is graphed as supply and demand curves. Elasticity is tough to explain in a few words. You might research the term yourself.
- *Price elasticity of supply* attempts to measure how much a supplier might increase the amount of product or service she desires to supply as prices are going up, or cut back production as prices are going down.
- *Price elasticity of demand* attempts to measure how much consumer demand will go up or down as price changes. Typically, as price goes up, consumer demand tends to go down; and as price goes down, demand tends to go up.
- Learn about an anomaly of price elasticity when higher prices are charged to create a perception of higher quality, thereby stimulating higher demand by people who can

afford to pay for what they perceive to be higher quality (e.g. certain beauty products, and certain medical and legal products and services).

In regard to the purchase of a specific item, price is a function of:
- Degree of desire of a buyer to buy and the buyer's financial ability to pay.
- Degree of desire of a seller for a buyer's money.
- Seller's business strategy, e.g. sells higher volume of products or services at a lower price on each item sold, or sell lower volume at a higher price.
- Prices that the seller's competitors are charging for comparable products or services.

Priceless: one-of-a-kind artworks, irreplaceable historical artifacts, and other such rarities are often said to be priceless or invaluable. But if a seller wants to sell and a buyer wants to buy nothing is actually priceless.

Value: *things only have the value that people think they have*. Value is relative. Nothing has value on its own – not a dollar bill, not gold, not diamonds, not oil – nothing.

The word value is used in many different ways, including:
- Economic value: the price that people agree goods and services have when they are trading with each other. Supply and demand typically determine economic value.
- Utility value: the amount of use a person can get from a product or service.
- Sentimental value: the strength of emotional feeling that a person has for something; the better something makes a person feel, the higher the sentimental value it has for her. Your favorite old toy from childhood may have zero economic value for anyone else, but it is priceless to you because of its sentimental value – you wouldn't exchange it for any amount of money.
- Current book value: an accounting term; the way that assets are valued on a financial statement (purchase price of the asset minus depreciation).
- Current market value (actual value): estimate of the price a buyer would pay today; usually established by recent sales of comparable assets, e.g. houses are priced for sale based upon the current sales prices of comparable houses.
- Estimated future market value: a "working" guide as to what actual value (price) might be at a future time if a sale were to take place.
- Intrinsic value (of an investment asset): a favorite term of investment analysts; too complex to explain in the limited space of this book. Learn about it.
- *Best value*: that combination of price paid and utility gained (i.e. satisfaction, use, or benefit) that would provide a buyer an optimal return on the money she spent.

Money is something that people agree to use as a standard means of exchange in order to buy and sell goods and services among each other. Money can take different forms in different societies:
- Currency: paper bills and coins issued by governments.
- Credit cards, checks, and notes that represent currency.
- Hundreds of years ago the Native American people in New York used beautiful beads carved from clam shells (called wampum) as money.
- When I was a kid I remember being fascinated by pictures in National Geographic of people on the island of Yap using giant stone wheels as money.
- I have heard that prior to 2004 inmates in the Federal prison system used cigarettes as money because they were not allowed to have cash. And, then after smoking was prohibited in 2004, prisoners switched to using cans of mackerel as their money.

- "Virtual" currencies created on the internet.

The currencies of most countries – including the United States – do not have a fixed value. The value of the currency of each country "floats" up and down in relation to the currencies of other countries based upon <u>supply</u> (how much currency a country prints or coins) and <u>demand</u> (the degree of desire people have to own the country's currency and use it). Demand is typically a function of political stability and economic stability of the country. The US Government prints dollar bills and mints coins that are backed by the "full faith and credit" of the United States and the strength of the US economy.

Lost opportunity cost: once you spend money on one thing, you lose the opportunity to spend that same money on another thing.

Law of diminishing marginal utility
- The greater the amount of something that you have, the less satisfaction (utility) you gain from acquiring each additional unit of that thing.
- The more you have of something, the more additional units it would take to satisfy you.

Inflation: a general rise in prices of goods and services in an economy over time.

Deflation: a general decrease in prices of goods and services in an economy over time.

Behavioral economics and the corollary study of **behavioral finance**: emerging fields of study based upon real life observations of how people actually behave with money.
- In real life we flesh and blood people don't always behave with money:
  - o The way that economic theories predict that we will behave.
  - o The way that we say that we will behave.
- Behavioral economics mixes in the fields of psychology, sociology and social psychology to help us better understand how we might actually behave with our money.

After people develop spending, saving, and other money management habits, they tend to keep on doing things in the same habitual way, even though they say they will change their ways. If you have developed any money management habits that you would like to change, study:
- How experts recommend we try to change our behavioral habits in other parts of our lives, e.g. diet, exercise, smoking, gambling.
- Behavioral modification programs such as Twelve Step programs and mindfulness.
- *Cognitive behavioral therapy*.

"New paradigm": scary words to prudent business managers and financial professionals.
- New paradigms in science and in manufacturing often really are new and better ways of doing things. However, <u>so called</u> new paradigms in economics and behavioral economics seldom, if ever, really are new.
- Times change and technologies change, but human behavior with money is not likely to change much in your lifetime.
- *"It's different this time"* is the stuff of which investment bubbles are made, e.g. the new paradigm technology stock bubble of the 1990's; the new paradigm mortgage securities bubble of the late 2000's.
- Whenever you hear the words "it's different this time" be skeptical, very skeptical.

Types of economies: learn enough about the pros and cons of each of the following types of economies to develop a well-informed, well-reasoned opinion about the type of economy you think will provide the best opportunities for you to live the life you dream of living.

- *Market economy*: a "free market" in which business is governed by supply and demand.
  - o "Free market" of privately owned businesses operating with minimal government involvement and regulation.
  - o Capitalism: features private ownership of the means of production (property, factories, etc.), and the ability of individuals and companies to sell goods and services they produce for a profit and accumulate financial wealth (a/k/a capital).
  - o Barter economy: people exchange products and services without money (a farmer trades a chicken in exchange for a toolmaker's ax; an electrician trades his services for an accountant's services); "swapping". Mankind's original economy.
  - o Cash economy: instead of swapping goods and services, a buyer pays cash money for the products or services of a seller.
- *Planned economy*: a government plans the economy and owns the means of production.
  - o Socialism: in its ideal form, all citizens would work together cooperatively to provide the goods and services that each person needs. People elect their own democratic government, and their government owns the means of production. Workers are paid. People can own private property. Learn about the rise and demise of Utopian societies in the United States in the 1800's.
  - o Communism: extreme form of socialism; authoritarian central party control; no private ownership of property (in theory) - everything owned communally.
- *Mixed economy*: combines traits of both a market economy and a planned economy. Most countries have mixed economies that blend in capitalist private ownership of property with socialist social welfare programs and some amount of government planning of the economy, e.g. tax policy, trade tariffs, investment in infrastructure to facilitate economic growth, central bank influence on monetary matters.
- "Black market" (underground) economy: exchange of goods and services that "skirts the law" outside of a government taxed and regulated economy.

Degree of competition among suppliers determines how much "freedom of choice" consumers have in purchasing products and services:

- *Monopoly*: no effective competition; consumers are stuck with only one supplier.
- *Oligopoly*: a limited number of suppliers from which consumers can choose.
- *Free market*: many suppliers from which consumers can choose.
- *Government regulated utility*: no competition, but government regulates the prices that the regulated supplier can charge and geographic area in which the supplier can operate.

Taxes are fees that governments assess citizens in order to pay for services that governments provide to citizens. *Think of taxes as the "dues" we pay to be citizens.* Learn about:

- Types of taxes and reasons why each type of tax is used, e.g. income taxes, sales taxes, real estate taxes, special purpose taxes on products such as tobacco and alcohol.
- Learn about two types of income tax rates:
  - o Graduated (a/k/a progressive) tax rates - increase in stair stepped fashion as a person's income increases
  - o Flat tax rates - same tax rate on every dollar of every person's income.
- Role taxes have played in American history, from British taxes on their colonies (e.g., taxes on stamps and tea) to the establishment of a permanent Federal income tax in 1913, to today's incredibly complex tax code that is loaded with tax credits and tax incentives.

Governmental economic policy: learn about the current economic policies of your elected government representatives, and develop opinions about policies you think they should adopt.

- Types of taxes and tax rate structures that should be used to finance the economy of your local, state, and national governments?
- What should government do for people? What should people do for themselves (self-reliance)? How much financial support can a government supply to how many people?
- Global competition - for jobs, wealth, natural resources needed for manufacturing.
- Global cooperation - free trade agreements such as the North American Free Trade Agreement (NAFTA); European Union.
- To stimulate your thinking about the economic policies you would like your government to adopt, learn about the economies of some other countries that have vibrant economies, and the degree to which free market capitalism and government planning mix in those economies. Do some compare and contrast studies of current American economic policies with the governmental policies in other countries, such as:
  - o Germany: role of labor unions in a vibrant mixed economy.
  - o Norway: a vibrant mixed economy that features a heavy dose of socialism, e.g. social welfare programs and economic planning.
  - o China: a government trying to steer evolution of a planned economy away from iron fisted Communist Party control toward a more mixed economy as they try to accommodate the demands of a growing middle class and a wealthy elite. Learn about common criticisms of government practices.

Social responsibility of citizens in capitalist democracies
- In order for a capitalist democracy to prosper over the long term, each citizen must believe he has a social responsibility to abide by the society's laws and behave in an ethical manner.
- <u>People must be able to trust each other to "do the right thing"</u> if they are to continue living in harmony with each other and continue doing business with each other.
- Each citizen also should believe he has a social responsibility to help provide economic opportunity, and financial assistance as needed, to people who truly need help.
  - o Social responsibility is essential for maintaining social and economic order.
  - o Think about all the rebellions that have happened throughout history after enough citizens began to think and feel that there was too much income inequality between rich and poor, and that they didn't have a "fair" opportunity to get good jobs that would provide them a good income.
  - o Learn about two types of "re-distribution of wealth" - from people who have more money to people who have less money:
    - Statutory re-distribution through taxes, e.g. income taxes and estate taxes.
    - Voluntary re-redistribution through philanthropy, e.g. financial contributions to charities and religious organizations.
- <u>Understand the benefits of "benevolent self-interest"</u> (a/k/a enlightened self-interest) – learn how doing good things for fellow citizens typically comes back around to benefit a person in the long run.

Economies evolve over time. Learn how various professional economists and experts in different fields of study envision the future of the local, state, national, and global economies in which you will be living, working, and managing your investment portfolio.

Marketing

Marketing is a planned effort to influence how people think and how they spend their money.
- Companies use marketing to influence consumers to buy their products and services.
- Politicians use marketing to influence people to vote for them and to fund their campaigns with financial contributions.
- Charitable and religious organizations use marketing to raise money to fund their good works.

Marketing is applied psychology. It's all about mind games. It's fun to study.

Components of a comprehensive marketing program might include:
- *Creating a culture of excellent employee performance*: typically the most productive and profitable component of a comprehensive marketing program. Each employee contributes to either a positive or negative impression of the company (a) directly through contact with customers and others outside the company, or (b) indirectly through the quality of work that is contributed to producing the products or services sold). Creating a "culture of excellence" in which each employee contributes to a positive image helps generate:
  - Repeat business from satisfied customers.
  - "Word of mouth" referrals to new customers made by satisfied customers as well as the company's suppliers, subcontractors, and other people who have observed or heard about the company's excellent performance
- *Advertising*: topics to study are suggested in a few pages.
- *Sales*: topics to study are suggested in a few pages.
- *Signage and name placement*: signs, vehicles, employee uniforms, naming rights on buildings and sports stadiums, sponsor names on sports team uniforms and equipment.
- *Product placement*: getting actors or other public figures to use a company's product in TV shows, movies, and other venues where the product will be noticed by the public.
- *Pricing*
  - Pricing can be used as a marketing tool in various ways, such as:
    - Deep discount pricing or free samples that get people to try a product ("try it, you'll like it").
    - Loss leaders: one or more select items priced below cost in order to attract customers and get them to see and buy profitable items.
    - Low price on each unit sold to create an image of "good value" and generate a high volume of sales.
    - High price on each unit to create an image of high quality.
  - Learn about "price point" – how a product is priced relative to its competitors.
- *Doing good works* that get employees and their employers talked about in the community, in their industry, and in the media, such as:
  - Employees volunteering time and talents with community and industry organizations.
  - Employers sponsoring programs and events.
  - Learn how the military uses "psychological operations" to "win the hearts and minds" of a local population (target market audience) - often using covert tactics that are not perceived by the target market audience as direct attempts to influence their thinking and behavior.

"Target marketing" involves:
- Segmenting an entire population into "target market" demographic subgroups who are

identified as people being most likely to become customers or contributors;
- And then crafting a marketing program tailored to influence the thinking and spending behavior of that specific target market.

Branding: creating name recognition for a person, product, or organization. A "brand" is:
- The public image of a person, product, or organization.
- An image that creates a favorable impression of the person, product, or organization.
- The first thought that pops into people's minds when they hear the brand name.
- The image that sticks in people's minds.

Elevator speech: a sales pitch that could be delivered during a 30 second elevator ride (hence the name) to concisely summarize whatever is being sold and interest a listener in hearing more.

Talking points: pre-planned comments designed to:
- Guide the communications of an entire organization.
- Guide the communications of individual employees with people outside the organization.
- Keep everyone in an organization "on the same page" saying the same things.

External marketing: directed at people outside the organization - prospective customers and business partners such as suppliers, subcontractors, and professional service providers.

Internal marketing: directed at people inside the organization - employees and other people considered to be members of an organization's business team. Internal marketing is a key element in creating a culture of excellence.

Internal marketing tools include:
- Publications: employee manual, intranet, newsletters.
- Employee training programs; mentorship of new employees.
- Incentive compensation programs and contests designed to motivate employees to contribute to the organization's culture of excellence.
- Employee suggestion programs and open door policies of senior managers that solicit employees' ideas about how to improve the organization's culture of excellence.
- Providing a work environment in which employees enjoy working.
- Community service programs, clubs, and other activities that develop esprit de corps.

Focus group: a group of people that marketing professionals bring together in order to get feedback (opinions, suggestions for enhancements, etc.) on a new product, service, advertising program, packaging, etc. Focus group participants are encouraged to talk with each other so that they stimulate each other's thinking as they share their thoughts about the subject matter.

Test market: selling a product in a limited geographic area or to a sample demographic group in order to gauge consumer interest before rolling it out for wider scale distribution.

Creating cultural demand
- The best marketing programs move past just creating demand in individual consumers.
- They create a cultural demand for a product or a service in an entire society – they are "game changers".
- Learn about marketing geniuses who created cultural demand, such as *Edward L. Bernays (nephew of Sigmund Freud), Albert Lasker,* and *Steve Jobs.*

Advertising

Advertising is a marketing communication designed to deliver a specific message to a specific target market audience.

Psychology and behavioral economics are key elements in the creation of advertising. Advertising professionals study psychology and behavioral economics to learn what motivates consumers to spend money and buy certain things, and techniques they can use in advertising to manipulate (influence) consumers' thinking and spending behavior.

Every word, image, color, note of music, and person in an advertisement is carefully selected by advertising professionals to influence the thinking and behavior of their target market audience in the way that the advertiser wants their thinking and behavior influenced.

Advertising typically is designed to appeal to emotion more than rational thinking.
- Typically, advertising professionals are not given enough time or space to provide all the facts and complete explanations that target market audience members would need in order to make well-formed, well-reasoned purchase decisions.
- Rather, they are typically given limited time or space constraints within which to craft effective advertisements, e.g. 30 seconds on TV, one page in a magazine, shared space on a computer screen.
- So, they typically go for emotion grabbers that entice consumers.

Subliminal advertising is a "message within an advertising message" that appeals to people's subconscious minds, most famously to the human instinct of sexual attraction. Many people doubt that subliminal advertising is actually used. I ask skeptics to try to explain why smart advertising professionals who have studied psychology would not try to appeal to people's subconscious minds and conscious minds in the same ad. (Read Vance Packard's book *The Hidden Persuaders*.)

Advertising "vehicles" are chosen for the delivery of advertising messages based upon where advertising professionals think their target market audience is most likely to see or hear their advertisements. Commonly used advertising vehicles include:
- Newspapers and magazines
- Radio and television
- Signs and billboards
- Internet

"Word of mouth" advertising occurs when people tell other people about a product service.
- People will say either good things or bad things about a person, organization, product or service based upon their personal experience and what they hear other people say.
- Creating a culture of excellence within an organization helps make people outside the organization think good things - the key to generating good word of mouth advertising.
- Benefits of word of mouth advertising include:
  - o It typically is more effective than paid advertising because people tend to believe it more. It is especially effective when it comes from a person who has first-hand experience with whatever she is talking about and the listener knows and trusts the opinions of the person who is doing the talking.
  - o It's free, and it amplifies the effect of paid advertising.
  - o It can travel fast "through the grapevine".

<u>Sales</u>

Sales methods include:
- *Generating "repeat business" purchases made by satisfied customers - typically the most profitable sales method.* Creating a corporate culture of excellent employee performance is a key element in getting customers to come back time and again to buy.
- *Referral sales* (word of mouth advertising) generated by satisfied customers and other people who have learned about the quality of a company, its people, and its products or services.
- *Person to person sales* by salespeople or independent marketing representatives.
- *Indirect sales*: passive selling through advertising, a company's website, etc.
- *Direct mail*: sent directly to the homes of prospective consumers (a/k/a junk mail).

Two broad categories of person-to-person sales:
- *"Soft sell": "consultative" selling targeted at the rational thinking* of prospective customers; explaining the logical reasons why a decision to spend money would make prudent economic sense for the customer.
  - o Soft sell is based upon getting to know and understand a buyer's needs and wants, and then explaining how the company's products or services can satisfy those needs and wants (and in some cases of outstanding consultative selling, explaining why those products or services are not the best fit to satisfy the buyer's needs and wants at the present time – think of the goodwill this builds).
  - o Soft sell builds trust in the buyer that the salesperson will only recommend what she thinks is truly best for the buyer.
- *"Hard sell": "manipulative" selling targeted at the emotions* of prospective customers.
  - o Hard sell often tries to convert a buyer from thinking about something as a want into thinking about that thing as a need (conversion of "I'd like to have that" into "I need to have that").
  - o Hard sell typically uses the words "How does it <u>feel</u>?" more than "What do you <u>think</u>?"
  - o Hard sell often includes the following technique:
    - ▪ Get the buyer into a buying frame of mind by engaging in "small talk" that gets the buyer to "feel good" about the salesperson, and then asking a series of questions that generate "yes" answers (e.g. "don't you agree that …") that make the buyer feel that they both think alike. These questions can start "way out in left field" and then gradually come around to a series of questions that lead up to the "sales pitch".
    - ▪ The sales pitch concludes by offering the buyer a choice between two purchase options, e.g. "now, would you like to buy Option A (a widget fully loaded with all the bells and whistles") or Option B (basic model widget) rather than just asking if she wants to buy a widget.

Negotiation: study the art of negotiation (and the art of debate) from the offensive perspective of a seller and the defensive perspective of a buyer.

Body language: during person to person sales transactions (and conversations among family members) people communicate in both verbal language and body language. Good sales people learn to use and to read body language. So should you.

Risk Management

Risk management: the study of how to manage what could go wrong in our imperfect world.

Financial risk management is a key element in the business of professionals such as insurance agents, bankers, and financial advisors. Pick the brains of these professionals to get a practical education in financial risk management.

Insurance people think of risk as the probability that something undesirable (a peril) might occur and cause financial harm. They talk about risk management in terms of:
- Risk identification: what perils could occur and what is the probability of their occurring?
- Risk avoidance, e.g. "No you can't have a BB gun. You'll shoot your eye out."
- Risk transfer: transferring risk to others by means such as buying insurance policies to transfer specific risks to insurance companies, or hiring experts to do work that would be "risky" for you to do yourself.
- Risk management: managing risks that you decide to accept (or can't avoid or transfer).

Risk management
- *Think like a chess player* - think one or two moves ahead. Anticipate what could go wrong (with your job, your investments, the economy, etc.) and cause you harm. Then plan how to avoid, transfer or minimize the risks of those things harming you.
- *"Enterprise" risk management*: corporate risk managers try to think holistically about every possible risk their employers' companies (enterprises) might face. As you make each decision, consider the degree of risk your decision might introduce into your life.
- *Loss control plan*: objectives, strategies, and action plans designed to minimize the risk of suffering losses, be those losses financial, emotional, or any other type of loss.
- *Contingency plans*: in our imperfect world plans don't always work out as expected, people don't always perform as expected, and unexpected events happen. Having a "Plan B" in mind helps minimize the risk of getting hurt when the unexpected happens.

Risk-reward: generally speaking, the greater the potential reward the greater the risk of something not working out well. Evaluating potential risk versus potential reward should be a key factor in making our decisions (choices) about our lifestyles, careers, financial management, etc.

Risk transfer through insurance
- Buy insurance from financially strong companies that have earned good reputations for customer satisfaction and claims payment, and are likely to remain in business to pay any future claim you might have - especially important for life insurance companies. Learn about A. M. Best ratings of the financial strength and stability of insurance companies.
- Policies of the same type (auto, homeowners, etc.) provided by different insurance companies can have different coverages (risks they will cover), different exclusions (risks they won't cover), and different deductibles. Learn about these differences before buying.
- *Prices charged by an insurance company (insurer)* are based upon factors such as:
  - Actuarial projections of insured losses that the insurer expects to be incurred by members of large groups of statistically similar people (law of large numbers).
  - Each policyholder's loss history and "risk profile" for projected future losses.
  - Prices charged by the insurer's competitors; learn about the insurance market cycle of hard markets (increasing prices) and soft markets (decreasing prices).
  - Investment income of the insurer – both current and projected future income.
  - Insurer's corporate objectives for "return on capital employed".

Work/Study Program

Work/study programs: many employers and colleges have established work/study programs in which students get jobs that become an integral part of their studies. Employers and educators have learned that the workplace provides a great hands-on learning laboratory for students who might become future employees. Work/study programs allow students to:
- Learn how classroom material can be applied in real world business situations.
- Learn things through "on the job training" (OJT) in the real world that they couldn't learn in a classroom, e.g. practical job skills and street smarts.
- Learn how knowledge gained in the "liberal arts" such as psychology, sociology, philosophy, English, history, and geography can be applied to making money in the business world.

Establish a work/study program for yourself as a part of your business school curriculum.
- If you currently have a job, use it as a work/study program.
- If you don't yet have a job, get one.
- If you are too young to go to work for someone else, start your own business (with your parents' consent, of course), e.g. cutting lawns, shoveling snow, babysitting, pet-sitting.

If you currently have a job, use your workplace as a "learning laboratory". To paraphrase a gross old figure of speech, *"suck all the financial and business management marrow" that you can out of the bones of your employer's organizational body.*
- Observe and listen to what is going on - what people say and what people do. Try to gain exposure to workplace skills and management practices that may not be directly related to your job but will help increase your future value in the job market, perhaps in subjects such as marketing, negotiation, finance, accounting, human resource management, law and regulatory control.
- Ask questions. Be curious. Pick the minds of co-workers and supervisors to gather all the potentially useful information that you can.

If you are a student in high school or college, try to tie your school work and a job together as much as possible.
- An ideal job might be in an industry you would like to explore with a good employer who might be able to offer you a job after you graduate.
- Try to identify ways that class material could be applied in your employer's organization.
- Ask your teachers for their thoughts about how class material might apply to your job and your employer's operations.
- Ask people at work how they think class material might apply to your job and your employer's operations.
- You might use your employer as a case study in class papers or projects.
- If you have the opportunity to do a class project, consider preparing a paper that you could also submit as a suggestion in your employer's suggestion program

Caution: take care to not divulge to classmates or teachers any of your employer's confidential information, e.g. trade secrets, proprietary operating systems, new products or services in the development pipeline, or any other internal-use-only information. Be prudent. Use common sense. *Ask your supervisor what information that you learn at work must be treated as strictly confidential and what information could be shared with your class.*

Chapter 4. Business Plans & Financial Budgets

A few personal business planning basics

A personal business plan is a roadmap that will help you get where you want to go in life - a guide to making your dreams come true.
- Two old adages offer great advice:
  - o "You need to know where you want to go before you can get there."
  - o "If you don't know where you want to go, any road will take you there."
- Experience with people I have known tells me:
  - o Most 22 and 32 year olds don't think much about what life will be like at 62.
  - o By age 42, after the realities and responsibilities of life have begun to sink in, such thoughts cross people's minds more frequently.
  - o By age 52 most people have been doing a lot of thinking about what their lives will be like in a short 10 years when they get to age 62.
  - o The earlier in life that you start to plan for your future, the more likely you will be to lead the comfortably satisfying life you dream about living.
- People who don't have a plan for their lives leave their financial destiny to fate. To a large extent, they put their future in the hands of other people.

Wishing works only in fairy tales.
- We can't just wish we had more money and expect to get it. In real life we must decide how much money we want, plan how to get it, and then take action to go out and get it.
- *Be realistic.* Successful business people face the realities of life head-on, and plan their businesses so as to manage those realities.
- *Financial planning won't guarantee you get rich.* The cold reality of statistical fact is that most of us won't get "rich" - depending of course upon how each of us defines rich.
- *However, most of us are likely to live happy, financially comfortable lives if we use a business planning and financial budgeting process over a long enough period of time.*

Planning should be a continuous loop process, not a one-shot thing. You can't just write a plan, put it away in a desk drawer, and then expect miracles to happen.

Below is a suggested six step planning process (which you can revise as you think will work best for you).
- *Step 1. Objectives*: decide what you want to achieve in life.
- *Step2. Inventory*: identify what you have to work with today – your financial assets and liabilities, current income, personal strengths and weaknesses, what you value most in life, things that you love to do, risk tolerance, etc.
- *Step 3. Strategy*: decide how you want to live your life in pursuit of your objectives.
- *Step 4. Action plan*: decide what steps to take toward achieving your objectives.
- *Step 5. Monitor*: *keep track of* your progress toward achieving your objectives.
- *Step 6. Revise*: start at Step 1 again and revise your plan as needed based upon changes in the objectives you want to achieve, progress you have made toward achieving your objectives, lessons you learned, changed conditions in your life and the economy, etc.

Two integral parts of a personal business plan:
- *Business plan* = the words part
- *Financial budget* = the numbers part

Think of the interrelationship of plans and budgets this way:
- Plans without budgets won't help us figure out the money we will need to have in order to do the things we are planning to do.
- A budget without a plan is just a bunch of numbers on paper with no idea about how to actually bring that money into our lives.

A personal business planning process will help you tie together into one holistically coordinated plan a number of elements that some people talk about as being separate plans:
- Budget management plan
- Financial plan / investment management plan
- Life management plan (such as a "life coach" might recommend).
- Career path plan
- Risk management plan
- Estate plan

<u>**Ease into your planning process**</u> – and have fun doing it – the more fun we have doing something the more likely we are to keep on doing it and trying to get better at it.
- Just as no ship's captain can "turn an ocean liner on a dime" nobody can turn an unplanned life into a well-planned life overnight. If you tried to change too fast, you'd probably drive yourself nuts, get frustrated, and quit using "that darned" planning process. Let's exaggerate to make the point. Think about a person trying to go from one extreme of planning to the other extreme - a total free spirit consciously trying to become an obsessive compulsive planner of every little detail in his life (like anyone would ever want to). It's not going to happen anytime soon – probably not until pigs fly. And, even if it did happen, the newly obsessive compulsive planner would want to quit being so manic as soon as he realized the monster he had created.
- Enjoy the act of planning. It gives us an opportunity to focus our thinking on how we can make our dreams come true. That's fun. And life should be as much about the journey as it is about the arrival at our dream objective destinations. Plan to enjoy every day that life gives you as you use your planning process to guide your journey toward your dreams. Death has an inconvenient way of ending the journey through life for some of us way sooner than we had planned.

<u>**Keep your plan short and sweet**</u>.
- *<u>A good bit of my personal business plan is still in my head and not on paper because</u>:*
    - It's a continual work in progress. New ideas and insights regularly come to mind.
    - The more details that I tried to write, the more I found I had to revise those details because of changing circumstances.
- <u>Your entire plan and budget might be written on just a few pages</u>. *The idea is to focus your thinking, and provide you a written reminder of what you were thinking.*
    - *<u>Start by writing down your dreams</u> about what you want to do in your lifetime (your "bucket list"). These written dreams can then become long term and ultra-long term objectives in your plan - guide stars to use in steering the course of your life toward realization of those dreams.*
    - Pick one or two of your most important dream objectives, and write down a list of things that you think you would need to accomplish at some point in time in order to eventually achieve those dream objectives. These to do lists can become your short term and mid-term objectives. Don't get hung up writing these lists – you can expand and revise them over time as you work your planning process.

o   Then begin compiling your "strategy" - a list of guiding principles for the way you want to live your life as you go about achieving your objectives.

o   Then prepare an initial action plan – a "to do list" of things that will help you achieve of your short term and mid-term objectives.

- *Don't try to plan every single detail and every single minute of your life.*

    o   Identify enough action plan steps to achieve your objectives, but leave yourself enough unplanned "free time" to take advantage of opportunities as they present themselves, and to enjoy the fun times that a life well-lived has in store for you.

    o   Make sure you understand the difference between being "efficient" and being "obsessively compulsive".

    o   *Keep a healthy sense of perspective on the amount of your precious time that you invest in planning.* As John Lennon sang to his son Sean in the song *Beautiful Boy,* "*Life is just what happens to you while you're busy making other plans.*"

    o   "Don't lose sight of the forest for the trees". The idea is to plan to live, not to live to plan.

Plan to be as good as you can be, not better than anybody else. Be like the weekend warrior runners who seek personal best times in each race rather than trying to beat other runners.

Plan for trade-offs. *We can plan to have a lot, but we can't plan to have it all*. Make sure you understand the term *lost opportunity cost* in economics.

- *Economic trade-offs*: we each have a limited supply of money. Once we spend some of our money on one thing we lose the opportunity to spend that money on something else. We must plan to trade-off not getting certain things that we want in order to have enough money to pay for what we want more.

- *Compromise trade-offs*: in order to get most of what we want in a business transaction:

    o   We may need to give up getting some of what we want, and accept some things we want less or don't want at all; and

    o   Allow the person with whom we are negotiating to get some of what he wants.

- *Risk-reward trade-offs*: if we are unwilling to accept a higher risk of loss, we must be willing to accept the probability of earning less reward (return on our time and money).

Planning for trade-off decisions requires that you fix in your mind a priority order ranking of:

- *Things you value most in life* (maintain a list of the things you value most in life in the personal inventory section of your plan - more on this in a few pages).

- *Objectives you consider most important to achieve.*

Plan for the future.

- <u>*The world of your future is going to be different from the world as you know it today*</u>.

- Visualize the world in which you will be living in 10 years, 30 years, and more.

- Learn as much as you can about what experts in various fields think the world of the future will be like, and how they think people should plan to prosper in that future world.

Plan ahead, the way a chess player plans his moves. Anticipate what might happen.

- What will the economy be like in the future for earning income each year and for managing your investments?

- How are current events in your life, your country, and the world likely to play out?

- How are trends and cycles that you know about likely to play out in the future?

- What resources are you likely to have available to work with in the future, e.g. expertise you plan to acquire, new people in your life, wealth you plan to amass?

- How are people likely to react to decisions you make – your family, co-workers, boss?
- If you currently have a job, how might your job be changed by technology; what new job skills might you need to learn; what might future market conditions be like for your employer; how might your industry be evolving?
- How might changing demographics affect your future competition for jobs?
- How will your employer's operations and the ways you spend your money impact the vibrancy of the economy and the social order of the community in which you will be living?
- What can you do today to make the world of tomorrow a better place for you to live and to achieve your business plan and projected financial statement budget objectives?

Life is long, and it keeps getting longer.
- Learn about average human life expectancy today and the factors that are likely to help it continue to get longer, e.g. medical discoveries, better healthcare, better nutrition.
- *Plan for a life longer than the current average human life expectancy.* The younger you are, the longer the life you should plan on living.
- *Tomorrow may never come; life must be lived today.* But, most of us are going to live a lot of tomorrows. We must plan to spend enough money today to live happy lives "in the moment", while we plan how to pay for all the tomorrows that we are likely to live.
- *Our human bodies grow older each day.* As time passes the probability increases that we could become physically unable to continue working at jobs to actively earn a predictable stream of annual income, and the probability also increases that we will need to spend a lot more money each year on medical expenses. While we are physically able to do so, we should plan to build investment portfolios that would be able to generate enough passive income to make us feel that we have comfortable financial security blankets.
- *Consider planning* to have *"financial freedom" rather than "retire"* - financial freedom to do whatever you want to do during the "next chapter" of your life. Consider the financial planning benefits of planning a career path toward a job that you love so much that you wouldn't want to retire from it; a job that could provide a predictable stream of revenue as far out into the future as you think prudent to plan (see Chapter 17).

To minimize risk in your life, plan for gradual evolution of your life.
- Typically, gradual evolution of lifestyles, careers, and investment portfolios is less risky than radical revolution. "The longer the leap, the harder it is to leap successfully."
- Plan for *segues* – gradually easing away from doing one thing into doing the next thing.
- As your life is evolving, consider tinkering with your plan rather than overhauling it.
- Beware the dangers of a radical reaction to events, such as dumping a trusted advisor who had served you well over a long period of time just because one thing didn't work out the way you had wanted (I have heard this regrettable story too many times).
- In certain exceptional situations, (e.g. your company being acquired and new management asking you to move to a new town) you MAY need to make exceptionally rapid revisions to your plan. In these cases be on high alert for the dangers that can come from significant changes over a short period of time. Talk to as many confidants as you think prudent to get different perspectives on your situation. Ask for advice. Don't try to carry heavy mental burdens alone if you don't have to.

If you have an epiphany (an "aha" moment), in which you suddenly see yourself or the world differently, be careful about the speed with which you act upon that epiphany. It could be a "false epiphany" - you could be wrong. Talk with at least one confidant whose judgment you trust to get his thoughts about an epiphany before making a major overhaul in your plan or budget based upon that epiphany.

- If your epiphany is that honesty is truly the best policy, then by all means start being more honest immediately.
- If your epiphany is about a major career change, it might be wise to go slowly; to take some baby step feelers in that direction before taking major strides.

Have a "Plan B". Plans can sound great in our heads, look good on paper, and then not play out in the real world as we had thought they would. Be a pragmatic realist. As you plan for things that would have significant impact on your life, think about Plan B options you might implement if your Plan A wasn't working out as planned.

Old habits die hard.

- Planning habits acquired over a lifetime are not likely to change the minute you begin using your planning process. Give yourself plenty of time to practice using your planning process. Just as with everything else people practice, the more you practice using your planning process, the better you are likely to get at using it.
- The longer you use your planning process, the more it is likely to become a comfortably ingrained habit in your life, and the more long term objectives you will likely be able to comfortably work toward achieving.
- The more time you spend using your planning process, the more time that focused thinking about your plan will be percolating in your brain, and the more likely it is that:
  - o You will be able to identify action plan steps that will enable you to make progress toward your long term objectives.
  - o You will develop a progressively more holistic plan that links together your objectives and action plans to achieve those objectives.
  - o Your action plans begin to overlap so that taking one action plan step will advance you toward achieving multiple holistically-linked objectives.

Don't use planning as the sole excuse for not acting.

- Don't put off doing things that you know you should do, but are uncomfortable doing or scared to do, by rationalizing that you need to think more about it and do more planning(e.g. confronting a co-worker who is not treating you right, or a spouse who is behaving in an unacceptable manner).
- If you tend to be a perfectionist, don't put off taking action plan steps until you think you have a perfect plan. There are no perfect plans. There are just lots of good plans that keep on getting better as people revise them.

You can't just copy a plan out of a book and expect it to work for you!

- Each of us is a unique person who has unique life circumstances, a unique set of skills and abilities, and a unique financial position.
- There are too many variables in each person's life to allow a "one-size-fits-all" plan to work for everyone.
- Each of us should have a uniquely personalized plan for managing our lives and money.

Use this book as a tool to get started in developing your business plan and projected financial statement budget, and learn all you can about planning from all the other resources available.

- Learn how experts in various fields advise us to plan, e.g. professional financial advisors, management consultants, life coaches, and other professional service providers.
- Use the vast quantity of how-to-plan resources available in books, classes, and websites

Magic in written plans and budgets

There is practical magic in writing a business plan and a projected financial statement budget. The physical act of writing will help you:
- Crystallize and organize your thoughts about your life.
- Interpret your dreams in real world terms.

Writing a plan and budget can help you:
- Lay out a series of shorter term objectives that lead up to achieving your long term dream objectives.
- Manage the human weakness of forgetfulness that we are all prone to experience. Regular reading of a written plan and budget can help prevent your mind from:
  - o Forgetting altogether what you originally planned to do.
  - o Playing tricks on you such that you don't do all the things you had planned to do, or do some things you hadn't planned to do that may not have been good for you to do.
- Strengthen your self-discipline to stick to your written plan and budget. Regularly reading your plan and budget will help keep them in the forefront of your mind.
- Do the mental gymnastics with numbers needed to make budget management decisions. *There is special magic in writing the numbers in a budget* because it so awfully hard for so many of us to manage numbers in our heads, e.g. remember and keep track of all our current revenue and expense numbers as a year progresses, and make a reasonably accurate projection of what we can make those numbers become at the end of the year.
- Make better decisions (see Chapter 7).

Don't get me wrong. It is possible to run a successful business without a written plan and budget. I've observed successful business owners do it. However, they were exceptional people. They had natural gifts of brain power that most of us don't have:
- An ability to develop a plan in their heads that included most of the elements that should be included in a good written plan and budget.
- An ability to retain the details of their plans and budgets in their heads.
- Self-discipline to stick to their plans and budgets without written reminders.

The above said, most of these people became even more successful after they began preparing and using written plans and budgets.

Planning Process Step 1: establish your business plan objectives

Make your dreams your objectives.
- *Open your mind to dream about whatever you desire to do and to have in your life*.
- "Follow your bliss." What would bring you the greatest joy and satisfaction you can imagine? What achievements would make you feel as contented as a cat sleeping on a sunny window sill?
- Dream big. Dream expansively about all that you would like to do during your life, all the income you would like to earn, and all the wealth you would like to accumulate
- Dream big, BUT, and this is a Big BUT, *never plan to live beyond your current means*. Dream big, but plan a financially prudent lifestyle.
- To spur your dreaming:
  - o Ask older people who are closer to the end of the line than you are what they would do in life if they could have a do-over.
  - o Brainstorm with family, advisors, and close friends in whom you can confide. Ask them what they would do if they could do whatever they dreamed of doing.

Don't put artificial limits on your dreams, and don't let anybody else try to do it either.
- Don't tell yourself "I could never do that." *Maybe you couldn't do it this year, or next year. But maybe you could do it after 5 years, 10 years, or 20 years of diligently working at learning new skills, practicing the skills you learn, gaining life experience, and surrounding yourself with good people who would help you achieve your dream objectives*.
- Free your mind of any limitations that you may have been placing upon yourself, or limitations that other people may have tried to place upon you.
  - o Don't let the expectations of family, friends or anyone else become your expectations for your life.
  - o Don't let your potential be defined by anyone but you.
  - o Don't succumb to feeling typecast, stereotyped, pigeonholed, or relegated to any role in life other than the role you dream about for yourself.
  - o Don't ever feel limited by your current education level, age, sex, or anything else.
- There is a lot of truth to the saying "you can be whatever you want to be if you try hard enough".
- Library shelves are full of biographies of people who had a dream, were told they couldn't do whatever it was that they dreamed about doing, and then they went out and did it anyway.

Putting your dreams into words might be tough.
- Some people might run into a mental roadblock when trying to put their dreams into words because they can't get visions of the great lives they think other people are living out of their minds (beware feelings of envy). Focus on your vision for your life.
- And some people just haven't given themselves the freedom to think about what they would do "If only … wasn't stopping me". Plan how to get past "if only's".

Set your sights high, but understand that time will limit how many of our dreams each of us can fully achieve in the one lifetime we get.
- If you could live enough years, and you used your planning process diligently enough, you could achieve pretty much every objective you set for yourself.
- However, given the different starting points in life from which each of us begins to use a

formal planning process, how far each of us will have to go to get to our dream destinations, and the limited years of life each of us will have to get there (some will get more years, some will get less years), most of us won't have <u>all</u> the time we would need in order to achieve <u>all</u> of our dream objectives – but we will get as close as possible.

- *"Life is more about the journey than the destination"*. Plan to enjoy every single day. Be a happy, optimistic pragmatist who understands "you can only do what you can do."

Describe the evolving lifestyle you dream of living as you age. *Hindsight is 20/20, but foresight is 20/400* – use your planning process as binoculars to help you see the lifestyle you desire to be living in 10 years, in 20 years, in 30 years, and the last year of your life.

- *The younger we are, the more difficult it is to visualize ourselves at an older age.* An 18 year old may hear mom and dad talk about concerns of theirs and not fully understand those concerns. By age 50 it is likely he would have a far better understanding.
- *The older we get the smarter we get about the past.* How many times have you looked back on what you did when you were younger and said to yourself "What was I thinking?" or "I should have done ..." Well, now is the time to flip your view of life around. Instead of looking back, look ahead to your future. What will make the older you say "I'm glad I did that years ago"? *Using a planning process will help make us smarter about our futures*.
- Read Aesop's Fable about the Grasshopper and the Ants. It speaks directly to planning for future financial security and doing things today to provide for that future security. It is brutally tough to picture ourselves in the future having a lot less money than we need - living in fear of how to pay for food, medicine, and shelter as limited savings run dry. Picture the Grasshopper and the Ants instead. Plan accordingly.
- The act of writing a business plan and projected financial statement budget will help focus your thinking on the evolving lifestyle you want to be living as you age and how much money it will take to finance your lifestyle at various stages of your life.

Don't get stuck in your past as you dream about your future. The past has only two uses:
- Memories to enjoy.
- Lessons to learn.

Lay out a progression of objectives to achieve over the course of time that will advance you from where you are today toward the eventual achievement of your dream objectives. The easiest way to plan this progression of objectives might be to <u>start with your dream objectives</u> to achieve in the future (where you want to go) and work your way back in time with increasingly realistic objectives (steps to take to get there) in a reverse order of "planning periods" (segments of time).

- *Ultra- long term objectives*: last year of your estimated life expectancy - the <u>dreams you aspire to make come</u> true by the end of your life.
- *Long term objectives*: roughly 5 to 30 years out into the future - big picture <u>"aspirational" objectives</u> that help you (a) look down from the proverbial vantage point of "30,000 feet" to visualize the path you would like to take through life toward your dream objectives (e.g. career, marriage, children, good works that help others) (b) visualize the lifestyle you want to be living at various ages as you grow older and (c) lay out a progression of mid-term and short term objectives that lead toward achieving your dream objectives.
- *Mid-term objectives*: roughly 2 to 5 years; more detailed objectives to achieve in a more foreseeable timeframe in order to stay on track to achieve your long term objectives.
- *Short term objectives*: 1 to 2 years; describe in specific detail exactly what you think you will need to accomplish in order to stay on track to achieve your mid-term objectives.

The further out into the future that you plan, the more your objectives will serve as aspirational guideposts to strive toward. The closer to the present that you plan, the more your objectives should become realistically achievable.

Developing a tiered progression of objectives makes good business sense for two reasons:
- First, ultra-long term and long term objectives will give you points of reference in the distant future from which you can backtrack in time to the present. This will help guide your thinking about things you will need to accomplish as you progress through life in pursuit of your dreams.
- Second, the further out into the future that you try to plan, the more likely it is that:
    - o Unexpected stuff will happen that will:
        - ▪ Create new opportunities that you can't foresee today.
        - ▪ Detour you from your plan, and require you to revise your plan in order to get back on track toward achieving your objectives.
    - o You will change as a person and your objectives will change along with you. As we grow older (and hopefully more mature), most of us experience changes in what we value most in life and what we dream about accomplishing in life.

Ultra-long term and long term objectives *are more about "what you want to do" than "how you will do it".* Don't get hung up on trying to figure out the exact details of what you will need to do in order to achieve your long term objectives.

Ultra-long term and long term objectives are your dreams that you want to make come true. Try to describe your dreams in real world terms. What real world achievements will make you feel you have lived a happy, satisfied life? To stimulate your thinking, you might try to describe:
- *Dream amounts of net worth and annual income* that would provide you a feeling of financial freedom to do whatever you dream of doing.
- *Dream job* - a job you would gladly do for free if your budget could afford it, perhaps turning a favorite hobby into a career.
- *Dream relationships*, e.g. happy marriage, children who love you (and listen to you), close circle of friends.
- *Dream home in dream location.*
- *Dream vacation.*

Mid-term objectives: objectives that you think you would need to achieve within the next 2 to 5 years in order to stay on track toward your long term and ultra-long term objectives. Examples:
- Get the educational degree or certification of technical training that you think you will need in order to secure a job you would like to have as you advance along a career path toward your dream job (see Chapter 14 for more on career path planning).
- Secure that next job along your career path.
- Contribute the maximum allowable amount to the tax advantaged savings plan(s) your employer offers (especially if your employer matches employee contributions).

Short term objectives
- *Develop your business plan in the way that most successful athletes develop their training programs* - plan a progression of shorter term, realistically achievable objectives that advance you toward ultimately achieving your longer term objectives (athletes try to progressively stretch their capabilities rather than pushing themselves "too hard" all at once and risk hurting themselves).
- *"Every journey starts with a single step."* People get to their destinations by taking

enough small steps in the right direction.

For each mid-term objective, lay out a series of detailed, small step objectives that you can realistically expect to achieve over the next one or two years that will advance you toward achieving that mid-term objective. Business people often refer to this progression of small step objectives as establishing "mileposts" (follows with the transportation analogy). Keys to setting a sequence of mileposts:

- Mileposts must be realistically achievable. They shouldn't be pie-in-the-sky hopes. Think of setting achievable objectives as tempering your dreams with the realities of life.
- Milepost objectives must be measurable so that you will know when you have achieved each successive milepost and can move on toward the next milepost.
- Begin with mileposts you can start working toward immediately - things you don't have to wait to start doing. Then shift your focus out over the next few months and year.
- Understand that milepost objectives (and action plans to achieve them) can be the trickiest part of planning because they need to be delineated clearly enough to actually act upon within a relatively short period of time, and they require us to allocate precious time to taking action plan steps to achieve them.
  - o There are only 24 hours in each day. There is a limit to how much you can do in one week, one month, and one year.
  - o Don't try to do too much too fast. "Don't bite off more than you can chew".
  - o *Think of milepost objectives in terms of a "to do list". Don't put "too many" items on your list.* If your list got "too long" you might discourage yourself from trying to achieve some or all of those objectives.
  - o Mileposts (and action plans) are continual works in progress that we can revise based upon changing conditions in our lives, changes in our personal inventories of resources, and the milepost objectives that we have already achieved.
- Don't sweat it if you can't seem to lay out a complete progression of milestone objectives that lead toward each mid-term objective. Just write down those mileposts that you can think of today. The further you progress down the road toward each mid-term objective, the more clearly you will be able to identify the next mileposts you will need to get to.

Following are a few suggestions of short term milepost objectives to spur your thinking about milepost objectives to include in your plan.

- Develop a formal decision making process (see Chapter 7).
- Learn how to use the financial management tools available on the websites of the financial institutions with which you do business.
- Learn how to reconcile your checkbook with your bank statement and do it each month.
- Maintain a running total list of your credit card purchases each month (like recording checks in a checkbook register) and reconcile your purchase records each month with the statement that your credit card company sends you.
- Pay in full the balance due on your credit card(s) each month.
- Identify the maximum compensation available to a person in your current job, e.g. your employer's matrix of salary ranges for each position/job level in the organization.
- Develop a plan with your employer to earn that maximum compensation
- Develop the initial draft of a career path plan that would advance you toward your dream job (see Chapter 14).
- If you are expecting to earn a pay raise at work during the next year:
  - o Contribute one third of that raise to whatever tax advantaged savings plans are available to you.
  - o Invest another one third of that pay raise in a cash reserve savings account.

Planning Process Step 1a: establish projected financial statement budget objectives

FYI (For Your Information): The following is just a brief introduction to budgeting. It is meant to spur your interest in learning more about how to prepare and use a budget. I can't do justice to this expansive subject in such limited space. Seek the advice of savvy business people you know and perhaps a financial advisor. A sample format is on this book's website (www.ymiyb.com).

Budgets quantify the money you will need in order to finance living the lifestyle you are planning to live at each stage of your life. A written budget will:
- Provide clearly defined dollar number short term and mid-term objectives that should be achieved by specific dates in order to stay on track to achieve long term objectives.
- Help temper your financial dreams with the practical realism of hard dollar objectives you will need to achieve within specific periods of time.
- Help you harness the power of visualization as a tool to use in making your financial dreams come true (more on visualization in Chapter 5).

Budgets are projected financial statements – specific dollar number objectives to be achieved on future financial statements. Just as historical financial statements have two integral parts, so too projected financial statement budgets should have two integral parts:
- *Projected statement of income and expenses*: this is the only budget part that most people have in mind when they think about and talk about budgets.
- *Projected balance sheet*: this is *the second part that most people don't think about nor talk about as being an integral part of a budget.* You should!

Projected statement of income and expenses (or projected "income statement"): tells you how much revenue (income) you should generate and how much money you could spend during the last one year of a planning period in order to finance the lifestyle you are planning to live during that year, and stay on track to achieve your long term wealth accumulation objective.

Projected balance sheet: a snapshot of the balance sheet you want to have as of the last day of a planning period. A projected balance sheet:
- Identifies wealth you want to accumulate and debt you want to eliminate.
- Converts the percentage numbers in an *"investment asset allocation plan"* into dollar numbers of cash, stocks, bonds, real estate, etc. (see Chapter 15).
- Typical entries include:
  - Current assets: cash and other assets that could be converted into cash in a short period of time, e.g. certificates of deposit, treasury bills, stocks, bonds.
  - Non-current / capital assets: property and equipment intended to be owned for a relatively long period of time, e.g. real estate, cars, boats.
  - Loans payable
  - Deferred income taxes
  - Net worth

Means and ends
- A *projected income statement* details the _means_ to achieve
- the _ends_ of *projected balance sheet* objectives.

Chicken or egg - balance sheet or income statement? Don't get caught up in the mind game of "which came first, the chicken or the egg" as you plan projected income statement and projected balance sheet objectives. Plan both sets of objectives concurrently.

- Projected income statement objectives and projected balance sheet objectives are inextricably linked together by income statement net profit that carries over to balance sheet net worth.
- Projected income statement objectives provide a guide to help decide upon projected balance sheet objectives; and
- Projected balance sheet objectives provide a guide to help decide upon projected income statement net profit objectives.

Prepare a six column, projected financial statement budget "spreadsheet" - one column for an historical financial statement (which sets up the format and the starting point for your budget) and one column each for five (5) budget planning periods [sample formats at (www.ymiyb.com)].
- Within your spreadsheet, set up one page for the balance sheet part of your projected financial statement budget and another page for the income statement part.
    - o In the first column of the balance sheet page, prepare an historical balance sheet as of the last day of the previous calendar year.
    - o In the first column of the income statement page, prepare an historical income statement for the previous calendar year.
- Budget numbers for each of the five (5) budget planning periods should be as follows:
    - o <u>Balance sheet</u> numbers - as of the <u>last day</u> of each planning period.
    - o <u>Income statement</u> numbers - for the <u>last year</u> of each planning period.
- In the second column on each page write realistic estimates of what you think you can make the historical numbers become during the next 1 year planning period.
- In the sixth column on the far right of each of the two pages, write your ultra-long term dream objectives for the last year of the lifespan you can reasonably expect to live.
- In the middle three columns, establish budget objectives for three intervening planning periods – perhaps 3 years, 10 years, and 20 or 30 years depending upon your age.
    - o Having your <u>realistic 1 year</u> objectives and your <u>dream ultra-long term</u> objectives on the same page will help you project budget objectives that you should strive to achieve during the intervening three planning periods.
    - o The side by side presentation of planning periods will help you work back in time from the distant future to the present.
- Keep in mind that the farther out into the future that budget planning periods go:
    - o The tougher it is to make accurate financial projections; and
    - o *The more that budget objectives become aspirations.*

Projected financial statement budgets are built upon:
- *Business plan objectives* you want to achieve in your lifetime.
- *Strategies* you want to use to achieve your objectives.
- *An historical financial statement for the prior year* that provides:
    - o The format for projected financial statements.
    - o Starting point numbers from which to project objectives.
- Historical financial statements for more than one prior year would be a big help. <u>The more years back in time you can prepare historical financial statements, the easier it will be to identify historical trends in your money earning, spending, and saving behavior and money management habits you might need to change in order to achieve your objectives.</u>

There is a good bit of business management "art" involved in projecting budget objectives (see the Business Management section of Chapter 3 for more on the art and the science parts of management). The more you practice using your budget planning process, the better you are likely to get at the art of establishing achievable budget objectives.

Planning process Step 2: take a personal inventory

Take an inventory of what you have to work with in developing your plan - money, skills and abilities, strengths and weaknesses, level of financial literacy, beliefs, etc. It can be tough for us to take an objective look at ourselves. It might be helpful to discuss your inventory with a confidant who knows you well. Other people can be more objective about us than we can be about ourselves. They can help us identify things such as strengths on which we can capitalize and weaknesses we should work on strengthening, things we are good at doing and things we are not so good at doing, etc.

What do you value most in life? Your plan should flow from what you value most – from what gives your life the most meaning and satisfaction. Maintain a list of what you value most in a priority order of importance to you, such as:
- Spiritual life.
- Family life.
- Physical and mental health.
- Self-fulfillment - a comfortable feeling that you are living a good life.
- Money and the material things money can buy.

Writing this list and periodically reviewing it will also help you keep your priorities in mind as you make decisions that generate optimum joy, satisfaction, and practical use for you.

What is your current financial position? Prepare an "historical" financial statement as of the most recent year end, and perhaps the most recent month end - balance sheet and statement of income and expenses formats are on this book's website at (www.ymiyb.com).
- Balance sheet:
  - How much do you own?
  - How much do you owe?
- Statement of income and expenses:
  - How much money can you reasonably expect to earn this year?
  - How much of that money do you expect to spend this year?

What do you believe about money? Your beliefs about money may be the single most important factor in how much income you earn and how much wealth you amass.
- If you believe that money is a tool that can be used to do good for yourself and for others, you are likely to capitalize on opportunities that come your way to maximize your income and your wealth.
- If you believe that money is the root of all evil, you are more likely to put up conscious or subconscious psychological barriers to maximizing your income and wealth.
- If you are a practicing member of a religion, what does your religion teach about money? It's tough for people to live in dissonance with the religious bedrock of their beliefs.
- What do you believe about the responsibility of each person to be self-reliant - to provide for his own financial well-being?

To stimulate your thinking about what you believe about money:
- What are your opinions about the following statements:
  - Money isn't the cause of bad behavior, human weakness is.
  - Money is just one of the many things in life that can lead us to bad behavior unless we have enough self-discipline to manage our behavior.

- o Money has the power to mess with a person's mind in much the same way as power, alcohol, and other addictive substances can mess with it.
- Ask some people older than you how their thinking about money has evolved as they have physically aged, mentally matured, and gained experience in life.
- Learn what religious leaders of different faiths have to say about money and what people should do with the money in their lives (you are likely to hear a common theme of using money to do acts of good in the world).

Based upon my years of observing people, it seems to me that the happiest people tend to believe that money is just one of the tools that they can use to help themselves live satisfying lives. They feel good about the money in their lives because they plan to use it to *"do well by doing good"*.

What are your strengths and weaknesses?
- *Plan to capitalize on your strengths.*
- *Plan to strengthen your weaknesses.* Don't kid yourself about having weaknesses. We all have them. It's tough to face up to our weaknesses, but, it's empowering to do it. Smart business people continuously seek to identify the "weakest parts of their game", and then work to strengthen those weaknesses. *"You're only as strong as the weakest link in your chain."*
- Personality
  - o More the self-confident, outgoing type, or more the shy and retiring type?
  - o More of a take-charge leader, or more of a follower?
- Self-discipline: how good have you been at sticking with resolutions and plans you have made in the past? How well do you resist temptation?
- Self-motivation: how passionate are you about improving the way you have been managing the money in your life, and achieving objectives you set for yourself?
- Would people describe you as someone who has the good common sense to "do the right thing" most times?
- Skills and abilities: what do you do well? What are you not so good at doing?
- Book knowledge acquired in classes, self-study, etc. It is important to be self-honest about what you know, AND, perhaps even more important, to know what you don't know. Pride, ego, and self-deceit have caused misery for many a person.
- Street smarts acquired through experience in the real world "out on the street" away from the protective nests of family and school?

What do you love to do?
- What would you do if you could do anything you wanted to do?
- What activities provide you the greatest joy and satisfaction?
- How would you describe your dream job?

How do you feel about your life and about the money in your life?
- Do you feel happy, and satisfied that life is treating you pretty well? Or, might you feel that you have gotten the raw end of the deal too often?
- Do you feel happy and satisfied with your job and your income? Or, might you not be as happy with your job as you would like to be, or not making as much money as you would like to be making?
- What do you like most about your life?
- What might make you feel better about life if you could change it?
  - o Does anything make you feel unhappy?

  o   Do you have any fears?
  o   Does anything ever cause you to lose sleep?
- Do you feel you are worthy to have a lot of money?
- Would you feel guilty about becoming wealthy?
- Do you feel pretty good about the way you have been managing your money and just want to get better at it? Or, might you be concerned by the way you have been managing your money and worried about the financial position you are in today?
- Do you feel worried that at this stage of life you haven't accumulated as much of an investment nest egg as you think you should have?
- Do you feel worried about the risk of losing your job?
- Do you feel worried about the risk of losing money on your investments?

What emotions are tough for you to control - love, anger, fear, insecurity, enthusiasm?
- What emotions pose the most risk of interfering with your rational thinking and negatively influencing the way you manage your money?
- What emotions could marketing, advertising and sales people target as "emotional spending triggers" in their efforts to get you to spend your money the way they want you to spend it?

To help stimulate your thinking about how your emotions might influence the way you manage your money, ask yourself what might make you:
- Feel a desire to have it whenever you see it?
- Feel you must do something whenever you see people doing it?
- Feel you just want to get away from it all?
- Feel a need to fill a longing in your heart?
- Feel the need to "buy the love" of another person?

Who are the people closest to you – family, friends, neighbors, co-workers?
- Are you surrounded by people who are positive influences on you and your money - people who are likely to help you achieve your objectives?
- Are there any people who have been negative influences - people who might be likely to lead you astray from your plan and budget?

What image do you think you project to the world? People get "vibes" about each other. What vibes do people get from you? The image that you project influences how people react to you, and what they may or may not do to try to help you achieve your objectives.

When people look at you what image do you think they see:
- A happy person who makes people feel good and attracts them or a sourpuss who repels people?
- An inner sense of happiness and satisfaction emanating out as warm, inviting energy?
- A glass half full optimist or glass half empty pessimist?
- A "people person" who enjoys the company of other people or a loner who doesn't seem to enjoy being with people?
- A curious, non-judgmental student of life who invites other people's thoughts and opinions or a know-it-all who doesn't care much what other people think?
- A generous person who tries to "share the wealth" by making win-win decisions or a stingy narcissist who is only looking out for himself?

What is your risk tolerance level? How much risk can you tolerate without getting stressed out or losing sleep?

What is your risk tolerance in regard to job income?
- How much risk in job security would you be willing to accept in return for an opportunity to earn more money? Would you prefer the higher compensation potential of a job with a relatively high risk start-up company in an emerging new industry or the somewhat lower compensation potential of a job with a relatively low risk, well-established company in a more mature industry?
- Would you prefer the relative comfort and security of a steady 9:00 to 5:00 job as a non-managerial employee, or the exciting challenges and risks of being a manager?
- If you were promoted to a managerial position, would you feel comfortable accepting the responsibility for, and the consequences of, the actions of all the people you managed - all that your people did and all that they didn't do?
- Would you be willing to take the risks associated with a new job with a new employer?
- Could you handle the risks of becoming an entrepreneur starting up a company with the intent of that company becoming your primary source of income?

What is your risk tolerance in regard to investment return?
- How well would you sleep at night if you lost money on an investment?
- Would you rather accept a lower risk of losing money in return for a lower rate of return on your money, or take a greater risk of losing money in return for a chance to earn a greater rate of return?

What financial management expertise and experience do you have?
- *Expertise?*
  - o What is your current level of financial literacy?
  - o How much do you know about business and financial management?
  - o How good are your current financial management skills and abilities?
- *Experience?*
  - o How much experience do you have managing money?
    - ▪ Bank account management?
    - ▪ Credit or debit card management?
    - ▪ Budget management?
    - ▪ Investment management?
  - o How well have you done at managing your money?

What is a reasonable estimate of money that might be coming into your life in the future?
- Income potential from your current job with your current employer?
- Income from future jobs along the career path you are planning?
- Investment income?
- Inheritance?

Process Step 3: determine your strategy

"Your strategy" is the way you want to go about living your life in pursuit of your objectives. When we use the word "strategy" in general in this book, as in "your strategy", we mean a composite blend of interconnected individual strategy pieces – a set of guiding principles that you think are the good and right ways to live your life.

This book offers suggestions of a number of individual strategy pieces to consider blending into your composite strategy.
- Be yourself.
  - o You are a unique person. There is no one else exactly like you on the planet. Develop a strategy for living your life the way you think you should live it.
  - o Let your financial literacy, your experience, your personality, your risk tolerance, and everything else that is you dictate your strategy.
  - o Your strategy should enable you to live a happy, satisfying lifestyle.
- *Ask people who you think have lived good and satisfying lives for their advice about individual strategy pieces to consider.* But, be careful about trying to copy exactly anyone else's composite strategy. Each of us is a unique person who has a unique set of life circumstances. Another person's strategy might work for him but not work for you because you are a different person who has a different set of life circumstances.

A written strategy can be a valuable tool to use in a number of ways, including:
- To help guide planning your objectives and action plans.
- To help guide your decision making (see Chapter 7).
- To serve as a component of your behavioral control system (see Chapter 5).
- To help prevent people from manipulating your thinking and behavior (see Chapter 12).

Following are some individual strategy pieces to consider blending into your composite strategy.

Plan to do things that bring you joy and satisfaction.
- *It's human nature to* seek *pleasure and avoid pain* – to *do things we enjoy, and avoid doing things we don't like to do.* Planning to do things you enjoy doing will make it easier to stick to your plan.
- *Plan to have fun.* Life is short, and you only get one.
- Plan to seek the satisfaction of self-actualization – to become what you dream of becoming (learn about self-actualization).
- *"Follow your bliss" in planning your career path.* If you plan to do things you enjoy doing, and making money and accumulating wealth are among your objectives, it is likely you will find ways to make money and accumulate wealth. The happiest of the successful business people I know seem to enjoy doing what they do. Aspire to find a "calling in life" rather than just seeking a job. (Joseph Campbell coined or popularized "follow your bliss". Learn about him and why he thought it was so important to follow your bliss.)

Value people more than money - be others oriented.
- *Money has diminishing economic utility* – the more money you have, the less additional satisfaction each additional dollar is likely to generate for you (learn about "marginal utility"). If your income doubles, your joy and satisfaction are not likely to double.
- *But, making a child smile and helping someone in need* will never lose their ability to provide the rich reward of making you feel good.

- *Self-centeredness is self-defeating.* Over time, self-centered people tend to turn off the type of others-oriented people who are most likely to help them succeed.
- Heed this ancient advice "it is more blessed to give than to receive". People tend to get far more joy and satisfaction out of giving than receiving.
- Think about what President John F. Kennedy meant when he told the American people *"Ask not what your country can do for you, but what you can do for your country."*

Value the quality of your life more than the money in it.
- "Quality of life" has become a popular catch phrase. What does quality of life mean to you?
- Money can be used to help increase the quality of life, but "money alone can't buy happiness".

Value the quality of being more than the quantity of doing.
- Plan for the quality of your experience in doing each thing you do more than the quantity of how many things you can squeeze into your schedule.
- Don't rush through life. Take time to "stop and smell the roses".
- Live in the moment. Each moment is precious and we can never know how many of them we will get to live. Learn about and practice mindfulness – being in the moment.
    o The younger you are, the tougher it may to be to fully understand this strategy.
    o The older you are, the easier it is likely to be to understand this strategy. Experience is likely to have taught that "a bird in the hand is worth two in the bush" - *the moment we have here and now is more valuable than future moments we may never get.*
- *A 15 year old high school student is likely to think that 50 years is forever. A 65 year old is likely to ask how 50 years could have flown by so fast.*

Don't try to micro-manage your life.
- Plan, but don't try to over-plan every little detail of life. Let your dream objectives guide you to plan in enough detail to make progress toward your dreams without getting bogged down in trying to plan what you will do every day of every month. Two good reasons to avoid over-planning:
    o Situations and circumstances in life can change so often and so fast that overly-detailed plans can become outdated and unworkable almost "before the ink is dry on the paper".
    o You'd probably drive yourself nuts if you tried.
- Manage your life, but don't try to micro-manage everything and everyone in it. Seek a balance in management of your life such that the people who know you best might say of you that you are "in control" of things without being a "control freak".
- "All things in moderation".

Surround yourself with good people (see Chapter 8).
- Develop a "business team" of good people to help you succeed - people who are good influences on your money, e.g. friends, role models, co-workers, workplace managers, professional service providers.
- Don't try to do it all by yourself. Business owners don't have to be experts at doing all the things that are necessary to run a successful business. Smart business owners hire smart people who have expertise and experience that they don't have. You don't need to know it all. Hire people who know what you don't know. Use their expertise and experience.

Motivate those good people to help you succeed by tapping into the internal motivation that most good people have to help others.
- *Help other people.*
  - o "You get back more than you give."
  - o "What goes around comes around."
- *Be so nice that everyone who gets to know you can't help but feel a desire to help you.* Practice what you were taught while you were growing up about how to treat others - smile, be kind and compassionate, say please, say thank you, etc.

Create your own good luck.
- *Think positive and do good things.* Good luck tends to come to people who do. Flush negative thoughts out of your mind with a steady stream of positive thoughts (see Chapter 5 for more about creating good luck).
- *Adopt a mindset of abundance.*
  - o Believe that there is enough abundance available in this world to provide every person with prosperity.
  - o The philosophy of living life with the expectation of abundance (be that an abundance of joy, satisfaction, love, money ...), and sharing the abundance they receive, has been around for thousands of years in religious texts.
  - o *Make win-win decisions* - each person can help create the good luck of abundance for himself by means of helping to create abundance for others.
    - ▪ When we try to help other people come out as winners in our decisions, they tend to become motivated to reciprocate and help us come out winners in their decisions.
    - ▪ *Compromise* as needed to achieve win-win decision outcomes. Giving up a little bit today can get you back good luck in return tomorrow.
    - ▪ A reputation for making win-win decisions will help attract people into your life who also use a win-win strategy - people who are likely to help you create the kind of good luck that brings abundance into your life.

Plan for the long term.
- *The tortoise beat the hare* - slow and steady perseverance tends to win more often than fast and furious. Treat wealth building as a long term marathon, not as a short term sprint. Most wealthy people didn't get rich quick. It is not likely that you will either. *Plan to get richer – not rich - each year.*
- Beware get rich quick schemes – they usually hurt more people than they help.
- The business world goes through a repetitive cycle of economic good times followed by not such good times. Companies that have been successful over the course of many years typically plan how to prosper in the economic good times and weather the tough times.
- If you experience financial difficulties, plan to correct the *root causes* of those difficulties over a reasonably long enough period of time. Don't just treat the *symptoms* of difficulties with quick fixes.
- *Give a well-thought plan enough time to work before making any significant revisions.* One key trait that most successful people share is the self-discipline of consistency. They give their well-thought plans time to work, while making occasional minor tweaks to adjust for changing circumstances. Successful people don't "abandon ship" too soon.
- Time has made many a decision that didn't appear to look so good at first, turn out to look pretty good in the long run.
- *"Time heals all wounds.*

Plan a sustainable lifestyle. Consider the impact of the lifestyle you plan to live today on the world in which you will be living in the future. Plan to do all you can to help make the future world in which you will need to live as good as it can be. Ideas to stimulate your thinking:

- Economy: plan to do what you can do to make the economy as vibrant as possible as far out into the future as possible.
- Society: the business world and the communities in which business is conducted are dependent upon bonds of trust, civility and fairness that allow people to live in close proximity and interact with each other. Plan to do all you can to strengthen the social bonds that connect people in your local, state, national and global communities.
- Environment and natural resources: we live in a closed biosphere here on planet Earth. There is a limited supply of arable land, fresh water, clean air, fossil fuels, metal ores, timber, and all other natural resources. And human life requires a healthy biodiversity of plant and animal life.
    - o "Don't foul your nest." Plan to minimize the pollution in your home here on Earth -keep your planetary home as clean and well maintained as you can.
    - o Plan to be a good steward of the world's limited supply of natural resources.
        - "Waste not, want not." Plan to squeeze out every bit of use you can from the natural resources that you consume today.
        - Plan to do what you can do today to conserve the world's remaining natural resources, and to maximize the quantity of these resources that will available for use in the future by you and everyone else who shares the planet with you.

Life is long. Plan to live a long time. As you make decisions, consider how actions you take today might play out many years into the future.

Planning for short term gratification at the expense of long term gratification can be a fool's game. A series of decisions guided by short term gratification, and lacking the direction of a long term business plan and budget, often leads to financial danger. Examples:

- People who spend every nickel of current income and never accumulate a savings nest egg to help provide for their future financial security.
- Employers who have exploited past employees and can't attract quality new employees.
- Governments that run deeply into debt by spending too much money trying to please voters in the short term without having made hard decisions about how to raise the tax revenue that will be needed to repay that debt over the long term.

Plan for change. Change is inevitable. *The world of tomorrow will NOT continue on exactly as you know it today.* Become a futurist. Anticipate and plan for change. *Change in life-as-we-knew-it* will be a function of many things, including:

- An accumulating body of knowledge and human experience spawning an accelerating pace of invention and discovery in telecommunications, medicine, biotechnology, nanotechnology, cryotechnology, etc.
- Relatively rapid changes in the social and geo-political order of the world that are being spurred along by dissident activists in many countries. These activists for change are being enabled by the rapidly evolving global telecommunications and transportation networks to share information and coordinate their efforts to change the world.
- Demographic shifts in populations of communities and countries around the world caused by changing birth and death rates.
- Life cycles of individual companies and entire industries.
- Cycles of economic expansion and recession; inflation and deflation; rising and falling

stock markets.
- *Nature's "cycle of life" - birth, growth and death.* Change is nature's way to renew itself. Plan for the evolutionary changes in life that come to all of us, e.g. physical aging; mental maturation; comings and goings of the people in our lives; demographic evolution of our communities.

Seek projections of the future from experts in various fields: economists, financial advisors, professional risk managers, medical and biotech experts, technology experts, physicists, ecologists, climatologists, geologists, oceanographers, demographers, agronomists, foresters, social psychologists, and every other type of expert you can think of who might offer an interesting perspective on the future. Also seek their advice about what we can do today that will help us prosper in the future:
- What do they think the world will be like in the future? How do they think future living conditions will impact the lifestyle you dream of living and the money you dream of having?
- How do those experts define "sustainable lifestyle" from their various perspectives?
- What advice do they offer about sustainable lifestyle choices we should be making?
- Pay the most attention to the projections and advice of those experts who you can reasonably expect will receive the least financial gain from the advice they provide.

"Go with the flow" of change in the world. Consider planning lower risk, gradual transitions and segues in your life, and avoiding the higher risk that can come with making radical changes.

Practice social conformity and intellectual independence. *Rebels have a much more difficult row to hoe in the business world than social conformists.*

Social conformity in this book means:
- Abiding by the generally accepted rules of proper behavior, dress code, vernacular language, etc. of each group to which you want to belong (e.g. family, club, team, work group, neighborhood, community, nation) – behaving well enough to live together, work together, and accomplish group objectives together.
- Conformity does NOT mean becoming a mindless pawn of society.

Intellectual independence in this book means:
- Thinking for yourself rather than blindly accepting what you are told.
- "Thinking outside the box" to look at challenges from other perspectives.
- Cultivating and using your creative powers. Whenever you catch yourself thinking "I wish there was a better way" or "there ought to be a better way", shift your thinking to ways it actually could be done better or made better; seek to "build a better mousetrap".
- Projecting how current events, current trends, and historical cycles are likely to play out in the future in order to identify new opportunities, and planning how to profit from those new opportunities rather than just going "along for the ride" through life with the crowd.
- Constructive critique of your employer's operations and the way you were taught to do your job. "The way we have always done it" may never actually have been the best way it could have been done when the "way" was first implemented. But it worked back then, so people kept on doing it that "way", and the "way we do it" wound up becoming institutionalized. Try to find a better way to do it that you can suggest.

Take care of "first things first".
- List your objectives in priority order from most important down to least important. Then, allocate your resources (time, effort, money, etc.) so as to provide yourself the greatest opportunity to achieve your highest priority objectives. Then allocate your remaining resources to achieving your lower priority objectives.
- To maximize the compensation you receive from your employer, allocate your time and effort in a way that provides you the greatest opportunity to exceed your employer's expectations while achieving your most important objectives and performing your most important duties. Then allocate your remaining resources to achieving your least important objectives and performing your least important duties.
- On your projected income statement budget, list the expenses in your fixed expense and discretionary expense categories from largest expense items to lowest expense items. Focus your attention on how you might minimize your largest expense items first.

Look for good opportunities presented by "bad" news. You can be pretty well assured that when you hear bad news, two things are happening:
- Some people who let their emotions influence their decision making are going to be making some bad decisions that cost them money.
- Some smart, rationally thinking people are looking for opportunities to capitalize on the bad news and make money from it.

One example - "buy on the bad news, sell on the good news" is common investment advice advocated by many financial advisors, e.g. buy after the media have been slamming a specific investment or an entire class of investments, and sell after the media begin to heap praise upon it.

Beware talk of "new paradigms" of human behavior, especially human behavior with money. "There is not much new under the sun" when it comes to human behavior, especially behavior with money. When pundits and "experts" say "it's different this time" in regard to money, it rarely is.

A few expense management strategies to consider:
- *Live below your means*. Don't spend every penny of every paycheck. <u>It is easy to fall into the habit of telling ourselves "Oh, I have plenty of time to save for the future. I'll start saving money tomorrow." Unfortunately for way too many people, tomorrow becomes next month, which becomes next year, which leads to never having saved enough.</u>
- Save up cash reserves to pay for "big ticket" (expensive) purchases, and to serve as a contingency fund to pay unplanned expenses.
- Avoid debt to the greatest extent possible.
- Buy best value, not lowest price.
    - o Think in terms of net value gained more than price paid.
    - o "Don't buy cheap."
    - o "You get what you pay for."
    - o Pay good people a fair price for their work.
    - o Don't buy for show or prestige.
    - o Best value usually is somewhere in the middle between the lowest price and highest price.

A few revenue management strategies to consider:
- Making a living should include a whole lot more than just making money. Seek a job that provides three types of compensation that combine to form an optimum "total

compensation package".
- o *Money* (revenue) enough to achieve your projected financial statement budget objectives.
- o *Satisfaction* enough to achieve your business plan objectives.
  - ▪ Job satisfaction; enjoyment of your work; opportunity to "be all you can be".
  - ▪ Social satisfaction: enjoyment of the time you spend with people at work.
- o *Free time* enough away from work to do all the other things besides work that would make your life good and satisfying, e.g. attend to spiritual life, build and maintain relationships with family and friends, savor peace of mind, experience the joys of recreation and creative hobbies.
- Seek to exceed your employer's expectations of you.
- Don't spread yourself too thin at work by agreeing to requests to do too many things that aren't directly related to achieving your work objectives and exceeding your employer's expectations of performance of a person in your job position.
- Don't work so many hours and create so much such stress for yourself that you burn out.

A few investment / wealth management strategies to consider:
- *Hire a professional investment advisor*!
- Save at least 10% of your annual revenue.
- Maintain a cash reserve as a contingency fund to use in the event of things such as (a) an interruption in your stream of income caused loss of your job or a long term disability, (b) an uninsured medical emergency, (c) all the expenses you would incur if your home was destroyed in in a catastrophic storm or fire. I have heard professional financial advisors recommend a cash reserve in the range of 3 to 12 months of annual income.
- *"Don't lose money"*.
  - o Learn what legendary investor Warren Buffett has to say about not losing money.
  - o Consider seeking prudent returns on your investments over longer periods of time rather than making "get rich quick" bets.
  - o Keep in mind the principle of risk-reward, "the greater the potential reward, the greater the risk".
- Buy low, sell high; buy on the bad news, sell on the good news.
- Consider mutual funds more than individual stocks and bonds.
- Don't try to beat stock market averages.
- *Invest money today in ways that will help you make even more money tomorrow.*
- To maximize the power of compound earnings, don't touch your invested principal.
- Maintain an age appropriate, well-diversified investment portfolio (mix of cash, stocks, bonds, etc.). Typically, the younger you are the greater the percentage of your investment portfolio might be in stocks, and the older you are the greater the percentage might be in cash and bonds.
- Buy a house to serve as a home more than as an investment.

Have a "Plan B" contingency plan in mind for what you might do to achieve your higher priority objectives if your "Plan A" doesn't work out as planned.
- As you are developing "Plan A" action plans to achieve objectives that will have significant impact on your life it would be prudent to think about what you could do if Plan A isn't working as planned.
- Ask yourself "what could I do if …?" Think about options you might have for a Plan B you could begin acting upon quickly.

- Having contingency plans already in mind can provide multiple benefits, such as:
    o Speed your response if a Plan A isn't working.
    o Minimize any financial or mental harm that might otherwise have come to you.
    o Provide the peace of mind that can come from confronting your worst fears, e.g. loss of your job, sudden death of a spouse.
        ▪ Facing up to fears is the best way to manage them.
        ▪ You are likely to gain peace of mind by having thought through ways you might deal with the worst if the worst ever did happen.
    o The mental exercise you get from thinking through Plan B options is likely to help you:
        ▪ "Think quick" "when you need to "make lemonade out of lemons" "on the fly".
        ▪ Develop the mental toughness that would be needed to deal with the stressful times that can come after realizing that Plan A isn't working.

As you think about Plan B options, don't dwell on all the negative things that MIGHT happen in your life. The idea is to understand that:

- It is a fact of life that we live in an imperfect world in which some unexpected "stuff" is going to happen in everybody's life at some point in time.
- We need to be ready to deal with bad stuff as quickly and efficiently as we can after it starts to happen in our lives and then move on to continue living happy, satisfying lives.

Planning Process Step 4: develop an action plan

An action plan is a series of things you to do that you think will advance you toward achieving your objectives.

Tailor your action plan to fit your life - comfortably – an action plan that fits well with your personality, your current skills and abilities, your life circumstances, your objectives, and your strategy. There is no way that this book could or would attempt to suggest a specific set of action plan steps for you. Each person's life is so unique that it would be impossible to even suggest a one-size-fits-all action plan.

A few thoughts to consider:
- Keep your action plan short and sweet. Don't plan to do too many things too fast.
- Plan to do enough things to advance toward achieving your objectives, but don't try to plan every little thing you do every day.
- You might start by picking a few of your most important dream objectives and writing a list of things you can think of immediately that you would need to do at some point in time in order to eventually achieve each objective. Don't get hung up writing this initial list. You can expand and revise it over time as you work your planning process.
- Keep in mind that the further into the future you try to develop action plans, the more likely it is that things will happen that will require you to revise those plans.

Plan for the unexpected to happen as the result of actions you take.
- *Law of Unintended Consequences*: unintended things that we couldn't conceive of happening while we were planning sometimes do happen as the result of actions we take.
- *"The devil is in the details"*. Action plans often look really good on paper. Then, when a person actually starts doing the things she planned to do, she discovers that she hadn't thought of all the little things that go into doing what she planned to do.
- *Murphy's Law* - "if it can go wrong, it will go wrong". Not true all the time, but true enough, often enough, for us to plan to be alert for things going wrong when we act according to our plans.

Be prepared to take corrective action "on the fly".
- Think about this - unexpected stuff happens on a space flight even after the best experts in the world have planned every miniscule detail for every minute of the flight.
- When action plans start to go awry, you might want to ask for a time-out or a do-over, but don't plan on getting one. "Time waits for no man."
- Learn to be flexible and adaptable – "like a willow in the wind, be prepared to bend, but don't break".
- Be ready to "put your thinking hat on" and find workable solutions to "unworkable problems".
  - o Train your mind to "think quick".
  - o Learn about the term "Yankee ingenuity", and how often it is that successful people must use Yankee ingenuity to get their "missions accomplished".
  - o Use the street smarts you have gained through your experience in life.
- "Plan B": as we said on the previous page, it would speed your ability to take corrective action on the fly if in advance you had thought through Plan B alternative action plans while you were developing Plan A action plans to achieve those objectives that will have the greatest impact on your life.

Planning Process Step 5: Monitor your progress

Monitor your progress toward achieving your objectives. A few ideas to consider:
- Prepare written management reports on a regular basis. Two suggestions:
  - o Regarding your business plan objectives, use your written objectives and action plan as a checklist, and check-off your completion of action plan steps and achievement of "milestone" objectives.
  - o Regarding annual budget objectives, prepare financial statements [format on this book's website (www.ymiyb.com)]:
    - ▪ As you begin using your budget, prepare a financial statement each month to keep track of your progress toward achieving your objectives.
    - ▪ Consider preparing monthly financial statements until using your budget becomes a habit - until you "get the hang of" sticking to your budget.
    - ▪ Thereafter, you might consider preparing financial statements quarterly to track your actual progress toward achieving your annual objectives.
- Read your business plan and projected financial statement budget frequently enough to develop a "feel" for how well you are progressing toward your objectives as you go about your daily activities.
- Reconcile the monthly statements you receive from banks, credit card issuing companies, investment advisors, etc. with your own records of your financial transactions.
- Conduct a "self-review" performance review of your performance as president of your company. Sit down with your written plan and budget and critique how effective your current strategy and action plan have been in helping you achieve your objectives.

Your job performance reviews as an employee of your employer should be an integral part of your system for monitoring your performance as president of your company.
- There is likely to be a significant carryover effect in your performance as an employee of your employer to your performance as president of your company. The same skills, abilities, behavioral habits, etc. that are important for success in your role as an employee are likely to be important for success as president of your company.
- Your employer's reviews of your job performance will also indicate how well you are doing at achieving your projected income statement budget objective for actively earned income.

Ask people who know you well to help you monitor your performance (see Chapter 9).
- Other people can be more objective than we can be in monitoring our performance. They are not burdened by the human weaknesses of self-delusion and blindness to our own shortcomings that we all are prone to suffer.
- Ask for their objective observations and constructive critique of the way you have been living your life and managing your money. Ask these people to be as candidly honest as they feel comfortable being. Make sure they understand that you want to hear things about yourself that they might think you wouldn't want to hear. Make clear that you need to hear their honest critique in order to learn what you need to work on in order to become the best person and best money manager you can become, and achieve your objectives for your life.

<u>Planning Process Step 6: revise your plan</u>

Revise your plan and budget as needed in response to things such as:
- Progress you have made toward achieving your objectives.
- Expertise and experience you have gained.
- Changes in your personal inventory, e.g. personal relationships, job, financial assets and liabilities, annual income, beliefs, behavioral habits.
- Changing conditions within your employer's organization, your industry, the economy.
- Changing conditions in the world around you, e.g. family, home, community, country, the world; new discoveries and new technologies; people in your life.
- Unexpected events and unintended consequences of your actions.

Think about how sailors tack into the wind to get where they plan to go.
- Long term objectives are guide stars that keep us headed in the direction of our dreams.
- Occasional course changes will be needed in order to keep advancing toward our dream objectives.
  - o When "the winds of fate" shift in our lives.
  - o To get around obstacles and challenges that we couldn't see from the positions we were in at the time we made our plans.

Life has a funny way of working out so that we sometimes accomplish our long term objectives in ways that we couldn't have even conceived of, let alone planned, when we first set those objectives 10, 20 or 30 years earlier.

Plan evolutionary revisions, not revolutionary changes.
- By all means, revise your plan as quickly as needed to manage rapidly changing conditions in your life or action plans that have gone seriously awry. Exceptional situations may require you to make significant changes in your plan over a short period of time, e.g. management change in your company leading to intolerable working conditions, a family emergency requiring a move to a new town. If a significant change is required in a short period of time:
  - o Be on high alert for the dangers that can come from radical change – emotions getting the better of rational thinking, unforeseen consequences of snap decisions, etc.
  - o Try as best you can to plan prudently in the short time you have available.
  - o Ask for the opinions and advice (and help if applicable) of at least one of your business team confidants.
- The above said; try to structure plan revisions that enable your life to evolve gradually. Most times it is better to tinker rather than overhaul - not always, but most times.
- Typically, the more radical the change, the greater the risk. The more radically and the faster a person attempted to change her life, the less time she would give herself to prepare to successfully manage those changes.

Keep on challenging yourself.
- After you achieve one objective, set another more challenging objective.
- "Once you stop growing, you start dying".

Get Started

"KISS" – keep it simple to start.
- *The big thing is to put your dreams in writing and get them fixed in your mind* so that they can:
  - o Guide your planning.
  - o Guide your decision making.
  - o Reinforce your self-discipline to stick to your plan taking the actions needed to make your dreams come true.
- Regarding your initial business plan
  - o After you write your list of long term dream objectives, pick one or two objectives you want to work on first and make lists of short term and mid-term objectives and "to do list" action plan steps that will begin advancing you toward those dream objectives.
  - o You could probably write your initial short term objectives, mid-term objectives and initial "to do list" on just one or two pieces of paper.
  - o Then start a lifelong process of compiling and tweaking your "strategy" - a list of the guiding principles by which you want to live your life.
- Regarding your initial projected financial statement budget:
  - o Be sure to include each "fixed expense" – expenses you <u>need</u> to pay.
  - o Then add discretionary expense items on which you <u>want</u> to spend money.
  - o You could probably write your projected income statement on one piece of paper (or software spreadsheet) and your projected balance sheet on another sheet.

Over time, you can <u>gradually</u> flesh out your plan with more detail.
- Have fun adding objectives to work on and greater detail – but be careful not to get bogged down in working on too many objectives (at least at the outset) in too much detail.
- You might have fun adding greater detail to your plan by visualizing yourself writing the <u>outline</u> for the "biography of a life well lived" that your grandchildren could write about you years later.
- Just be careful about adding "so much" detail that you begin to detract from the functionality of your plan.

Final thoughts:
- This book is only an introduction to the vast quantity of planning and budgeting information, advice, and help that is available.
  - o Learn what professional financial advisors, life coaches, business consultants, and other professionals have to say about planning and budgeting.
  - o Use all the "how to" resources on planning and budgeting that you can find to help you develop a planning and budgeting process that works well for you.
- The more detail I might have tried to offer about preparing your unique plan for your unique life, the more I might have steered you away from the objectives, strategies and action plan items that will work best for you to help you make your dreams come true.
- Planning is like any other life skill. The more you learn about it, and the more you practice it, the better you are likely to get at doing it.

Chapter 5. First, Manage Yourself

First and foremost - don't be your own worst enemy. Over 2,000 years ago Hippocrates advised doctors "first, do no harm." His advice serves us equally well today when paraphrased into "first, do yourself no harm", because, when it comes to money, most of us are our own worst enemy. We do things we wish we hadn't done, and then later ask ourselves:

- What was I thinking?
- Why did I do that?
- How could I have made such a dumb mistake?

A few classic examples of people who had been their own worst financial enemies:

- People who buried themselves under a mountain of credit card debt.
- College students who took on student loan debt without thinking through how they would be able to use their degrees to earn enough money to pay back their loans.
- High income earning couple who have a minimal investment nest egg because they spent every penny of their high income on expensive things such as a big house in an upscale neighborhood, luxury cars, country club membership, and private schools for their kids.
- "Instant millionaire" male athletes who signed multi-million dollar contracts and then blew it all on young men's fancies – wine, women, fast cars, …

The fastest way most of us can improve our financial management is to avoid doing ourselves harm – "don't shoot yourself in the foot". The more unhappy you are with your financial lot in life, the more important it probably would be to NOT do anything involving significant amounts of money until you develop the first draft of your written business plan and projected financial statement budget. Don't shoot again until you have aimed.

"It's easier said than done." It's easy for people to tell us to stop doing ourselves harm. But if we don't have a plan for what we should be doing, then it's pretty darn tough to do it. And even when we do have a plan for what we should be doing we may not do it for a number of reasons, including:

- Our hormones and emotions get the better of our rational thinking minds.
- Family or peer pressure makes us do things that we wouldn't have done otherwise.
- Advertisers, marketers, or salespeople influence us to spend our money the way they want us to spend it rather than the way we had planned to spend it.
- Serious stuff can happen in our lives that causes us to delay doing things that we had planned to do, or causes us to do things we hadn't planned to do.

Six suggestions that might help you manage yourself:

- Use a business planning and budgeting process (see Chapter 4).
- Use a decision making process (see Chapter 7).
- Adopt a scientific approach to gathering and evaluating the information upon which you base your decisions (see Chapter 8). Question the validity of all the information, ideas, suggestions, and advice you gather – including everything written in this book. Test the validity of information by seeking confirmation from multiple sources, e.g. other experts in the field of study, people you know who you think are well-informed about the matter at hand, the internet. Think for yourself.
- Surround yourself with good people to advise and help you (see Chapter 9).
- Learn the "best practices" of successful business people and use them (see Chapter 10).
- Heed consensus advice offered by the financial service industries (see Chapter 15).

Adopt a business mindset

Success starts in the mind. Successful business managers, consultants, and athletic coaches all preach this. Countless books, classes, and seminars do too. Skim through the books on the Business Management, Sports, and Self Improvement shelves in your local library or bookstore. Look for threads of common advice that weave through the books regarding success starting in the mind, such as:

- Make a conscious decision to succeed.
- Accept responsibility for your success or failure.
- Believe you can succeed and visualize yourself succeeding.
- Commit yourself to doing what you need to do to succeed.

Make a conscious decision to succeed in managing your money. Adopt a winner's mindset. Tell yourself "I can succeed, I will succeed, I am succeeding" over and over again until you begin to really, truly believe down to the core of your being that you will succeed in achieving your business plan and projected financial statement budget objectives.

There is no conspiracy of forces holding anybody down. The only thing that can keep you from succeeding in the life you plan is you. *Rid your mind of negative thoughts such as*:

- "I'm trapped by" … my job, a mountain of debt, being stuck in this town with no way out, a lifestyle that everybody expects me to maintain, etc.
- "I'm a victim of circumstances." "Poor, poor pitiful me." "If only …"
- "I'm just no good at" … my job, managing my money, etc.
- "I can't win because they don't want me to"; "they're out to get me"

Heed what President Franklin Delano Roosevelt told the American people when the country was reeling from the financial devastation of the Great Depression *"The only thing we have to fear is fear itself."* His message - we are a strong and resourceful people; if we don't let this depression crush our spirit, and we all work together, we will get through it and prosper in the future. And they did.

Commit yourself to doing what it takes to achieve your objectives. Commitment is the internal driving force that powers the actions needed to succeed. You may have heard commitment referred to as will power, fire in the belly, passion to succeed, or can do attitude. I particularly like "can do attitude" - it conjures up the idea of mind over matter. With a can do attitude we can overcome any challenge or hardship that life tosses into our paths.

Coach yourself up to be a winning money manager. Successful athletic coaches find ways to get their players to use their minds as well as their bodies. Get some self-coaching ideas (as well as inspiration) from books written by great coaches. Two suggestions to stimulate your thinking:

- Dean Smith, *The Carolina Way*, Penguin Press, 2004
- John Wooden, *Wooden*, McGraw-Hill, 1997

Practice - with a conscious intent to develop better financial management habits. Some people don't understand the huge difference between:

- A. *Repeating* - doing the same old thing the same old way over and over again without any thought about trying to get better at doing it; and
- B. *Practicing* – doing something over and over again with a conscious intent to get better at doing it each time.

Practice practicing.
- Practice doing all the routine little things you do in your daily life, e.g. practice brushing and flossing your teeth the way dentists recommend we brush and floss, practice picking out fruits and vegetables at the market the way that well experienced grandmas and produce managers recommend. Coach John Wooden had his UCLA basketball players practice how to put on their socks in order to avoid getting blisters.
- Practicing the routine little things can help you improve your techniques for practicing bigger, more complex things like financial management.
- *Adopt a mindset of practice, not repetition.*

For those on the shy and retiring side, work on re-gearing your mind to become as outgoing and humbly assertive as you can be in the human interaction part of managing your life and money - <u>acting as president of your business</u>, managing people, negotiation, networking, etc. The more shy and retiring that you are, the more important it will be to "look inside and reach out".
- *Look inside yourself*: What genetic inheritance and/or life experiences might have led you to be more on the shy and retiring side rather than the outgoing and assertive side? What might you work on to become more outgoing and assertive about what you want?
- *Reach out to good people* to help you work through your shyness. Develop a confidential relationship with at least one person with whom you feel comfortable talking about why you are the way you are, e.g. spouse, friend, religious leader, or professional counselor. Two minds are likely to be better than one at working through your shy and retiring nature to become more effective at the human interaction aspects of managing money.

When dealing with hyper-assertive Type A, alpha dog, power tie wearing, dominant personality people, pay heed to what countless football coaches have told countless teams to boost players' self-confidence before playing higher ranked teams *"we all put our pants on one leg at a time."*
- *Don't be timid* – stand your ground – speak up for yourself – go for what you want.
- *Don't be intimidated* - don't let yourself be pushed around - by anyone - ever.

Don't ever let the thought of coasting enter your mind.
- Money has a habit of disappearing pretty quickly after people begin to think they "have it made" and they can finally kick back and ease up on doing ALL the little things that made them successful.
- Money can't take care of itself. We must continue to take pro-active care of our money until the day we die.

Success is a continuous journey, not a destination.
- You can't just get "there" to success, and then stop.
- They say success is fleeting in Hollywood. Well, financial success is fleeting in all parts of the world for people who think they have finally made it to Easy Street. "Easy come, easy go." *<u>Prudent businesspeople know that the wolf lurks around every corner on Easy Street</u>*.
- No matter how successful you become, keep on reminding yourself that all you have done so far is take a progression of action plan steps toward realizing your next dream objective.
- *"The game isn't over until the fat lady sings"* – *and she won't sing until you croak.*

As you become successful, don't let money or the power of any position you acquire in a promotion at work get into your head and corrupt your business mindset. Read Chapter 6 and prepare yourself for gaining and sharing ever greater wealth and success.

Prepare your written plan and stick to it

People who are concerned about their current financial positions might find it prudent to not do anything further that would have significant impact on their money until they wrote the first draft of their business plans and projected financial statement budgets.

"Stay focused like a laser on your plan" is common advice in business management literature for a good reason – it works. Your decisions and actions should be guided by your well-reasoned plan, not by your emotions or how you feel at the moment.

Three things that are likely to help you stick to your plan and budget.
- Plan to do what you love to do.
    - o *It's human nature to do things we enjoy and avoid doing things we don't enjoy.*
    - o Plan objectives and action plans that will give you a warm glow of satisfaction and joy.
    - o "Follow your bliss." Plan ways you can make your dreams come true.
- *Read your plan and budget on a regular basis.* Business plans and budgets can't do much good if they get tucked away in drawers.
    - o The more often you read your plan, the more it will become fixed in your mind, and the less time you will need to spend reading it each subsequent time. Think about the way a little kid memorizes his story books so that he knows when mom or dad skips over a word or a page when reading the book to him.
    - o Reviewing your business plan at regularly scheduled times (once a month, once a quarter) can help prevent you from getting pulled too far off plan.
    - o And if you recognize that you are being pulled away from your plan, or somebody on your business team tells you that you are (a key reason to have good people on your team), reading your plan will help guide you back on plan.
- Surround yourself with people whose company you enjoy, and who have enough concern for your well-being to tell you when they see you drifting off your plan.

Use the power of positive thinking

Examples of the power of positive thinking abound:
- *Entrepreneurs* who had big dreams and then went out and made them happen even though people kept telling them that they were crazy or that it couldn't be done.
- *Underdogs* who upset big dogs in sports because the underdogs thought they would win.
- *Karate experts* who break boards with their bare hands.
- *Firewalkers* who walk barefoot across red hot coals.
- *Martin Luther King* and *Mahatma Gandhi* who led massive changes in the social order of their countries in the face of massive opposition.

Create your own good luck.
- Some people think "He has all the luck." Well, no, actually, no one has all the luck. *There is a virtually endless supply of good luck for each of us – when we create it for ourselves.*
- *The luck I mean is a stream of good things happening over a long span of time.* I don't mean hitting the lottery.
- I have observed this good luck coming to positive thinking people time and again over the course of many years. These positive thinking "lucky" people tend to have a lot in common as to what they believe, how they think, and how they act, and so do the not so lucky, negative thinking people.
  - o *Positive thinking optimists* tend to expect good luck and they usually get it. Characteristics they seem to share include sunny dispositions, smiles on their faces, expect the best, consistently appear to be content, thankful for their good luck in life.
  - o *Negative thinking pessimists* tend to expect bad luck and they usually get it. Characteristics they seem to share include gloomy dispositions, glum looks, expect the worst, consistently seem to be complaining that something just went wrong or that things didn't work out right, wish they had better luck.

Creating good luck works. Wishing for good luck does not work. <u>What may look like pure luck usually turns out to be the cumulative effect of a whole lot of good things the lucky person has been doing over a long period of time.</u> Creating good luck is not just a story line in *Pollyanna* (read the book or see the movie – a good life lesson).

Positive thinking provides two powers to create good luck in your life:
- *Active creation of* good luck
- *Passive attraction* of good luck

Power # 1: active creation of good luck

Positive thinking helps us actively create good luck by:
- Guiding our decisions and actions toward positive outcomes.
- Helping us recognize opportunities as opportunities present themselves. Expecting good luck to come opens the mind to recognize good luck when it arrives. Negative thinking people can watch an unexpected gift horse come walking right up to them and not recognize it. Wise people over many generations have advised that the answers to prayers don't always arrive in the form that people were expecting.
- Tapping into inner resources we hadn't yet discovered within ourselves.
- Helping to generate the self-confidence needed to take the action needed to create good luck.

- Helping to create the will power - the "force of will" – needed to meet the challenges and overcome the obstacles that might otherwise hinder us in creating our own good luck.
- Helping us maintain the peak mental and physical health that we need in order to put our best efforts into doing the good work needed to create good luck.

Visualization *is pro-active optimism.* "Visualize" means picture in your mind that you have successfully done whatever you want to do before you actually do it. A classic example is a golfer seeing in his mind that his ball has gone where he wants it to go before he swings – "see the ball, be the ball".

- Visualization is a <u>key element in sports psychology</u>. Learn about this burgeoning field of study. Colleges are offering programs in sports psychology, and individual athletes and entire teams are hiring sports psychologists to help athletes optimize their performance.
- Libraries and bookstores are loaded with books written by athletic coaches, business consultants, psychologists, and all sorts of other authors who advocate for the power of visualization to help people improve their performance. Read some of these books.

Visualize yourself achieving your business plan and projected financial statement budget objectives. A few examples of visualizations:
- Smiling at your monthly bank statement because you have exceeded your cash savings objective each month for the past year.
- Receiving your fifth straight employee of the year award.
- A happy holiday meal in your dream home surrounded by your loved ones.
- Executive director of your favorite charity thanking you for being their largest donor.
- Your family, friends, and business team gathered together to celebrate the success of the company you founded in order to turn your favorite hobby into a business.

Affirmations *are cousins of visualizations.* They are personal pep talks. Affirm to yourself that you already are the money manager you want to be and you have done what you planned to do. *The simple act of telling yourself that you already are the money manager you want to be and that you have done what you planned to do programs your mind to cross over the bridge from where you are to where you want to be.*

Saying affirmations to yourself each day can help:
- Reinforce your can-do attitude to achieve whatever objectives you visualize yourself achieving.
- Crowd out any existing negative thinking from your mind and prevent new negative thinking from taking root.
- Create a positive reinforcement loop – as affirmations help you achieve the objectives you visualize achieving, your mind will be getting programmed to believe ever more strongly that affirmations and visualization work, which is likely to make affirmations and visualization increasingly more effective as tools in achieving your next objectives.

Studies I have heard about indicate that unhappy people start feeling happier almost immediately after they force themselves to smile. Just as telling themselves to smile can help make people feel happier, affirming to yourself that you are a good money manager is likely to help program your mind to think the way a good money manager would think. A few examples of affirmations:
- Wealth flows abundantly to me as I live the good life that I have planned to live.
- I am a good steward of the wealth with which I have been blessed.
- I prudently use the wealth I have amassed as a tool to help other people prosper.

- I am a smart businessperson who makes good decisions.

Learn how to write and use affirmations to help accomplish the objectives you visualize accomplishing. There is a vast amount of information about how to use affirmations available from bookstores, libraries, and online.

You might try keeping a few written affirmations handy on a piece of paper by your bed or at your workplace. Reading those affirmations can help re-energize your positive thinking any time you catch yourself with a negative thought such as "I'm no good at …" or "I can't do …"

"What goes around, comes around." Doing good things for people will help motivate many of them to "return the favor" and do good things that result in good luck for you. Learn about:
- Ancient wisdom such as Karma, "do unto others as you would have others do unto you", and Native American teachings that each person should do what is good for all.
- What science teaches about the interconnectedness in life and the universe (a) in biology – ecosystems and the biosphere, (b) in physics - quantum entanglement.

Power # 2: passive attraction of good luck

The pheromone effect.
- Good business people are drawn to each other by positive vibes in much the same way that bees are drawn to each other by the pheromones they emit.
- We humans are drawn to positive thinking, happy people who emanate "good vibrations".
- Positive thinking will attract the type of good people who can help bring you good luck.

Metaphysical "law of attraction"
- Countless practical people in the practical real world have reported that some form of power in the "universe" helped them gain prosperity, be that power a spiritual entity or a secular humanist power, the law of attraction worked just the same. People believed they could attract good into their lives, and into their lives it came.
- Learn about the New Thought school of thinking and religion that developed in the mid to late 1800's.
- Learn about the magnetic power of a "mindset of abundance" to attract good luck.
- Read:
  - *The Power of Positive Thinking* written by Norman Vincent Peale, one of the most famous books about positive thinking.
  - *The Secret* written by Rhonda Byrne, a huge best seller that tells us about the Law of Attraction.
  - Any of the numerous other self-help books that talk about how to attract prosperity.
- Open your mind to consider the metaphysical power of the law of attraction to help you attract prosperity into your life. Try using the power of positive thinking to attract prosperity. It can't hurt, and it is likely to help. Just give it time to play out.

Self-fulfilling prophecy: we tend to create self-fulfilling prophecies for the outcomes of our lives through the way we think about ourselves and about our lives. *Harness the power of positive thinking to create a powerful self-fulfilling prophesies of good luck in living your life and managing your money.*

Control your emotions

Excessive emotion and business don't mix - like drinking and driving, like oil and water. Excessive emotion can impair, and seize control from, the rational thinking mind that is required for prudent business decision making. Physical crimes are often described as "crimes of passion". Well, we could call a great deal of the financial harm we cause ourselves "fiscal crimes of passion" because they are a result of excessive emotion.

Excessive emotion is hard to define. For the purposes of this book let's define emotion as being excessive if:
- (a) You can't seem to think rationally; or,
- (b) Someone observing you would say you're getting too emotional.

Coaches tell athletes "*play with passion, but play under control*". That's good advice for business people too. Business requires us to dance into certain areas where rational thinking and emotions must mix together under control, such as:
- *Passion* for what we are doing. Passion in the context of this book means degree of desire to become as good as we can get at managing our personal financial management companies (see the "art" part of the Business Management section of Chapter 4).
- *Compassion* - feelings of concern for other people such as empathy and sympathy.

Conscious recognition of our emotions that might affect our thinking and behavior to an excessive extent can help us control those emotions. Identify and write a list of emotions you are prone to feel to excessive levels – both negative emotions (e.g. fear, panic, anxiety, worry, revenge, and jealousy) and positive emotion (e.g. irrational exuberance). Include this list in the Inventory section of your business plan (see Chapter 4).
- Take the emotion of fear as an example. Some of us can get so afraid of certain things, that we can't think clearly about planning how to control our fear. Writing down fear as an emotion to be dealt with pulls it out of the dark recesses of our brains, and "puts it up on the table" where our rational thinking minds can dig into the reasons why we have become excessively fearful in the past (e.g. lack of self-confidence, lack of knowledge about someone or something), and then plan how to manage our fear(s).
- This inventory might be tough to do (maybe even emotion-tweakingly tough), but doing it is likely to pay you big dividends. Talking to a confidant who knows you well (or a professional counselor) may be a big help in preparing this list and planning how to manage the emotions on it.

"Irrational exuberance" is the positive emotion of enthusiasm taken to an excessive extent.
- When we think about emotions getting out of control, we tend to think about negative emotions. But make no mistake, excessive enthusiasm – irrational exuberance – can be seriously harmful to your financial position.
- The possibility of a good outcome can get some people so excited that they become blinded to the possibility of a bad outcome. They can see only the pros of a prospective decision option and not the potential cons.
- Too much of many good things isn't good for us, like food, wine, and sun. Too much emotion can be flat out bad. As the ancient Greeks said "*all things in moderation*".
- *Enthusiasm is great to have, just don't let it snowball into irrational exuberance.*

Classic examples of irrational exuberance:
- *Investment bubbles are poster children for irrational exuberance.* People who got so

enthusiastically swept up in a buying frenzy that they totally forgot about basic economic fundamentals and their own common sense.

- People who went ga-ga over promises made by a new employer during the hiring process for a new job, and didn't bother to do enough research into the pros and cons of their new employers and their new jobs. Then after starting their new jobs they sadly discovered the undesirable realities of the employers and/or the jobs.
- People who decided to get married while they were still blinded by infatuation (puppy love – "she's so pretty"; "he's so nice"). Then after being married for a period of time they got to know each other well enough to begin recognizing their differences and each other's annoying behavioral quirks, and wound up in financially messy divorces.

Develop an emotion control system. Research emotion calming techniques, and use your experience to learn what techniques work best for you. A few suggestions:

- Take a deep breath and put a smile on your face. Smiling has great calming power.
- Step back from the situation mentally and physically to "give yourself room to think".
- Take a walk around the block, or exercise in some way, to get good hormones working.
- Take a mental time out to enjoy a soothing cup of tea.
- Listen to soothing music. It is said "music has the power to soothe the savage beast."
- Talk things out with a confidant whose judgment you trust.
- Sleep on it. A good night's sleep can work miracles to restore rational thinking.

Meditation and mindfulness

- Learn how all sorts of successful people use meditation and mindfulness to help keep their emotions under control. Learn how Russell Simmons says we can use meditation.
- Learn what many business consultants have to say about how people can use meditation and mindfulness to help control their emotions and improve their job performance. I have seen mindfulness featured in a "Health and Wellness" calendar given to employees.
- Learn how psychologist Ellen Langer says we can use mindfulness.
- Read *The Miracle of Mindfulness* by Thich Nhat Hanh.
- Learn how "mindfulness" coaches (such as George Mumford, author of *The Mindful Athlete: Secrets to Pure Performance*) coach people as varied as business leaders, athletes, and attorneys to use mindfulness to sharpen thinking and help achieve success.

Surround yourself with good people who will tell you when they see your emotions getting the better of your rational thinking and will try to help you regain control of your emotions.

"Control yourself" has been said by countless mothers to countless kids. Pay attention to Mother.

"Don't sweat the little things, and remember, everything is little."

- Don't take this adage too literally and go overboard in the direction of becoming nonchalant. Just use the adage to help maintain perspective on how events that can seem so earth shatteringly big at the moment aren't really so big in the grand scheme of life.
- *Emotions can deceive us into thinking that a relatively minor event in life is a major event*, e.g. getting all worked up and spending an imprudent fortune on a loved one's birthday (be both thoughtful AND financially prudent); road rage after "some idiot" does something so "crazy" that it drives a good driver to do something expensively stupid.

Vent stress - don't let it build up. Everybody feels some level of stress at times. Stress can lead to bodily illness that increases medical expenses and cuts short working careers and lives. Pressure from stress can lead to mental blow-ups and doing all sorts of things that can cause financial harm. Find ways that work for you to vent stress, such as:

- Exercise. It's almost impossible to remain stressed while exercising – ask any jogger or power walker.
- Talk to a confidant. "Don't suffer in silence". The act of telling someone your troubles can work wonders as an escape valve for mental steam. And, getting input from another person can help in planning the best way to address the source of your stress.
- Don't let problems fester. Face problems head on and get them resolved ASAP.
- Hire people to do work for you that would stress you out if you tried to do it yourself, e.g. tax return preparation, investment management, home renovation work.

Manage your mistakes. Mistakes can create mental danger zones in which emotions run wild. We are prone to spending money imprudently as we try to correct our mistakes or make amends to others for any hurt our mistakes may have caused them.

After you think you <u>may</u> have made a big mistake, no matter how bone-headed dumb, ashamed, embarrassed, or angry you may feel:

- Don't do anything until you have used your emotion control system to calm down and get into a rational thinking business mindset. "Don't jump out of the frying pan into the fire."
- Make sure you actually made a mistake. Sometimes things aren't what we thought they were at first. Sometimes we think we made a mistake when in fact we hadn't.
- If you did indeed make a mistake, "don't cry over spilt milk." Put the mistake in perspective. See it as just one small detail in the big picture of your whole long life.
- Figure out how you can correct the mistake, if correction is possible. If you have time, talk to at least one confidant to get an objective perspective, and perhaps advice and recommendations.
- Forgive yourself, no matter how bad the mistake seems to have been. Don't keep on kicking yourself over and over. Once is enough. Self-forgiveness is strong medicine for mental health.
- Learn from the mistake. Analyze what you did and why you did it, and determine how you can avoid making the same mistake again.
- *The bright side of making a big mistake is that the bigger the mistake, the more likely you are to remember lessons learned from it.*
- If you hurt someone, apologize, sincerely.
- *Find a way to laugh about it. Sooner or later we can laugh about most of our mistakes. Make it sooner.* "Laughter is the best medicine."
- *Put the mistake behind you. Move on.* A mistake becomes history the moment after it is made. Nobody can change history. Don't let "if only I had …" get on a continuous playback loop in your mind. Let go of any control the past might have over you. Don't let the past keep you from living your life the way you want to live it in the present.
- Revise your business plan if needed.

Understand that EVERYBODY makes mistakes. Nobody is perfect.

- *<u>This book is loaded with lessons I learned from mistakes I made</u>.*
- Tell yourself "it wasn't my first mistake, and it won't be my last".
- There are billions of people in the world today, and virtually every one of us makes mistakes every day. Maintain a healthy sense of perspective that the world won't end just because of the mistakes that one person makes. Morning will continue to dawn after every night.

- If you get to thinking "I'm the only one who could have ever made such a stupid mistake" remind yourself that with the billions of people alive today, and the billions more ancestors who preceded us, odds are that many people have made the exact same mistake. Take comfort in statistics (did I really just say that?). It is likely that there are lots of other people out there living their lives after having made the same mistake you made, and even more likely, many other people recently made much bigger ones.
- *You can also be comforted in the fact that right now there are sophisticated professionals all across the country who are about to make mistakes that will cause them to think "I can't believe I made that mistake" at some time in the future.*

The positive spin on mistakes is that sometimes it takes a mistake for us humans to:
- Learn lessons that parents, teachers or supervisors had tried to teach us.
- Learn that the advice people had given us had been advice we should have taken.
- Learn lessons that we hadn't been able to learn any other way.

Manage your fears and worries.
- One of the greatest causes of fear is the unknown. One of the very best ways to manage a fear is to learn all that we have the time and resources to learn about whatever we fear. By means of learning about something we have feared:
  o We may discover that it is not really something to fear.
  o We may learn how to deal with whatever we feared.
- Make elimination of each fear and worry that you listed in your personal inventory (see Chapter 4) an objective in your plan.

Develop a problem solving process. Below is a suggested eight step process you can tailor to your own liking (pretty much the same as the decision making process covered in Chapter 7).
- Step 1. Calm down and get into a rational thinking business mindset.
- Step 2. Determine if you do have a real problem, or just a false perception of a problem.
  o If it is a real problem, define as exactly as you can the nature and scope of the problem - what is the problem, what caused it, what are the ramifications, etc.
  o If it is only a false perception of a problem, seek ways to change your thinking that would help you avoid future false perceptions.
- Step 3. Identify the options you might have for prospective solutions of the problem.
- Step 4. Evaluate the likely outcome of each option from which you could choose.
- Step 5. Make a decision – choose the option you think will have the optimum outcome.
- Step 6. Take action on the problem solving option you choose.
- Step 7. Critique your decision. Learn as much as you can from the outcome.
  o Determine if you were contributing to the problem - and oh so often we have at least some part to play in each of our problems either because of things we did or things we didn't do. If you were, seek ways to change your thinking and behavior to help avoid similar problems in the future.
  o We must be careful about laying too much blame for our problems on other people. Remember this old chestnut *"when you point the finger of responsibility at someone else, you have three fingers pointing back at you"*.
- Step 8. Put the problem behind you and carry on with your life. Don't dwell on the past.

Don't compare your life to anyone else's life.
- Comparisons can make us miserable. They can lead a person to think all sorts of negative emotion laden thoughts such as "I am not as likeable as she is, or not as good as she is at

playing this game, or not as good at doing my job".
- No one can ever be exactly like someone else. Each one of is too unique - we each have a unique life history, unique personality, unique skill set, and unique life situation.
- What we all can be is thankful to have this wonderful gift of life that presents an almost boundless opportunity to become the person we dream of becoming, provided we use a planning process, work diligently on our action plans, use a decision making process to make prudent decisions, and are blessed with enough time to achieve our objectives.

Accept the reality that the world is not a perfect place.
- Life is not a perfectly smooth road of only good things. We all experience bumps in the road of life.
  o When you catch yourself feeling you were knocked down on the road of life, "just pick yourself up, dust yourself off", and move on to the bigger and better things that await you just around the bend.
  o Believe that when you finally get to the end of your road in life and look back you will see that there had been a lot more good than not-so-good.
- Don't get excessively emotional about events over which you have no influence or control. Think about words attributed to Reinhold Niebuhr "God, grant me the serenity to accept the things I cannot change, the courage to change the things I can, and the wisdom to know the difference." *"You can only do what you can do."*
- Don't get sucked into believing the false images of a perfect world that entertainment, advertising, and marketing professionals try to create. Movie and theatre people talk about getting audiences to "suspend disbelief" in order get them immersed in stories. It's OK to let your mind go in order to enjoy a story or an entertaining television commercial (think Super Bowl ads), but then snap back to an awareness of the reality of your life and the life going on around you.
- The seemingly "perfect" families in your community almost undoubtedly have far from perfect stuff going on in their lives behind the veneer of public appearances they put on.
- In the business world you are going to encounter people who don't seem to have all the expertise, experience, or communication skills that you would expect people in their positions to have. Don't get frustrated or annoyed by people who are in positions in which you think they should know more than it appears they know. Just think about how The Peter Principle might apply – many people have risen through their organizations to jobs in which they really don't know what they are talking about or what they should be doing.

Accept that "bad" things happen to good people (however you define "bad"). That's life. For whatever reasons, things we don't want to happen do happen to all of us. Accept that "bad" things will happen to you. Most times will be good, but some will not.
- Don't get mired in feeling sorry for yourself. *Pity parties are expensive.*
- Put this positive spin on bad things – without at least a few bad things, we couldn't fully appreciate all the good things in our lives. *Consider bad things to be just a pinch of bitter seasoning that the world tosses into your life stew, and that after a lifetime of cooking along with all the good things that you put into the pot, your stew will wind up being pretty tasty.*

Manage bad things that "happen to you" pretty much the same way you manage mistakes.
- As soon as you feel like a bad thing is happening, be alert for emotions kicking in. Bad can go to worse if we allow emotions to interfere with our ability to think clearly and rationally about how to get through the bad time. Keep your wits about you.

- Determine just how bad "bad" really is. *Bad is in the eye of the beholder. What might seem catastrophically bad to one person might not seem so bad to another person.* "Looks can be deceiving." Things aren't always what they appear to be at first."
- Put bad events in their proper perspective.
  - o *Emotions can lead us "to make mountains out of molehills".* As big as any bad event may seem at the moment, it is not likely to look nearly so big when seen in the context of the grand scheme of your life.
  - o Most "bad" things won't "ruin your life", no matter how bad the situation feels at the moment - they may change your life, but they won't ruin your life.
  - o And, after enough time passes, most of us can find humor in even the worst "bad" things that happened to us. *If you are an adult, think back to when you were a teenager. How many times did you feel "doomed" by something that you laugh about today?*
- Find life lessons to learn. Become wiser for the experience. Many a millionaire has earned a fortune, lost a fortune, earned it back, and died wealthy.
- *Business people often say that they learn the true measure of a person by observing how she responds to being "behind the 8 ball".*

Adages and song lyrics offer sound advice:
- "If it doesn't kill you, it will make you stronger."
- "Time heals all wounds."
- "Look for the silver lining in clouds."
- "Don't cry in your beer."
- "The sun will come out tomorrow" (yes, Little Orphan Annie in the song *Tomorrow*.)

Expect the best, but be prepared to deal with the worst.
- The "worst" is going to happen once in a while. That's life. Stuff happens - the job we had tried so hard to get turns out to be killing us, the love we thought would last forever turns around and walks out the door, the investment we thought was going to make us rich turns out to be a big loser.
- The bigger the magnitude of the event, the more important it is to not let it get you down.
- Take comfort in the fact that no matter how bad you think you may have it at the moment, there are many, many other people who have it worse than you do, and they are still out there getting on with their lives as they deal with their challenges. Be thankful you don't have to deal with their situations.

Keep in mind that the "worst" may only be the worst in our minds at the moment it happens. The "worst" has a funny way of sometimes turning out to actually have been the best thing that could have happened, when looked back upon from the vantage point of the future. Lots of stories and songs have been written about this amazing phenomenon of life. "Thank God for unanswered prayers" has earned its place in the pantheon of folk wisdom for good reason.

And, w*ith all due respect to some hard core athletic coaches and motivational speakers who say "failure is not an option", failure IS an option* with which we must be prepared to deal.
- In real life people do fail to achieve some of their objectives. "You can't win 'em all."
- The best laid plans and best informed decisions don't always play out the way we thought they would. When plans and decisions don't play out the way you thought they would, keep your rational thinking wits about you, evaluate the circumstances with which you have to deal, revise your plans accordingly, and then go out and take action to make good things happen.

- Aspire to succeed at everything you plan to do, but be realistically prudent enough to have a Plan B for the times that you do fail.
- Study history to learn how so many successful people have gone through times of both "agony and ecstasy" on their way toward achieving success in the long run.

Don't get rattled by unexpected events, especially by times of "crisis". When times of crisis appear to be darkest it is most important for us to maintain our composure, keep our wits about us, think rationally, and resolves the crisis. "The darkest hour is just before dawn."

It pays to have a thick skin and an open mind. Business is like a schoolyard at times. Just like kids, adults sometimes say all sorts of mean and nasty things. "Don't let what people say get under your skin."
- Look in the mirror. People may just be reacting to the way you have been treating them.
- Understand that people occasionally say and do things that they haven't thought through, or that they don't really mean.
- "Walk a mile in the other person's shoes." Have empathy and sympathy.
  - o Sometimes people are just having bad days and lash out at whoever crosses their paths.
  - o Sometimes people are motivated by an inner anger at things that have nothing to do with the people to whom they say mean and nasty things.
  - o Some people have inferiority complexes that cause them to think other people are a threat to them.
- If anyone insults you or taunts you as a manipulation technique to disrupt your thinking and get you to do something your rational thinking mind wouldn't allow you to do (like athletes talking smack on the football field) remember two old playground adages:
  - o "Sticks and stones may break your bones, but names will never hurt you."
  - o "Let it roll off your back like water off a duck."

Don't let what anyone says or does "get you down", or "make you so angry you can't see straight."
- Understand that life isn't always "a bed of roses", and that you have no control over what people say or do. You can only control how you react to what other people say or do.
- To help keep your composure, think about the title of the song "Heaven Is in Your Mind" from back in the late 1960's.

Take criticism well.
- *Use criticism as a window to see yourself from a different perspective.* Ask the person criticizing you "why do you say that?" Try to find out what prompted the person to criticize you. Did you really "screw up", or, were you really "so ignorant", or were you really "so mean"? Is there a lesson to learn or a behavior for you to change?
- Even if a person is being something of a jerk in the way she is criticizing you, try to keep your cool and see if there are kernels of truth in what she is saying (tough, I know).
- If you hear the same criticism different times from different people, you can be pretty sure that there is something you need to learn about yourself.

Don't hold a grudge, hate, or seek revenge to get even. Such negative thinking injects emotional feelings into rational thinking.
- A grudge poisons the mind and saps the mental energy of the person holding the grudge.
- And, with a touch of irony, the person who incited the grudge may be completely oblivious to the grudge.

- Overt displays of hate or revenge might provoke people to do you further harm. It is never good for a person's pocketbook to have somebody actively trying to do him harm. Revenge can start a Hatfields & McCoys style feud of tit-for-tat, mutually harmful retribution to "get even".
- *Getting even doesn't get a person ahead - it usually sets a person back.* Getting even costs in terms of the lost opportunity cost of the time, effort and/or money that is spent doing whatever is done to get even.
- Heed this old wisdom "turn the other cheek" and "don't burn any bridges".

Practice forgiveness. Forgiveness has been taught by spiritual leaders for thousands of years because of its near mystical powers.
- Forgiveness helps clear the mind of negative thoughts and restore the positive attitude and rational thinking mindset needed to learn from a hurtful experience and move on wiser for that experience.
- The act of forgiveness can help release internal stresses that make us feel ill about something somebody did. Forgiveness can help us feel better physically.
- Forgiveness helps restore relationships between people who have no recourse but to maintain social or business relationships.
- There is great power in the ancient advice to "love your enemies".

Learn why so many people say we are all connected to each other. "What goes around comes around". What you "have done unto others" may just be coming back to you.
- Study some of the ancient wisdom about the interconnectedness of life, such as:
  - o   Native American beliefs about the interconnectedness of all life.
  - o   Karma
- Learn what experts in quantum mechanics (quantum physics) have to say about entanglement - the connectedness of things in the physical world.
- Watch the movie "I am".

Study history to mellow your emotions.
- The "good old days" often look better in the rear view mirror of memory than those days looked to the people who were living them.
  - o   Studying history will help you learn (or remember) what life actually was like back in the good old days of the past.
  - o   THESE are the good old days that you will be remembering some day.
- People in the past endured lots of adversity in their lives. Some people persevered and succeeded, some didn't. Learn how people succeeded.
- Read some rags-to-riches biographies of successful people (ask your librarian for some suggestions). People who had been thinking that the deck had been stacked against them since they were little kids are likely to learn that no matter how bad they think their lives have been, their lives have not been as bad as the lives of many people were before they pressed on to become successful.
- Talk to some older folks about the tough times they have experienced in their lives, seen other people experience, or heard about, and what they learned from those tough times.

Avoid getting swept up in the excessive emotions of other people. To help minimize the risk of other people's emotions impacting the way you think, feel, or behave:
- Surround yourself with as many prudent, independent thinkers as you can; people who are not prone to getting excessively emotional; people who have a relatively low

susceptibility to being influenced by the excessive emotions of others (see Chapter 9).
- Talk to the most level-headed people you know about current events that seem to be stirring up excessive emotions in other people. Ask them to critique your thinking about these events. Ask if they think you might be getting swept up in the emotions of others.
- Review your written business plan frequently enough to keep your mind focused on what <u>you</u> think and believe, <u>your</u> objectives, <u>your</u> strategy, and <u>your</u> action plan.

Determine if what you love to do is good for you to do.
- One of the key points in this book is to do what you love to do. But some of the things we may "love" to do may not actually be "good" for us to do.
- Run your feelings for what you love to do through the filter of your rational thinking mind. Ask yourself:
    o Is what I love to do advancing me toward achieving my objectives?
    o Does what I love to do fit in with the strategy I have written in my business plan?
    o How might doing what I love to do impact me and the lifestyle I plan to live later in life, for example:
        ▪ Is spending too much money on my love of travel keeping me from saving enough money for my future financial security?
        ▪ Is continuing to play the sport I love as often and as hard as I played it when I was younger doing damage to my body (e.g. knee or back injury) that will cost me a ton of money in future medical bills?
        ▪ Is doing what I love to do contributing to the degradation of the environment (the air, the water, or the land) in which I will be living in 30 years? As is said "what will the world be like for your children"?
- Learn how various philosophers advise us to think about what is "good" for us.

Don't get "blinded by your own brilliance".
- More than once in my life I have observed a person delude himself into thinking he was smarter than he really was, and that self-delusion came back to bite him.
- Don't live life thinking you are the smartest guy in the room. Adopt the attitude that there is always someone smarter than you are in any group, and you would be smart to get those smarter people on your side helping you achieve your objectives.
- The smarter a person thinks he is, the easier it can be for someone else to outsmart him

Don't let life get you down. Feeling depressed about what is happening (or not happening) in their lives can hurt people's management of their money in at least three ways:
- Some unhappy people try to buy happiness.
- Feeling depressed can adversely impact people's ability to think rationally and make well-informed, well-reasoned decisions.
- Unhappiness can blind people to great opportunities staring them right in the face – opportunities to make life better if people would just take advantage of them.

Some people who aren't happy with their lives fight admitting to themselves that they aren't "happy campers". They just put on a happy face to show to other people, and "soldier on", slogging through their lives feeling blah. Two suggestions for these people:
- Get happy – use ideas in the next section as you see fit.
- If you feel so "down in the dumps" that you just can't seem to get yourself happy, it might be money well spent to talk to a professional counselor, therapist, or doctor who specializes in working with people who feel depressed.

Get happy

We humans tend to be motivated to do things we enjoy doing and avoid doing things we don't enjoy.
- *We seek pleasure and avoid pain.*
- Gear your business plan toward doing what you love to do.
   o Beginning to plan doing things you would love to do is likely to start making you feel happier immediately. Just as part of the fun of a vacation is planning where to go and what to do, so too our spirits are likely to be lifted as soon as we start planning the journey toward the things we love in life and making our dreams come true.
   o Developing an action plan of things that will make you happy will help motivate you to follow through on your plan to actually do what you planned to do.
   o *Givers (people who give of themselves) tend to be the happiest people.* Plan to give of your time, talents, and money to help other people. Feel the joy of doing well for yourself by doing good for others.
- Surround yourself with people whose company you enjoy.
- Make "happy" lifestyle choices about where you live and what you do.
- Have fun in a lifelong journey of continuous continuing education.

"The best things in life are free". Find the true happiness in simple pleasures such as:
- *Being grateful (thankful) for all that you have today, especially for the gift of life.*
- Relationships with family and friends.
- Good conversation.
- Putting a smile on somebody else's face; it will put a bigger one on yours.
- Practicing "random acts of kindness", e.g. while driving in traffic that is crawling along, let a car that has been waiting at a cross street enter traffic in front of you.
- Stopping to "smell the roses" as you walk, marvel at a butterfly, or luxuriate in a warm sun and gentle breeze.
- Singing and whistling to yourself.

As you make your lifestyle choices keep in mind the "dark side" power of money to lead us to feel stressed and unhappy with our lives.
- Beware being held as "financial prisoner" by places of privilege such as country clubs, private schools and gated communities where people are more likely to feel:
   o Peer pressure to spend money that their budgets can't afford.
   o Stuck in ruts of materialism and "keeping up with the Jones".
- Avoid being seduced by the lure of a job that pays "big money" but which you don't think you would truly love. The more of your precious time that you might invest in a job for the sole reason of making money, the less time you would have to do all the other things in life that could bring you greater joy and satisfaction.

Have a light heart and a good sense of humor.
- *A sense of humor is an invaluable business asset.*
- Humor has great power to help us keep our emotions under control.
   o Finding the humor in things that people have said or done that we don't like is a great antidote to emotional knee jerk reactions - fuming, screaming, crying, gnashing teeth, whatever – none of which are financially productive and all of which can lead us to make expensive mistakes.

- o Laughing helps blow off emotional steam and restore a rational thinking business mindset.
  - o As I heard storyteller and writer Kevin Kling say "when you laugh at something, it can't control you any more" (learn about Kevin Kling – he offers us some great advice).
- Laughter helps clear mental blocks. If you don't understand something that seems perplexing, step back and have a good laugh about something, anything. Then you can come back to the matter at hand with a clearer mind and take a fresh look at it.
- Laughter helps us maintain a sense of perspective on how small each single event is in the grand scheme of a long life.
- "Laughter is the best medicine."
- And, best of all – it's just plain fun to have a good sense of humor.

Having a sense of humor doesn't mean being a comedian or the class clown.
- In this book, a sense of humor is more about the ability to find the humor in the ways we humans act and the current events we read about in our newspapers, and finding joy and happiness in all the little things of daily life.
- A sense of humor is an internal thing that you know you have. It is not an external thing that you need to show to anybody, although it is good to keep a smile on your face.

Make yours a kind spirited, compassionate sense of humor.
- We all must live together on this spaceship Earth. We can't just "stop the world and ask to get off". And we all do things all the time that have the potential to drive each other nuts - I do, you do, we all do.
- Gentle, good natured humor works two ways:
  - o It helps all of us get along together here in our confined space on Earth.
  - o It will help you maintain your sense of perspective about sharing the experience of life with the rest of us imperfect people.
- *Avoid sarcastic, biting humor.* It can come across as mean spirited, and repel the type of good, compassionate people who have the internal motivation to help you succeed.

Don't take yourself too seriously. Laugh about your human weaknesses, a/k/a foibles – a humorous sounding euphemism. Say "foibles". Sounds funny, doesn't it? Foibles are more fun than weaknesses. We all have foibles – and to know them is to love them. They are part of what makes each of us the special person that she is.

Try to see the humor in your world the way that a good professional humorist would see it. At the risk of becoming dated, a few suggestions to stimulate your thinking:
- Watch TV shows that feature well intended satire (as opposed to mean and nasty sarcasm); the kind of satire that can make public figures laugh at themselves.
- Read political cartoons, and comic strips such as Doonesbury, Dilbert, and Zits.
- Learn about authors Will Rogers and Mark Twain (and read some of their work too).
- Read "The Onion" online.
- Listen to podcasts and radio shows that feature a humorous take on life.

We can laugh at almost anything after enough time has passed to get some mental separation from it.
- We humans have the gift of being able to laugh at just about any personal tragedy after enough time passes, e.g. investment loss, business failure, divorce, serious illness, loss of

a loved one who has passed on (think Irish Wake). We should use that gift of laughter.
- I've heard humorists talk about how much time must pass before people can start laughing about catastrophes and tragedies. To me, the right time to start laughing about painful events is as soon as possible. *Right now, today, ask yourself "what can I find in any situation that pains me today but might make me laugh in one year, ten years, or twenty years?" Then laugh today. Why wait?*

Think of life as a game that you enjoy playing.
- Consider every day that you wake up as an opportunity to start a new game.
- Make it a fun experience to think up ways to increase your income, decrease your expenses, and increase your net worth each year. Think of financial statements as score cards.
- Think about your job as another one of the many small games you get to play within the grand game of life. Very few jobs are matters of life and death. Even if you "struck out" on one job and lost that one "game", you could learn from the experience and move on the wiser to find a job better suited to you and play a better game at that next job.

Change things that make you unhappy. *Don't stew, do!* The mental burden of unhappiness can be as much of a hindrance to achieving business and financial management success as carrying a 100 pound box of rocks would be to walking up the stairs in the Washington Monument.

In the "Planning Process Step 2, take a personal inventory" section of Chapter 4 we suggested writing a list of things that have been making you unhappy (e.g. things that might make you think "I'm worried; I'm scared; I'm trapped; I have no alternative; I don't like …" Writing this list might be tough because it will make you think about things you might have been trying to avoid thinking about. But writing it might provide benefits such as:
- The act of writing the list can help shine light into the dark corners of your mind to help you see more clearly any specific stuff in your life that that you aren't happy about.
- You can then make it an objective in your business plan to resolve each thing you identified.
- Getting negative, burdensome thoughts out of your mind and on to paper will free up space for positive, productive thinking about what to do about them.
- You are likely to start feeling better just knowing that you have begun to do something about those things that had been making you feel unhappy.
- To help keep yourself in a positive thinking mindset while you are identifying things that had been making you unhappy:
  o Give yourself pep talks (say affirmations) about how you love your life today and you are using your planning process to bring ever greater amounts of joy into your life each new day.
  o Tell yourself that you are good person, and good things happen to good people who think good thoughts, plan good things, and do good things.

If you buy a product or service and you are not happy with it:
- "Get it off your chest." Tell the product supplier or service provider about your dissatisfaction. Good people may well ask how they can "make things right" for you. You might then tell them what they could do to make you feel better, and perhaps tell them your thoughts about how to make a better product or deliver a better service
- Think about how you would "build a better mousetrap". How would you make a better product or deliver a better service? Aside from being a creative way to vent your dissatisfaction, it might just stimulate some new career path planning ideas for you.

Challenge yourself to improve each day

Plan to become more successful each day, each month, and each year. *"There is always room for improvement."* The most successful people don't rest on their laurels. They are always trying to get better.
- Professional golfers take hundreds of practice swings every day.
- Master violinists practice hours a day.
- A karate master once told me that after a student achieved a black belt the student had just attained a physical level that would enable him to start learning karate.
- So too, most good business and financial managers live lives of continuous continuing education – continuously working to improve their business and financial expertise.

Make life an exciting learning adventure:
- Be curious. Little kids who are mesmerized by butterflies, ants, and bees offer a great role model for having fun learning new stuff each day.
- Talk to people about what they do for a living, why they do it, and how they might try to get better at doing it – you are likely to get some great stories and some good ideas to use.
- Learn how smart thinkers through the ages have learned to learn and to fuel their creativity, from Socrates to Leonardo da Vinci to Benjamin Franklin to Thomas Jefferson to Thomas Edison to Warren Buffett to Steve Jobs.

Take a scientific approach to life.
- Scientists continuously seek new knowledge - new ideas, new insights into the way the world works, new discoveries, and new inventions. So too should we continuously seek new knowledge.
- Scientists continuously test the validity of old knowledge – e.g. principles, theories, findings of prior experiments and studies. Ask people for constructive critique of your thinking and the ways you have been doing things as a means to help you test the validity of your thinking and your old ways of doing things, and perhaps learn new information and new and better ways to do things.
- Seek "a-ha" moments – those times when you "get it" – when you get a new insight or you learn something new that "makes it all click into place" in your mind.

Gently push out the bounds of your comfort range.
- Think about schools - each year's classes are built upon the foundation of prior years' classes; after students become acceptably proficient in the subjects taught at a certain grade level, they are promoted to the next grade level the next year. At each grade level students are introduced to progressively more complex and sophisticated course work in each subject area, e.g. basic addition and subtraction gradually leads up to calculus.
- To improve your proficiencies and self-confidence, it might be best for you to gently stretch out the bounds of your historical comfort range.
  - o Gradually increase the level of complexity and difficulty of things that you attempt do as you become increasingly proficient in your skills and abilities.
  - o Try to do some new things that you had not previously attempted to do.
  - o Learn to recognize limits you may have been imposing on yourself just because you thought you wouldn't be able to do certain things, or people told you didn't have the ability to do certain things. Then try doing some of those things - especially the ones you have always dreamed about trying.
- Given that all things in life are connected, working to improve how well you do one thing is likely to have carryover benefit to help you improve how you do other things.

- Learn how Outward Bound challenges people to stretch their limits.

BUT, take care to not stretch the limits of your capabilities so far that you over-extend them.
- *"Don't stretch your rubber band so far that it breaks."*
- Over-extension of a person's capabilities is one of the biggest causes of failure.

Seek to become better each day.
- Seek to become a better person each day – a better spouse, parent, friend, community member, co-worker, money manager, etc.
- *Seek personal bests.* Use joggers as a role model. Most joggers don't try to "beat the competition" in races they run. They just try to improve upon their personal best time at running a particular distance. Try to become as good as you can at whatever you do.
- "Once you stop growing, you start dying". This old adage applies to mental health as well as physical health. Muscles atrophy when they aren't exercised. So too our minds need daily exercise in order to stay sharp.
- *Don't become a dinosaur* stuck in a rut doing the same old things in the same old ways who gradually becomes functionally extinct in the evolving world of business, financial, and life management.

Practice is a key element in developing good habits and improving performance.
- There is a big difference between repetition and practice.
  - o Repetition is doing the same old thing the same old way over and over again without any effort to improve doing that thing.
  - o *Practice is a concerted effort to get better at doing something.*
- Through practice we develop good habits for doing whatever we practice.

A few ideas about practice to consider:
- Break down whatever activity you want to practice into its component details - the little things - the fundamentals. Practicing each of the component fundamentals will result in improvement in doing whatever activity you practice.
- Seek the help of coaches and mentors.
- Ask people who are good at doing whatever you are practicing for constructive critique of your practice. Also ask if they would be willing to share some tips on how they do it.
- Observe people who you think are better at doing whatever it is that you want to do better – learn through observational osmosis.
  - o Observe at a "macro" level the big picture of how they do it, e.g. how a football wide receiver runs his pass routes and catches passes.
  - o Then do some analytical observation at a "micro" level. Try to spot all the little details that go into the way they do it, e.g. the little things that the wide receiver does with his feet, hips, head, and hands on each play in order to get open, and how he uses his hands to catch the ball.
- Trial and error during practice might help you discover better ways to do something. By trying various tweaks to the way you had been doing something you might discover adjustments that help you improve your performance.

Develop "standard operating procedures" (SOP's): an SOP is a set of steps you decide is best to take to do a specific thing or to respond to specific circumstances:
- A checklist of steps that you can commit to memory.
- The component elements of SOP's can be practiced in order to get better at doing things.

A few more best practices of successful people

Behave the way you were taught to behave while you were growing up. *While parents, teachers, and other community members were teaching us how to be good people, good students, and good citizens, they were also teaching us how to become good business managers:*
- Mind your manners. Say please, and say thank you. Apologize and say you're sorry.
- Use common sense.
- Treat people the way you want them to treat you (mothers often flip this one around – "how would you like it if Johnny did that to you?").
- Do your homework.
- Don't put off until tomorrow what you can do today.
- Waste not, want not.
- A penny saved is a penny earned.
- Put a smile on your face.
- If you don't know, just ask.
- Will you please listen to what I am saying?
- Pay attention. Keep your eyes and ears open.
- Practice makes perfect.
- Did you think about the consequences of what you were doing?
- Don't open your mouth until your brain is engaged.
- Share that with your brother. Don't hog it all.
- Be fair about it.
- Keep your nose to the grindstone (work diligently).

Words of wisdom like the above have been passed down from generation to generation because they have worked in each succeeding generation to help people get along with each other and succeed in making a living. *Many business consultants and motivational speakers have built profitable careers upon the foundation of such age old wisdom.*

Civility pays.
- If you treat people well they are likely to reciprocate and try to do well by you.
- People who can help you succeed will be attracted to you.
- It feels good to be a civil person who treats people well. Since we tend to continue doing things that make us feel good, if you feel good about the ways in which you do business, you are more likely to stick to your plan and achieve your objectives.

Be proactive, not passive. You have two choices about how to manage your life and money:
- *Proactive management - the positive choice*: well-planned action that seeks to control what happens in our lives typically generates better financial results than re-acting to events that happen. And, proactive management provides a comforting feeling of control.
- *Passive management - the negative choice*: passive managers often use the excuse that they are so busy doing their daily work that they don't have enough time to plan. Day after day they just re-act to whatever life throws at them. Passively managed businesses tend to get buffeted about and damaged by winds of economic fate because no one is steering safely toward success and prosperity.

A proactive manager is "captain of her fate".

Be humbly assertive.
- Observation of many people over many years tells me that people who are nice and humbly assertive in the workplace tend to have happier, more satisfying lives than self-centered people who are rudely pushy at work.
  - The relatively few pushy people who achieve business success over the long run tend to do so by trading off the warmth of human relationships that can make life so satisfying.
  - When you run into a person who is rudely pushy in business think about the personal life she is likely to go home to each day.
- Be humble enough to motivate people to help you achieve your objectives.
- Be assertive enough to communicate clearly:
  - That you want people to do what you think is the good and proper thing to do.
  - That you will not be pushed into doing something that you don't think is the right thing for you to do.

Ask for the best deal. Don't be shy. Good business people respect customers and clients who politely establish at the outset of a business relationship that they expect to be given the best value in product or service being purchased.

Surround yourself with people who have enough concern for you and your well-being to offer you honest, constructive critique of your thinking and your behavior. It helps greatly to have people in our lives who will give us constructive critiques of our thinking and behavior. *Our human weaknesses can make self-evaluation of our thinking and behavior tough to do.*
- *"Psychological blinders"* can prevent us from seeing our weaknesses and shortcomings.
- *"Funhouse mirror effect"* - we might see a distorted vision of ourselves when we look in the mirror while a person standing by our side can see us as we actually are.

Earn a good reputation. The people around you are observing what you do, listening to what you say, and talking with each other about what they see and hear. Make it good talk.

Earning a good reputation will:
- Attract good people to you – "birds of a feather flock together". Good business people like to work with people with whom they feel they could do business on a handshake (if their attorneys would allow them).
- Demonstrate to your employer that you are a "keeper"- that your employer should do all they can to keep you happy in order to keep you from leaving the company.
- The most desirable career promotions, the biggest pay raises and the best business deals tend to come to those people who have the best reputations for being trustworthy.

Be trustworthy - trust in each other is the foundation of business.
- Be honest. Look what a good reputation did for Abraham "Honest Abe" Lincoln.
- Don't lie. Lies are almost always discovered. And, after a person tells a lie, she must carry two burdens:
  - Trying to remember who she lied to about what.
  - Living with herself as a liar.
- *If you promise to do something, do it*. If you don't have the time or ability to do something, be honest and say you can't do it. Good business people don't like to be "stiffed". And, they have memories like elephants. "Let your word be your bond".

Be a "straight shooter".
- Don't tell a person what you think she may want to hear if it isn't what you actually think. Say what you honestly think in a tactful, empathetic way. Offer your evaluation of the situation at hand and your suggestions for what you think should be done.
- *Don't be a "yes man".*
  - o Don't be afraid to disagree.
  - o Don't roll over and agree with a decision that you don't think is in the best interest of everyone concerned.
  - o Just be tactful and respectful in presenting your opinion.
- Independent thinking is a highly prized commodity among the kind of smart people with whom you should be surrounding yourself. If a person doesn't respect that you don't always agree, take that as a signal that this may not be a good person to have in your life.

Don't "fake it."
- Faking it is almost always discovered in the long run, and it comes back to bite the faker.
- If you are asked to do something that you know you don't have the expertise or experience to do well, say so.
  - o If the person knows you well enough to trust your business smarts, intellect, and motivation to succeed, she may just tell you to go ahead and give it a try anyway.
  - o If you both agree that it would be best if you did not attempt to do it, your honesty is likely to earn her respect and trust for doing similar things in the future after you gain the expertise and/or experience to do them.
- If you don't know the answer to a question, just say "I don't know. I'll find out, and get back to you." Good business people respect and appreciate that kind of honesty.

Play by the rules - social conformity is usually the best way to achieve success in life.
- Play by the generally accepted rules of good behavior (<u>ethical norms</u>) in the social groups of which you are a member, e.g. your family, community, and workplace.
  - o Become known as a person who has impeccable ethics. Let "high ideals" guide your behavior. "Take the high road" every time.
  - o "Work within the system" and "make the system work for you".
- Obey the law. Avoid "bending the law". Don't "skirt the law".
- Rebels who "buck the system" occasionally find success in life, but more often rebels lose their battles with the social order and flame out in failure.
- *You can march to the beat of a different drummer, but if you do, the music you make should harmonize with the music that other good people are making.*

Think before you speak.
- Think about what you want to say before you open your mouth to say it – especially in business conversations. "Don't put your foot in your mouth."
- Prepare for each business conversation before you walk in the door or pick up the phone. Plan what you want to say. Think through questions you may want to ask and questions you might be asked.
- Some people talk too much. They drone on and on with meaningless small talk and irrelevant chit-chat. Stay alert for this very human condition. If you think you may talk too much, work on saying less. After business conversations critique yourself on what you said. If a colleague or friend was with you, ask them to critique what you said.
- On the other hand, polite conversation usually involves introductory pleasantries to break the ice and set a civil tone before getting to the meat of the matter. Use common sense.

- If you feel your emotions percolating up during a conversation, try not to say anything more until you can calm down your emotions and you can think rationally about what you want to say; you might try excusing yourself for a bathroom break or whatever else you can think of to give yourself time to compose your thoughts.

Think before you act. "Look before you leap."

Henry David Thoreau said "simplify, simplify, simplify".
- Don't make life more complicated than it needs to be.
- Don't make plans so complex that you can't possibly put them into practice.

My mother said "Eschew obfuscation". In the business world people say "KISS", an acronym for "keep it simple stupid".
- Clear and simple requests and instructions minimize the chances of being misunderstood.
- Keep business communications "short and sweet". Don't ramble.
  o The more words you use to make your point, the greater the chance your point will get lost.
  o The more that the facts of your message are obscured by excess words, the harder it will be for people to understand what you want them to understand.

Adopt an "others oriented" strategy in your life.
- "The more you give, the more you get." It's amazing how often the good that we do for other people comes back to us in ways we hadn't expected. *Do good things for other people without expecting anything back in return and you are likely to be pleasantly surprised by just how much you do get back in the future.*
- A "me first" strategy doesn't help a person maximize her well-being, and it can hurt.
  o A "me first" strategy typically turns off the type of others-oriented people who are most likely to do what they can to help others succeed.
  o Self-centered people tend to get stuck with other self-centered people.
    ▪ People not likely to think much about the well-being of others.
    ▪ People more likely to make win-lose decisions in which they maximize their well-being to the detriment of others.
- Business transactions require "give and take". If there is too much take by one person the other person is likely to be more guarded about how much she will offer to give in the next transaction, that is IF she decides to do business again; and she may well tell people she knows to be careful about doing business with the person who tried to take too much – not a good reputation to build.

Welcome change.
- Change is the central theme in the cycle of life - birth, life, and death. Change is going to happen. So, don't fight it. Use it. "If you can't beat 'em, join 'em".
- Anticipate change. Keep track of current events and how they might fit into trends and cycles you know about. Think about how those trends and cycles are likely to play out in the future and changes that might be taking place as a result.
- Be vigilant for opportunities that change might be creating.
- Pay special attention to opportunities in new technologies, discoveries, and new ways of doing old things – somebody may have "built a better mousetrap" that you can use.

See the sunny side of change:
- *Change keeps healthy fresh air circulating in the waters of life.* A stagnant pond of status

quo will smother the life in it over time.
- Go with the flow. Don't try to swim against the stream of change in life.
- Look for the silver lining. See the glass of change as half full.
- See the good old days as pleasant memories to enjoy, while you are in the process of making each new today another pleasant memory for future enjoyment.

Seek ways to get out in front and lead the pack. When you are out in front leading the parade of your life you avoid all the dust that a herd of people could kick up to obscure your view of opportunities that lay ahead. Successful business people typically seek to:
- Stay ahead of job seeking competitors by striving for continuous self-improvement as they aspire to be the best at what they do.
- Find new and better ways to do old things.
- Dream up creative new ideas, new products, and new technologies.

Don't blindly follow the herd.
- Don't do what you think "everybody else" is doing just because they seem to be doing it. Blindly following the herd without making a well-thought, well-reasoned decision can lead to some serious financial damage. As the old wisdom advises, "don't be a lemming who follows other lemmings over a cliff".
- *Don't do anything with your money based solely upon what you think everybody else is doing.* Whenever it might appear that everybody else is doing something with their money, and you begin to think that maybe you should be doing the same thing with your money, try to identify exactly who "everybody" else is, exactly what "they" are actually doing, and why "they" are doing it. Gather enough information to make your own well-informed, well-reasoned decision about what you should do (see Chapter 7).

Most of us use the word "they" pretty loosely. As a kid, when I said "they" are all doing something, my mother would say:
- You are not they; and
- Exactly who is this "*ubiquitous they*"?

I didn't like what my mother was saying then, but I do now. She was trying to teach me to think for myself, to identify exactly who was doing exactly what. Thinking for yourself will help you steer your financial ship away from danger that "everybody else" may be about to crash into.

Many people make the mistake of hearing what a few people are talking about, or seeing what a few people are doing, and use that small sample of the total population as the basis for a false assumption that a much larger group (the mythical "everybody else") thinks it or is doing it.

Be alert for opportunities that might be had by "going against the grain" – by going a different way than the crowd is going.
- Regarding your career:
  o Think supply and demand.
  o Fewer people seeking jobs in an industry means employers have a more limited <u>supply</u> of job seekers from which to satisfy their <u>demand</u> for new employees; and the more limited the supply of prospective employees, the better the compensation packages that employers may be willing to provide to attract talent.
  o There are great opportunities to be had for good career paths in staid, old "mature" industries (e.g. banking, insurance, construction) that the herd doesn't find exciting or attractive.

- Regarding investing, you might consider a "contrarian" investment strategy:
  o Buying when others are selling – prices are likely to be dropping.
  o Selling when others are buying – prices are likely to be rising
  o The best time to invest in a certain type of assets might be right after an investment bubble bursts, IF, the underlying drivers of future economic value of that type of assets are strong.

Consider developing plans and making decisions that allow your life to flow along smoothly.
- The smaller the steps you plan to take, the smoother your walk through life is likely to be; the longer the steps, the more likely you might trip over a bump in the road.
- Don't react in haste to circumstances you don't like - *"don't jump from the frying pan into the fire"*.
  o "Don't do anything rash" while under the influence of excessive emotions.
  o "The devil you know may be better than the devil you don't".
  o "The grass might look greener on the other side of the fence", but if you jump the fence it might not actually look greener after you land on the other side."

Don't micro-manage your life.
- Seek Aristotle's "golden mean" of moderation in managing your life:
  o Enough planning to prudently steer your ship of life toward realizing your dream objectives.
  o Enough unplanned "free time" each day to enjoy your ride on the river of daily life as it flows along toward your dream objective destinations. Immerse yourself in the spontaneous joy of the moment as events happen.
  o Make it an ultra-long term objective for the final year of your life to be able to say it had been a great ride.
- Avoid becoming an obsessive compulsive planner who people describe as a "control freak".
  o Don't drive yourself nuts trying to plan and control every little detail of every day.
  o Don't over-think every little thing that you do each day. Practice doing things that you do on a regular basis to develop good habits in doing them - so that they become "second nature" to you – so that you can do them with a minimum amount of time spent deciding what to do and planning how to do it.

This is a long book that contains many ideas and many suggestions to consider.
- <u>Be judicious in choosing the number of suggestions in this book that you decide to try, and in how rapid a succession you decide to try them</u>.
- Use only those suggestions that you think make good sense for you to try.

If you are a student – don't drop out of school without thinking long and hard about the consequences!
- If the thought of considering a decision to drop out of school has crossed your mind, be sure to consider ALL the potential cons of such a decision. If you dropped out of school today, you might be shooting yourself in the foot and hobbling your ability to maximize your prosperity in the future.
- Many of the best paying jobs require high school, trade school, or college diplomas. If you dropped out you might not be able to qualify for a job you would really like to get at some time in the future.

<u>Old habits die hard</u>

We humans are creatures of habit and our old habits tend to die hard.
- Think about all the New Year's resolutions people make and then break within a few weeks (e.g. resolutions to change diet, exercise, or smoking habits).
- After our rational thinking brains make good decisions about changing old behavioral habits our brains must get our bodies to actually change our behavior.
- Financial management habits can be among the toughest habits to change.
- Lifestyles are comprised of a whole bunch of interconnected behavioral habits (learn about holism and the interconnectedness of the parts of our lives). In order to change our money management habits, it is likely we will need to change some other habits too.

Learning what we should be doing and then doing it are two entirely different things.
- It is far easier to identify what financial management habits we should be changing, and to think about making those changes, and to talk about making those changes, and to plan to make those changes, than it is to actually change our behavior.
- Also, we are susceptible to deluding ourselves into thinking that we are changing a behavioral habit when in fact we are not.

There are many sources that offer excellent money management advice - professional financial advisors, books, classes, websites, etc. We can talk to the best financial advisors in the world and read the best-selling financial management self-help materials, but, we must actually act on that advice in order to actually improve our money management behavior. Keep in mind these adages:
- "It's easier said than done."
- "Actions speak louder than words."
- "Talk is cheap."
- "You can lead a horse to water but you can't make him drink."

To help change money management habits you think you would do well to change:
- Learn how psychologists, counselors, consultants, and other experts in the field of human behavior recommend that we go about trying to change habits we want to change.
- *Study sports psychology.* Most of the ideas for changing performance habits in sports apply to changing money management habits.
- <u>Learn about cognitive behavioral therapy</u>.
  - o Changing the way you have been thinking about money might help you make improvements you would like to make in the way you have been managing the money in your life.
  - o Beginning to think that <u>"your money is your business"</u> might pay performance improvement dividends to you.

Some habits will be easier and faster to change than others. Maintain perspective on just how tough it is for each and every one of us humans to change our behavior. Life is long. Give yourself time to change habits you want to change.

A series of little changes over time can culminate in a making big change. A proven way to modify any behavioral habit is to break own the desired change into a series of small, achievable steps. As the old folk wisdom says "every journey starts with the first step".

"Two steps forward, one step back."
- Most of us make progress toward changing our habits by taking a certain number of steps

forward and then taking an occasional step backward.

- The greater the magnitude of change you plan to make in a money management habit, the more internal resistance you are likely to encounter, and the more likely you will be to take at least one step backward. It's a fact of life. Accept it.
- Accept each backward step as a learning opportunity - <u>learn from it</u> - and go easy on yourself - "you're only human".
- Focus on the progress you have made from where you started. Be happy about that progress and encourage yourself to keep moving forward according to your plan.

For example, if you "blow your budget" for a month (and you will – we all do) learn from the experience. Successful business managers learn from their inevitable missteps.

- Analyze why you spent more money than you had budgeted to spend.
- Figure out how you can prevent it from happening again.
- Then use the lesson(s) learned to help you do a better job of sticking to your budget in the next month and future planning periods.
- Revise your budget if you need to, and then work at sticking to that revised budget.

Treat yourself the way a good athletic coach would treat you.

- Learn the fundamentals (good habits) of good money management.
- Practice those fundamentals. "Practice makes perfect" (actually, as good as you can be would be more accurate since few people are ever perfect at anything [and what is "perfect" anyway] – but "practice makes you as good as you can be" isn't as catchy a phrase).
- Work on improving the weakest parts of your money management game (your worst habits) and capitalize on your strengths (what you find you are good at).
- Be your own best cheer leader. Pat yourself on the back for each step you take toward changing your behavior.

Don't wait any longer to begin using your business planning and projected financial statement budgeting process to change old money management habits that you want to change. If you stick to using your planning and budgeting process over enough time, your old habits are likely to begin changing, and your financial management performance is likely to improve.

No matter how old you are, it's never too late to start.

Chapter 6. Plan Ahead to Manage Greater Wealth and Success

Plan to have greater wealth and success before you get it (success meaning achieving a position that confers the power of authority to direct people's behavior). Understand that you are likely to achieve greater wealth and success if you use a business planning and projected financial statement budgeting process diligently enough over a long enough period of time. Prepare to manage this future prosperity.

Money and success have nasty powers to change people for the worse. Wise elders have been warning generation after generation for thousands of years about the dangers of money and success with words such as "… it is easier for a camel to go through the eye of a needle than for a rich man to enter the kingdom of God."

I have seen too many people have the misfortune to acquire too much money too soon - before they were prepared to cope with having what they perceived to be "so much" money. Some of them began to do some pretty creepy things and lost friends and some lost most of their money. You may have known a nice person who got decidedly less nice after acquiring a lot of money, or heard about people who frittered away new-found wealth after their brains got addled by "all that" money (many professional athletes and celebrities made a ton of money and then wound up losing it all because of financial mismanagement).

Alone, or in a tag team combination, money and success can play on human weaknesses to make people:
- Do things that they never would have thought of doing while they were on their way to gaining their wealth and success.
- Get greedy, and being greedy can cause all sorts of financial problems.
- Get cocky (overly confident about their capabilities), which can lead to:
  - "Getting too big for one's britches" and making financial mistakes.
  - Thinking they are better than other people - becoming haughty and alienating "the little people" below them in society.
  - Forgetting how people helped them get where they are, and beginning to think that they no longer need anybody else's help to stay successful.
  - Driving away the good people who helped them succeed and who would be best able and most motivated to help them hold on to their prosperity.
- Become blind to their shortcomings and human weaknesses, and begin to think:
  - I'm so smart, so rich, and so powerful … that I could never have financial problems.
  - I'm "too big to fail" now.
  - I'm invincible, infallible.
- Become self-centered - think they are the center of the universe and that the world revolves around them. They lose their sense of perspective on how the real world works. Their emotional self-love fogs their rational thinking.
- Get lazy - ease up on how hard they work and let down their guard against all the mean and nasty things in this world that can make money and success disappear.
- Become a magnet attracting "hangers on" - a "posse" of "fair weather friends" who are more interested in sharing in a person's newfound wealth than they are with developing a quality relationship with him, e.g. long lost sleazy Cousin Willy shows up wanting to be best buddies and get some of the money.

Different amounts of money can trigger negative personality changes in different people.
- For some people the trigger might be an inheritance that they get to spend on all sorts of

things that they had not been able to afford in the past.
- For others the trigger might be a promotion at work that provides them greater power of authority and pays them more money than their co-workers and neighbors earn, which allows them to buy stuff that their co-workers and neighbors can't afford.
- For others it might be getting salary increases that allow them to join country clubs and send their kids to private schools.

A few words of caution on job promotions:
- Promotions to positions higher up the "corporate ladder" typically confer increased "authority of position" – meaning that people in higher positions are conferred with the power of authority to tell people in lower positions what to do. Having a position that confers the authority to "order people around" can "mess with a person's mind" and give a person a "king complex" – a feeling that he rules his subjects in his kingdom - be his kingdom a work group, department, division, or an entire company.
- *A promotion can erase a person's memory of exactly how much help he needed from other people to get the position to which he was promoted.*
  - o A person can become deluded into taking too much credit for his own success.
  - o He can also become so deluded about his own capabilities that he forgets how much help he will continue to need in order to continue achieving his new objectives in his new position.
- Well liked, well respected co-workers have become disliked butts of derisive jokes after they morphed into insensitive, pushy bosses.

Personality changes often occur at an insidiously slow creep.
- A person "afflicted" with increasing wealth and success, as well as those closest to him, may not be able detect personality changes creeping in over long periods of time.
- Relatives and friends who are "too close to the forest to see the trees" may see personality changes as just isolated little personality quirks in Good Old Joe. And then one morning they wake up and suddenly realize that Good Old Joe has turned into a dislikably different person, a la Doctor Jekyll and Mister Hyde.
- *Scrooge wasn't always a mean and crusty tightwad. He got that way over time.*

Ten point wealth and success management system

Following is a ten point internal control system that you might consider using to help you manage yourself as you are acquiring wealth and success.

1. Treat money and the power of authority as <u>intoxicating</u> and <u>addictive</u> substances.
2. Cultivate a belief that you are not the center of the universe.
3. Include in your business plan at least one "higher purpose" objective to help make the world a better place in which to live.
4. Adopt an "others-oriented" strategy for living your life.
5. Spend some of your precious time helping to improve the lives of people who have been less fortunate than you have been.
6. Inoculate yourself against wealth and success - success in this book meaning achieving a position that confers the power of authority to direct people's behavior.
7. Seek role models of people who remained good hearted after they acquired significant wealth and success, and continued to make prudent financial decisions.
8. Don't flaunt it after you have gotten it.
9. Set up an early warning detection system that will alert you to unwelcome changes in your thinking and behavior that might be creeping up on you.
10. Ask people with whom you have close relationships to monitor your personality and behavior, and advise you about any changes they might observe in your personality or behavior.

Point 1. Treat money and success as <u>intoxicating</u> and <u>addictive</u> substances. Treat money and success with the same respect and caution that prudent people treat wine and pharmaceutical drugs.

- When used as recommended they have wonderful powers to enhance life.
- When used improperly they have destructive powers to harm life.

Point 2. Cultivate a belief that you are not the center of the universe. Make sure you understand that the world does not revolve around you, your needs, and your wants. Borrow a preventive step from the classic Twelve Step behavioral modification program of AA - adopt a belief that there is a power greater than yourself in this world however you understand that power, be it spiritual or secular.

Practice your "religious" beliefs in your daily life – religious in the sense of your most deeply held beliefs, not in the sense of any religious institution (although they could be one in the same). Fight the human tendency to get caught up in the swirl of events going on around us and forget our core religious beliefs. Pressing problems, rapid and unwelcome changes, aggravations, and other types of "personal problems" all have a way of making us act like someone other than the person we are down deep.

Caution: religious beliefs are a highly personal matter. Act on your beliefs, but don't push your beliefs on anyone else. Be especially careful about preaching to other people about your beliefs that underpin your life. Many people get turned off or offended by preachy people. *Preach by action, not by word.*

Point 3. Include in your business plan at least one "higher purpose" objective to help make the world a better place in which to live - an objective that guides you to continue "doing the right thing" and making decisions that enable you to "take the high road" through life.

Point 4. Adopt an "others-oriented" strategy in living your life.
- Adopt the strategy of using the wealth and success you accumulate as tools to help others, thereby helping to make it a better world in which to live and prosper.
- Seek win-win decisions. Seeking the greatest good for everyone impacted by your decisions is a powerful antidote to the psychological poisons of self-centered greed, avarice, narcissism, and haughty airs of superiority.
- *"Share the wealth."*
- "Do unto others as you would have others do unto you."
- "Put yourself in other people's shoes." Try to see yourself through their eyes.
- Be empathetic and sympathetic.

Point 5. Spend some of your precious time helping to improve the lives of people who have been less fortunate than you.
- Volunteer to do community service work.
  - o Support one or more charities with your precious time as well as your money.
  - o If you belong to a religious organization, support it with your time as well as your money.
- If you can help pull someone up the ladder of economic prosperity, the act of pulling that person up the ladder will help keep your feet planted firmly on the ground – as you are pulling up with your hands you will be pushing your feet back down onto the ground.
- If you can help someone learn how to achieve the prosperity he has dreamed of having, the act of helping him will help you keep in mind all the good things you should keep on doing in order to maintain and increase your own prosperity.
- As you get to know people who don't have as much money as you have:
  - o It will help you see the world and your life from their perspectives.
  - o You may well see that having less money has led them to place a higher value on the blessings of life that money can't buy.
  - o Keep your wealth and success in its proper perspective in a life well lived.
- The good feelings that you get will keep you in touch with the age old wisdom that the best things in life can't be purchased with money alone.

Many resources can help connect you with opportunities to volunteer your time and talents, such as:
- Religious institutions.
- Local governments.
- Schools and colleges.
- Internet sites and library bulletin boards.
- Non-profit organizations themselves, e.g. food banks, soup kitchens, homes for battered women and children, homeless shelters, Habitat for Humanity, Salvation Army, mentor programs, adult reading programs, English as a second language programs.

Point 6. Inoculate yourself against wealth and success. Consider an analogy between "germs" and "wealth and success". Disease causing germs are all around us. Our bodies build up resistance to physical disease causing germs through gradual exposure to those germs in the world around us and through inoculation. To protect yourself from the mental disease-causing germs of "wealth and success" (a) expose yourself to these germs in the world around you by observing how wealth and success have "sickened" people you know and know about, and (b) inoculate yourself by studying how wealth and success have infected others.

- Learn about:
  - o Behavioral economics.
  - o Psychology of personality change.
  - o Cognitive dissonance.
- Clip out stories from newspapers and magazines about wealthy, successful people who have been acting like crooks or creeps. Do some research on their lives to find out if they started out as nice people and they began changing for the worse after they began acquiring wealth and success.
- Read biographies and novels about people whose lives were changed for the worse by money and/or power. Get recommendations from librarians and bookstore employees.

Point 7. Seek role models of people who remained good hearted and continued to make prudent financial decisions after they acquired wealth and success.
- People you know first-hand, perhaps friends, relatives, neighbors, or co-workers.
- People you learn about second hand e.g. actor Paul Newman and President Jimmy Carter.

Point 8. Don't flaunt it after you have gotten it.
- Don't advertise that you have money. Avoid "conspicuous consumption". Play your "money" cards close to your chest.
- The more money that it appears you have, the more people might be tempted to try to get some of your money, e.g. relatives or acquaintances asking for gifts or loans; hucksters and scam artists who are drawn to money "like flies drawn to honey".
- And the more that people try to get some of your money, the greater the potential that their efforts might sour you on life – *the initial joy of having attained wealth and success can turn into the "curse" of having it.*

Point 9. Set up an early warning detection system that can alert you to unwelcome changes in the way you think and act that might be creeping up on you.

1. *Write two lists of things that might indicate changes in the way you think and act*:
   - People and things in your life for which you are most thankful.
   - Specific behaviors of people who you don't think are handling their wealth and success very well – behavior you want to avoid after you gain greater wealth and success.

Then, each year at the same time of year (such as the week of your birthday), write two new lists. Save your lists from prior years but don't look at those lists immediately before writing the current year's lists. <u>After</u> you write the current year's lists, compare the two current lists with the lists written in prior years. Look for changes in the lists from year to year that might indicate wealth and success have begun to change you in negative ways. You might also consider reviewing your lists with a trusted confidant (e.g. family member, close friend, financial advisor, or religious leader) who could provide you with an objective, tough love critique of variances he identifies in your lists.

2. *Keep copies of your plan and your historical financial statement as of the end of each year*, and look for tell-tale changes in them from year to year:
   - In your business plan, look for tell-tale changes in your:
     - o Objectives - what you planned to do.
     - o Strategies - how you planned to live your life in pursuit of your objectives.
   - In your year-end balance sheets, look for tell-tale changes in the type and prices of assets you have been buying and the amount of debt you might have been accumulating.

- In your year end income statements, look for tell-tale changes in the types and amounts of your expenses that would indicate changes in your lifestyle choices and behavior, and the amounts of money you have been saving each year.

3. *Once a year compare your current circle of friends with friends you have had in the past.*
   - Have there been any significant changes in your circle of friends?
   - Are there any noticeable differences in the characteristics of the people you have befriended recently, e.g. beliefs, values, priorities in life, lifestyle, social status?
   - Have you begun associating with people who might not be such good influences on your money management?
   - Are you losing touch with good people with whom you shouldn't be losing touch?

4. *Make a list of words and terms you might use to describe a person whose behavior had been negatively influenced by money and success, and define these words and terms in your own words.* A few words and terms to spur your thinking:
   - Conspicuous consumption, ostentatious, living high on the hog.
   - Status seeker, snob, air of superiority, acting high and mighty.
   - Materialistic, money hungry, sold out (for money).
   - Scrooge, tight fisted, greedy.
   - Cold-hearted.
   - Covetous, avaricious.

Then at least once a year do some soul searching, introspective analysis as to how your current thinking and behavior stack up against your original definitions.
   - Could people be using any of these words or terms when they talk about you?
   - A good time to do this might be at holidays that can be excessively commercialized such as birthdays and Christmas.

Point 10. Ask people with whom you have close relationships to monitor your personality and behavior and alert you to any changes they observe creeping in. You might share this chapter with them and discuss it so they fully understand what you are trying to do. Ask them to be candidly honest with you.
   - *Personal confidants*: family members, friends and co-workers with whom you have close relationships, religious leader, etc. Ask them to tell you if they observe changes in your personality, the way you treat people, the way you talk about money and behave with money, or the way you might have been handling any increased power of position (authority) you might have gotten through a promotion at work.
   - *Professional service providers*: ask them for constructive critiques of your money management and personal behavior from their professional perspectives.

Chapter 7. Decision Making

Decision making should be a process

Decision making should be an ongoing process.
- Nobody can make a "perfect" decision every time. But we all can get better and better at making "good" decisions (*well-informed, well-reasoned decisions that result in good outcomes*) if we develop and use a formal decision making process.
- Each new decision should be <u>informed by the outcomes of prior decisions</u> and <u>guided by a business plan and projected financial statement budget</u>.

Decision making is a critical life skill. Each person owes it to herself to:
- Learn all she can about how successful people make their decisions and what experts in various fields say we can do to improve our decision making, e.g. psychologists, athletic coaches, business consultants.
- Develop her own decision making process.
- Practice using her decision making process with the intent of getting better and better at making good decisions.

This chapter came about because I have known too many people who just couldn't seem to make good decisions.
- A common trait these people seemed to share is that they didn't have any sort of "mental checklist" process that they went through to make each of their decisions, be the decision a little tiny one (cereal or eggs this morning) or a really big one (take this job or not).
- It seems they "acted without thinking", or reacted in the heat of the moment based upon emotion, or just went along with what they thought "everybody else" was doing.
- Too often they "shot themselves in the foot" by making decisions that wound up causing themselves harm.
- It seems that their decisions were not well enough informed nor well enough reasoned.

Developing a personalized decision making process can be as simple as writing down a checklist of steps to go through when making each of your decisions. Below is a suggested nine step checklist to consider, and perhaps tailor to your own liking:
- Step 1. Get into a rational thinking business mindset.
- Step 2. Identify factors that should govern your decision.
- Step 3. Gather relevant information.
- Step 4. Identify the decision options from which you could choose.
- Step 5. Evaluate the likely outcome of each decision option.
- Step 6. Make the decision.
- Step 7. Take action.
- Step 8. Critique the decision's outcome and learn from the experience.
- Step 9. Put that decision behind you and clear your mind for the next decision.

A written checklist:
- Can provide a standard operating procedure (SOP) that can be practiced, and, as with all things we practice diligently, the better you are likely to get at making decisions that result in optimal outcomes.
- Can be committed to memory as a mental checklist which programs your brain computer with decision making software and it can be read as needed to refresh your memory.

Process Step 1: get into a business mindset

Get yourself into a rational thinking business mindset.
- Clear your mind of any emotional junk that may be rattling around in there. Get cool, calm and collected.
- Engage your rational thinking mind.
- If you can't get yourself into a clear thinking business mindset try to postpone making the decision until you can.

The advice to clear your mind of "impetuous desire", and think through decisions with "calm and prudent forethought" goes all the way back to our ancient ancestors.
- A few years ago I was browsing through an old book store and came across the book *Treasury of Thought, Forming an Encyclopedia of Quotations from Ancient and Modern Authors*, written by Maturin M. Ballou, published in 1875, in Boston, by James R. Osgood and Company, late Ticknor & Fields, and Fields, Osgood, & Co.
- Ballou quoted the ancient Greek historian Thucydides from the 400's BCE "You are convinced by experience that very few things are brought to a successful issue by impetuous desire, but most by calm and prudent forethought."
- What Thucydides thought was good advice in the 400's BCE, Ballou thought was equally good advice in the 1800's, and it remains good advice today.

When making your larger, more substantive decisions, you might try doing what many successful athletes do prior to playing their games - visualize yourself being in a calm, rational thinking mindset making a well-informed, well-reasoned decision.

Excessive emotion and rational thinking mix like oil and water – they don't. Excessive emotion interferes with:
- The ability to clearly identify and define the decision to be made.
- Gathering information that would be useful to have in making the decision.
- Identifying potential decision options from which to choose.
- Evaluating the likely outcome of each decision option.
- The brain's ability to make a well-reasoned choice of the decision option that is most likely to result in the most favorable outcome (think about Spock in Star Trek).

Process Step 2: identify factors that should govern your decision

Magnitude of the decision: put the decision's outcome in its proper perspective relative to its likely impact on your life and your financial well-being.
- Major impact on your life and money – potentially life changing consequences, e.g. change your career, get married.
- Relatively inconsequential - no big deal, e.g. which socks to buy.

Scope of the decision:
- Complex: many factors that should be considered - many possible permutations on potential decision options, e.g. a decision about buying a car.
- A simple "cut and dried" yes or no, e.g. a decision about buying a candy bar while waiting in a grocery store check-out line – buy it or don't buy it.

Time frame within which the decision should be made:
- Plenty of time to gather all the information you think you should have in order to become well-informed, identify decision options, and evaluate the likely outcome of each decision option?
- Snap decision needed immediately, e.g. buy a sweater you see in a store window while walking down a street in a town you are visiting?

Will anyone else's life be impacted directly by the decision? If yes:
- Whose lives – family, friends, neighbors, co-workers?
- To what degree will their lives be impacted?
- Should these people be given an opportunity to provide:
  - o Information to consider in making the decision?
  - o Opinions, advice, and/or recommendations regarding decision options.
  - o Help in evaluating the likely outcome of decision options.

Process Step 3: Gather information relevant to the decision

Good decisions typically are well-informed decisions.
- Understand that everything in life is connected either directly or indirectly, and every piece of information you have ever downloaded into your brain computer will have some degree of connection to every decision you make. Some of this information will be directly related to the decision at hand and some will be so distantly related that it will be functionally irrelevant to the decision.
- As you go about your daily life, be a curious student of life learning as much as you can about as many things as you can.
- As you prepare to make each individual decision, seek to gather enough additional information specifically relevant to the matter at hand to make a prudently well-informed decision.
- Chapter 8 provides more depth on gathering and managing information.

As you think about what constitutes a well-informed decision, think about flowers and mutts:
- Cross-pollination: flowering plants prosper when bees pollinate one plant with pollen from other plants. So too a person's decision making ability prospers when her brain is cross-pollinated with information she gathers from different sources.
- Hybridization: different species of dogs can be bred together to create new hybrid species that are well suited for specific purposes; and some say that mixed breed mongrel mutts are the healthiest and best dogs. So too mixing ideas from different fields of study can help our minds breed the most creative and best decision option ideas

As you think about what constitutes a well-informed purchase decision involving a significant amount of money, also think about the folk wisdom to "follow the money".
- Follow the trail of money as it would flow through the prospective purchase transaction, e.g. from raw materials suppliers, to manufacturer, to retailer, to individual salesperson, to you.
- Who would get how much of each dollar you spent?
- Would you be making a best value purchase?
  - o Would each party in the money trail be earning a fair profit?
  - o Is there some fat in somebody's profit margin that could be trimmed?

As you think about using the internet to gather information directly relevant to the matter at hand be aware that the sheer mass of information available on the internet can be both a blessing and a curse.
- *Blessing*: the internet can provide massive amounts of potentially useful information.
- *Curse*: the massive amounts of information available can seem so overwhelming and intimidating that some people can get frozen into inaction by a feeling that there is more information that they should be gathering before making a decision.

Understand that it is important to gather enough information to make a well-informed, well-reasoned decision, but, we can't gather ALL the information that might be useful to have.
- In a perfect world a person would be able to have perfect knowledge of all the information relevant to every decision she makes. But, we don't live in a perfect world. We live in the real world, with real world limitations on how much information a human can gather and fully understand. We can be well-formed, but not perfectly informed.
- It is unlikely we would have enough time and money to gather ALL the useful information that could be gathered somewhere from some source at some expense at

some moment in time; and even if we did for that moment in time, the world is generating potentially useful new information every minute of every day that we would have no practical means to know about and gather immediately after it was generated.

- *We don't know what we don't know*, therefore we may not know about the existence of information that would be useful to have.

Set practical limits on the amount information you try to gather for each decision based upon factors such as:

- Magnitude and scope of the decision:
  - o The greater the magnitude and more complex the scope, the more you should try to gather as much information as you can from as many sources as you can.
  - o The smaller the magnitude and less complex the decision, the more you might rely on memory, experience, and what your gut tells you to do.
- Time frame in which the decision should be made.
  - o It might be prudent to take months (or longer) to make a decision about a career change or marriage.
  - o But don't spend an hour deciding between a one scoop cone of vanilla ice cream or a two scoop dish of chocolate ice cream.
- Time, effort, and money that would be prudent to spend on gathering information.
- Information sources available to you prior to the time the decision should be made, e.g.:
  - o Memory
  - o Your files and records
  - o Sources available for research of information specifically relevant to the subject matter of the decision, such as.
    - ▪ Books
    - ▪ Internet
  - o People who have relevant expertise or experience.
- How much help of other people would be prudent to request, and how much time and effort could you reasonably expect them to provide?
- Is the decision big enough and complex enough to warrant paying a professional expert for her advice and recommendation?

The more that a decision might influence the big picture direction of your life, and the more money that is involved; the wiser it might be to seek information, advice, and recommendations from people who have:

- More expertise and experience than you have in the matter to be decided.
- A track record of making good decisions.
- Different perspectives on the matter to be decided.
- Greater objectivity about the matter to be decided (because they have less at stake with the decision's outcome). You might be "too close to the forest to see the trees".

Be guided by practical expediency - <u>do the best you can with the time and resources you have available to gather enough information to make a prudently well-informed decision</u>.

Process Step 4: determine your decision options

What options do your business plan and projected financial statement budget suggest?

What decision options does society suggest?
- What does the law say you should do?
- What would be the ethical thing to do?
- What do the generally accepted rules of good and proper behavior in your community say you should do?
- What would your family and close friends want you to do?

What options does the consensus opinion of experts in the subject matter suggest? A majority of the professionals in most professions are likely to agree on certain generally accepted advice. For example:
- Medical experts typically advise:
  - o Eat a varied diet that includes plenty of vegetables, fruits, whole grains, and low fat proteins.
  - o Exercise, but don't over-do it.
  - o Get plenty of sleep.
- Management experts typically advise:
  - o Prepare a written plan and stick to it.
  - o Learn from the outcomes of previous decisions.
  - o Anticipate change and prepare to capitalize on that change.
- Financial planning experts typically advise:
  - o Live below your means - spend less than you earn each year.
  - o Build cash reserves appropriate for your unique life circumstances.
  - o Maintain an age appropriate, well diversified portfolio of investments.

What options do your business team members suggest from their varied perspectives (read about assembling a business team in Chapter 9)? In particular, if you have hired professional service providers who have expertise and experience in the matter, what options do they suggest?

What options do historical precedents suggest?
- What options do your prior decisions suggest? If you have made a similar decision in the past about a specific matter, what options does the outcome of that decision suggest?
- Most likely other people have had to make similar decisions in the past. If you can identify one or more historical precedents in which people made decisions similar to the decision you are about to make, try to determine the decision options from which they could have chosen, and the outcomes of the options they chose.
- If you know a person who has made a similar decision, and know the person well enough to talk to her about her decision, you might ask her:
  - o What decision options were available to her.
  - o Why she chose the option she chose.
  - o What she learned from the outcome of her decision.
  - o Which option she would choose today.
- You may not have to "re-create the wheel".

What options does "the book" on the subject suggest, e.g. textbook principles, theories and predictive models.

- Caution: I strongly recommend that you do not rely _solely_ upon what "the book" says to do. The "textbook" answer is not always the optimal decision option.
- During my career I have observed and heard about some amazingly bad decisions made by "book-smart" MBA's in "ivory tower" corporate home offices. These executives were likely to have made their bad decisions based upon what "the book" they studied in school indicated would be a good decision. But, they lacked a "streets smarts" understanding of how textbook principles, theories and predictive models were likely to play out in the real world with real people.

What options do your "street smarts" experiences in life suggest?

What options does common sense suggest?
- What would your mother tell you to do (OK, some moms have better common sense than others, but in general, our culture gives mothers credit for having good common sense)?
- Just as good common sense tends to lie at the heart of making good decisions about personal relationships, so too good common sense tends to lie at the heart of making most good business and financial management decisions.
- Using common sense can help with the "art part" of management" - applying textbook principles, theories and formulas to determining optimal decision options in real world situations.

What options does your "gut instinct" suggest?

What options do your subconscious mind and dreams suggest?
- Our brains store vast quantities of information that our subconscious minds can link together to suggest good decision options when we give them the opportunity to do so during:
  - A good night's sleep; or
  - Relaxing "down time" such as meditation, jogging, or a leisurely walk around the block.
- When you have time, sleep on a decision and see what your subconscious mind might suggest in a dream. There are countless stories of creative ideas, solutions to problems, and decision choices that have come to people while they were sleeping.

Can you craft a win/win option?
- Try to craft a decision option that has the greatest potential to generate the greatest good for the greatest number of people impacted by the decision.
- _Compromise_ is often a key part of crafting a win/win option during a negotiation.
  - Compromise occurs when each party involved with the negotiation gives up a little of what she wants in order to get most of what she wants in a business transaction in order to get the deal done.
  - It is said that "the best compromise often occurs when neither party is completely happy with the decision outcome."

Process Step 5: evaluate the likely outcome of each decision option

Evaluate each decision option in relation to your business plan and projected financial statement budget.
- Objectives: how well would each option advance you toward your objectives over the course of your short term, mid-term, and long term planning periods?
- Strategy: how well would each option conform to your strategy for living your life?

If the magnitude and scope of the decision warrant the time and effort, write a list of your decision options along with the pros and cons of each option.
- Which options have the most in their favor? The least against them?
- What could go right? What could go wrong?
- In a risk driven decision, which option has the lowest risk of a negative outcome?
- In a reward driven decision, which option offers the greatest potential reward?
- Potential upside gain? Potential downside loss?

Regarding identification of items on the con side of the ledger:
- The greater the impact of a decision on your life and your money, the greater the benefit might be to write this list of pros and cons of each decision option.
- The act of writing the cons can be a good emotional control for irrational exuberance.
- If the magnitude and scope of the decision are such that the decision outcome would not have significant impact on your life or your money, but would have a noticeable impact, it might not be prudent time management to write down the pros and cons of each option, but it would be prudent to take enough time to at least think through each of your options.
- Be an optimistic pessimist. Stay in your optimistic, positive thinking business mindset as you try to identify the potential downsides of each decision option. Don't let thinking about potential negatives suck you down into an emotionally depressed mindset in which you may not be able to think clearly. Just give healthy consideration to the potential downside of each decision option.
- Identifying the pros and cons of multiple options can help you formulate a contingency Plan B for the next best thing you could do if the outcome of the Plan A option you choose doesn't play out the way you thought it would.

When making decisions of significant magnitude and scope, keep in mind the *law of unintended consequences* - outcomes we didn't intend to happen might happen as the result of decisions we make.
- Stretch your brain to think of potential unintended consequences of each option.
- Evaluate each decision option from as many different perspectives as you can think of.
- Ask members of your business team, and perhaps a professional service provider who has greater expertise and experience in the decision's subject matter, "what do you think could possibly go wrong if I decide to ..."

Evaluate the "trade-offs" (lost opportunity cost) of each decision option.
- *Economic trade-offs*
  - Once you spend money on one thing, you lose the opportunity to spend that same money on another thing.
  - We each have a limited amount of money - "we can't have it all". We must trade off the opportunity to buy things we want less in order to have enough money to buy things that we want more. For example, if a person decides to buy a dress

that looks beautiful in a store window she gives up the opportunity to invest that money in a retirement savings account that would help her secure greater financial freedom later in her life.

- *Joy and satisfaction trade-offs*: in order to spend some of your valuable time doing something that you think would give you greater joy and satisfaction, you would have to give up the opportunity to use that time to do something that you think would give you less joy and satisfaction, e.g. on the same night at the same time you couldn't go out on a very special romantic date and have a girls-night-out with your friends.
- *Risk-reward trade-offs*: in order to seek a greater reward (return on our money) we should be willing to accept a greater risk of losing some of our money. How much potential reward would you be willing to give up in order to have less risk of losing money?

Consider the impact that each decision option might have on other people.
- Try to project the likely impact of each decision option on the lives of others.
- Try to project how people are likely to react to the likely outcome of each decision option.
- Try to determine which decision option would generate the "greatest good" for the greatest number of people.

"If it sounds too good to be true, it probably is".
- The better a decision option seems to be at first, the harder we should probably try to identify potential downside risks. Potential negative impact may not be readily apparent, and it might even be intentionally hidden from us.
- *"The grass may look greener on the other side of the fence", but sometimes it's an optical illusion.* Try to look over the proverbial fence from a different angle of vision (to get a different perspective) to see if you can see any brown spots in the grass on the other side from that different angle before you try to climb over (have you ever noticed how something can look a certain way when sunlight is sparkling off of it and then it looks different when you move and can see it from a different angle at which the sun isn't reflecting off of it?).

Process Step 6: make the decision

Lean toward the decision option that best fits your business plan and budget.
- Objectives: option likely to have the greatest impact on achieving your objectives.
- Strategy: option that best conforms to your strategy for living your life, such as:
    o Provides you the greatest satisfaction.
    o Provides you the greatest economic value (utility).
    o Generates the "greatest good" for the most people impacted by your decision.

Lean toward choosing the option that a "prudent person" would choose - "prudent person" being loosely defined because of its subjective nature. Research the term "prudent person" and develop your own working definition. I think of a "prudent person" as being a reasonably intelligent, reasonably well-informed person who has a track record of making decisions that have had reasonably good outcomes for both herself and the people impacted by her decisions.

Lean toward choosing an option on which there is a consensus of opinion among your business team members, professional service providers, materials published by relevant professional trade associations, etc.

When there is not a consensus opinion about which option to choose, try playing a mental game in which you are a judge in a court making a decision about a "case".
- Think of all the sources from which you gather useful information as being witnesses presenting evidence to you.
- Seek additional evidence to fill in any holes in the story that leave you wondering about what to decide.
- If the decision is important enough to warrant the time and expense, seek a recommendation from another "expert witness" - a specialist who has even more expertise and/or experience in the subject matter than anyone who has already provided you advice or a recommendation, or a different perspective than other experts. (Certain people in virtually every profession have carved out specialized market niches within their industries, and gained more expertise and/or experience in that particular market niche than their peers who have not specialized).
- Make your decision based upon the "preponderance of evidence" in favor of one of the decision options.

Be extra careful when considering the choice of a decision option that runs counter to:
- *Consensus opinion of reputable experts* in the subject matter of the decision to be made; and
- *Best business practices* that have proven to generate successful outcomes for most successful people over long periods of time.

Be extra, extra careful when considering an investment recommendation that was made by a "lone wolf" financial guru if that recommendation differs from:
- Consensus opinion available on the websites of highly reputable companies in the financial services industries.
- Generally accepted best practices advocated by the financial services industries.

If a lone wolf seems to make sense to you, dig deeper to see if you can gather more information that would support the validity of the lone wolf's recommendation.
- Seek "second opinion" critiques of the lone wolf's recommendation from confidants who

have track records of making good financial decisions, and from at another professional financial advisor if possible.
- Bear in mind, *no investment guru has ever achieved perfect investment enlightenment.*

What do your street smarts, common sense, and gut instinct / intuition tell you to do?
- Keep in mind what we said in Chapter 3 about business management being part science and part art. After you have done all of your "science part" facts-and-figures analysis and evaluation of decision options put your decision options through the "art part" filters of your common sense, street smarts, and gut instinct / intuition.
- The common sense "we were born with" and the street smarts we acquire and refine through our experiences in the real world might be the most accurate predictors of how a decision will play out with real people in real life situations. Sometimes business people get so caught up in the mental machinations of crunching numbers and applying textbook predictive models that they lose sight of a decision making directional signal that the proverbial wise old farmer would see as clearly as a giant flashing neon sign.
- You might "trust your gut" to "go against the grain" of your "scientific" analysis and evaluation to the extent that you have:
  - o Expertise in the subject matter to be decided.
  - o Experience in the subject matter.
  - o Had historical success at making good decisions based upon trusting your gut. The more that past decisions have worked out well by trusting your gut, the more you might trust your gut.
- But, be careful about trusting your gut if you think you might be overly influenced by emotion - "knee jerk reaction" or "snap judgment" decisions made "in the heat of the moment".
  - o All too often people lament making "ill informed decisions" because they were too excited "to think straight".
  - o "Feel good" decisions that "just feel right" made because a person feels good about what another person is saying, or feels the other person is a good person who wouldn't "steer her wrong", or feels the other person is trustworthy.

Athletic coaches push their players to learn the fundamentals of the game and practice those fundamentals so often and so well that their players can make split second decisions that SEEM to be made "without thinking" in game situations.
- To paraphrase what some football coaches have been known to tell their players, "I want you to be able to react to game situations. You don't have time to think as a play is happening. When you think, you make mistakes."
- Good athletes learn to recognize situations and think so fast that it seems they are reacting intuitively to situations such as:
  - o In football, how a cornerback would defend against a roll-out option play.
  - o In baseball, what a third baseman would do if a ground ball was hit to him in a one out situation with base runners on first and third.
- In most cases when athletes seem to be making split second decisions without thinking, they have actually spent a great deal of time:
  - o Studying how coaches teach players to perform the fundamentals and how the best players at their position perform the fundamentals.
  - o Practicing the fundamentals in as many different game situations as possible to learn what would be the optimum thing to do in each situation.
  - o Learning the "tendencies" of what opposing players and teams are likely to do in various game situations by studying what they had done in the past in such

situations, and how well those players and teams had done those things.
- o   Developing a "game plan" for how they will react in various game situations if the opposition does any of the things that they can reasonably be expected to do.
- Malcolm Gladwell's book *Blink*, and Daniel Kahneman's book *Thinking, Fast and Slow* are great reads that expand on the old adage "think fast".

Many a great business decision has been made by chief executives based upon a hunch that went against conventional market research. Research the biographies of successful people who are said to have had a:
- "Good nose for business".
- "Midas touch" – everything she touched turned to gold.

Exceptions to the rule: there are exceptions to virtually every decision making "rule of thumb". Special situations sometimes dictate choosing a decision option other than the option that the usual rules of thumb indicate should be made. Let's call this the *"Yes, but ... rule"*.
- Societies develop all sorts of rules of good and proper behavior, and virtually every one of those rules has exceptions. As an example, people will sometimes tell a "little white lie" rather than telling the pure unvarnished truth that would likely hurt another person.
- And the imperfect business world has a way of creating situations in which the best decision options are exceptions to generally accepted rules. As an example, many entrepreneurs have had gut instincts that told them to do things that ran counter to what all their professional advisors and experts recommended, and those gut instinct decisions turned into pure gold.

"Most decisions aren't pure black or white, they are shades of gray".
- Most decision options aren't 100% THE right decision or 100% THE wrong decision– they aren't all good or all bad, completely "right" or completely "wrong" (however you define right and wrong). "Good" options may have potential for mostly good outcomes but also some degree of potential for bad outcomes too.
- A decision option might have a largely positive outcome for you while it is having somewhat of a negative outcome for somebody else.
- You might have a fabulous time, but it will cost so much that you will need to re-work your budget by cutting back on some other expense items in order to fit in the cost.
- <u>Choose the option that you think has the greatest potential to generate the "optimum" outcome – "optimum" being the option that has the greatest potential to generate good for you and people impacted by your decision and the least potential to hurt anyone.</u>

On big picture, potentially life changing decisions the best decision might be to wait on making a final decision (e.g. changing jobs, getting married, buying a home), if:
- There is not a consensus opinion among your closest confidants and professional advisors about which decision option to choose, or their consensus opinion is to wait.
- Common sense tells you that you shouldn't rush into the decision.
- Your gut instinct tells you to wait.
- You have a nagging feeling that you don't have all the information you should have.

If you decide to wait on making a final decision about the matter at hand, it might be helpful to:
- Seek new information that gives you a fresh insight into the optimal decision option to choose.
- Seek "second opinion" type advice and recommendations from people who have even

more expertise or experience in the subject matter of the decision than the people who have already provided you advice and recommendations.
- Re-evaluate each decision option to see if you can get any fresh insights.
- *"Sleep on it"* and let your subconscious work on it.

BUT, don't procrastinate.
- *There is a big difference between a well-reasoned decision to wait and procrastination.*
  - o Waiting is a positive decision to gather more relevant information and to give more rational thought to evaluating decision options.
  - o Procrastination is a negative decision to dodge responsibility for making a decision that should be made.
- Procrastination can "weigh on the mind". Undecided matters have a way of creating stress and unease in our minds when we know we should make a decision.

Don't get frozen into indecision by:
- *Thinking there is still more information you could get* – just one more piece of advice, just one more set of facts, ... whatever. The best decisions are <u>well</u> informed decisions, <u>not perfectly</u> informed decisions. Use the lessons you have learned from making prior decisions, the street smarts you have gained from your experience in life, and your common sense to help you determine when enough information is enough.
- *Not liking any of your decision options.*
  - o Life will go on whether or not you make the decision. Better to steer the outcome toward the best of bad options and minimize the pain.
  - o Learn about "Sophie's Choice" – a novel that was made into a movie about a mother who was sent to a Nazi concentration camp and forced to choose which one of her two children would be allowed to live and which child would be put to death immediately. The term "Sophie's choice" has since come into the vernacular to describe a situation in which a person must choose the less undesirable of two undesirable outcomes.
- *Fear of being wrong.*
  - o This often happens when there is a heavy duty decision that must be made, and the outcome could be life changing, such as to leave a current job.
  - o The worst that can happen is that you make a mistake. Fine. We all make mistakes. That's life. When our well thought decisions turn out to be mistakes, we can deal with our mistakes, learn from them, and move on with our lives.
- When a decision needs to be made, make it.

Two suggestions that might help you make a decision about which you have been "waffling" (going back and forth in your mind about which decision option to choose):
- Try to explain your thoughts about your decision options to a close confidant. As you go through the mental machinations of explaining your thoughts about your options, the "right" choice may well separate itself from the other options.
- *"First thought"* rule of thumb: when "you are sitting on the fence" and can't seem to make a decision, but the situation requires an immediate decision, the best choice may well be your first thought. It is said that the first thought that popped into a person's mind is often the best decision option to choose; not always, but often.

Process Step 7: Take action

A decision is just a mind game until you take action.

In order to achieve your objectives you will need to take action on your decisions.

Process Step 8: Critique the decision's outcome

Critique the outcome of each decision.
- Critique your decision - seek lessons you can learn from the experience of making the decision and living with the outcome of the decision.
- Ask business team members for constructive critique of your decision, and when prudent, ask people who were impacted by your decision for their thoughts.

Process Step 9: Put the decision behind you

If the decision outcome was good:
- Be grateful for your good fortune.
- Thank people who gave you good advice and recommendations.
- Don't begin to think "I'm so smart" and develop a cocky attitude. Maintain a mental line of distinction between a healthy level of confidence and an overly confident attitude that could cause you to "slip up" on making your next decision.
- Don't brag, or do anything else that might stir up feelings of jealousy or annoyance in anyone who might have to listen to you or live with you.
- "Don't rest on your laurels."
- Treat the decision as good practice for making good decisions in the future.

If the decision outcome wasn't so good:
- *Understand that you made the best decision you could at the time that you made it.* Even if in retrospect you feel you didn't make the best decision that you could have made, it is important that you understand you did the best you could with what you had to work with at the time, such as:
  - Your decision making skills at that time.
  - The experience you had in making the same type decision.
  - The information you had.
  - The advice and recommendations you had received
  - Your physical and mental condition.
- Learn whatever lessons you can from the decision and be wiser for the experience,
- Let it go.
  - The past is past. There is nothing you can do to change what has happened to date as a result of the decision.
  - Don't second guess yourself. Beating yourself up with thoughts such as "I could have done this" or "I should have done that" can make you miserable, and fog your ability to think rationally about your next decision.
  - Don't harbor grudges against anyone or anything.
- Move on with your life.

Chapter 8. Gathering & Storing Decision Making Information

Brains Operate Like Computers

The quantity and quality of information you gather and store in your "brain computer" is a key factor in the decisions you make.
- Quantity: the more data you store in your brain's computer memory, or can access quickly from external information storage formats, the more data your brain can draw upon to compute decision options and the potential outcome of each decision option.
- Quality: the more closely that information is related to business and financial management, to current affairs in the world around you, and to other fields of intellectual enrichment, the more likely that information will prove to be useful in decision making.

Consider sorting out the sources of decision making information from which you could choose along a continuum that runs from high use potential sources on one end to low use potential sources on the other end.
- "Useful information" and "use potential" are highly subjective terms – a source that you think offers potentially useful information for making your future decisions might not be a source that I would think of as a source of potentially useful information for my decisions. The movie *Working Girl* offers an insightful lesson as to what might be useful information for one person but not for other people.
- Evaluate the likelihood that each information source available to you could provide you with information that would be useful in making business and financial management decisions, and assign each source a place along your continuum.
- Toward the high use potential end of your continuum you might place sources generally thought to have a target market audience of people seeking information aimed at their intellect, sources recommended by successful people, and sources that have provided you with information that you found to be useful in making previous decisions, perhaps editorials, columnist opinions, investigative reporting, intellectually stimulating interview shows, classes, trade association meetings, non-fiction books, museum visits.
- Toward the low use potential end you might place sources generally thought to have a target market audience of entertainment seekers, perhaps magazines that focus on news about the lifestyles of celebrities, and many reality television shows.
- To help maximize the number of your decisions that result in optimal outcomes, *consider investing more of your precious time and money gathering information from sources closer to the high use potential end of your continuum and less time and money gathering information from sources closer to the low use potential end of your continuum.*

Gather and store as much information as your time and money allow regarding subjects relevant to business management and financial management, such as:
- Economic supply, e.g. improvements in productivity, manufacturing facilities being built, employment statistics, discoveries of new sources of natural resources, depletion of natural resources, increasing or decreasing agricultural yields and fish stocks.
- Economic demand, e.g. population growth or decline, increasing or decreasing usage of natural resources, popularity of consumer goods, income and wealth of various demographic groups such as populations of developing countries.
- Job availability and pay ranges, e.g. new employers moving to locations within a reasonable commuting distance for you, types of jobs moving out of your commuting range and country; local, national, and global income levels and cost of living.
- Changes that might create opportunities, e.g. discoveries, new inventions, current trends,

evolution of companies and industries, start-up companies based upon interesting new ideas, changes in political leadership.

Keep in mind the adage *"you are what you eat."* Health professionals tell us that our bodies are made up of the food and drink we put into them – a healthy diet helps build a healthy body. Business people would be wise to *paraphrase "you are what you eat" into something like "your thoughts are what you watch, listen to, and read"*. Feed your mind a well-balanced diet of nutritious information that it can use to make prudent decisions and develop profitable ideas.

You can't know it all, but you need to know enough.
- We live in the Information Age. There are innumerable sources that can provide you with useful decision making information.
- There is more information available today to more people from more sources than there has been at any time in history. And, the quantity and availability of that information is increasing at an accelerating pace. Technology has made massive quantities of information available instantly and globally.
- Business is being transacted in some time zone on this planet every hour of every day. The term "24 x 7 world" was coined to describe this global linkage and aliveness. So too, in places around the world tonight thinkers are thinking, discoverers are discovering, writers are writing, and doers are doing things that might be relevant to decisions you will be making tomorrow.
- No matter how much you know today, there will always be more to learn tomorrow. And some of today's potentially useful information will have become obsolete by tomorrow.
- *Become an information sponge.* Soak up all the potentially useful information you can reasonably gather and store.
  - o Seek to learn something new every day.
  - o Develop a continuous continuing education program for yourself (the idea of a "business school in your head" that we discussed in Chapter 3).
  - o Maintain a level headed perspective on just how much potentially useful information you can reasonably gather and store.
- *Keep in mind that everything in life is connected either directly or indirectly.* Every piece of information your brain has ever absorbed might be helpful in making a future decision. To stimulate your thinking, research *"the butterfly effect"*, an old story line about how different life might be today if just one tiny little thing was changed in the past.
- But, there is so much information that might possibly be useful in making our future decisions that nobody could gather and store all that information. We need to be selective in choosing the information we pro-actively seek to gather.
- *Seek an optimum quantity of information, of optimum use potential, gathered in an optimum amount of time, at an optimum price.*

Following the computer analogy, program your brain to link new information with information previously stored in your memory files. Determine how new information relates to information you already know, be that a new idea, new insight into previously stored information, additional detail, new link between different groupings of information in your mind.

Information gathering and storage decisions to make include:
- *How important is it to you to increase the number of your decisions that result in more desirable outcomes*?
- How much of your precious time are you willing to spend each day, each week, each year gathering potentially useful information?

- How much of your budget money are you willing to allocate to gathering information?
- From what sources will you get your information? What mix of information sources will provide you the greatest amount of potentially useful information?
- What information do you think would be prudent to get from first-hand sources – "direct from the horse's mouth"?
- What information do you think would be prudent to get from second-hand sources, e.g. news sources, professional service providers, classes, friends, websites? Sources that:
    - Have ready access to useful information to which you don't have access.
    - Have the time and expertise to distill vast quantities of hard-to-understand information within their area of expertise into a useful summary.
    - Interpret the jargon of a profession or industry in words you understand.
- How will you store various types of information so that it will be readily available when you need it: memory, paper records, computer or other electronic device, etc.?

Each person's ability to gather and store information is limited by a unique combination of factors, such as:
- *Inherited genetic capability*, such as:
    - Senses of sight, hearing, smell, touch, and taste.
    - Memory.
    - IQ (intelligence quotient) - learn what psychology and medical professionals have to say about how the information gathering and processing capabilities of our brains may vary in different people.
- *Acquired learning skills*, e.g. observation skills, conversation skills, reading speed and retention, computer skills.
- *Expertise that a person has in subjects to which the information might have relevance.*
    - The expertise that a person has in a particular subject (business management, playing a musical instrument, etc.) helps the person recognize potentially useful new information and integrate that new information into information already stored in his memory files.
    - Learn about the term "*level of understanding*" as used in education.
    - As an example, my experienced contractor clients who have construction expertise that I don't possess have walked me through construction job sites and pointed out construction issues that they saw in an instant that I walked right by.
- *Preconceived ideas and biases - we tend to see and hear what we are programmed to see and hear.* As the old saying goes "you see what you want to see, and hear what you want to hear." All sorts of games and parlor tricks are based upon this. Think about how sleight-of-hand magicians make a living by playing tricks on our eyes.
- *Time available*: there are only 24 hours in a day. We each have a limited amount of time we can allocate to gathering and storing information that has high use potential.
- *Budget money available to pay for*:
    - *Information*, e.g. subscriptions, classes, books, professional advice and services.
    - *Information gathering and storage equipment*, e.g. computers and hand held devices, file cabinet, file folders, book shelves.

Know what you know, and, know what you don't know.
- Knowledge is "money in the bank" to savvy business people. They learn to be honest with themselves about what they know and what they don't know. They try to surround themselves with people who are "smarter than they are" – people who know what they don't know.
- Don't kid yourself about knowing more than you really know. The less working

knowledge that you have about the subject matter of a decision, the more beneficial it can be to reach out to people who know more than you know about that subject. <u>Don't get blinded by your own brilliance</u>.

- How often have you heard people say about someone "he doesn't know what he is talking about"? Don't let that someone be you.

<u>*Question what you think you know*</u>. As Euripedes said in 400s BCE Greece "*Question everything.*"
- Maintain a sense of "scientific objectivity". Keep an open mind.
- Don't get stuck in an intellectual rut with preconceived ideas.
- Don't blindly accept dogma. Question dogma in the sense of intellectual growth - a trait highly valued by smart business people. Dogma that goes unquestioned can be used by proponents of that dogma to lead "unquestioning" believers like sheep.
- Ask people to critique your thinking.
    o Ask them to ask you questions about why you think what you think.
    o Seek their opinions about how much they think you really know about what you think you know.

Project an image of being curious and non-judgmental.
- Project an image that invites people to share their ideas, insights, advice, and opinions.
    o Let people know you are open to whatever they have to say.
    o Be as open minded, non-judgmental, objective, and unemotional as you can be.
- People who know potentially useful information are much more likely to share what they know when they feel comfortable that they won't be criticized or judged, nor have their veracity challenged.

Avoid projecting the image of a "know-it-all".
- Adults don't like it when a kid tries to act like he knows more than everybody else knows. Same goes in the business world.
- Smart business people know that there is too much to know for anyone to actually know it all. The type of good people with whom you should be surrounding yourself tend to be put off by folks who profess to know it all. Experience teaches smart business people that know-it-alls tend to make poor decisions on occasion precisely because they don't know it all. Smart people tend to avoid doing business with know-it-alls who they can reasonably expect to screw up eventually and hurt people in the process.
- A person who acts like a know-it-all hangs a sign around his neck saying "I'm gullible".
    o Know-it-alls tend to be seen as "patsies" (attractive targets) by bad guys who seek to take advantage of know-it-alls who are blind to what they don't know.
    o Socially irresponsible bad guys try to size up just how much their patsies don't know, and then figure out ways to exploit them by selling them such things as inferior quality goods, over-priced things the patsies don't need, or even fraudulent deals like "selling them the Brooklyn Bridge".

Take time each day to let your brain process information and think creatively.
- *Get enough sleep.*
    o Our human brains evolved to require sleep in order to maintain peak operating efficiency and to process the information they take in each day. Learn how important sleep is to brain efficiency.
    o Use the information processing powers of sleep and dreams.
        ▪ Learn how different people use dreams (e.g. people who practice

different religions and members of different aboriginal nations) and how various professionals say we can all use our dreams.

- If you aren't remembering your dreams:
    - Try training yourself to get better at remembering them.
    - It may be a signal that you aren't getting enough sleep.
- Unplug your brain from all your electronic gear long enough each day to allow your brain to do its work the way it was biologically designed to work.
    - o Electronic information technology tools and toys can have addictive power to hijack our lives and make us slaves to texting, social networking, playing games, and all their other intoxicating attractions.
    - o As this book is being written I am struck by the number of people who walk our streets and sidewalks with their eyes glued to hand held devices, oblivious to the world passing them by. These folks could be doing themselves a triple disservice:
        - Missing out on valuable information processing and creative thinking time their brains could have had.
        - Missing out on observing and listening to all the new, potentially useful information their surroundings are offering them.
        - Missing out on the pure joy of a nice walk.
- Plan "down time" each day to walk, jog, paint, meditate - whatever activity allows your brain to relax (decompress) enough to let information soak in and get processed.
    - o Give yourself enough time to be in your own head with your own thoughts so that your brain can digest all the information you have been feeding it.
    - o "Take time to smell the roses."
    - o Most joggers and walkers I know (those who exercise unplugged from electronic gear) say that one of the things they love most about jogging and walking is the time it gives them to think about things, to process information, and to come up with creative ideas and solutions to challenges.

This chapter is intended to:
- Encourage you to think about:
    - o *The economic value of information.*
    - o The quantity and quality (usefulness) of information you gather and store for use in making your decisions.
- Provide an introduction to gathering and storing information in a businesslike manner.
- Share some of the "best practices" I have observed successful business people use to gather and store their decision making information
- Offer a few information gathering and storage ideas of my own.
- Encourage you to develop a personalized system for gathering and storing information that helps you maximize the number of your decisions that result in optimal outcomes.

This chapter is NOT intended to tell you what to watch, what to listen to, nor what to read. It simply offers some ideas about gathering and storing potentially useful information that might help you increase the number of your decisions that result in optimal outcomes.

Gather information from a varied mix of sources

A varied mix of information sources will help you:
- Gather information from one source that another source doesn't have.
- Gain access to the special expertise and practical experience of different people.
- Corroborate the validity of information received from one particular source.
- Get reports on the same current event from different perspectives.
- Gather opinions, advice, and recommendations from varied points of view.
- Balance out the biases and self-interests of sources, such as:
  - "Left leaning liberal" and "right leaning conservative" political biases.
  - Self-interest of an industry's marketing and lobbying efforts.

Cross-pollination of information from different sources helps people make some of their best decisions, and come up with some of their most creative "new" ideas.
- Mixing bloodlines and genetic pools in animals tends to breed the healthiest offspring. So too mixing information from different sources can help generate the best decisions.
- Almost no creative idea is entirely new. Most "new" ideas are rooted in other people's older ideas. As an example, in this book I re-worked and built upon information I have gathered from many, many different sources during the course of my life.
- Try learning who inspired your favorite song writers, authors, and painters and how each person's work was influenced by others.

Let the experience you have gained from making your prior decisions guide you in developing a varied mix of information sources that helps you maximize the number of your future decisions that result in optimal outcomes.

Parents and teachers: it's their "job" to help their children and their students gather and process information. If you still have these folks in your life, reach out and ask them to teach you all they can. By the way, *asking parents and teachers to share their wisdom is one of the nicest things you could ever do for them.*

Good schools are learning institutions, not dogma memorization factories. They:
- Encourage students to question information that is taught in classes and textbooks rather than just parroting back that information from rote memory on tests.
- Encourage a free flow of ideas.
- Encourage students to open their minds, let down their self-defense mechanisms, and welcome new ideas that challenge their current ways of thinking.
- Encourage freedom of thought to look at things from different perspectives, to develop well-informed well-reasoned personal opinions, and to think creatively.
- Offer a non-judgmental environment for students to test their understanding of newly acquired information and to test the validity their own opinions and ideas.

Good teachers are dedicated professional "educators" whose business it is to help their students maximize the educational value that students get from the school experience. Good teachers:
- Endeavor to:
  - Get to know each student (to the best of their ability given class size and student personalities) and to personalize class presentations in ways that help each student learn all he can from class material.
  - Encourage students to think independently and creatively.

o Encourage students to "learn how to learn", and motivate them to embark upon a life of continuous continuing education.
- Seek to lead class discussions that encourage students to think for themselves and contribute their thoughts and opinions to the discussions.
- Help students learn how to critique and question information.

Classmates can help each other by providing:
- Information classmates know that isn't in class materials.
- Opportunities to learn:
  o Which information each classmate thinks is useful to learn.
  o How to see the world through other people's eyes as classmates provide their opinions about and critiques of information presented in class.
- Role models for good learning habits.

"You get out of it what you put into it." We take away from school in direct proportion to the effort we put into it. A few suggestions:
- Pay attention in class.
- Ask questions to get:
  o Explanations that clarify your understandings of class material.
  o Additional information about topics that interest you.
  o Greater insight into how one topic relates to other topics.
- Ask teachers and classmates for constructive critique of your ideas and your understandings of class material.
- Ask for suggestions of information sources for self-study of subjects that interest you.
- Get all you can out of homework and special projects.
- Participate in extracurricular activities, e.g. athletics, clubs, community service projects.

Use as many senses as possible when learning new things, i.e. sight, hearing, touch, smell, taste.
- Learn what educators have to say about the benefits of multi-sensory learning.
- Learn how using multiple senses can increase the different types of connections our brains make with new information, thereby improving our understanding and retention of that new information.
- Take written notes of information you hear in class and read in textbooks.
- Ask teachers and classmates' questions about information you hear in class and read in textbooks. Crafting questions will help your mind process that information (and the answers are likely to provide additional information about and insight into the subject).

You are never too old to go back to school, for just one class or for an entire degree program.
- Learn new skills and polish up old skills.
- Stimulate your creative thinking.
- Learn how to learn better (good learning habits are good business habits).
- Expand your network of business contacts with teachers and fellow students.

Older people in your community have a wealth of knowledge they have accumulated through the years. Older people have:
- "Been there, done that" and "seen it all".
- Learned how to adapt to changes in their lives and in the world around them - inventions that changed the way they had been living life, changes in political leadership, impact of wars and the aftermath of wars, etc.

- Lived through the ups and downs of economic cycles of expansion and recession.
- Experienced countless fads come and go.
- Seen investment bubbles come and go.

Pick their brains. Ask questions such as:
- What do you value most in life? How important is money in your life?
- What did you do during your working career (or what are you still doing)? Why?
- What are the most valuable lessons you have learned:
    o About living a satisfying life?
    o About having a satisfying career?
    o About money management?
- Did you make any mistakes in managing your life and your money that I should try to avoid making?
- What would you do differently if you could have a do-over in life?
- What would you do if you were me?

Listen to their stories. Their perspective and wisdom can be amazingly educational, and a lot of fun. The older that folks get the less inhibition they tend to have about saying exactly what's on their minds You are likely to enjoy the experience and so will they. (When I was in my 40's and my father was in his 70's we starting talking far more than we ever had before. I asked him questions about his younger days that I had never thought to ask when I was younger. I had never known what a wild and crazy guy he had been when he was young, and how much he knew about the way the real world works. I had only known him as a workaholic corporate executive who wasn't home much. I learned a lot.)

Profit from their experience.
- Emulate the smart things they did.
- Learn to avoid making the mistakes they made.

It is said that "youth is wasted on the young." Learn why. At some point in the aging process it dawns on many of us that *"the older we got, the smarter our parents and elders got"*.

Religious leaders: until the printing press came along, religious institutions were primary repositories of the knowledge that civilizations accumulated over the centuries. It has been the job of religious institutions and their leaders to pass down "institutionalized" information from generation to generation from the perspective of each religion. Whether you study religious teachings from a secular or a spiritual perspective, these teachings contain a wealth of information as to the ways people have learned to live together and do business together successfully through the ages. Be aware that some religious leaders are more dogmatic and evangelistic about their religious beliefs than other religious leaders. *As a businessperson, sift through religious dogma to find the ecumenical wisdom at its heart.*

People within your current network of business contacts and new people you meet:
- Be as gregarious as your personality allows. Talk with as many people as you can. You never know who might turn out to be a valuable source of fascinating and potentially useful information.
- Practice picking peoples' brains with tactful questions.
    o Try to get them to talk about their ideas, their opinions, their plans.
    o Ask for advice or a recommendation about how to do things that interest you.
- Project an image of being curious and non-judgmental that encourages people to open up

and tell you what they truly think.
- At business events and social events meet new people and talk with them – don't just talk to people you know.
- Pay the most attention to people you think have good business minds and appear to be living financially prudent lifestyles.
- When shopping, you might try asking fellow shoppers what selling points led them to choose whatever they are buying, what drew them to a particular store, and what might be some other good places to do comparative shopping.

Role models:
- *Positive role models* of thinking and behavior to emulate.
- *Negative role models* of thinking and behavior to avoid.

Role models might be:
- First-hand: people you know and can observe yourself.
- Second-hand: people you only learn about from reports or stories about them.
  - o Keep in mind that information you receive second hand has gone through the filters of one or more other people.
  - o You may not be getting the 100% unvarnished truth about a person's actual thinking and behavior. Important details might have been embellished, edited, censored, or unintentionally omitted.
  - o Second-hand stories often embellish the truth in order to make the story more interesting (and less accurate) - an average person can be built up to sound like the greatest thing since sliced bread - a near perfect person who doesn't have any character flaws or other human weaknesses.
  - o Beware "storybook heroes" – people whose behavior in real life was significantly embellished in stories about them (as a Baby Boomer, Davy Crockett and Wyatt Earp immediately spring to mind). Beware also idealized media reports of the behavior of the rich, the powerful, and the famous.

Mentors - people willing to advise you and help you learn what they know. All sorts of people can be valuable mentors, e.g. relatives, friends, coaches, co-workers, and supervisors.

Professional service providers can provide all sorts of valuable information, advice, and recommendations.

Observation and listening
- Keep your eyes and ears open to everything going on around you. When most of us were kids we were taught to "*stop, look, and listen*" before crossing a street or railroad tracks. We learned to keep track of what was going on around us in order to avoid getting hit by an oncoming vehicle. The same stop, look, and listen lesson applies in the business world. *Smart managers keep track of what is going on in the world around them in order to avoid getting hit by oncoming economic conditions or competition that they should have seen coming.*
- Take in the life going on around you. You never know when or where the next piece of useful information might pop up, or what might stimulate a new idea in your mind.
  - o Something you hear on the radio while driving to work.
  - o Something you see or hear while you are away on vacation.
  - o Something you see written on a book cover in a store window.
  - o A conversation with a neighbor on the front lawn.

- o A movie or a television show (I have picked up many a good idea this way).
- *It is uncanny to me how "fate" so often seems to guide us to just the right piece of information at just the right time*, such as when flipping through a newspaper or magazine in a doctor's waiting room, or turning on a radio at just the right moment. Over the years many people have told me that they have been struck by how often fate seems to have guided them to just the right piece of information at just the right time.
- *"See the forest for the trees."* As you are taking notice of all the fascinating little details of daily life going on around you (the trees) also take notice of the "big picture" context (the forest) in which those little details are going on.

Practice the art of "active observation".
- By active observation I mean paying close enough attention to what is going on in the world around you to absorb the information that your senses are sending to your brain, and to link that information to information previously stored in your brain computer's memory as applicable.
- Train your brain to notice as much detail as possible in what you see and hear, and to remember as much of that new information as possible. <u>Think about spy and detective movies in which the hero seems to see and hear everything going on around him, and he remembers every little detail</u>.
- Don't wander aimlessly through life oblivious to what is going on around you.

Practice the art of "active listening".
- By active listening I mean <u>keeping your mind focused on a conversation partner</u>.
  - o Listen to what the person <u>is saying</u>.
  - o <u>And</u>, what I find intriguing as I age and gain more experience in life, what a person <u>is NOT saying</u>. Words not spoken can be an indication that he might:
    - ▪ Not know as much about the subject of the conversation as a person who is well-informed about the subject would probably be saying.
    - ▪ Not be understanding what you are saying, and that you should try to clarify what you are trying to communicate.
- Don't let your mind wander to other things while the person is talking. Learn how practicing certain mindfulness / meditation techniques might help you stay focused in the moment during a conversation. Just as our minds are prone to wander during meditation, so too our minds are prone to wander during conversation to thoughts that divert us from focusing on our conversation partner, e.g. "what was it that I was supposed to buy on the way home; what is my sister doing with that guy; what should I say in the meeting tomorrow".
- Look your conversation partner in the eye. You can read a lot in the eyes.
- Listen to what the person is saying with his body language as well as to what he is saying with his spoken language. Learn about the importance of body language in face-to-face communication.

Conversation: <u>practice mining for nuggets of information gold in streams of conversation</u>.
- *Get out of your head and into the other person's head.*
  - o *You already know what you know. You don't know what he knows.*
  - o Pick his brain. Learn what he knows.
  - o Minimize what you say about yourself. Try to say just enough about yourself to keep the conversation flowing.
  - o Do not "lecture" the person, or try to "show him" how much you know.
  - o Don't try to "one up" the other person in the way that kids often do on the

playground, e.g. "that's nice, but I did such and such that was even better."
- Practice asking questions to help confirm your understanding of what your conversation partner is trying to communicate and to learn more about subjects that interest you.
  - o Direct questions to get specific information, e.g. to a banker - what are the interest rates on your different types of bank accounts?
  - o Open ended questions to get whatever information a person thinks is relevant to your question, e.g. to the same banker - what do you suggest I do with my money? Open ended questions can yield all sorts of information, including:
    - Information that you wouldn't have thought to ask about.
    - Whole worlds of new ideas and new ways of thinking about things.
    - Different ways people have linked information together in their minds.
- When you have a difference of opinion seek to learn what makes your conversation partner think differently than you do. Avoid arguing that you are right and he is wrong. Argument is not conducive to good conversation, unless you have a tacit agreement that you are debating a point in civil fashion.
- To help motivate your conversation partner to open up and tell you what he truly thinks:
  - o Project an image of being curious and non-judgmental.
  - o Learn to use empathy and sympathy to connect with people.

Small talk (chit chat) is meant for being sociable, but it also can serve as an icebreaker that leads into an educational conversation. For instance:
- After meeting someone at a party, you might try asking a question about him and his life. People can get pretty interesting after they get started talking about themselves.
  - o A starter question might be along the lines of how he knows the host, where he grew up, what brought him to where he lives now, or where he went to school and what he did while he was there (many people have great school stories that could lead a conversation in all sorts of fascinating directions).
  - o And there is always "so, what do you do?" Talking about a person's job can yield all sorts of fun and useful information.
- When chit-chat is about a current event in the news, you might try asking your conversation partner questions such as what he thinks about the news, what makes him think that, how the news might impact his job or his life, and what you both might do with this knowledge of the news, if anything.

When you want to know about just about anything – just ask. *Try a simple progression of questions:*
- Start by asking a person you think might know what you want to know.
- If that person doesn't know, ask him who he thinks might know. When asked nicely, most good people who don't know an answer will refer you to someone they think might know. Be sure to say thank you for the referral.
- Contact this second person, tell him who referred you, and politely ask your question.
- If the second person doesn't know, ask him who he thinks might know.
- And if that third person doesn't know, keep on following the question progression until you finally get to a person who has the information you want.
- To make this progression work:
  - o Be polite and respectful, and say thank you.
  - o Be brief and to the point. Don't waste people's time with idle chatter.

Practice asking "why" with an obvious intent to learn.
- Little kids can be a role model for adults. Kids are great at asking why. It's a natural way for young minds to learn. Then, as we grow up, many of us seem to lose our natural human curiosity - probably because we were answered "because" and "because I said so" so often that our natural curiosity got stifled.
- But, be careful to not be perceived as a pain in the neck who is just asking "why" in the way that some kids repeatedly ask "why" as an attention getting (but annoying) little game.

Your experience in life.
- "Profit from your experience".
- Think of each day that you wake up and draw breath as being the next day in life-long "on the job training" in business and financial management.
- *We can hear something in a class or read something in a book but not learn a lesson until we have the experience of doing something ourselves.*
  - o We can be led to the water of knowledge but no one can make us drink it.
  - o Real life experience is often the best teacher of the lessons we couldn't or wouldn't learn any other way.
- Be alert for "teachable moments" for yourself.

Mistakes and bad experience can be better teachers than successes and good experience.
- Life sometimes is a "school of hard knocks."
- *The more painful the mistake or experience, the greater our incentive to learn how to avoid repeating the same mistake or going through the same bad experience again.*
- Ask people you know and trust for constructive critique of your mistakes.
  - o Ask what they would have done differently in your situation. Ask what they recommend you do differently if a similar situation should arise in the future.
  - o Ask if there was information you could have had, and should have tried to get, before deciding to do whatever you did.

Keep in mind that "some people never learn" (how often have you heard that one?).
  - o Some people don't pay enough attention to what they are doing to learn from their experience.
  - o Some people can work at a job for 30 years but gain only one year's experience 30 times.

Other people's mistakes and bad experiences can offer way less painful lessons than our own! We can learn a lot about life, business management, and financial management from observing other people's mistakes and bad experiences, and from hearing about and reading about other people's mistakes and bad experiences.

Books: being well-read is considered one aspect of being well-educated for good reason - books offer us the great ideas and wisdom that mankind has accumulated over the centuries, as well as a vast resource of current practical advice.
- Learn about the resources available to you in your local libraries and bookstores.
- Ask librarians and bookstore employees for suggestions of books that can help you learn about subjects that interest you.

"Trade press" publications of your current industry and any other industry you want to learn about, e.g. websites, blogs, and magazines.

Computers, hand held devices, and the internet: be sure you understand the pros and cons of computers, hand held devices, and the internet, such as:
- Pro: amazing abilities to help gather and store vast quantities of information.
- Con: potentially addictive power to drag a person into obsessive-compulsive use that could:
    o Bury him under an overload of information, and
    o Cut him off from personal contact with human beings who might be even more valuable sources of information.

Set prudently reasonable limits on the time that you allocate to using electronic devices.

Mass media "news" sources – discussed in a separate section later in this chapter.

Mass media "pop culture" entertainments – internet, television, radio, movies, and magazines
- Be wary of how the things we see, hear, and read in the fantasy world of "pop culture" entertainments (content intended primarily for entertainment not for edification) can skew the way we perceive and think about the real world in which we actually live, thereby influencing our thinking, our decisions and our actions.
- *Don't let fantasy distort your thinking about reality.*
- Keep in mind that what we see and hear in fictional TV shows and movies are "make believe" stories portrayed by actors – not real people in real life.
- "Separate fact from fiction": useful information can be gleaned from some fiction when we are careful to not let that fiction skew our perceptions of reality and the way real life plays out with real people in the real world.
- Learn why some critics say that too much of today's pop culture "dumbs down the population".
- Learn about the schooling and popular entertainments of "educated" people in the 1600's, 1700's and 1800's and then do some "compare and contrast" study of today's pop culture and the pop culture of past times.
    o Learn how the pop culture music, literature, and theatre at various times in history has tended to reflect life in those times.
    o Shakespeare may have touched on some raunchy subjects in his time, but in such a well written way that we consider his works to be masterpiece staples of English literature today.
- While we are making our choices of mass media pop culture entertainment, we might be wise to consider what "redeeming value" people 100 years from now might see in the entertainment in which we are considering an investment of our precious time.

Your financial records and reports: develop and maintain records of your financial management performance "that talk to you" in terms you understand.

<u>**Evaluate the source**</u>

Does the source communicate in language you understand?
- Does the source use words you usually understand?
- Does the source explain things in such a way that you usually understand what he is talking about?

Expertise and experience - does the source actually know what he is talking about?
- How much expertise does the source have in the subject matter?
- How much experience does the source have with the subject matter?

Reliably accurate?
- Source's reputation for providing reliably accurate information?
- Length of time the source been developing his reputation?
- <u>Source's track record of providing you with information that has proved reliably useful to you in making your decisions</u>?

Reasonably objective as opposed to overtly biased?
- Biases of individual people and entire organizations operate as internal censors of information they choose to communicate and how they choose to communicate it.
- We all have biases that influence our thinking and our communications to some extent – even if we don't recognize that we have those biases.
- Try to identify the underlying biases of each information source.
- The best intentioned people, who have the highest aspirations to present objective information, might be subconsciously influenced by their personal biases to present you subjectively slanted information.
- Certain news media organizations, as well as individual commentators and reporters, have gained reputations for displaying overt political biases in the news they choose to report and how they report that news. They provide a steady stream of information that seems biased by their "left leaning liberal" or "right leaning conservative" political beliefs, and seems to be aimed at target market audiences who staunchly support their liberal or conservative positions. *They slant the news in the direction they think their target market audience leans.*
- *As you read this book evaluate how my biases have shaped the book's content* (e.g. my bias toward a low to moderate risk lifestyle) - *especially my biases that I might not yet have recognized but which some readers are likely to tell me they recognized.*
- On an "objective – subjective continuum", seek sources that have track records of providing information toward the objective end of the continuum.

Seek sources that are more "open minded" and objective than overtly biased and subjective. Minimize the attention you pay to people and organizations that:
- Follow the "party line" in presenting information that supports their dogmatic beliefs and the "group think" of followers who share their beliefs.
- Appear to have an "I'm right, and you're wrong if you disagree with me" attitude. They may offer tidbits of useful information, but they can also pollute an objective, rational thinking business mindset.

Motivation – why did the source invest the time, effort, and perhaps the money required to present the information?

- A desire to make money – personal profit?
  - o Companies and salespeople typically are motivated to make money.
  - o Writers, public speakers, and others who seek to be paid for the information they provide might be motivated to communicate with a slant or style intended to differentiate themselves from their competitors for the money of a target market audience (paid directly through sales of subscriptions, tickets, etc. or indirectly by payments received from advertisers and sponsors who want to reach a target market audience).
- Industry trade associations typically are motivated to provide information that supports the best interests of their association members, which may or may not be in your best interest.
- A politician might be motivated by a commitment to public service, a desire to be elected or re-elected, a need to raise campaign funds, or lining up a new job in the private sector after his term in office ends.
- A desire to be "in the spotlight" of public attention?
- A desire to gain an audience for artistic expression?
- A desire to educate the general public - you and me?

Motivation that is good for you:
- Altruistic desire to provide objective information that helps educate the general public.
- Self-actualization.
- Job satisfaction.

Motivation that may not be so good for you:
- Money – a desire to make money – personal profit.
- Power - a desire to influence what people think, believe, and do.
- Attention and fame, e.g. news personalities on TV or radio who say outrageous things in order to attract the biggest audience possible and create reputations for themselves that they can parlay into making money for themselves.
- *Ulterior motive or "hidden agenda"* - the actual motive behind an apparent motive. Ulterior motives typically are intentions to generate greater benefit for the information source than would appear to be the case "on the surface" to a casual observer.

Training that the source might have had in how to influence people's thinking?
- Formal training in marketing, advertising, psychology, rhetoric, etc.
- Mentor who taught the source "tricks of the trade" in how to influence others.
- Role models: people who were good at influencing others.
- Debate training: debaters are trained to prepare convincing arguments.

Be especially wary of information provided by people who have gained reputations as:
- *"Spin doctors"*: people trained in how to put the best "spin" on information in order to present that information in its most favorable light.
- *Propagandists*: people trained to provide information that influences people to think the way that the employers of propaganda writers want those people to think.

First-hand or second-hand information?
- *First-hand information* comes directly from the source – "straight from the horse's mouth"; the purest form of information
- *Second-hand information* is passed along by a source other than the original source.

When evaluating second-hand information, keep in mind:
- Second-hand sources filter original information through their preconceived ideas, biases, expertise in the subject matter, etc. Try to determine a second-hand source's:
    o Expertise and experience in the subject matter.
    o Expertise and experience in gathering complete and accurate information from first-hand sources.
    o Point of view, biases, preconceived ideas, etc.
- A potentially positive aspect of second-hand information can be that people who know more about a subject than we know can summarize, interpret, and/or edit information so that it is more user-friendly and understandable than it would have been if we had gotten it straight from the horse's mouth. Think about which would be more useful to you – trying to read and understand Einstein's Theory of Relativity on your own, or having an experienced teacher explain the Theory to you in simple layman's language.
- Potentially negative aspects of second-hand information might be that second-hand sources:
    o Might have misinterpreted the first hand-source's original information to the point that the second-hand information is inaccurate, or
    o Might have edited the information with a conscious intent to communicate only information that he wants to communicate.
    o Second-hand information might not even be second-hand:
        ▪ It might be third-hand - someone who heard it from someone,
        ▪ It might be an unfounded rumor or gossip - "hearsay" that the source heard "on the grapevine".
        ▪ It might be just a figment of the second-hand source's imagination, i.e. "I think I remember him saying …"

The parlor game "telephone" provides an excellent example of how second-hand information can get distorted by people who don't correctly understand what they were told by a first-hand source and/or don't remember exactly what they heard, and then pass along incorrect information. If you are not familiar with this game, learn how it is played.

Filter the content of incoming information

Adopt the mindset that information you receive <u>might be</u> less than 100% complete and less than 100% accurate.
- *We don't know what we don't know.* Therefore it's virtually impossible for us to know for sure if new information we receive is 100% complete and 100% accurate.
- It's human nature to "color the facts".
- People sometimes forget to say things they meant to say.
- People sometimes fake or guess at an answer to a question when they are too proud or too embarrassed to admit that they don't know for sure.
- Just about everybody tells little white lies, and some of those little white ones can grow into pretty big whoppers.
- Sometimes people will edit (self-censor) their communications in order to communicate only as much of what they know as:
    o They think other people really want to know.
    o They think other people should know.
    o They think others will understand.
- Some people won't "tell the truth, the whole truth, and nothing but the truth" in their efforts to protect themselves or to motivate you to do something that they want you to do. They may withhold or alter key facts. They may prevaricate (euphemism for "lie") through:
    o Omission: not telling all the truth they know.
    o Commission: telling falsehoods. They might provide:
        ▪ Misinformation that is just plain incorrect, or
        ▪ Disinformation that deliberately attempts to steer you to a wrong conclusion.
- Sometimes news sources don't have enough time or space to provide us all the potentially useful information they know, and sometimes they are just plain wrong.
- Marketing materials and advertising often "stretch the truth" as to the quality and/or capabilities of products and services.

Also understand that experts can have different interpretations of the same set of facts. For instance, in the same newspaper on the same day:
- One economist might say the economy is heading deeper into a recession while a second economist says the recession has bottomed out and times will be getting better soon.
- One analyst might say gasoline is at an historic high while a second analyst advises us that the inflation adjusted price is actually lower than in the past.

Question incoming information in the polite, civil tone of intellectual pursuit.
- Learn about *Socrates and the Socratic method of using questions to seek the truth.*
- Learn about the *scientific method* and how scientists use it to test the truth of information with which they work - theories, principles, and the results of other scientists' studies. Sometimes after questioning and testing enough times, they discover that what they thought was true, isn't true, or what they thought would happen, doesn't happen.
- *Qu*estion dogma. Just because you were taught that information is true and correct doesn't mean that it is true and correct.
- Question what "everybody else" seems to be thinking.
- *Questioning people in the polite, civil tone of intellectual pursuit doesn't mean you don't believe what a person is saying. Rather, it simply means you have learned to not blindly*

accept everything you read and hear. Smart business people recognize and appreciate questions that are intended to give questioners a better understanding of what they had been trying to communicate or to get additional information.

- *You might provide a critique of information people provide you but don't criticize them.*
- <u>*Question things I wrote in this book*</u>. <u>Put my thoughts and suggestions to the test. Ask successful business people you know for their critique of the book. Ask them to corroborate or correct specific things I wrote.</u>

Understand we humans have tendencies to:
- "See what we <u>want</u> to see, and hear what we <u>want</u> to hear."
- See what we <u>expect</u> to see, and hear what we <u>expect</u> to hear.
  - o Learn about the term "selective attention" in psychology.
  - o Check out "The Invisible Gorilla" video on YouTube.
- Consider to be true what we want to be true or expect to be true.

The fewer the times you have to say "I was misinformed" or "I was misled" the better your decisions and your money management are likely to be.
- Seasoned business people learn to take information "with a grain of salt" (a healthy sense of skepticism) when it comes from sources that they haven't grown to know and trust, until they can confirm the accuracy of the information with other sources.
- "If it sounds too good to be true, it probably is".
  - o The better a deal sounds, the harder you should try to find potential negatives.
  - o The higher that the potential return on an investment is touted to be, the harder you should try to identify the potential investment risks.
- P.T. Barnum warned us all with his famous line *"a sucker is born every minute"*. Don't get "suckered" into any business or investment transaction.

Context
- To fully understand a spoken comment, an excerpt from a written communication, or an event, it is important to understand the context in which words were spoken, words were written, or an event occurred. Information taken out of context can lead to a misunderstanding of that information.
- Context of spoken words?
  - o Target audience - to whom were comments addressed?
    - ▪ Different audiences can influence a person to convey the same message with different words and different slants.
    - ▪ A person might say something in the presence of people from Group A but rephrase the message to people from Group B.
    - ▪ For example, a politician speaking to a small group of financial contributors might say something in a different way than he would say it in a televised broadcast.
  - o Purpose of the comments – what was the speaker trying to accomplish?
  - o What was the content of the entire communication?
- Context of written words?
  - o Target audience?
  - o Purpose of the entire written communication?
  - o If the written words were just an excerpt from a more comprehensive communication, what was the content of the entire communication? As an example, it is said that people can use excerpts from the Bible to justify almost anything by citing one verse taken out of the context of the entire Book (chapter)

in which it was written and the entire Bible taken as a whole.
- Context of an event?
    - o What led up to people doing what they did, or to an event happening?
    - o What prior events might have led up to this event?
- *Seek the "back story" – the full story behind the story.*
- To fully understand information seek to understand the information's context, such as:
    - o "Gotcha" sound bite quotes taken out of context by someone who wants to "get" someone else.
    - o "Selective excerpting": a few words excerpted from an entire written communication in such a way that people who didn't read or hear the entire communication would construe the excerpted words to mean something different than the communicator intended.
    - o Numbers excerpted from a complete set of statistics for a specific purpose.
    - o Video clips that don't show the totality of what was going on at the time.

Confirm you have the correct understanding of information.
- Communication requires a message sender and a message receiver.
- *Effective communication requires that the receiver understand the message as the sender intended the message to be understood.*
- Ineffective communication can result in the famous line from the movie *Cool Hand Luke* "What we've got here is failure to communicate". Two examples:
    - o Things we don't want to happen might happen as the result of our doing things based upon incorrect understandings of information.
    - o We might miss out on taking advantage of an opportunity because we didn't understand that "it was right there for the taking".

To confirm your understanding of information you have heard you might:
- Repeat back to the speaker in your own words what you think you heard him say. You might ask something like "Did I understand you to say …"
- Ask the speaker to clarify what he said. Perhaps ask him to put it in different words.
- Ask follow up questions to determine if you are on the "same wavelength" as the speaker or if you are "off track" in your understanding.

To confirm your understanding of information you have read you might:
- Explain your understanding to people who you think have greater expertise and/or experience in the subject matter and ask them to confirm or correct your understanding.
- Ask people for their understanding of what the author wrote.
- Read other materials that were referenced by the author.
- If you are a student, ask teachers for their understanding.

Ask "dumb questions".
- *I use the term "dumb question" to mean a question that that might make you feel "dumb" about asking it because you assume everybody else knows the answer and you don't.*
- Too often we are embarrassed to ask a good question because we assume it will make us sound dumb. Big mistake!
    - o At almost every class, seminar or meeting I attend I am amazed by the questions people do NOT ask. An entire audience will sit listening attentively to a speaker, often nodding in agreement, when, in fact, most people didn't understand something that the speaker said.

- o The truth comes out after one brave soul asks a simple question such as "Would you please explain what you mean by that?"
- o After the ice is broken by that first question other audience members typically chime in with follow up questions that they had been reluctant to ask.
- There is no such thing as a dumb question when a person has a sincere intent to better understand what a speaker said or to learn additional information.
- Smart business people recognize and appreciate questions that are intended to give audience members a better understanding of what they had been trying to communicate or to get additional information.
- Questions you feel dumb about asking may the best questions you could ask. When you feel dumb about not understanding something that means you have something to learn. Seize the learning opportunity.

A few dumb question guidelines:
- Ask questions that are earnestly intended to help you learn.
- Ask questions that aim to "get to the heart of the matter".
- Ask questions that guide a speaker to:
  - o Explain or clarify what he said or meant to say.
  - o Elaborate on something he said - provide additional detail.
- As an example, good dumb questions to ask at a seminar might be:
  - o What does that mean?
  - o Why is that important to us?
  - o How can we use that?

Talking points (a/k/a "the company line" or "canned remarks"):
- Provide key points around which marketing and political campaigns are designed.
- Present a consistent, favorable image of an organization or person.
- Typically woven into all marketing communications.
- Provide broad brush generalities that help avoid "getting pinned down" on specifics.

Try to dig past the surface of talking points in order to get to the underlying motivation and business plan of the organization or person using the talking points.

"Numbers don't lie, but some people do". It is likely that statistics have been manipulated for self-serving purposes since our ancient ancestors first began compiling facts and figures for the purpose of doing business with each other.

Learn what the business term "massage the numbers" means, and how the term came into being.
- "Numbers crunchers" (people who work with numbers) such as accountants, actuaries, and economists have been known to interpret and manipulate (massage) statistics to say what their employers want those statistics to say.
- There are a mind numbing number of statistical databases from which people can extract numbers to support just about any point they want to make. They can do this by:
  - o Selectively extracting certain statistics from a complete set of statistics.
  - o Providing their interpretations of statistics in the way they want those statistics to be interpreted by an intended audience.

Numbers that we don't count ourselves are subject to the human error and the human weaknesses of the people who provided the numbers to us.
- Numbers presented to us by other people can be influenced by their:

- o Expertise and experience in accurately gathering numbers.
- o Motivation to present the numbers.
- o Biases.
- o Interpretation of the numbers.
- Consider how often we hear complaints about errors in government censuses.
- Computer programs sometimes have glitches that result in inaccurate numbers.
- People might even present numbers for the purpose of deceiving a specific target market audience. For instance, in regard to item counts in company inventories:
  - o Company owners have been known to inflate the dollar value of company inventories to investors.
  - o Embezzling employees have been known to lie to their employers about the actual number of items that are still in company inventories.

Surveys and polls generate findings from statistical sample groups of people who are selected to be representative of entire populations. The thoughts and beliefs of an entire population are extrapolated from a sample group.

- Surveys and polls can be hazardous to our independent thinking in that they can exert peer pressure that steers us toward thinking the same way that the findings indicated a majority of survey or poll respondents thought.
- When you are trying to understand and analyze the findings of a survey, poll, or certain research studies, ask yourself:
  - o What purpose was it intended to serve?
  - o Who paid for it?
  - o What motivated the funding party to spend the money it spent?
  - o Who was chosen to conduct it?
  - o How much was the surveyor paid for his services?
  - o What is the surveyor's reputation for generating impartial, objective findings and providing accurate interpretations of findings?
- In cases in which money could be made or lost as the result of the findings:
  - o *Findings typically "support the hand that feeds them"*: findings that get published for consumption for an intended audience typically support the position of whoever funded the survey, poll, or study. This is typically the case when a survey, poll, or study is conducted with an express intent to generate findings that can be used to help market a product, support or oppose a piece of legislation, etc.
  - o Findings that didn't support the position of whoever funded the survey, poll, or study probably wouldn't need to be made public and we wouldn't get to know about the existence of those findings.
  - o A survey or study can be designed to gather information from a carefully selected sample of people with the intent of getting the findings that the people who paid for the survey or study wanted to get.
- In cases in which a funding party has a well-intentioned motive to educate the general public, keep in mind:
  - o Each parson selected to be a participant in a survey or poll will have his own set of human weaknesses.
  - o People are prone to changing their minds, often quite quickly. Surveys and polls taken one week might generate different findings the next week.
  - o Some people might give the "socially acceptable" answers that they think they are supposed to give, rather than say what they truly think.
  - o People may not tell the whole truth about what they really think, even if their

          answers will remain anonymous.
- o   Think about why the findings of political polls turn out to be wrong so often.
  - ▪ It might not be useful to spend much time dwelling on the findings of one single political poll.
  - ▪ It might be more useful to make a quick mental note of the findings of that one political poll, and then give more credence to those findings as additional polls provide findings that corroborate the findings of the initial poll.

A few final thoughts about filtering information:
- *"Read between the lines."*
- Think about what's behind euphemisms.
- Seek:
  - o   Root causes and central truths that underlie the details.
  - o   Objective reports, analysis and opinion.
  - o   Differing points of view and differing opinions on the same current event in order to gain a broader perspective on the event and a greater understanding of the "gray" nuances of information that may have presented in a more "black and white" manner.
  - o   Differing projections of the future outcomes of current events.
  - o   Behavioral tendencies of the individual people and/or groups of people involved.

A business approach to gathering news

News suppliers are businesses.
- News suppliers are in the business of selling news product.
- As with all businesses, *the law of supply and demand governs the news business*.
- The objective of news suppliers is to supply news content that a target market audience will demand - that is, people will want to watch it, listen to it, or read it.

Learn about the role that money plays in the news business – revenue and expenses.
- Revenue: the amount of revenue news suppliers can generate is a function of the number of customers they can attract and the price customers are willing to pay for their news.
- Expenses: it costs money to supply news product.
  - o News suppliers must generate enough revenue to pay all of their expenses.
  - o Commercial news suppliers (for-profit companies) must also earn enough profit to satisfy their owners' desires for a satisfactory rate of return on investment.
- There are a limited number of potential customers, and each potential customer has a limited amount of time and money he can afford to spend getting his news.
- Therefore, news suppliers compete to attract customers at different "price points" (price ranges) - prospective customers who have more money can afford to pay more for their news than prospective customers who have less money can afford to pay.
- Study how commercial radio and television news has evolved as result of the visual images that TV could bring into people's home, the profit generated by the TV show *60 Minutes*, innovation of the 24 hour a day news channel CNN, and availability of news *"on demand"* on the *internet supplied by a vastly increased number of new sources*.
- Watch the movie *Network*.
- Read Howard Kurtz's book *The Fortune Tellers*.

Make a game of analyzing the business plan of each news supplier.

Revenue
- Two basic "business models" for generating revenue.
  - o *For-profit commercial business model*: sources of revenue include advertisements, subscriptions, one-off purchases (e.g. magazines at newsstands; articles from a website). Prices determined by many factors, including:
    - ▪ How much money people are willing to pay – customers and advertisers.
    - ▪ Prices charged by competitors.
  - o *Non-profit public service business model*: National Public Radio (NPR) and Public Broadcasting Station television (PBS), etc. provide the news as a "public service" funded by sources such as listener/viewer memberships, philanthropic funding, corporate sponsorships, and government.
- Customers - target market audience?
  - o People seeking potentially useful information, entertainment, both?
  - o Target market demographic groups, e.g. age groups, income brackets, male or female, political beliefs and party affiliation, or special interests such as sports fans. Indicators of target market demographic groups include types of products advertised, sponsorship announcements, and the placement of advertisements and sponsorship announcements on different television and radio programs, and in different websites and blogs, and within specific sections of newspapers and magazines.
    - ▪ *Advertisers and sponsors spend a lot of money trying to figure out the*

places in which their target market demographic groups are most likely to see or hear their advertisements and sponsorship announcements.
- ▪ Try to figure out which demographic groups advertisers and sponsors are trying to attract:
  - • With what types of news and/or entertainment programming at which times of the day.
  - • In which type media - newspapers, magazines, websites, blogs, etc.
- • Product: what news product are they trying to sell to their target market audience?
  - o Information rich reports and in-depth analysis?
  - o Headline/sound bite news within a varied product mix of other types of content, e.g. news, sports, and celebrity/entertainment pieces?

Expenses: what does it cost them to supply their news product to us?
- • How much does it cost to:
  - o Gather "raw data" news - reporter salaries, transporting reporters and equipment to sites of events, etc.
  - o Produce "final copy" news product for broadcast or publication.
  - o Distribute that news product to you.
- • What constraints does expense management place on the news product they can supply, such as:
  - o Number of reporters they can afford to hire (aggregate compensation they can afford to allocate among all reporters).
  - o Time they can give each reporter to spend researching each news story.
  - o Amount of air time or print space they can afford to allocate to news.

Profit
- • Dollar profit:
  - o Needed to remain in business.
  - o Needed to pay for human resource and capital asset investments needed to assure future viability of their news business – staffing, equipment, etc.
- • Return on investment: the owners of news sources typically have multiple options as to how they could invest their money. If owners aren't earning a satisfactory rate of return on the money they have invested in their news business, they are likely to cut back or close down news operations and reallocate their money to different programming content or to altogether different business investments that might generate a higher rate of return.

"You get what you pay for."
- • <u>We get the news content that we are willing to pay for</u>:
  - o *With our money* – (a) subscription prices we will pay, and (b) contributions we make and our tax money that we approve being appropriated to fund to public radio and television.
  - o *With our time* - amount of "air time" to which we will pay attention to programming, and amount of advertising and/or sponsorship announcements we will tolerate.
- • *Bad news must sell better than good news.* If there wasn't demand for bad news (e.g. crime, catastrophe, terrorism, war) news sources wouldn't supply so much of it. Think about why drivers slow down to gawk at car accidents.
- • *News targeted at emotions must sell better than news targeted at rational thinking.* Sex, violence, personal tragedy, celebrity, and sensationalism must sell better than

dispassionate reporting of facts and analysis of current events, discoveries in science and technology, etc. or there wouldn't be so much of it.

- It seems that "personality trumps content" in some television news programming - the emphasis of such programing seems to be on placing good looking people who have engaging personalities in front of viewers more than it is on presenting viewers with impartial, informative news content that has relatively high use potential.
- *If more of us become more willing to pay more (in terms of money, listenership, or viewership) for more in-depth news reports, well-reasoned editorial opinion, and "think piece" news that has high use potential, the more likely it is we would get more of it.*

Think for yourself. Don't sit back passively and let broadcasters, writers, and editors tell you what to think.

Question news stories with the "reporter's best friends" – who, what, when, where, why, and how. Ask yourself questions such as:
- Who is the news supplier? Who was the reporter? What reputations have they built?
- Who is involved in the story – individual people, demographic group(s), organization(s)?
- What happened? Where did it happen? How did it happen? Why did it happen? If it was an accident or catastrophe, how can I prevent the same thing from happening to me?
- When did the news event occur? Is it stale old news or new news?
- How much time might the reporter have spent on the story - gathering the facts, fact-checking the accuracy of facts, analyzing the facts, determining the meaning and significance of the facts, and preparing the story?
- Who is the target market audience for the story?
- Why did the editor approve presentation of this news piece?
- How should I interpret the information presented in the story? What can I learn?
- How can I link any new information to information already stored in my memory files:
  - o To flesh out more detail on the bones of a story I already know something about?
  - o To identify a trend as it is developing?
  - o To come up with creative ideas?
- *Why might this information be important to me?* What is the context of the story?
  - o <u>Relationship to the big picture of life on this planet</u> - on a scale that runs from changing life on Earth as we know it down to the fifth marriage of a famous celebrity?
  - o <u>Relationship to my life</u> – what impact might the story content have on my life and my money - big impact or negligible impact?
  - o Relationship to whatever else is happening in my community and in the world?
  - o Relationship to historical precedents?
  - o Relationship to current trends and historical cycles?
- *How could I or should I use this news?*

"Fact check": news reporters are supposed to "fact check" (confirm their facts) with at least two reputable sources whenever possible prior to publishing a story. So too we news consumers should try to fact check news information with least two reputable sources before using that information to make significant decisions.

"It's the same old story."
- *Learn to recognize the relatively few story plot lines (patterns of human behavior) that have been playing out over and over again in the "human drama" throughout history,*

with only the characters and specific details changing in each story, e.g.:
  o Repeated / ongoing conflict over the same old things between the same two countries, or the same two religious groups, or the same two political parties.
  o Expensive disaster caused by business managers who sought to enrich themselves by doing things they should not have been doing or not doing things they should have been doing.
  o Poor boy pulls himself up by the bootstraps to become successful.
• If you are not yet aware of how the plots of news stories can sound so strikingly similar, it might stimulate your awareness if you read two books written about fiction:
  o *The Seven Basic Plots*, by Christopher Booker.
  o *20 Master Plots and How to Build Them*, by Ronald Tobias.
• Learn why the adage "history repeats itself" came into being.
• *One of the benefits of getting older is that we can say to ourselves "Hey, I've heard this story before" with increasing frequency.*

Be guided by the word "new" in "news" and "news-papers". Seek:
• New details about current events.
• New information regarding old stories.
• New perspectives on current events.
• New takes on old stories that stimulate your thinking in new ways.
• New discoveries, new technologies, new ideas.
• Newly emerging trends that might influence future events.
• Newly developing changes that may be creating business opportunities.

Diligently practice becoming a progressively better user of "the news". Just like with every other life skill, if we consciously practice gathering and filtering useful news information, it is likely we will become better, faster and more efficient users of "the news".

Following are a few suggestions for using the news:
• Control your emotions - don't fret about doom and gloom news, and, don't go ga-ga for over-hyped rosy outlook news.
• Manage your scarce resource of time.
  o *Practice identifying stories that are different enough from stories you have heard in the past that they warrant investing your precious time, and stories that are so similar to stories you have heard in the past that they warrant less of your time.*
  o Don't spend too much time on stories that are just developing while there are few factual details and much conjecture about what the actual facts might be.
• Seek objective reporting to get salient facts.
• Seek investigative reporting about issues that affect your life.
• Seek editorial opinions that differ from your opinions; editorials that make you think.
• Sift out nuggets of useful new information from repetitive recitation of old information.
• Project out into the future how each story is likely to play out, but be careful about jumping to a conclusion too soon on stories that are still playing out (and perhaps acting too hastily on what you know to date) – there are surprise endings to many stories that seem predictable right up to a surprise plot twist at the ending.
• Seek the "back story", e.g. how and why events happened, how people did things.
  o As each story actually plays out, seek new details that help you fill in the backstory.
  o Seek well thought analysis and opinion that helps you understand the backstory.

- Seek lessons about human behavior.
- Seek risk management lessons in stories about crimes that you can apply in your life (e.g. robbery and fraud), accidents people have had, catastrophic weather events, etc.
- Create mental storage files for different types of stories. Run a quick mental scan of your brain computer's storage files to see how you might link new information with information you already have stored (e.g. link current events with trends you know about, and determine how those trends might fit into historical cycles you know about, and use the context of those trends and cycles to help project how current events are likely to play out in the future.
- Learn or re-learn how reading teachers suggest we can improve our reading skills, e.g. speed, comprehension, and retention.
- Scan the headlines and perhaps the first few paragraphs of written stories to identify the type of story, the probable plot line, and the probability that it might provide useful information.
- A practical rule of thumb - *the louder the voice of a newscaster on TV or radio, the more likely the news is meant to appeal more to your emotions than to your rational intellect.*

Consider skimming through certain stories in search of nuggets of useful new information:
- Stories having "the same old story" plotlines that make you think "I've heard this story before".
- Stories that follow-up on old stories that are beginning to get stale.
- Stories that emphasize and sensationalize relatively useless details of big, important stories rather than providing dispassionate reporting of more useful but less emotion grabbing details, such as the reporting of:
  - o "Pay to play" - one government official getting caught accepting money in return for "political favors", rather than reporting how many other government officials are routinely "bought off" and how to stop money from corrupting government.
  - o Horrific act committed by one soldier in a war, rather than reporting all the horrific things that the soldier had experienced which may have led him to do what he did, and how other soldiers in the current war or previous wars may well have done the same thing.
  - o Sordid details of the personal life of a company's president, rather than reporting the business reasons that actually led to his company's problems.
- Stories and editorials that feature dogma you have heard restated over and over again.
- *Stories that feature the words "best ever" or "worst ever"*: these attention-getting words are used in error way too often (usually to hook into our emotions). Precious few things truly are the best ever or the worst ever of its kind (the words best and worst are "superlatives" - learn what superlative, comparative and declarative mean in grammar).
- Stories that create an impression that "everybody" is buying a specific type of investment such as technology stocks or real estate. If you spot a significant volume of stories touting a certain type of investment, take it as a warning that an investment bubble may be inflating.

Consider skipping altogether:
- Stories that rehash the same old information that has already been published or broadcast umpteen times, or just reinforce opinions you already hold.
- Stories about previously newsworthy events that have long since evolved into "human interest" soap operas that offer negligible useful news as they just try to pluck emotional heartstrings, e.g. plane crash, bridge collapse, hurricane, earthquake.

- "Scare stories" that dwell on financial calamities or economic doom and gloom.
- "Fluff" stories about the love lives, outrageous behavior, or mental meltdowns of celebrities.
- Financial and political pundits on TV and radio who have obvious biases and are obviously trying to appeal to a like-minded audience (that is, skip over their comments after you have heard these people enough times to have gotten a feel for their dogmatic positions on issues and you pretty well know what they are likely to say).

Beware "sound bite" excerpts from entire oral communications – they can be misleading.
- Along with the proliferation of instant internet-connected communications devices and the news sources that have arisen to populate that space, it appears there has been a proliferation of sound bite/headline-only type news that doesn't provide much useful information. This proliferation of sound bite news is likely to have come about for reasons such as:
    o Sound bites are easier for broadcasters to sandwich in between commercials.
    o Sound bites can be recycled over and over again to fill air time and print space.
    o Sound bite news must sell better than longer, more in-depth think-piece news that requires a longer attention span.
- Sound bite excerpts from an entire communication can be used to steer a news consuming audience toward conclusions the sound bite provider wants that audience to draw.
- Sound bites can be used <u>by public figures</u>. If they stick to carefully scripted talking points, public figures can create favorable impressions in the minds of the general public without getting into the details of what they actually think (especially details which might anger or annoy key segments of the general public).
- On the flip side, sound bites can be used <u>against public figures</u>.
    o Victims of sound bite quotes often complain that their words were taken out of context and do not accurately convey the entirety of what they said and think.
    o Media savvy public figures know that words and images captured by the internet are out there forever, and that their words might be "sound-bited" for use against them in the future. It seems that many (if not most) of these media savvy people have found that the less they say and the closer that they stick to their sound bite friendly "talking points", the safer it is for them - the less that they say to the public about what they truly think, the less ammunition they give opponents to shoot back at them.

If you hear a sound bite snippet of information that you think might be useful:
- Try to find out more about the source's complete communication so that you can put the sound bite excerpt into its proper context.
- Research what else the person might have said (or done) relative to the subject – their "entire body of work" so to speak – to corroborate your understanding of the information.

Do NOT confuse frequent stock market updates with useful business news.
- *Frequent stock market price updates may be called "business news", but it probably would be more appropriate to call them "stock trader updates".*
- Frequent stock market updates on what "the market" or "investors" (typically large corporate and institutional investors, not Average Joe amateur investors like you and me) are doing every few minutes are, at best, useless chatter for many of us amateurs, and at worst, dangerous motivation for some of us to make investment management mistakes.
- The simple fact that the Dow Jones Industrial Average moved up or down during any given hour or any given day doesn't tell us much if anything about what the future market

values of our stock investments are likely to be if we are planning to hold them long term, and perhaps sell them months or years in the future. Let the investment professionals you hire worry about minute to minute and hour to hour stock price updates.

- The hourly and daily ups and downs of common stock prices don't account for all the other factors that drive the price of common stocks, e.g. the impact of decisions made by a multitude of business and government leaders, currents events in the politics and economies of countries around the world, trends and cycles, game changing innovations and inventions, and discoveries.

News stories can contribute to self-fulfilling prophecies. If enough people are led to think and behave the way that news sources steer them to think and behave (especially people who "follow" certain reporters, pundits, and commentators steeped in dogma), then their "group think" and collective "herd behavior" can ripple through a society thereby contributing to make happen what pundits and commentators prophesied would happen.

Regarding the prices of investments:
- Investments only have the value that people think they have (please go back to Chapter 3 and read about money, value and prices in the Economics section, and do as much additional study as needed to be sure you understand what money is and why money only has the economic value that people think it has).
- IF enough people let pundits and commentators do too much of their thinking for them, then those pundits and commentators can have a significant influence on the prices of investments. The movie *The Big Short* offers a great lesson on the valuation of investments.

Regarding an entire economy:
- If enough people believe what they are being told about the economy doing well:
  o The resultant "wealth effect" (a good economy, a feeling of job security, increasing value of their investments, and money in the bank) is likely to make people feel more comfortable spending their money.
  o Manufacturers are likely to continue making their products while they are expecting consumers to continue buying.
  o Retailers are likely to continue building their inventories in order to satisfy the demand they are expecting to continue.
  o And as money continues to circulate through the economy, economic expansion is likely to continue.
- Vice versa with recessions

A few thoughts about choosing news sources:
- *Develop "go to" news sources:*
  o Sources that maintain good reputations for:
    ▪ Objective reporting of facts.
    ▪ Providing well-informed, well-reasoned analysis and opinion
  o Sources that have provided you information that has proven useful to you in making your previous decisions.
- Choose those news sources that you think:
  o Provide the most useful information for you in making your financial management decisions.
  o Are best suited to your daily schedule and budget.
- Choose specific sections in newspapers and magazines, specific time slots on radio and

TV, podcasts, reporters, blogs, and other specific news sources that "speak to you" in language you understand.

- Choose different sources that provide different perspectives on the news, e.g. sources that have developed reputations for being politically liberal, conservative, or moderate.

A few news source suggestions
- Newspapers, magazines, podcasts, blogs, and other online content that you think is targeted at "thinking" people who enjoy learning - a target market audience of people seeking a broader education in all sorts of subjects that feed the intellect, e.g. science, technology, economics, business management, personal financial management.
- Editorial and opinion pages of newspapers and online equivalents.
- Investigative reports.
- Talk shows hosted by people who use well-modulated voices – hosts who avoid rants; shows that feature civil discussion of books, new ideas, current events, and other subjects that might have high use potential for you - perhaps shows featuring people who use satirical humor to get us to think about newsworthy events.
- Non-fiction book reviews can provide some great information and ideas in a concise summary format.

And close to my heart, the sports sections of newspapers
- The worlds of sports and business are closely linked in the ways people think and act.
- Many sports reporters and columnists:
  - o Make savvy observations of the way people live their lives as athletes, athletic team owners, managers, coaches, and fans.
  - o Extend the breadth of their observations and opinions past the world of sports into the worlds of business and society in general, and the human condition that underpins all of life.
- We can gain valuable insights into business and financial management:
  - o How successful team owners and senior managers run the business side of team operations.
  - o Lessons to learn from the mistakes of not so successful team owners and senior managers.
  - o How coaches manage the performance of individual players and entire teams.
  - o How athletes manage their careers, personal lives, and financial affairs.
- Thomas Boswell's columns in *The Washington Post* are a great example.

Store your information where you can get it when you need it

There are many ways to store your information, including:
- Memory.
- Paper records you store at home, e.g. in file folders, file cabinets and/or a desk.
- Personal records stored electronically on your own computer or other electronic device, or "the cloud".
- The universe of information stored on internet websites.
- Books you own and store in your home and books stored in local libraries.
- Outsourced to professional service providers.

Choose a combination of storage methods that works well for you.

A guiding principle for choosing the way you store information is that relevant information should be readily available at the time you need to make your decisions.

Memory has the great benefit of being instantly available.

However, *memory also has at least two significant downsides:*
- *It has a habit of playing tricks on us – we misremember.*
- *It fades – we forget.*

Each of us has a different capability to use memory to store information.
- Be honest with yourself about how good your memory is.
- Some people have a photographic memory. They can remember vast amounts of information.
- Other people have a much more limited memory.
  - Some people have memory lapses such that on occasion they have a "brain-fry" and can't remember a fact or a name that they know they know.
  - As many people age their memory diminishes.

Learn about neuroplasticity and how our brains evolve as we age.

Learn how experts in their fields say we might be able to improve our memories by exercising and training our brains.
- Think about all the memory games you have played or heard about, and speed reading classes that have helped people read faster and remember more of what they read.
- Learn about benefits that some people say we can gain from:
  - Challenging our brains to learn new skills and abilities, such as learning to play a musical instrument or learning a new language
  - Doing crossword and Sudoku puzzles and other "brain teaser" games.
- Learn about mnemonics (mnemonic devices) – techniques that help us remember information, such as creating rhymes or acronyms, and word associations.

Paper records - bank and broker statements, tax receipts and tax returns, your personal financial statements, etc. These records can be stored at home, in a safe deposit box, or at a professional service provider's office.

To gain perspective on the importance of written records, learn about the historical origin of written records. My thought is that one of the first uses (if not the first use) of writing was as a

business tool. It may be that:
- As greater numbers of people lived in towns and cities an increasing number and size of business transactions was pushing the outer limits of merchants' memories as an effective information storage tool. Written records increased their information storage capacity.
- Written records helped them conduct business by providing:
  o Inventory lists of merchandise they had available to sell.
  o Documentation of transactions that could be used to reduce the number of after-sale disputes over exactly what buyers and sellers had agreed to do.

Regarding written paper records that you decide to store at home:
- Store them in a container such as:
  o File cabinet or desk.
  o As a no cost alternative, cardboard boxes work just fine.
  o Consider storing critical papers in a fireproof container.
- Within the storage container organize papers in separate file folders. As a no cost alternative to store bought file folders, large envelopes you receive in the mail can be slit open with a knife and recycled into functional file folders.

If your budget can afford it, you might consider storing critical papers in a bank safe deposit box, e.g. birth and marriage certificates, military discharge papers, social security card, title to your home, and mortgage documents.

Do not let yourself get buried under paper.
- Try to file away bills, statements and other financial papers as soon as possible after receiving them. A few innocuous pieces of paper left untouched on a desk can have a magical procreative power to multiply into forbidding stacks of paper.
- "It's tough to drain the swamp when you're up to your butt in alligators." Same goes for good decision making when you have so much unorganized paper that you can't find the information you need.

Chapter 9. Surround Yourself with Good People

Good people can help you succeed in many ways. They can:
- Provide good role models for your lifestyle choices and money management behavior.
- Provide expertise and/or experience to do things for you that you couldn't do as well yourself.
- Provide advice and recommendations.
- Share life lessons they have learned from their successes and mistakes, and the successes and mistakes they have observed other people make.
- Be confidants with whom you can discuss your financial affairs, talk out things that weigh heavily on your mind, and be sounding boards for your ideas.
- Take some of your workload off your plate thereby increasing the time you have available to do other good and satisfying things. "Many hands make light loads."
- Critique (NOT criticize – big difference) your thinking and behavior - financial management and otherwise.
- Become part of your internal control system:
  - To help you manage your performance as president of your company and the performance of your other business team members.
  - To help protect you from yourself. Good people who have care and concern for your well-being (and the guts to be honest with you) can tell you when they think you are straying from your plan, or doing things that they don't think are good for you to do. They can serve as "Dutch uncles" or "alter egos".

Don't be a "Lone Ranger". The ancient book of Proverbs 12:15 advised "The way of a fool is right in his own eyes, but a wise man listens to advice." And Abraham Lincoln is said to have advised "He who represents himself has a fool for a client."

Don't be intimidated by talent, recruit it.
- Most successful business owners I know have learned that it is easier to succeed when they have a team of top quality people helping them succeed.
- Know what you know and what you don't know; know what you are good at doing and what you are not so good at doing - and - *be smart enough and self-confident enough to surround yourself with people who are smarter than you are, know more than you know, and are better at doing certain things than you are*.
- Think about a good football coach who has a good game plan. That coach would give himself the best chance to win if he could put the best players in the league on his team to implement his good game plan. Same goes for putting the best available people on your business team to help you implement your business game plan. Aspire to assemble a team of all-stars. Having a good business plan is important, but it takes good people executing a good plan to create success in life and in money management.

Take a close look at the people in your life. Ask yourself:
- Has everyone been mostly a good influence on the way I manage my money?
- Has anyone been a particularly bad influence on my life and my money management?

The less satisfied you are with your life in general, and your money management in particular, the more beneficial it would probably be to take a close look at the people in your life, and decide if you would be better off if you changed the nature of your relationship with anyone who has been having a bad influence on you, or perhaps even terminated the relationship. Like a habit that's hard to shake, the longer and closer a relationship has been, the tougher it can be to change or terminate it. Two suggestions that might help make changing the nature of a relationship or terminating the relationship as easy as a tough task can be made:

- Talk to a close confidant whose judgment and decision making you respect or a professional counselor who specializes in relationship counseling. Such a person can:
  - o Help you analyze the relationship as objectively and dispassionately as possible – analyze how you got into the relationship and why you have maintained it.
  - o Provide objective third party advice and recommendations about what you might do, if anything.
  - o Bolster your resolve to change the relationship as needed or terminate it.
- Focus on your well-being, and the room you would be making for new people to come into your life to be more positive influences on your life and your money.

Don't make the mistake of continuing a relationship that hasn't been good for you because you hope a person will change her behavior just because you want her to change.

- *Each person is the only person who can change her own behavior.* Just as you are the only person who can change your behavior, so too another person must have the internal motivation to change her behavior.
- You can talk to a person until you are blue in the face about how you want her to change, but that person won't change her behavior until she becomes motivated to change.
- *You can't change anyone else's behavior.*

If the relationship that hasn't been good for you is with a friend, analyze what ties have bound you two together.

- Was the person a true friend who liked you for being you, or might she have been "using you" because of what she thought you could do for her?
- Were you motivated to be in the relationship because it helped you feel socially accepted? If so, you might have a personal issue to work on.

If you think the person is indeed a true friend with whom you want to maintain a relationship, you might try talking openly and honestly with her about the ways in which you think her behavior hasn't been good for you. Then if you don't see her begin to change her behavior, it might be wise to begin making a decision as to whether or not you would be better off by stepping back from the closeness of the relationship or possibly terminating it altogether. Two old adages provide excellent advice:

- *"Talk is cheap."* A person can talk a good game about changing her behavior, but it takes action to actually change behavior.
- *"The road to hell is paved with good intentions."*

If the relationship has been with your spouse or another family member, you might be well advised to talk with a professional who specializes in family counseling.

Organize the good people in your life into two groups:

- *Network* – all the good people you know. Add as many good people as you can.
- *Business team* - an inner circle of people within your network with whom you have the closest relationships - people who directly influence how much money you earn and spend, people you consider to be confidants and advisors, and professional service providers. The time and effort needed to develop and maintain close working relationships will put practical limits on the number of people you can include on your business team.

Build a network of business "contacts"

Networking
- "Contact" is a noun used in the business world to describe someone that a businessperson knows who might be able to help him either in the present or at some time in the future.
- "Networking" is a verb used in the business world to describe the process of building a network of contacts.
- "Birds of a feather flock together."
    - Nice people like to associate with other nice people.
    - Smart people like to associate with other smart people.
- Professional service providers who believe in delivering best value services are drawn to top quality service providers in other professions to whom they could refer clients if and when clients needed different skills sets of professional expertise or experience.
- Cliques develop in the business world just as they do in the high school world.

Networking is a normal human behavior. All of us already practice networking to some extent in our personal lives. We have:
- Families.
- Circles of friends.
- Communities of neighbors.
- Social networks on the internet.

People to consider including in your network of business contacts:

In your personal life
- Immediate family members and other relatives.
- People you know who have good business minds - friends, neighbors, etc.
- Professional service providers – both people you hire in their professional capacities and people you know on a social basis.
- Leaders and other active members of community service organizations of which you are a member.
- Religious leaders.
- Teachers and librarians.
- Sales representatives in stores where you shop regularly.

At work
- Your immediate supervisor and other managers.
- Co-workers.
- Suppliers, subcontractors, and other people who do business with your employer.
- Customers with whom you have enough regular contact to develop a relationship.
- Leaders and other active members of industry trade associations.
- Friendly competitors.

Your elected government representatives and their key staff members.

Two ways to add good people to your business network:
- Passively attract them.
- Actively recruit them.

To passively attract good people:
- Be a good person - the type of person that other good people want to be around - nice, trustworthy, fair, polite, etc.
- Treat everyone with dignity and respect.
  - o Understand that every person in every job is an important person in this world that we all share together.
  - o Have a "we are all in it together" attitude.
- Develop a good reputation for trying your hardest to do your best at whatever you do.
- Seek to do exemplary work that attracts the attention of good people.
- Present a personal appearance that advertises you are a good person who other good people should get to know.
- Emanate "good vibes". Think positive and maintain a cheerful, sunny disposition that makes people feel good.
- Use the visualization process we talked about in Chapter 5.
  - o Visualize yourself as the good-hearted, successful president of your personal financial management company with whom good people want to associate.
  - o Act like the president you visualize yourself being.
- Adopt the open, inquisitive demeanor of a successful entrepreneur who seeks and welcomes all the advice and help he can get.
- Keep your emotions under control. Good people tend to be attracted to calm, stable personalities and shy away from people prone to emotionally driven irrational behavior.

To actively recruit good people:
- Ask people in your network to refer you to people in their networks who they think you should know.
- Identify the leaders within your employer's organization (leaders in the formal power structure and leaders of informal groups) and seek to develop relationships with them.
  - o People who have the power of their positions to make decisions that impact you and your career.
  - o People who influence the people who have that power of position.
- Identify the people who are among the best at what they do in your community, company, and industry.
  - o Find people in your network who know the people you identify and ask for introductions.
  - o If no one in your network can make an introduction to a person you want to meet, research interest(s) you may have in common with that person, "cold call" the person and introduce yourself (learn about "cold calls" in sales). You might use your shared interest(s) as a conversation "ice breaker".
- Join at least one trade association in your industry. This is a great way to learn who industry "insiders" think are the best people in the industry.
  - o Get active on at least one committee to demonstrate that you are a good person who other good people should get to know.
  - o As you learn who the movers and shakers are in the association, try to get on at least one committee on which people you want to meet are members.
- Join at least one local community service organization, and get active on at least one committee (use the suggestions above for getting active in a trade association).
- Join and get active in a club or social group.

- Consider organizing your own club or social group to attract like-minded people who share your interests. To spur your creative imagination, learn how people in the past have organized groups such as:
    o The Lunar Society of Birmingham, England.
    o Ralph Waldo Emerson and the writers who gathered around him in Concord, Massachusetts during the mid-1800's.
    o Various groups and organizations founded by Benjamin Franklin.
- *At parties and social events, talk to people you don't know.* It's amazing how often that when we least expect it, fate connects us with people it is good for us to know.
- Attend continuing education classes and seminars. Instructors and classmates are often good prospects to add to your network. Also, ask instructors and classmates for referrals to people in their networks who they think you should know.
- Whereas networking is such a fundamental part of every job that involves sales, ask people you know who have sales oriented jobs for advice about recruiting people into your network.
- Learn how to use online social networking sites for business networking purposes. *Caution*: be careful what information you put out in cyberspace. What you think might be funny or attractive to friends today might repel a prospective employer or prospective client in the future. In particular, postings related to alcohol, pranks, and sex might kill potential business opportunities in the future.

Develop your casual acquaintances into influential relationships.
- *"It's who you know PLUS how well they know you"*. The better that people get to know you, the more likely they will be to think of you if an opportunity to help you arises.
- Smile and say hello every time you see a person in your network. If appropriate to the situation, stick out your hand to initiate a handshake. If the person doesn't seem to recognize you or know your name, help them out by saying "Hi" and then quickly follow up with your name and when and where you two have met before (e.g. Hi. I'm Jane Doe in the Accounting Department at Smith Company. We met at …). After a few "Hi's" the person is likely to recognize you as the sort of nice and friendly person who she would enjoy getting to know.
- Learn something about people's hobbies, their kids, high school, college, etc. Use this information as a quickie conversation starter when you see these people.
- Use superior performance to stand out from the crowd in each organization of which you are a member. Make it an objective in your business plan to earn whatever performance awards are given out by your employer and other organizations of which you are a member, e.g. employee of the month award, outstanding service award.
- Seek to help other people - stay alert for opportunities to help people.
- Introduce people within your network to each other when you identify opportunities for them to help each other.
- Thank people who have helped you or are helping you.
    o Seek opportunities to say "thank you" for simple things such as a person's cheery smile that brightens your day each time you see her.
    o Let people know how grateful you are for their contributions to your joy, satisfaction, and success.
    o Letting people know that you appreciate them will help get them more invested in your well-being.

Distill a team from your network

Team building involves developing and maintaining closer relationships with a select inner circle of people within your network. Prospective team members might include those people:
- Who exert the greatest influence on your life and your money.
- With whom you have developed the closest relationships.
- Who have expertise and/or experience to provide you with sound advice and help.
- With whom you have the most regular contact.

Choose business team members:
- Who have expertise and experience that you don't have.
- Whose strengths complement your weaknesses.
- Whose company you enjoy.
- *Who have enough care and concern for your well-being to tell you things they think you need to hear even if they think you might not want to hear what they have to say.*

Do not pick "yes-men" who agree with every single thing you say and do, and tell you only what they think you want to hear. Yes-men are not likely to offer you ideas that might be better than your ideas, nor warn you when they think you are about to do something that they think you shouldn't do.

People you might consider putting on your business team include:

Family members:
- Immediate family members probably exert the most influence on your money, e.g. how much of your money is spent each year, how much money you save each year, and net worth you accumulate.
- Other relatives who have proven to be good managers of their lives and their money.

Friends and neighbors (a) who have good business minds, (b) who have demonstrated good decision making skills, and (c) with whom you have developed close relationships.

"Choose your friends wisely."
- They can be powerful role models of good behavior to emulate.
- They can grow into close confidants with whom to share your innermost thoughts.

People at work
- Your immediate supervisor and the senior managers to whom she reports.
- Co-workers who have good work habits and do their jobs well.
- "Champions" - well placed, influential people who can help pull you up the corporate ladder.
- Suppliers, subcontractors, or other people who do business with your employer, who have been in the business long enough to learn the best practices of people in your industry, and who are willing to share their knowledge with you.

Paid professional service providers
- It is rare for any of us to have ALL the skills, abilities, knowledge, and resources that we need to optimize our success in managing our money, for instance:
  - Financial management expertise and experience.

- o Access to valuable sources of information.
- o The time needed to do all we would need to do to optimize our success.
- We can "outsource" various duties to paid professional service providers in order to gain the benefit of their skills, abilities, knowledge and resources. Add paid professionals to your team based upon:
  - o The degree of need you have for their services, and
  - o Money available in your budget to afford the cost of their services.

Professional service providers to consider adding to your team include:
- Banker(s) within the local office of the bank(s) with which you do business.
- Property and liability insurance agent, e.g. automobile and renters / homeowners insurance.
- Life insurance agent.
- People who maintain your fixed assets: automobile mechanic, heating & air conditioning service contractor, pest control contractor.
- Financial advisor.
- Tax advisor.
- Realtor.
- Attorney specializing in family law and/or personal financial matters, e.g. prenuptial agreement, living will, will, estate plan.

Successful business teams and sports teams share many characteristics, such as:
- Team members who:
  - o Are committed to contributing their unique individual skills and abilities to help their team achieve the team's objectives.
  - o Are committed to working together as one coordinated unit rather than as a bunch of talented individuals.
  - o Have the social skills needed to work together and "maintain harmony in the clubhouse".
- A team manager who motivates and coordinates team members.

Qualifications to seek in professional service providers

A top quality employer that has earned a reputation for providing top quality service.
- An employer's good reputation is earned by good employees doing good work.
- Professional service companies that have earned the best reputations in their industries typically employ teams of the best people in their industries.
- Top quality employers typically (a) motivate employees to become as good as they can become at doing their jobs, and (b) provide employees access to the best training available to help them stay up to date with best practices in their industry and to become as proficient as they can become in their profession.
- Top quality employers typically provide top quality "back office" support services that enable their "client-facing" employees to deliver best value services to their clients.

The less an employer's business model allows you to develop a personal relationship with a specific professional, the more important it would be to research that company's reputation and historical performance track record. A few research suggestions:
- Seek the opinions of people you know who have good business sense; preferably people who have had first-hand experience with the company.
- Analyze the company's marketing and advertising program.
   - A relatively low key advertising program that focuses on the importance of its people and their long term relationships with clients is likely to be a good indicator of top quality employees.
   - *A personal rule of thumb - the louder and brasher the advertising of a professional service provider company, the tougher it is likely to be for the company to attract and retain top quality professional employees.*
   - Do not make a decision about a professional service provider based solely upon the image that marketing and advertising professionals seek to create for the company.
- Try to talk with more than one of the company's employees – perhaps make two or three separate telephone calls. Tell people you are doing research to decide about doing business with their company. If people seem open to talking, ask if they can tell you:
   - *The average length of time licensed professional employees have been employed* (the type of licensed and certified employees who would be helping you). Low employee turnover tends to be a good indicator of a top quality employer - top quality employees tend to remain with top quality employers. They don't need to move to competitor employers to find desirable jobs. Conversely, the best people in an industry generally don't stick around too long with less than top quality employers.
   - *The average length of time the company maintains relationships with clients – the longer the average relationship, the better the indication of a good employer.*
   - What they say and the way they say it (i.e. friendliness and level of enthusiasm for their employer) can be good indicators of the quality of the employer.

Good character - the single most important quality for a person to have in business.
- Seek professionals who have earned good reputations for trustworthiness, morality, responsibility, diligence, humility… the same character strengths that we talked about in Chapter 5 as being important for you to have as president of your business.
- You must be able to trust professional service providers to actually have the expertise and experience that they "profess" to have and to do what they say they can do.

Expertise - compared to her professional peers, how good is the person at what she does? Indicators of expertise might include:
- References - from people you know, her satisfied clients, and other professionals.
- In conversation, she exhibits:
  - o A well-rounded knowledge of current events, the arts, sports, etc. - typically a good indicator of a curious, intelligent mind that strives for professional expertise.
  - o A desire to take continuing education classes in order to gain greater professional expertise rather than taking classes just to earn the minimum continuing education credit hours required to maintain her professional license.
- Membership and participation in one or more trade associations:
  - o Membership in a trade association provides professionals with opportunities to gain expertise, refine their professional skills, and learn new and better ways to serve clients.
  - o Active participation often indicates an interest taking advantage of the opportunities to gain expertise.

Experience - seek professionals who have:
- A track record of maintaining relationships with satisfied clients over extended periods of time.
- Successfully guided clients through the tough times of at least one economic recession. The quality of good professionals tends to shine through during tough economic times.
- Clients who have life circumstances and financial positions similar to yours.

"Quantity doesn't guarantee quality" - years in business don't necessarily equate with quality of experience. Some professionals just repeat doing the same old things the same old way year after year. They don't practice their craft with a conscious intent to get better at their craft each year.

Regarding professional service providers who don't have much experience:
- Every one of today's all-star professional service providers started her career with few clients and little experience.
- Think about how baseball scouts have spotted all the prospects who eventually became major league all-stars. If you carefully scout prospective professional service providers you just might find a blue chip "rookie sensation" who can do a good job today while she is in the process of working her way toward becoming a future industry all-star.
- Some people are wise beyond their years.
- Some people are "naturals" – they are just plain good at their jobs soon after they start.
- A lack of calendar year experience can be outweighed by a combination of factors such as "natural" business smarts, common sense, great on-the-job mentoring by top quality professional colleagues, experience in other industries or military service, or experience gained in other facets of life (e.g. raising a family, volunteer work, leadership positions in school or on sports teams).
- A smart professional of any age or experience level typically will act as a "quarterback" who calls upon her colleagues and other business contacts as needed to provide any special expertise or experience that she may lack - she will "call in the reinforcements".
- Another personal rule of thumb: the more "generic" and less complicated a client's life circumstances, financial position, and professional service needs, the more likely that a "newbie" professional can offset her lack of experience by simply adhering to her industry's "best practices" and offering advice that is generally accepted as prudent within her profession.

"Best value" service provider
- *"Best value" in this book means an optimum combination of top quality services and fair price.*
- Top quality professionals typically know all about "best value" and adopt a best value strategy in their business plans.
- Ask professionals who you are thinking about hiring if they have adopted a best value strategy in their business plans. If they say yes, ask them how they define best value. Listen for qualities such as:
  - Top quality professional expertise.
  - Experience working with clients who have life circumstances roughly similar to yours, e.g. annual income, net worth, marital status, age, etc. Experience working with people in positions roughly similar to your position allows them to gain a more specialized expertise in matters relevant to people in your position.
  - *"Value added services"* - providing services over and above the specific services professionals are hired to provide.
    - Good professionals will try to get to know you and your objectives, and then proactively try to help you achieve your objectives.
    - Perhaps the most valuable value added service is to help protect you from yourself - to tell you things you may not want to hear but you need to hear, and to tell you when they think you are straying from your plan and budget. Providing such advice requires care and concern for client well-being, and it requires guts enough to risk angering a client and having the client terminate their relationship.
    - Another highly valuable value added service can be referrals to professionals in different professions as those services are needed.
  - Fair price for their services - reasonable, competitive, etc.

Fair price - best value service providers in each profession typically are:
- Business savvy enough to know the range of prices that competitors in the local market charge for comparable services.
  - *They typically charge somewhere in the mid-range of prices offered by competitors - not at the highest range of prices nor at the lowest range of prices - not too expensive, not too cheap, but just right – like in Little Red Riding Hood.*
  - They price their services fairly enough to retain their clients for many years.
- Self-confident enough about their track records of delivering best value services to charge a price their industry would consider fair for the value they deliver.
- Smart enough to have a pretty good idea how much the budget of a desirable client prospect could afford today, and how much future revenue that client prospect might generate over the years if the professional does her job well enough to retain the relationship.

A few thoughts to consider when evaluating pricing:
- *"You get what you pay for."*
- Be wary of cheap prices.
- Low prices tend to indicate lower levels of service – keep in mind a professional's dollar cost to provide her services and the lost opportunity cost of her time that she could be spending with other clients to generate revenue.
- Don't automatically equate best quality with most expensive.
- Consider the lost opportunity cost of the time you would need to invest, and aggravation you might endure, if you tried to do for yourself what a professional could do for you.

Network of top quality business contacts
- The quality of the people with whom a professional chooses to surround herself says a lot about her. Good people tend to associate with other good people.
- Networks of good professionals can help each of them become as good as they can each become at their professions by:
    - Providing each other good role models, good advice, and motivation.
    - Helping each other learn through their shared experience with mutual clients.
- Having a network of other top quality professionals will enable a professional to refer you to a person who has special expertise or experience as needed.

Business strategy that aligns with your strategy
- The closer that a professional's business strategy is aligned with your strategy:
    - The greater her motivation is likely to be to help you succeed.
    - The more likely you are to enjoy your business relationship.
    - The easier your management job is likely to be.
- Seek a professional who "practices what she preaches" and "walks her talk" – she lives her life the way she advises clients to live their lives, e.g. lives below her means, has a prudently unostentatious office, seeks to be nice to everyone.

Passion for doing her work
- The more that a person loves her job, the better the quality of work she is likely to do.
- If a professional doesn't sound and act like she loves her job, you might be better off not doing business with her.
- Beware doing business with anyone who you sense reluctantly accepted her job after being pressured into the job by a:
    - Family member who pulled her into the family business (nepotism).
    - Family member who pressured her to take the job for the money and/or prestige that the job could provide to that family member, e.g. "my daughter, the doctor".
    - Friend who pressured her to do what the friend does.

Good decision making ability, as evidenced by:
- A track record of success in business.
- The appearance of a happy, well-lived personal life.
- In conversation she:
    - Sees current events from a big picture, global perspective.
    - Demonstrates good common sense and street smarts.
- Maintaining her rational thinking composure in the face of challenging circumstances that might have caused other people to lose their composure and get emotional.

Good communication skills
- Uses clear, concise language that you understand.
- Avoids using industry jargon that you don't understand.
- Good listener who practices the "active listening" we discussed earlier so as to better understand you, your needs, your wants, your risk tolerance, etc.

Personality that you like - a person with whom you enjoy spending time.
- If you don't enjoy the person's company, it is less likely you will want to spend enough time with her to maximize her benefit to you as a professional service provider.
- You need to feel comfortable talking openly and honestly about your objectives,

preferences, risk tolerance, fears, worries, etc.

Try to avoid doing business with anyone who:
- Strikes you as too pushy – that is, she tries to push you into doing what she wants you to do rather than providing you with advice and recommendations and then allowing you to decide what you want to do.
    - There can be a fine line between being professionally adamant about what an advisor thinks is best for a client and being too pushy.
    - You might draw that fine line at having a comfortable feeling that you are being given enough latitude to make your own decision.
- Tries to make you feel obligated to do business with her, along the lines of "you owe me because of the time I have invested in you". You don't "owe" your business to anyone.

Professional certifications and designations
- Professional certifications and designations should be just one of the pre-qualification measures to use in choosing professional service providers.
- Professional certifications and designations do not necessarily indicate the capability of a professional to provide best value service.
    - Most professional certifications and designations are awarded based upon taking classes and passing tests – they are not based upon expertise as a practitioner applying classroom training to providing professional services and advice to clients in the real world.
    - Passing a test to get a license to practice her trade does not mean a professional is good at providing professional service.
    - During my career as a surety bond agent I have encountered many professionals who were book-smart enough to earn their educational degrees and get their professional certifications and designations, but who sorely lacked the business-smarts, street-smarts, common sense and/or communication skills that are needed to be good service providers and advisors.
    - Some professionals have walls full of diplomas and certificates, but they could hardly give a client good advice about how to cross the street successfully.
- Some professional service providers are just plain better than others at helping their clients succeed.

If a professional offers the name of a person to contact for a reference:
- Evaluate the qualifications of the person to provide a reference - that is, what qualifies the person to judge the character, expertise and experience of the professional?
- If a person providing a reference doesn't know much about what a good professional in a particular industry is supposed to do, the person has no frame of reference for evaluating how good the professional is in comparison to other professionals in her field.

"Caveat emptor" - buyer beware! I have had the opportunity to observe the work of a wide variety of professional service providers over the course of many years - CPA's, bankers, insurance agents, financial advisors, realtors, attorneys, etc.
- Many, many good professionals have provided their clients immeasurable help in achieving their objectives, but a few not so good professionals have played a big role in creating nasty problems for their clients.

Hiring a financial advisor

Two types of professional financial management help you might consider hiring:
- *Mutual fund company(s)*: a reputable mutual fund company does virtually all the work for you after you decide in which of their mutual funds you want to invest.
- *Investment advisor (a/k/a financial planner)*: to advise and assist in preparing a financial plan, and advise you on specific investment decisions; also an advisor will typically buy, sell, and hold investment securities for you.

If you decide that hiring a financial advisor would be prudent, "hire" a "registered investment advisor" who has a "fiduciary duty" to act in your best interest, not her best interest!
- *Registered investment advisors* must register with the United States Government Securities and Exchange Commission or a state's securities commission. They are regulated as to the advice they provide.
- *Fiduciary duty* means that a person has a legal obligation to offer you advice that is in your best interest, not hers.
  - o Not all professionals who offer financial advice have a fiduciary duty to offer advice that is in your best interest and not in their best interest.
  - o Research the term "fiduciary duty" to make sure you understand what it means, and the benefits of working with a person who has a legal duty to look out for your best interests rather than her own.

The type and number of prospective financial advisors from whom you can choose will be a function of your desirability as a client. Your desirability will be based upon factors such as:
- Each financial advisor's business plan.
  - o Put yourself in the shoes of each prospective advisor. Try to understand how each prospective advisor perceives your ability to help her achieve her business plan objectives.
  - o The advisor's need for new clients. The more she needs new clients, the more desirable you would likely be as a new client.
- Income she thinks you have the potential to generate for her today, and the income you might be able to generate for her in the years to come – how profitable you might be as a client.
- Your financial position:
  - o Your current "investable assets" (cash and other liquid assets you have available to invest). *The more money you have available to invest, the more desirable you are likely to be as a new client.*
    - ▪ Prospective clients having investable assets under $100,000 are desirable to certain advisors.
    - ▪ Prospective clients having investable assets in the range of $101,000 to $1,000,000 are desirable to many more advisors.
    - ▪ Prospective clients having investable assets greater than $1,000,000 are desirable to most advisors.
  - o Your current annual income coupled with her estimate of your potential future annual income - which serve as indicators of the money the advisor can reasonably project you will have available to invest in the future.
- The financial advisor's personal perception of your potential as:

- o A source of referrals to prospective new clients. The greater the number of desirable prospective new clients she thinks you might refer to her, the more desirable you would become as a client.
- o As a client with whom she would enjoy working:
  - Co-operative nature – you would be open to taking the advice she gave you).
  - Pleasing personality - the nicer you come across as being, the more desirable you are likely to be.

Perhaps the best way to find a good financial advisor is to ask for recommendations from those people in your network of business contacts who you think have a track record of making good decisions in their lives and who appear to have had success in managing their investments.

Ask each person who provides a recommendation for the reasons she recommended that particular financial advisor:
- First-hand experience as a satisfied client of the advisor?
- Second-hand reports from people they know who are satisfied clients of the advisor?
- Knowledge of the advisor gained by virtue of a "cross-referral" business relationship (they refer each other business), or being a friend, neighbor, or member of the same community service organization?

Another way to find financial advisor prospects is to use the financial advisor "finder" tools that financial planning professional trade associations have on their websites, such as:
- Financial Planning Association (FPA)
- National Association of Personal Financial Advisors (NAPFA)
- Personal Financial Planning section, American Institute of Certified Public Accountants
- www.letsmakeaplan.com (Certified Financial Planners)

Interview each prospective advisor. Questions you might ask include:
- *If she has a fiduciary duty* to put your best interests before hers.
- If she does have a fiduciary duty, ask her:
  - o How she defines fiduciary duty.
  - o How she manages the risk of "conflict of interest" - the breach of fiduciary duty that would arise if she advised you to buy an investment product that would generate greater compensation for her, rather than advising you to buy another investment that more appropriately fit your financial plan but would generate less compensation for her.
- *How she is compensated.* Make sure you understand all forms of direct and indirect compensation she would receive. Her compensation might be one of these methods or a combination of several methods:
  - o Fee:
    - Annual fee computed as a percentage of the dollar value of your investment portfolio. *A significant benefit of advisors compensated by means of an annual fee is that the greater the net worth they can help their clients accumulate, the more fee income they can earn.*
    - Hourly fee
    - Lump sum fixed fee
  - o Commission paid on each purchase and/or sale of securities, annuities, insurance, etc.
  - o Residual commissions or bonuses paid on sales made in prior years.

- o   Salary.
- o   Performance bonus based upon sales revenue or profit generated for her employer.
- Why she thinks her method of compensation is best for her clients.
- What she knows about behavioral economics and behavioral finance - fields of study that deal with how you might actually behave with your money despite what you say you will do with your money. It is important for a financial advisor to have a good understanding of behavioral economics and behavioral finance in order to help you protect yourself from doing things with your money that might cause you financial harm.

In regard to the cost of hiring a financial advisor:
- *Focus on the bottom line net return you receive,* not the top line gross price you pay - the dollar amount growth of your net worth AFTER paying all fees and expenses.
- Think about the mistakes you have made with money in the past, and how the services of an advisor might help you protect you from making costly financial mistakes in the future - a "priceless" service.

Chapter 10. Managing Your Business

Get organized

Create an office for your business in your home.
- Designate a specific place within your home to be your "office space".
- An office doesn't need to be an entire room. Many a company has been started at a kitchen table.
- Your office space could be just a corner in a room where you can gather your business things and sit on the floor to do your work.

If you live with family or roommates, let them know that when you are working in your "office" you would appreciate it if they did not disturb you– just as many people do when they are working remotely from home at their "9 to 5" jobs.

Office equipment that would be helpful:
- Flat surface on which to do your work - card table, kitchen table, desk, etc.
- Chair.
- Container in which to store your paper records, e.g. file cabinet or cardboard box.
- Telephone.
- Computer and/or other electronic device(s):
    - Explore all the ways you can use these tools to help manage your company.
    - Learn how to use the online account management tools your bank and other financial service providers offer.

Gather together all your financial records in your office space, such as:
- Checkbook and register.
- Credit card purchase receipts.
- Receipts for "big ticket" (large dollar) purchases.
- Monthly statements from banks, credit card companies, mutual funds and stockbrokers.
- Income and income tax papers, e.g. pay stubs, W-2 and Form 1099 forms, tax returns, deductible expense receipts.
- Employee benefit papers, e.g. retirement account, flexible spending accounts.
- Insurance policies.
- Copies of legal documents, e.g. mortgage, automobile title, will, family trust, living will, medical power of attorney (store the originals of legal documents in a safe deposit box if your budget can afford it).
- Social Security benefit statements received from the Government.
- Your business plan and projected financial statement budget.
- Your management reports, e.g. financial statements, schedule of your IRA contributions.
- Electronic files stored on your electronic devices.

Give your company a name.
- *Naming your company will help you visualize yourself as the owner and president of your personal financial management company.*
- Set up your company's books and records using your company's name. Each time you see your company's name you will reinforce your thinking that your money is your business.

Suggestions for managing your business

Management *is a pro-actively planned and coordinated process that seeks to control people and events for the purpose of accomplishing objectives (as opposed to a series of "one-off" spur-of-the-moment actions and reactions to events).* Each management decision should be informed by your prior decisions, guided by your plan, and advance you toward achieving your objectives.

Different managers combine different elements in their management process, but most good managers incorporate many of the same elements in their management process, such as:
- Using written business plans and projected financial statement budgets.
- Surrounding themselves with a team of good people.
- Leading team members with a combination of leadership techniques that suits the manager's personality, the people being led, and the situation at the moment (see the next section for more about leadership).
- Delegating responsibility and authority to each team member to achieve agreed upon objectives, and holding each team member accountable for achieving his objectives.
- Establishing a behavioral control system (called "internal controls" in the business world) to help coordinate and control the performance of team members.
- Providing coaching, counseling, and mentoring to help each team member achieve his objectives and improve his future performance.
- Conducting regular performance reviews with team members.

FAMILY and FRIENDS on your business team should NOT be "managed" in the same way that you manage employees at work nor the way you manage service providers you pay (see Chapter 16, Money, Love & Family).
- When "managing" the behavior of family and friends be judicious in using the ideas about management presented in this book.
- <u>Don't try to micro-manage your life nor the people in it</u> – if you did it is likely you would drive yourself nuts and drive away the people closest to you.
- Find a prudent middle ground between "laissez-faire" management (letting your life just unfold without direction) and obsessive efforts to control everyone and everything in your life (being a "control freak").

"Stay focused like a laser on your plan." This is common advice offered by business consultants because it is so easy for us to get diverted from our plans and budgets.
- Our emotions can get the better of our rational thinking and lead us to forget what we planned to do and to do things without thinking about what we are doing.
- Unexpected events and being manipulated by other people can:
  - o Cause us to do things we hadn't planned to do.
  - o Divert us from doing things we had planned to do.

Suggestions that can help you stay focused on your plan:
- *Read your plan and budget frequently enough to keep them fixed in your mind.*
- Plan objectives and strategies that make you feel good. We tend to think about and do things we enjoy, and avoid thinking about and doing things we don't enjoy.
- Surround yourself with good people who have enough care and concern for your well-being to tell you when they see you veering away from what they know about your plan, and doing things that they don't think are good for you to do.

Develop a contingency Plan B for what you could do if Plan A for the significant things in your life (e.g. your job) wasn't working out as you had planned.
- *Well-reasoned plans that look great on paper don't always work out in practice.*
- There are precious few "sure things" in life and financial management.
- "Nothing is guaranteed but death and taxes."

The better the character and capability of the people on your business team, the easier it will be to manage them.
- Character: the more you can trust people to do what they say they can do and will do, the less time and effort you will need to spend supervising their performance.
- Capability: the better the expertise and experience of people at doing what you expect him to do, the less time and effort you will need to spend training and coaching them.

Develop a behavioral control system (internal control system) to help manage the performance of your business team and yourself. Behavioral controls are important because:
- Managers must temper their optimism and trust in people with pragmatic realism in order to manage the risk of human weaknesses.
- Everybody makes mistakes.
- Good people sometimes crack under pressure and their performance suffers.
- People don't always do what they say they will do – people sometimes forget, get swamped by other work, change their minds, or "promise more than they can deliver" (they can't really do what they say they can do).
- Some people lie, cheat, steal, embezzle, commit fraud …

An internal control system will help you:
- Provide an environment that encourages good people to do their best.
- Minimize the temptation for good people to do not such good things.
- Keep honest people honest.
- Prevent less honest people from doing the bad things they are capable of doing.

Good business people typically know a lot about internal control systems. Ask the experienced business people on your team for advice about how to set up and use your internal control system.
- Pick their brains about the internal control systems they use.
- Discuss news stories about financial misfortunes caused by professional service providers and ask for advice about how to prevent similar things from happening to you, e.g. Bernard Madoff defrauding investors, agents for athletes and celebrities who embezzled money from their clients, mortgage brokers who worked with mortgage lenders to make money by providing mortgages that shouldn't have been approved.

"Standard operating procedures" (SOP's) should be one element in your internal control system.
- A standard operating procedure is a set of steps to take to do a specific thing or to respond to specific occurrences – a checklist of steps that you and your business team members can commit to memory, i.e. "how we do things in this company".
- Each component step of an SOP can be practiced in order to get better at doing it.
- SOP's can be revised as you learn how things might be done better based upon experience, advice you receive, observation of people who are good at doing a particular thing, etc.
- Actual performance can be measured against performance step "standards" set in SOP's.

A system of "checks and balances" should be another element in your internal control system.
- Setting up a system of checks and balances entails splitting up job duties among different business team members so that no one person does everything for you, and everybody knows that other people are observing their behavior.
- *Checks*
    o Divide primary responsibility for doing different things among different people so that no one person could cause you devastating financial harm (e.g. spouse to serve as executive vice president, financial advisor to help with investment management, tax expert to prepare your taxes, attorney to handle legal matters, close friends and relatives to serve as an "audit committee" to keep a watchful eye on you and your business).
    o Each of your team members will know that other people are "<u>checking</u>" on his behavior - what he is doing or not doing.
    o Team members can provide you with constructive critique and advice regarding the behavior of other team members.
- *Balances*
    o Different people can provide advice and recommendations from their different perspectives so that you get "<u>balanced</u>" input for consideration in making your decisions.
    o If one person's advice regarding a significant decision "fly's in the face" of advice received from other team members, that person's advice wouldn't carry enough weight to sway your decision (at least not without gathering additional decision making information).

Maintaining regular contact with team members should be another element in your internal control system. Regular contact would provide you opportunities to:
- Deepen your relationship with each team member, which would likely help strengthen each person's sense of loyalty and personal responsibility for your well-being.
- Remind each person that you are counting on him to do his best.
- Remind each person that you are keeping a watchful eye on his performance.

Personal performance controls should be another element. A few suggestions:
- Adopt a formal business planning and projected financial statement budgeting process.
- Read your plan and budget frequently enough to keep them fixed in your mind.
- Adopt a formal decision making process to guide your decision making (see Chapter 7).
- Before deciding to do anything involving a significant amount of money:
    o Make sure of your motivation – why you want to buy it, do it, or invest in it.
    o Re-read your written business plan and budget, and think about how the proposed action would fit into your plan and budget.
    o Discuss the situation with at least one business savvy confidant who you think has a track record of making good decisions in his life.
    o Sleep on it. Try to avoid snap decisions on significant matters.
- Tell each team member that you want him to:
    o Provide you with constructive critique of your performance.
    o Tell you things he might think you might think are "bad news" – news that he might think you wouldn't want to hear. Be sure each person understands that you consider "bad news" to be critically important news that you need to hear in order to change behavior that would be prudent to change, or to revise your plan or budget as needed in order to achieve your objectives.
    o Tell you as soon as he thinks you might be starting to veer away from your plan.

- Periodically ask your team members how they think you might be able to do things better, and what, if any, new things you might try doing.
- Set up automatic electronic processing of regularly scheduled financial transactions to help minimize your risk of human error:
    o Direct deposit of salary or wages.
    o Transfer cash from checking account to savings account after direct deposit of paycheck.
    o Payment of monthly bills such as utilities and credit card balances.
- Create and maintain internal management reports to track your performance.

Beware the risk of overextending your resources - your time, money, personal skills, etc. (and overextending the capabilities of business team members to do work you ask them to do).
- Overextension may be the most frequent cause of business failure.
- Plan to do "*first things first*".
    o First, allocate your resources so as to achieve your highest priority objectives.
    o Then, allocate the remainder of your resources to your lower priority objectives.
- *Beware "executive burnout"*. Don't fry your brain by trying to accomplish too much too soon.
    o "You can only stretch a rubber band so far before it breaks."
    o "You can only do what you can do."
    o "All good things in time."

"Manage by exception"
- Management by exception occurs when a manager seeks to limit his active involvement in the duties of his team members to those exceptional times when situations dictate that he must get involved. The idea is for a manager to "work his way out of his job" to the greatest extent possible.
- Management by exception is the polar opposite of "micro-management" (being a control freak).
- Effective management by exception requires that a manager:
    o Surround himself with good people who have the expertise, experience, and motivation to do what they are expected to do.
    o Make sure those good people understand what the manager expects them to do.
    o Delegate as much responsibility and authority to team members as the manager can reasonably expect them to handle.
    o Let people do their jobs.
    o Have a prudent internal control system that alerts him to those exceptional situations in which he should get involved.
- Management by exception can provide two significant benefits:
    o Free up time for you to spend doing more of the things you desire to do.
    o Prepare your business team to step in and assume your duties as president of your company if you should ever become physically or mentally impaired to perform those duties yourself (see Chapter 17, "Develop a business continuity plan").

Seek to know as much as you can about what is going in on in each team member's head – to understand his perspective on his life, life in general, and his role on your business team.
- Seek to know "what makes each team member tick" - "where he's coming from" – his needs and wants, objectives, things he likes to do, things he doesn't like to do, what motivates him, biases, pressures and constraints he feels, etc.
- *Have empathy*: "put yourself in the other person's shoes." Try to see the world and your

relationship from each team member's point of view ("through his eyes"). Seek to understand as best you can the factors that lead each person to think, feel and act the way he does. Be sensitive to each person's needs and wants.

- *Have sympathy* for pressures and constraints each person might feel he is under.

Communicate clearly.

- Clearly communicate what you want team members to do, e.g. objectives to achieve.
  - o People need to understand what you want them to do if they are to do it.
  - o Confirm that people understand what you want them to do (one way is to ask them to repeat back to you in their own words what they think you want and expect them to do).
- Keep open lines of communication that make people feel comfortable telling you what is on their minds. Maintain an "open door policy".

Each person on your team needs to know enough about your plan and budget to do the work you expect him to do – BUT - everybody doesn't need to know everything.

- *Use "need to know" and common sense as guidelines* for the appropriate amount of information to share with each team member.
- Your spouse should know pretty much everything about you, your financial position, and your plans for your life and money. As a general rule, secrets are not good for marriages.
- Your financial advisor should know everything about your financial position and risk tolerance, and enough about your plan to help you achieve your objectives
- Children need to know enough to do what you expect them to do. The amount of information provided to a child should be appropriate to the child's age, maturity level, behavior expected of him, and ability to keep confidences.
- Other business team members (relatives, friends and neighbors, co-workers, professionals you hire, etc.) might need to know anywhere from very little to a whole lot about your business plan and budget, and perhaps your financial position - dependent upon the roles you want them to play as team members.

Coordinate team member activities.

- Let team members know who else is on your team, the role you envision each person playing on your team, and how you envision team members coordinating their work with each other.
- As appropriate for the role you envision each team member playing, keep him informed about what other team members have been doing and advising you to do.
- Ask team members for their thoughts about how you might improve the coordination of their activities and achieve greater synergy.

Motivate team members.

- The leadership style you adopt will be a key factor in the way you motivate your team members. See the next section "Be the leader".
- *Create an environment in which people want to do what you would like them to do.*
- *Make working with you an enjoyable experience.* People tend to be motivated to do their best work when they enjoy what they are doing.
  - o Try to create an excitement / fun factor for your business team members.
  - o Use your sense of humor to set a tone of joy that encourages people to have fun working with you.
  - o Don't take yourself too seriously. Let folks see that you can laugh at your human weaknesses while you are continuously striving to achieve your objectives.

Be a nice person who is easy to like and respect.
- It will easier to manage people if they like you and respect you.
- Liking and respecting a manager helps trigger the internal motivation in good people to try their hardest to do their best for their manager.
- Keep in mind the lessons your parents tried to teach about "playing nice". Those lessons carry over to the business world as people play the game of business. Practice the civil behavior you learned from parents, teachers, coaches, religious leaders and all the other elders in your community as you were growing up.

On the flip side, people are capable of doing nasty stuff when they don't like or respect their manager.
- Passive stuff
  - Do as little as they can get away with doing.
  - Don't speak up about incorrect things that they spot.
- Aggressive stuff
  - Do whatever they can to "make him pay" for whatever they don't like about him.
  - Sabotage their manager's performance.

Say "please" and "thank you". Smart managers know that in addition to being good manners, the words please and thank you are powerful motivators, and they cost nothing to say. <u>Good manners are good business.</u>
- *Please*: asking people to "please help me with …" taps into their human instinct to help a person in need of help.
- *Thank you*: people like to be recognized for their good work. Many people will work harder for a heartfelt "thank you" than they will for money.

Be trust worthy. *The foundation of business is the trust we have in each other.* People need to trust that you will be honest with them, do what you say you will do, as well as do what good ethics and laws say you should do. Good business people like to work with trustworthy people with whom they feel they could do business on a handshake (if their attorneys would allow them).
- *If you promise to do something, do it*. If you don't have the time or ability to do something, be honest up front and say you don't. Good business people don't like to be "stiffed". And, they have memories like elephants. "Let your word be your bond."
- *If you are asked a question and you don't know the answer, just say "I don't know. I'll find out and get back to you."* Good people respect that type of honesty.
- Be a straight shooter. Don't tell a person what you think he may want to hear if it isn't what you actually think. "Honesty is the best policy." Say what you actually think in a calm, considerate, respectful, and tactful way.
- Protect your good reputation. Don't lie, cheat or steal. Think about these two questions:
  - Would it be "backdoor stealing" if you knew a store clerk had given you more product than you paid for, or more change than you deserved on a cash purchase, and you didn't tell the clerk he had made a mistake?
  - Would you do business with a person if you had any reason to think he might try to take advantage of you ("not do right by you")?

Seek win-win decisions.
- "What goes around comes around."
  - A win-win decision typically makes you and the people impacted by your decision think that you came out winners.

- o   People who feel that you did your best to make win-win decisions that helped them are likely to be motivated to reciprocate by making win-win decisions that help you come out a winner in their future decisions.
- During the information gathering step of your decision making process, learn as much as you can about who is likely to be impacted by your decision (spending as much of your time and resources as prudent for the magnitude of the decision).
- As you develop decision options from which you could choose, consider the wisdom of developing a compromise option when there are differences in needs or wants - consider giving up some of what you want in order to get most of what you want.
    - o   Some people say that the best compromises occur when each party thinks that he gave up a little too much in order to get the deal done.
    - o   Keep in mind that success in life typically is not gained all at once. Success is typically gained as the result of good outcomes to a long, long series of decisions.
- *After you have identified and evaluated your decision options, lean toward choosing the win-win option which would generate the greatest good for the most people.*
- Seeking the greatest good for the most people impacted by our decisions typically makes us feel good, and that feel-good feeling helps generate a positive energy that helps power our efforts to do the best we can to achieve our objectives.
- Avoid win-lose decisions, e.g. "it's all about me and what I can get from you".
    - o   People who feel they lost typically try to avoid losing a second time. This is bad for maintaining relationships with the type of good people with whom you should be seeking long term relationships.
    - o   People who feel they lost are not likely to try to help you in the future, and they might try to get even or hurt you.

Manage the mistakes team members make. The suggestions below pretty much echo the thoughts offered in Chapter 5 about managing your own mistakes.
- If you think a mistake has been made, don't do anything until you get yourself into an emotionally calm, rational thinking business mindset.
- Then, clearly identify exactly what mistake you think was made, be it an error of commission (doing something) or omission (not doing something), and exactly who you think made the mistake.
- Then confirm that a mistake was actually made by the person you think made it. Sometimes things aren't actually what they appear to be at first.
- If a mistake was indeed made:
    - o   Don't blow up at the person who made the mistake.
    - o   Analyze what happened and why it happened.
    - o   Depending upon the gravity of the mistake, the position you are in after the mistake, and the time you have available to consider your options as to what to do (if anything), ask at least one confidant for his thoughts about what to do.
    - o   Forgive the person. "To err is human, to forgive divine." If correction is possible, forgiveness will help motivate the person to do all he can do to help correct his mistake and do better the next time. Forgiving the person will also help keep your mind in control of your emotions.
    - o   Find a lesson to learn. Determine what you can do to help prevent that person or any other team member from making the same mistake again in the future.
    - o   *Find a way to laugh about it. Sooner or later we wind up laughing at most mistakes. Make it sooner.* Laughter and forgiveness can combine to create powerful restorative medicine for rational thinking.
    - o   *"Don't throw good money after bad."* If the mistake was just the most recent in a

series of mistakes the person has made, <u>and</u> that series of mistakes was caused by pretty much the same type behavior that you two have discussed in the past, <u>and</u> the person hasn't demonstrated much effort to change his behavior, think about how your relationship might need to be changed or terminated in order to protect yourself and minimize the risk of future mistakes.

- Revise your business plan as needed.
- Put the mistake behind you and move on.

Be proactive.
- When you identify a situation that irks you, or behavior that you don't think is good and proper, plan how you can resolve the situation yourself or how you can mobilize other people to help you resolve the situation, and then take action on your plan.
- Don't just gripe about things that bother you - in the news, in your community, etc.
  - o "Get up out of your chair" and do something about things that bother you.
  - o Don't just sit stewing about it and leave it to "the other guy" to do something.
  - o If we each contribute our fair share of effort, we can make the world a better place in which to live and work, and to achieve financial prosperity.

If you become dissatisfied with someone, "get it up on the table" and get your dissatisfaction resolved as soon as possible.
- Don't keep dissatisfaction a secret. When you are dissatisfied with someone's general behavior or something specific he did or didn't do, say so.
- Communicate your concern in a calm, civil manner aimed at reaching a reasonable resolution of your dissatisfaction.
  - o Don't "get in anyone's face" or "raise your voice".
  - o If you feel your emotions may be influencing your rational thinking, wait to talk things out until you have full control of your rational thinking mind.
  - o The person may not have had a clue that you were dissatisfied. But if he had "picked up vibrations" that you weren't happy with him, he may very well feel relieved to finally talk about your perception of whatever he was or was not doing.
- In the context of managing your life and your money, rid your mind of negativity you might have attached to the term "confronting" someone.
  - o In management, confronting someone simply means telling a person that you are dissatisfied with what he has or has not been doing, and that you would like to "work it out".
  - o In management, confronting a person does not mean getting into a verbal fight.
- Ignoring less than desired behavior does nothing to improve it.
  - o The longer you ignore a behavior problem, the more time you give it to fester and hurt you.
  - o Don't let "a molehill grow into a mountain."
  - o "Nip it in the bud."
- There are two sides to every story. It might be best to concisely explain why you are dissatisfied and then ask the other person for his side of the story. It is likely that each of you will get valuable feedback about how you can work together to improve the current situation and avoid similar situations in the future.
- It can be pretty darn tough for some of us to speak up about what's bothering us. It gets easier with practice.

The greater the impact that a person's behavior can have on your life and your money, the more critical it will be to get your dissatisfaction resolved as soon as possible. Following are a few hypothetical situations and suggestions you might consider for resolving the situations:

- *Excessive spending of a family member*: review together the level of detail he had about the family budget and whatever agreement you two had about how he would help manage "family money" (i.e. your money). Work out a plan for him to do his part to bring the family budget back in line (perhaps read together relevant parts of Chapter 16).
- *Your perception of the way your supervisor at work is treating you*: <u>AFTER becoming confidant that you can talk openly and honestly with your supervisor</u> (see Chapter 14) you might try explaining your dissatisfaction as tactfully as possible. You might discover your boss wasn't aware of your dissatisfaction. While you are at it, you might ask your supervisor for his perception of your working relationship. You might get some valuable feedback about how your performance was influencing the way he was treating you
- *Unsatisfactory quality of service provided by a professional service provider*: tactfully explain to the professional why you have become dissatisfied. Good professionals want feedback from their clients as a means of learning how they might improve the quality of the professional services they provide.
- *Unsatisfactory quality of a product*: tell the sales person, retailer, and/or manufacturer about your dissatisfaction. Good businesspeople will typically say something like "thank you for bringing this to my attention" and ask "how can we make things right for you?"

Settle legal disputes out of court whenever possible.
- *"Nobody wins in court except the attorneys"* say most of the good attorneys I know.
- No matter how strongly you might feel that you were wronged, it might be best to try to negotiate a settlement rather than going to court.
- Don't let your emotions drive you into court. Beware:
  - Anger - "he's not going to get away with that".
  - Hurt pride - "I'll make him pay for making me feel like a fool".
  - Revenge - "I'll get him for that".
- Litigation can be expensive in three ways:
  - In money: attorney fees, court costs, uncompensated time away from work, etc.
  - In the lost opportunity cost of precious time: court cases almost always drag out longer than people expect them to last, and there are a lot better things to do in life than be tied up in a lawsuit.
  - In the toll taken on a person's life while legal proceedings are dragging out.
    - Like a sour lemon, litigation can suck the sweet joy out of a person's life.
    - It's tough to stay up in a positive frame of mind while the negative weight of a court fight is pulling a person's spirit down.
- Smart business people typically try to negotiate settlements rather than going to court. A number of times business owners have told me:
  - They had never been to court before.
  - How much the experience of going to court for the first time had sapped out of them personally and out of their companies.
  - How much they regretted having gone to court this one time.
  - That they would do whatever they could in the future to avoid having to go to court again.
- Good business people typically try to avoid doing business with people they perceive to be "litigious" - litigious meaning a person is more likely than most people to choose to go to court to settle a dispute rather than trying to negotiate an amicable settlement. A reputation for being litigious typically repels the type of good people with whom you should be trying to do business.

Be the leader

Lead.
- To lead means to motivate people to do what the leader wants them to do.
- *As president of your company, your job is to lead your business team to help you accomplish your objectives using a strategy that you would like them to use.*
- *Everything that happens, and doesn't happen, with the money in your life is your responsibility as president*.
- President Harry Truman said it concisely "The buck stops here." As President of the United States of America, Truman had a team of cabinet secretaries, advisors, and staffers to help him run the Government, but he made clear that he was the leader, that it was his responsibility to make the big picture decisions about what the Government did, and his responsibility to lead his team to accomplish the objectives he put forth.

Don't worry if you never thought of yourself as a leader.
- It's easy to be a leader. We all have it in us.
- *We are all "born leaders."* As babies and little kids we all learned techniques for leading our parents to do what we wanted them to do for us.
- If you tend toward the shy side, take heart in the fact that many of the best leaders exercise subtly quiet styles of leadership. Their leadership ability becomes more apparent the more that people interact with them.

Every leader has a different leadership style, but most good leaders tend to blend the following elements into their leadership styles.
- *Lead by example*: be a good role model of planning, budgeting, and decision making. Act the way you would like people to act, and do things the way you would like people to do them. Your business team members are likely to follow your lead.
- *Educate*: train/teach/describe/demonstrate how you would like things done. After good people learn how you want things done, they can do those things your way without being told exactly what to do - they can lead themselves with the least amount of your time and effort spent supervising them.
- *Use reason*: explain the reasons why it makes good sense to do what you want done; and in situations where it applies, explain how helping you achieve your objectives can help a team member achieve his objectives, perhaps situations such as:
  - *With your children*: "the more we save, the more money we will have in the future to pay for great vacations and to help pay for your choice of schools".
  - *With professional service providers*: "if you do right by me, I'll be your client until you retire, and I'll refer new clients to you as opportunities present themselves".
- *Inspire*: appeal to people's higher instinct. Explain how your objectives are intended to achieve "the greatest good for all" using strategies based upon high ideals. This will help people feel good about doing what you want done and feeling good is a strong motivator.
- *Tap into people's internal motivation*: put self-starters on your team who have an internal drive to do their best at whatever they attempt to do. Then stimulate their internal drive by delegating enough responsibility AND authority to get done what you want done. Delegating will require you to let go of some control, and letting go can be real tough for many people to do. But, if you have assembled a team of good people, and trust them enough, and let go enough, you free them up to do the good things they are predisposed to do. Of course, protect yourself with the type of behavioral control system we discussed a few pages back.

- *Build team spirit*, "esprit de corps": people typically try their hardest to do what their leader wants them to do when they think of themselves as a valued member of a team. They don't want to let down their leader and their teammates.
- *Reward*: expectation of reward can be a strong motivator. "A carrot is better than a stick". "You can attract more flies with honey than with vinegar." Different people are motivated to differing degrees by different types of reward, such as:
  - o Job satisfaction: put people in positions to do what they enjoy doing.
  - o Recognition: a heartfelt thank you or pat on the back.
  - o Money: often the least effective motivator of good people.
- *Authority conveyed by position* (power of position): your position as the "superior" in a relationship such as parent-child, supervisor-employee, client-service provider, or customer-salesperson, gives you the authority to direct the behavior of your "subordinates" in those relationships.
  - o Use the authority of your position as gently and tactfully as the situation at hand allows. One typically effective way for a leader to use the authority that a position confers is to suggest to a team member that he do what the leader wants done – smart subordinates will typically "get the message" to do what the leader suggests. Another effective means of asserting authority might be to raise your voice just enough to convey the importance of doing something.
  - o People in subordinate positions know you are the superior in the relationship - children know you are the parent, employees know you are the supervisor, salespeople and service providers know it is your money and you are the customer or client - and nobody likes to feel subordinate.
  - o Keep the authority to give orders in your hip pocket. Pull it out only when you absolutely must, such as to give an order to resolve serious differences of opinion that can't be settled by reasoning or negotiation, or in times of crisis management when decisions must be made and action must be taken immediately.
  - o Be extremely careful about giving orders such as "Do it because I said so." People don't like to be ordered. And, sometimes orders goad people into negative behavior such as rebelling (by children) or quitting (by people you pay).
  - o It is more effective to start out as the leader in a superior-subordinate relationship by being firm and then lightening up, than it is to start out with lax leadership and then trying to toughen up.
  - o Some business team members may try to test your authority, especially if they mistake your polite tact for weakness. If a team member does try to test your authority, immediately remind him that you are the leader and that you expect his support (in a tone of voice appropriate to the situation).
    - ▪ As your personality dictates, tactfully demonstrate that you have a strong "back bone" and that you intend to remain in control.
    - ▪ A classic example: high school students are famous for testing how much they can get away with when they have a substitute teacher. Students can get totally out of control when they sense that a timid substitute doesn't have the nerve to assert his authority of position as their teacher.

Power/force/fear - threatening a person - the proverbial stick in the "carrot and the stick", e.g. "If you don't do what I tell you to do, then you'll suffer the consequences."
- Threatening people with some type of harm – a financial, physical, or other "do it or else" threat - should be used only in specific situations that require its use as a *last resort when there is no alternative*, e.g. if a child does something exceptionally dangerous a second or third time, if an employee repeats doing or not doing something that could cause anyone

serious harm, or if immediate action is needed to respond to an emergency.
- Threats raise emotions, and you can never be sure of exactly how an emotionally charged person might react. It might just be a nasty reaction that hurts you badly. People might seek revenge, intentionally botch a job, quit in the middle of an important job, or sabotage you in ways you couldn't even imagine.
- If you start to think you may need to use the stick of a threat:
  o Be sure you can back up your threat by making happen whatever you say will happen.
  o Be prepared to carry out your threat – *don't make empty threats*. If you fail to carry out your threat then future threats are much less likely to be taken seriously. A classic example: a parent who threatens to ground a child for a month and then rolls over and makes an exception the very next day. Kids pick up on empty threats real fast, and they are likely to begin running right over parents who make empty threats and put "tire tracks on their parents' backs".

Let your leadership style flow from your personality. Be yourself. People can sense a phony who is trying to lead in a way that doesn't come naturally to the leader, and they don't respond to a phony as well as they do to a leader who leads from his own natural strengths.

Give strong consideration to developing a <u>humbly</u> <u>assertive</u> leadership style.
- If you tend toward being aggressively assertive, work on the humble part.
- If you tend toward being shy and retiring, work on the assertive part.
- In either case, emanate inner strength driven by confidence in yourself as a good person who has a well-reasoned business plan to do well financially by doing good for others.
- *Talk in terms of "we" more than "I".*
- *Politely ask people for their help,* e.g. "Will you please help me with this?"
- *Politely suggest what you would like people to do,* e.g. "How about if we do this?" And as an added benefit, politely suggesting a course of action leaves the door open for people to give you feedback as to what they think might be a better thing to do.
- As time and circumstances permit, *ask people for their advice and recommendations* as to what they think should be done to accomplish your objectives. Two powerful benefits of asking for advice and recommendations:
  o People might suggest a better idea.
  o People develop a sense of ownership in ideas they suggest, and that sense of ownership can be a powerful motivator for them to do their best at whatever they suggest.

Situational leadership - in certain situations it might be best to:
- *Emphasize different elements of your leadership style with different people,* e.g. your spouse (in the context of the family business), your children, paid professionals on your team, and people in physical danger during a hurricane.
- *Delegate leadership in specific situations to people who have greater expertise or experience* than you have in those specific situations:
  o For example, you might delegate leadership in financial planning to a professional financial advisor, or delegate leadership in the purchase and use of electronic equipment in your home to your children who are mature enough to handle that leadership responsibility (within the limits of a budget you provide them).
  o Keep in mind that after you delegate leadership responsibility to people, you, as president, retain ultimate leadership responsibility for their performance. Like a

ship's captain in the midst of a long voyage who delegates to a local harbor pilot the task of bringing his ship in to dock in a specific harbor along the way, you continue to be responsible for the course of your life after you let others take the wheel in specific situations.

A leader must stand up for himself when he has no alternative but to deal with aggressively dominant Type A personalities who try to get him do things he hadn't planned to do, or do things he doesn't think are in his best interest.

- *Keep in mind that <u>you are president</u> of your business.* Don't let a dominant person usurp your authority as president of your company to lead your life where you want it to go.
- Don't let anyone tell you what to do with your life or your money.
- Don't let yourself be intimidated or bullied into doing something that you don't think is in your best interest.

Despite your best efforts to avoid pushy, self-centered egotists it is likely that on occasion you will have no alternative but to deal with some of them - possibly a manager at work, a relative, or a neighbor. Don't let anybody intimidate you with:

- Shear strength of dominating personality.
- Loud voice and/or imposing physical size – someone who tries to impose his will on people with an attitude of "I'm the big dog in this pack".
- Physical symbols of wealth and success, e.g. power suits, fancy jewelry, luxury car.
- Dropping names of powerful "big shots" they know, e.g. "I was just having lunch with so-and-so" or "my client so-and-so".
- Bragging about how good he is at what he does, or all he has accomplished in life, or all the honors he has received.
- The power of his position, such as by a manager at work (see Chapter 14).

One way to build up your mental strength to stand up for yourself is to practice using a humbly assertive leadership style. Like an athlete gaining muscle strength through exercise, practicing a humbly assertive leadership in all areas of your life will strengthen your resolve to stand up for yourself when you must deal with a dominant personality.

Another way to strengthen your resolve to stand up for yourself is to think of a person's aggressively dominant personality as a weakness with which he must cope.

- Do what athletes do to as they prepare for a game – analyze the aggressively dominant person and try to identify psychological weaknesses in his game.
- Try to determine what has led him to have such an aggressively dominant personality, e.g. attempt to compensate for insecurities about physical or mental traits, unhappy childhood with dominating or abusive family, "spoiled rotten" by parents.
- Understanding a person's psychological weaknesses can help you:
  - o Reaffirm to yourself that no matter how much dominant people try to act like supermen, they are really just flawed human beings like all the rest of us.
  - o Understand that people who exhibit dominating personalities in their business lives typically carry over their dominating personalities to their personal lives, and a dominating personality in personal life typically precludes the type of warm and close human relationships that make life so rich and satisfying.
  - o *Gain feelings of sympathy and empathy for "this sorry person's" plight in life that squeeze feelings of intimidation out of your mind.*
  - o Feel good about the way you are living your life and leading the people on your team.

Control your emotions.
- Leaders must maintain control of themselves in order to effectively control others.
- In order to maintain an ability to make prudent decisions, leaders must be able to keep their rational thinking wits about them in pressure situations, in tough times, and during emergencies. They can't get rattled, flustered, perplexed, etc. to the point of not being able to think clearly – they must strive to stay "cool as a cucumber".
- Leaders who let people see them "losing it" risk driving away the type of level headed, top quality people who should be on their team.
- A leader who suffers from irrational exuberance can get so blinded by his expectations that he fails to see the dangers of the realities he is experiencing, and risk leading himself and his team into situations they shouldn't be getting into.

The emotions of even the best leaders can slip out of control on occasion.
- Don't get overly excited by amazingly good things that are happening, driven bonkers by people with whom you strongly disagree, stressed by thinking there is too much to do in too little time, flustered by unexpected stuff that comes flying out of left field, etc.
- *Don't let people get under your skin.* No matter what a salesman, co-worker, or boss says or does, don't let your emotions get the better of you.
- *Don't take business too personally.* Business people are dealing with you in the context of the business world, NOT in the context of your private life.

"If you are not part of the solution, you are part of the problem."
- As a leader, if you weren't leading people to help solve a problem that was stirring your emotions, you would be contributing to the continuance or worsening of that problem.
- By maintaining your composure when everybody around you seems to be losing theirs, you become a rock of stability around whom people can rally while you lead them toward doing things you think will generate the greatest good for everyone involved.
- If you don't like what is going on in a business or social situation, step up and take control of the situation to the extent that you can control it, don't let the situation control you. Seek the emotion calming control and mental focus that comes from working proactively to improve the situation.

Leaders must occasionally make tough decisions.
- During the course of your life, it is likely you will need to make some tough decisions.
- Leaders should take all the time needed to make well-informed, well-reasoned decisions, but they can't just idly procrastinate or avoid making tough decisions that must be made.
- As the old adage says *"a tough decision won't get any easier tomorrow"*.
- By all means ask for advice and recommendations from your business team members and other experts in the subject matter of a tough decision, but don't hand off to anyone else the responsibility of making a tough decision for you.
  - o There is a big difference between (a) considering a recommendation as just one piece of information you gather and evaluate in your decision making process; and (b) letting another person make a decision for you and telling you what to do.
  - o If you are not sure you understand the difference between (a) seeking advice and recommendations, and (b) doing whatever somebody else tells you to do, please re-read Chapter 7 about decision making.

<u>Manage Change</u>

"Nothing is constant but change".
- You are continuously changing.
- The world around you is continuously changing, and that pace of change is accelerating.
- The people in your life are changing – some changes being more noticeable than others.
    - People change as they grow up and mature. Nobody is exactly the same person as he was last year or ten years ago - some get wiser and more mellow, some get bitter and vindictive from being hurt, some get lazy from prosperity, etc.
    - People at work will retire or move on to new positions and new people will take their places.
    - Old neighbors will move away and new neighbors will move in.
    - Old friends will pass through your life and new friends will come into your life.
    - New generations of people are continuously being born and growing up to take their places in the world, while the old guard is turning over its roles in life to the next generations and eventually dying off - the cycle of life.
- Companies change as people come and go, as they grow, and as they adapt to the changing competitive marketplace and the changing needs and wants of customers.
- Governments change with each election.

Change creates opportunities for people who are alert to recognize those opportunities.
- Keep your eyes and ears open for the opportunities that change creates for you.
    - Make sure you can see a gift horse when it walks up and stares you in the face.
    - Getting out in front of change as it first starts to appear will give you a better vantage point from which to see opportunities.
- People being promoted or retiring at your place of employment, or a new position being created, might create an opportunity for career advancement.
- A growing company might offer a new and more desirable career path opportunity.
- New technologies, research breakthroughs, discoveries, and evolving demographics worldwide are leading to ever greater numbers of opportunities for you to prosper.
- Changes in climate and global weather patterns are leading to new levels of awareness and concern, which in turn are driving technology discoveries and creation of new businesses that are creating new career and investment opportunities.
- New technologies might create opportunities for you to:
    - Do your work faster and more efficiently.
    - Reduce your expenses.
    - Manage your money more efficiently.
- Some people get scared when they sense their lives are changing. They often rally around, and follow the lead of, people they think will help them get through the changes unharmed. Change might create an opportunity for you to lead such people to do what you think will be best for you and for them too – if you think win-win.

Don't fight change.
- Fighting change is a losing battle. Welcome change. Use change.
- We can't prevent change from happening no matter hard we try.
- *"If you can't beat 'em, join 'em."* Since we can't prevent change from happening, we would be smart to enter the ever-flowing stream of change and seek to control the direction of change in our lives to the greatest extent possible.
    - Nobody can completely control the stream of change in their lives, but if we use

a planning process and a decision making process to help direct the flow of that stream, then change is more likely to work out well for us in the long run.

- o The more good people with whom you surround yourself, the greater the mass of collective effort you will have available to help you control the stream of change.
- Too many people are hung up on the "good old days" and "the way we used to do it".
  - o They try to live in the world as they knew it in the past. But, that world is gone - it's history.
  - o Trying to live in the past leaves people vulnerable to a depressingly negative feeling that they are victims of circumstances - that life is doing things to them. That type of negative feeling can lead to all sorts of bad money management decisions.
- We would be smart to seek the new opportunities presented by change in the world around us, and use the lessons learned from life in the good old days to capitalize on those new opportunities in the great new frontier of the even better days that lie ahead.

Anticipate change - learn about likely changes in life as you know it and plan for those changes.
- *Learn all you can about how experts in various fields visualize life 10, 20, 30, or more years out in the future. How are changing conditions likely to impact the world in general, and your life, your job, and your money in particular?*
- Ask people how they visualize the world changing in the future, and how they think we should prepare ourselves to prosper in the changed world they visualize.
- Current trends and historical cycles are good tools to help project future changes.
  - o Identify as many current trends as you can.
  - o Learn about as many historical cycles as you can.
  - o Keep as up to date as your time and resources allow on what is new in the world (new discoveries, new technologies, new products, newly emerging industries, current events, etc.) and how those new things fit into the current trends you know about, and how those current trends might fit into historical cycles. That will help you project how changing conditions are likely to play out in the future.
- Plan for the changes in the global economy that the passions of today's political activists are likely to precipitate. Rapid evolution of global telecommunications and transportation networks is spawning rapid changes in the economic, social, and geo-political order of the world. In particular, the evolution of global telecommunications networks is making it easier and easier for dissident activists to organize and coordinate their efforts to change the world. Learn about social unrest that is being precipitated by what dissidents both here at home and abroad perceive as an inequitable distribution of income and wealth, and a lack of economic opportunity for large segments of populations.
- Minimize the number of surprises to which you must react.
- Adapt. Be flexible. "Be a willow in the winds of change. Bend, don't break".
- Plan for gradual evolution in your life to the greatest extent possible. Plan smooth transitions into doing new things and doing old things in new ways.
- Plan to avoid radical change to the best of your ability. Radical change tends to pose a greater risk of danger than well planned, gradual change.
- If you have an epiphany (an "aha" moment in which you see yourself or the world in a different light) be careful about the speed with which you revise your plan. Think through an epiphany carefully. Ask confidants on your business team to critique your epiphany. Time has a way of revealing many epiphanies to be false epiphanies.
- *"Be prepared"* as the Boy Scouts motto advises. Develop contingency Plan B's that prepare you to manage significant changes in your life as expeditiously as possible.

Reports, Meetings, Performance Reviews

Use the ideas offered in this section as appropriate to each of the three different roles you play as president of your personal financial management company.
- *As president of your family business* (please read and take to heart Chapter 16).
- *As an employee*, and perhaps manager, in your employer's organization (see Chapter 14).
- *As an employer* of professional service providers you hire and pay.

Many people don't think of reports, meetings and performance reviews as the valuable personal financial management tools that they are. It is likely these people have had workplace experiences that have caused them to perceive reports, meetings and performance reviews as pains in the neck, rather than as tools to use for their own benefit.

It seems to me that most people would prefer to <u>do</u> their work rather than:
- Report on their work.
- Meet to discuss their work.
- Sit through performance reviews of their work.

If you have developed a negative perception of reports, meetings and performance reviews during your career, work on converting that negative perception into a positive perception.
- *Adopt a mindset that these are valuable tools that you can use to help you achieve your objectives and realize your dreams.*
- Keep in mind that people on your business team (and at work) will take cues from you as to what they should think about the usefulness of reports, meetings, and performance reviews.

Reports can help you:
- Track your progress toward achieving your objectives.
- Reconcile your records of your money management performance each month with the statements you receive from financial service providers (e.g. banks, credit card companies, financial advisor) thereby helping you avoid unpleasant surprises.
- Evaluate the performance of people on your business team.
- "Prevent molehills from growing into mountains" by providing early warnings about potential problems so that you can take corrective action.
- Provide legal documentation if a need should ever arise.

Think of reports as scorecards you can use to keep track of how you're doing in the "game of life" as you manage your company through all the "planning periods" (months, calendar quarters, years) you are on this Earth playing the game of life.

Reports must be timely to be useful. Maintain your accounting records in orderly fashion so that you can prepare financial statements right after the close of whatever planning period you desire to prepare a report (as successful companies do).

Management reports to consider using include:
- External reports - statements provided by your financial advisor, banks, credit card issuers, and other professional service providers.
- Internal reports - reports you prepare for yourself, such as:
  - o   Financial statements.

o "To do list" of action plan items you can check off as items are accomplished.

o Running total summary of credit card purchases each month.

o Checkbook register.

o Retirement plan contributions you make each year.

Your personal (consumer) credit score and credit report.

- Personal (consumer) credit scores and credit reports are used by lenders, insurers, prospective employers and others to help them (a) evaluate a person's credit risk (likelihood of him paying his debts) and a person's personal life management skills, and (b) make a decision about offering the person credit, insurance, a job offer, etc.

- A credit score and credit report on your credit history is prepared by each of three major credit reporting agencies - Equifax, Experian, and TransUnion. Learn how these credit reporting agencies compute credit scores and prepare credit reports.

- Credit reports are prepared using information provided to the credit reporting agencies by sources such as major credit card companies, retail stores that issue their own credit cards, doctors, contractors, and other creditors (people to whom a person owes money) who have not been paid on time.

- Credit scores are computed based upon data such as the number of a person's creditors, amount of money owed to each creditor, pay record (prompt payments or late payments), and any loan defaults, lawsuits, prior arrest record, or bankruptcy.

- Credit scores range from 350 (worst credit risk) to 850 (best credit risk). The higher your score, the more desirable you are to lenders and the better the loan terms you are likely to be offered. (Credit scores are also called FICO scores because the first credit scoring model was developed by Fair Isaac & Co.)

Research how to manage your credit score. Advice I have heard includes:

- Learn about the Fair Credit Reporting Act (FCRA).
  - o The FRCA was created to help assure the accuracy and the privacy of information about us gathered by consumer credit reporting agencies.
  - o The Federal Trade Commission (FTC) is responsible for enforcing the FCRA.
- *Request a copy of each of your consumer credit reports each year at (annualcreditreport.com).*
  - o FCRA provides you the right to order one free report from each credit reporting agency every 12 months. A suggestion to help monitor your credit score is to order a report from one of the three credit reporting agencies every four months.
  - o The FTC's website has information about how to request free copies of your credit reports, and a warning to protect yourself from "imposter" websites that try lure you into paying for reports for which you hadn't intended to pay.
- Pay every bill promptly. Use automatic bill payments when possible to lessen the risk of making a late payment or forgetting altogether to make a payment.
- Limit the number of credit cards you have. Some people seem to sign up for every credit card promotion that offers them a free t-shirt or other "freebie" (freebies typically aren't free; almost always freebies are means for companies to "get their hooks into us" so that they can make a profit off of us in the future).
- Read each statement you get from each financial institution (bank, credit card company, investment companies) summarizing the activity in each account each month, and reconcile (compare) the transactions and balances that show on their reports with the transactions and balances you show on your internal reports.

Regarding reports prepared by employees you manage at work:
- Help people see the value of reports they are required to prepare by explaining how you and other company managers use the information in the reports they prepare.
- Within the limits of your managerial authority:
  - o Minimize the number of reports people are required to prepare.
  - o Make reports as simple and easy to prepare as possible.
  - o Make reports as functional as possible for your employees as well as for you and other managers who use the reports.
  - o Ask employees for their thoughts about how reports could be revised to make them easier to prepare and more functional.

Meetings: a few suggestions for leading effective meetings - primarily for use in meetings you lead at work, but also for possible use "in a watered down way" to guide family meetings.
- Schedule start times and completion times far enough in advance so that people can properly prepare for meetings.
- Start meetings on time and try to end them before the scheduled completion time. People love "early endings" - something akin to kids getting out of school early.
- Keep meetings short and sweet. My personal observation is that it is more effective to have more short and sweet meetings than it is to have fewer but longer and potentially more dreary meetings.
- Don't drone on. Don't lecture. Stick to the agenda - don't wander off agenda.
- Gear meetings toward how well "we" did and how we can all work together to do even better.
- Some people might be tougher on themselves than you might be – pump them up. Make each meeting as much of a positive pep talk as you can.
- Assign responsibilities for work that needs to be accomplished prior to the next meeting.
- At the end of each meeting set the date for the next meeting.

Encourage meeting attendees to come prepared.
- Prepare a written agenda and distribute that agenda to attendees far enough in advance that they can come prepared.
- If certain people have had difficulty achieving their objectives in the past, try doing some one-on-one coaching and counseling between meetings to help them get done what they will be expected to have done by the time of the next meeting. People dread being singled out if they have not met performance objectives and expectations. Try to avoid putting anyone on the spot in front his teammates.

Performance review meetings: Chapter 14 offers suggestions that might help you get the maximum benefit out of your employer's performance reviews of your work as an employee. Below are some suggestions you might consider using if you manage employees at work.
- *Promote performance reviews as coaching and mentoring opportunities intended to help each team member achieve his personal objectives.*
- Performance reviews are a continuous process, not a series of one-off, isolated events. *An employee's next performance review starts with his current performance review.* Lay the groundwork for the next performance review during the current meeting.
  - o Don't assume an employee understands what you expect him to do. Discuss his job description, job duties, and performance objectives.
  - o Establish a mutually agreed upon job description and objectives for the next performance review period.

During the interval between performance reviews:
- Lay the groundwork for making the next formal performance review meeting a positive experience for both of you by informally talking with each employee on a periodic basis.
  - o Let people know that you are trying do all you can to help them earn the best possible ratings on their next formal performance review.
  - o Coach and counsel people to help them do their jobs as well as possible.
  - o Constructively critique each person's performance in a tactful, supportive way. Try to point out positive things about each person's performance, and discuss ways performance might be improved. This is likely to motivate people who are doing a good job, and help people who are not doing such a good job improve performance that you think could be improved. It will also prevent your thinking from coming as a complete surprise during the next performance review.
  - o Letting people know that you care about them, and that you are trying to do all you can to help them, can help minimize the potential "dread factor" that you and each employee might feel as the time nears for his next performance review.
- The following suggestion might be idealistic for all employees in all job positions, but think about using it on a case by case basis as you see fit and your employer would allow.
  - o Ask people what their dream jobs would be within your employer's organization, and encourage them to work with you to prepare career path plans that will advance them toward their dream jobs (see Chapter 14).
  - o Work with people as best you can to help them implement their career path plans.
  - o The upside: if you can help an employee create a career path plan toward his dream job (a) you are likely to feel good about the good you are doing, and (b) he is likely to be more motivated to do the best that he can to achieve the objectives for which he will be held accountable.
  - o The potential downside:
    - ▪ You might eventually lose a valued employee to a promotion; or
    - ▪ If an employee realized that he might not be able to create a career path plan toward his dream job within your employer's organization, he might begin making plans to leave your employer in order to pursue his dream.
    - ▪ But if the employee wasn't enthusiastic about his job he might not have been working up to his full potential and you might be better off if he could be replaced with an employee who was more enthusiastic about the job and more likely to work up to his full potential.
- Near the end of each performance review period ask each person to do a self-review (using your employer's formal performance review form, if there is one). Interestingly, I have heard that many employees rate their own performance lower than their employers do. These self-reviews can serve two purposes:
  - o Help minimize unpleasant surprises during the performance review meeting.
  - o Provide you employee input to use in preparing for the performance review.

During each performance review meeting:
- Be honest, objective, tactful, and empathetic while you are presenting your evaluation of each person's performance. Offer constructive critique.
  - o People who are doing a good job are likely to be motivated to do even better.
  - o People whose performance you think could be improved need to know what improvement you think is needed. Let the person know you will do your best to help him improve his performance during the next review period.
- Ask each employee for his thoughts about your evaluation. Discuss any differences of opinion with the aim of trying to resolve those differences of opinion right then and there.

Chapter 11. Budget Management

Introduction to budget management

Budgets are <u>projected </u>financial statements:
- Projected financial statement budgets quantify:
    - o The money that will be needed to finance the lifestyles that people are planning to live at each stage in their lives.
    - o Dollar number objectives that will need to be achieved in order to achieve business plan objectives.
- Budget objectives should derive from business plan objectives.

Just as historical financial statements have<u> two parts</u> (statement of income and expenses and balance sheet) so too projected financial statement budgets should also have two parts:
- *Projected statement of income and expenses*: this is the only part of a budget that most people have in mind when they think about budgets.
- *Projected balance sheet*: <u>most people don't think about a projected balance sheet as being an integral part of a budget. You should!</u>

Three uses of historical financial statements in preparing projected financial statement budgets.
1. Enable people to see the results of their past financial management behavior and the current dollar numbers from which to project the future dollar numbers they want to achieve:
- *Historical statements of income and expenses* summarize how money flowed through people's lives over a specific period of time, e.g. the prior one year:
    - o Revenue (income) - how much money flowed in.
    - o Expenses: how much money flowed out – how much money they spent and on what they spent their money.
    - o Net profit (savings): how much money was saved from flowing out.
- *Historical balance sheet*s provide snapshots of what people had done with the money in their lives up until one particular day in the past:
    - o Types and dollar amount of <u>assets</u> people acquired.
    - o Money they owed (<u>liabilities</u>).
    - o Amount of money they would have remaining if they paid all the money they owed (assets - liabilities = <u>net worth</u>).
2. Help people identify financial management behavioral habits they might need to change in order to achieve their budget objectives.
3. Provide formats for budgets along with the starting dates from which to project numbers into the future.
- *<u>Projected statement of income and expense</u>* (projected income statement) - objectives to guide the flow of money through people's lives ***during*** a specific period of time - a "planning period" (typically one month, a calendar quarter, or one year).
    - o <u>Revenue (income) objective</u>: amount of money that people will need to generate during a planning period in order to finance the lifestyles they plan to live during that planning period - from a job, social security, pension, investments, etc.
    - o <u>Expense objectives</u>: amounts of money people will be able to spend on various things during that planning period, e.g. food, housing, utilities, healthcare, transportation, recreation and entertainment, etc.
    - o <u>Net profit (savings)</u>: amount of money people will need to add to their net worth during that planning period in order to stay on track to achieve their long term objectives for financial freedom and security.

- *Projected balance sheet budget*: objectives to achieve ***as of the last day*** of a planning period, such as:
  - o Amount by which to increase net worth.
  - o Dollar amounts to be invested in each of a diversified mix of investments in accordance with a person's asset allocation strategy (see Chapter 15).
  - o Amount by which to decrease debt.

Three main aspects of budget management:
- *Revenue (income) management*: generate enough money to pay the expenses of the lifestyles we desire to live while saving enough money to build enough net worth to provide a sense of comfort for our future financial security and financial freedom.
- *Expense management*: spending less money than we generate each year.
- *Investment portfolio management*: build investment portfolios in accordance with our asset allocation strategies that enable us to achieve our net worth accumulation and annual investment income objectives.

Take advantage of all the budget (and debt) management advice and assistance available to you from resources such as:
- Websites of banks, mutual funds, and other financial institutions.
- Your local banker.
- A professional financial advisor.
- Federal, state and local government resources. Check out the Educational Resources section of the Consumer Financial Protection Bureau (CFPB) website.

Consider preparing a six column projected financial statement budget spreadsheet (suggested formats for a projected statement of income and expenses and a projected balance sheet are on the Your Money Is Your Business website at www.ymiyb.com).
- As said in Chapter 4, keep it simple to start. You could probably write your initial projected statement of income and expenses statement of income and expenses on one piece of paper or software spreadsheet and your projected balance sheet on another sheet.
- In the first column of each document, prepare an historical financial statement for the most recent December 31st calendar year end.
- Then list budget objectives for each of five progressively longer planning periods in side by side columns on the spreadsheet.
- The further out into the future we plan, the more our objectives become "aspirational dreams" we desire to make come true.
- The closer to the present we plan, the more realistically achievable objectives should become.
- The act of preparing this spreadsheet will help your mind move more fluidly through planning stair-stepped, milestone objectives that will enable you to advance from your current financial position toward your financial dream objectives.

Following are suggestions for five planning periods to include in your budget spreadsheets.
- *Last year of the lifespan you can reasonably expect to live*: in the column on the far right of the spreadsheet write your ultra-long term "dream" financial objectives for the last year of the lifespan you can reasonably expect to live. These ultra-long term objectives will help you "back" into planning more specific milestone objectives that you should strive to achieve by the end of each planning period in order to actually achieve those ultra-long term objectives and make your financial dreams come true.

- *30 years* (or perhaps 20, depending upon your age and your business plan): in the next column to the left, financial objectives you will need to achieve in order to live the lifestyle you want to be living by that point in time.
- *10 years*: in the next column to the left, objectives that would give you the best shot at achieving your long term and ultra-long term objectives.
- *3 years*: in the next column to the left, realistic objectives that will enable you to live the lifestyle you want to be living by the end of this period of time.
- *1 year*: in the second column, next to the historical financial statement numbers, realistic estimates of what you can make your historical numbers become at the end of the year:
    - Revenue you can reasonably expect to generate.
    - Expenses you can reasonably expect to incur.
    - Savings you can reasonably expect to add to net worth.
    - Allocation of money to classes and types of assets in your investment portfolio.
    - Debt you can reasonably expect to eliminate (or will need to add).

Organize the expense items in your projected statement of income and expenses into three categories (suggested format only; different people may organize their expenses in different ways; you might experiment until you find a format that works best for you to manage your expenses.)
- *Fixed expenses*: expenses you NEED to incur in order to live the lifestyle you are planning.
    - Cost of living expenses, e.g. food, clothing, shelter (mortgage or rent).
    - Work related expenses, e.g. transportation to and from work, education or career training requirements (college degree or trade work certifications), uniforms or other business clothes, child care.
    - Repayment of debt, e.g. credit card, student loan, car loan, home mortgage.
- *Income tax expenses* - federal, state, local.
- *Discretionary expenses*: expenses you WANT to incur in order to live the satisfying lifestyle you desire, e.g. entertainment, recreation, travel.

Budget management is a function of:
- <u>Lifestyle choices we make</u>, including:
    - The jobs we choose (or passively choose to accept) and the revenue we generate each year from our jobs.
    - The expenses we choose to incur.
    - The money we choose to save and invest each year.
- <u>Strength of our self-discipline</u> to stick to our budgets and resist spending money we hadn't planned to spend.
- <u>Behavioral control (internal control) system we use</u> to manage our daily lives.

Think of your lifestyle choices as being on a continuum.
- *Survival existence lifestyle* at one end of the continuum: a lifestyle geared to <u>satisfying</u> the basic <u>needs</u> required to keep a human body alive and work at a specific job; the least expensive lifestyle a prudent person in her unique life situation could live; no frills. Choosing a survival lifestyle would maximize a person's ability to save money and amass net worth.
- *Luxury lifestyle* at the other end: a lifestyle geared to <u>satisfying wants</u>; a lifestyle that would have a person spend every penny she earned each year, and perhaps even go into debt spending more money than she earned; people who know her might describe her as being a spendthrift who has "champagne taste". Choosing a luxury lifestyle would

minimize a person's ability to save money and amass net worth.
- *Comfortably prudent lifestyle* somewhere in the vast middle between the two ends. Choosing a comfortably prudent lifestyle would allow a person to live a happy, satisfying life while being able to generate enough revenue each year and amass enough net worth to provide the level of financial security / financial freedom she desires in the future.

You might think of needs and wants this way:
- *Needs*: bare essential expenses that must be incurred in order to stay alive and work at a job.
- *Wants*: everything else.

Survival, luxury and comfortably prudent lifestyles are highly subjective terms.
- A comfortably prudent lifestyle for one person might be a survival existence lifestyle for another person.
- A "rich" person's idea of a survival existence lifestyle might be a "poor" person's idea of a luxury lifestyle.

Each of us is likely to define survival, luxury and comfortably prudent lifestyles in a different way based upon the unique circumstances of each of our lives, such as:
- Lifestyle to which we became accustomed as we grew up.
- Annual income we have grown accustomed to earning over the past few years.
- Net worth we have been able to amass and the sense of financial security it provides.
- Social pressure we get from family, neighbors, friends, co-workers.

We each must live with the consequences of the lifestyle choices we make.
- The more frugal the lifestyle you choose:
  - o The less revenue you will need in order to finance that lifestyle.
  - o The greater the financial freedom you will have to choose a career path doing work that you love.
  - o The less concern you will need to have for how much money jobs might actually pay in your chosen career path.
- The more luxurious the lifestyle you choose:
  - o The greater your need will be to choose a career path in which prospective jobs have the potential to pay well enough to cover all the expenses of that lifestyle.
  - o The greater your need will be to actually secure jobs in that career path that actually pay the money you plan to be paid for those jobs.

Beware two ways that our minds can blur the lines of distinction between a survival lifestyle, a comfortably prudent lifestyle, and a luxury lifestyle.
- *Rising expectations* can convert wants into needs. Let's say this a few ways to make sure you understand this critical point:
  - o As people's economic situations improve, luxuries tend to become necessities; things that were "wants" when people's budgets couldn't afford them tend to morph into "needs" after people become accustomed to having them.
  - o Price range of what people consider a "survival" level of need satisfaction tends to shift upward as income shifts upward
  - o People tend to desire to "move on up" in lifestyle as they move on up the income and wealth ladder, e.g. bigger home, pricier neighborhood, more expensive car, gourmet foods, fashion label clothes, expensive vacations.
  - o People tend to expect more as they can afford more.

- *Wealth effect*: the greater that people's annual income becomes and the more net worth that people amass, the more comfortable they tend to become with spending their money

Plan budget objectives that enable you to live a happy, comfortably prudent, and economically sustainable lifestyle. Nobody can give you exact hard dollar objectives to plug into your budget. You must decide for yourself objectives that will enable you to live the lifestyle you desire to live. But, there are certain guidelines that have worked for many people over many years. Ask your business team members for their advice about common budget objective guidelines such as:

- *Save 10 %*: generations of parents have advised their kids to save 10% of annual income. The concept of tithing 10% of income to higher purposes goes back to ancient times. You might think of saving as tithing to your future financial security. Try to work your way up to a projected income statement net profit objective of at least 10% each year.
- Cash reserves should be somewhere between 3 and 12 months of annual income.
- Home mortgage debt should not exceed 2 to 2 ½ times annual income (revenue).

Cash is a budget planning freedom machine.
- The more cash revenue that you can reasonably expect to generate each year; and
- The more cash that you have accumulated from year to year in your emergency reserve fund and in your investment portfolio,
- The more freedom you will have in planning your annual expense budget objectives.

Choose financially prudent, economically sustainable lifestyle strategies, such as:
- *"Life is about more than money"*. Life should be about generating as much joy and satisfaction as possible. Money should be just a tool to use to generate joy and satisfaction. Generate the greatest joy and satisfaction possible with each dollar spent.
- *Focus on parts of a satisfying lifestyle that can be lived with little to no money*: spiritual life, relationships with family and friends, learning, enjoyment of nature, creative arts …
- *"Live below your means"*: choose a satisfying lifestyle that costs less than you could afford to spend - spend less money than you earn each year.
- *"Do what you love to do and money will follow"*, if you want money to follow.
- *Surround yourself with people who are good influences on your lifestyle choices and your money.*
    - o "Choose your friends wisely". Choose friends who want to be your friend because of who you are as a person not because of your money. Money shouldn't matter among friends.
    - o Choose professional service providers who built their businesses based upon a strategy of providing best value to their clients; people who get greater satisfaction from helping clients than they do from the money they are paid for their services.
    - o Phase out people who have been negative influences on your lifestyle choices and your budget management decisions.
- Buy best value.
- "Waste not, want not." "Use it up, wear it out, make it do, or do without it."
- "Don't flaunt it after you've got it". Don't show off with things money can buy.
- Make budget management a game. We tend to do things we enjoy doing and avoid doing things we don't enjoy doing. Making budget management as enjoyable as possible will help you become as successful as possible at managing your budget. Don't compete against anyone else in your budget management game. Rather, do as most weekend

warrior 10K race runners do, have fun trying to achieve personal bests instead of winning an imaginary competition.

Choose strategies that help you achieve:
- Joy in the moment.
- Wonderful, lasting memories.
- Satisfaction of a life well lived.
- Your financial dreams.

Budget trade-offs = *lost opportunity costs*. No matter how much each of us would like it to be so, we can't earn the unlimited revenue that we would need to:
- Buy all the stuff we would like to have and do all the things we would like to do;
- Contribute to all the religious and charitable organizations we think could use our money;
- Provide all the financial support we would like to provide for family members; and
- Save all the money we would like to accumulate for our future financial security.

Budget management decisions require us to compute lost opportunity costs and make trade-off decisions:
- We must decide what we value most, need most, and want most.
- Then we must make trade-off decisions about getting the benefits of decision options we choose and losing opportunities to get the benefits of the options we could have chosen.
  - o When we choose to work at one job to generate revenue, we lose the opportunity to use that time to work at another job.
  - o When we choose to spend money on one thing, we lose the opportunity to spend that money on something else.
- "Every story has two sides." The other side of the "you're only young once" spending story is the "save for your future" savings story. Seek a satisfying balance between spending and saving.

Expense management trade-off examples:
- *Immediate gratification traded off against deferred gratification*: a person spending most of her income each year to support the lifestyle she desires to live today, traded off against the deferred gratification of saving money to provide future financial freedom.
- A person foregoing an expensive vacation in order to spend that money on classes that would help her acquire the education qualifications needed for a more desirable job.

Revenue management trade-off examples:
- Being paid a ton of money to slave at a job that makes a person miserable, traded off against being paid a whole lot less money to do a job she loves.
- Working every minute possible to make every dollar possible, traded off against earning less money but having more free time to maintain close personal relationships with family and friends.

Take care of "first things first".
- List your business plan objectives in priority order from the most important down to least important. Then plan a budget that provides you the best opportunity to achieve your most important business plan objectives.
- Revenue management - to maximize the money your employer pays you:
  - o Allocate your time and effort in a way that gives you the best opportunity to

achieve your most important objectives.
- o Then allocate your remaining time and effort to performing your lower priority duties and achieving your lower priority objectives.
- Expense management – to "get the most bang for your expense dollar bucks":
  - o List the fixed expense and discretionary expense items on your projected income statement from largest expense items down to lowest expense items.
  - o Focus your attention on minimizing your largest expense items first.

Sticking to a budget can be tough for all sorts of reasons:
- *Temptations* to stray from our budgets, such as:
  - o Seductive advertisements that try to make us feel that we owe it to ourselves to buy the nice things we see being advertised.
  - o Peer pressure exerted by neighbors who just bought something we would like to buy or did something we would like to do.
  - o News stories touting the high annual income potential of jobs in trendy industries (real estate, investment banking, high tech have all had their day) that lure people away from career paths in more stable, mature industries that offer more budget friendly, more predictable streams of future revenue. These alluring stories tend to multiply during the years and months prior to job market "bubbles" bursting in those trendy industries causing people who switched jobs to lose their jobs.
- *Excuses, excuses, excuses* - a human nature problem with which we all must deal.
- *Procrastination* - the "mañana" syndrome (mañana meaning tomorrow in Spanish), e.g. "I have plenty of time to save an investment nest egg. I'll start tomorrow". Well, tomorrow has a way of turning into next month, which turns into next year, then "after I get that promotion at work", and on and on. *There always seems to be plenty of time, until there is not*.

For some people, there never seems to be enough money no matter what stage of life they are in.
- 20's – when just starting out on their own, single people often feel a need to spend money on being a part of the "social scene", to keep up with ever changing styles, and to buy things they need in order to live out on their own away from home.
- 30's – a new family to feed, clothe, and house.
- 40's – college for the kids.
- 50's – renovating the house.
- 60's – taking that dream vacation while they still have their health.
- 70's and 80's - inflation chewing into their fixed income.

A few suggestions that might help you stick to your budget:
- Choose budget objectives that enable you to live a happy, satisfying lifestyle.
- Read your budget frequently enough to keep your budget numbers fixed firmly in mind. This will allow you to have a pretty good idea of how much money you have available to spend each time a thought about spending money enters your mind.
- Prepare financial management reports on a regular basis to compare your actual spending and saving behavior to your budget objectives.
  - o Prepare financial statements at least annually and perhaps quarterly or monthly as dictated by your track record of sticking to your budget.
  - o Design your own budget management reports as you find a need, e.g. maintain a running log of credit card purchases made each month.

Don't get imprisoned by your "stuff" (comedian George Carlin has a great bit about "stuff").
- Some people feel a need to buy a far bigger home than they need and to buy stuff to fill it –and then they get deeply attached to their stuff. They also have all that extra storage space that they can use to buy and store even more stuff that they don't use regularly.
- Some people feel so trapped by a need to own stuff (some of it requiring operating and maintenance expenses), and a feeling that need to keep on buying more stuff, that they feel they can't manage their budgets in a financially prudent manner, e.g. feeling trapped in a spiral of need to buy ever changing clothing styles and /or the newest electronic gear. Fashion trends and electronic technology change so fast that a person could literally go broke trying to keep up with buying all the new stuff that is out there to buy.
- *"Simplify, simplify, simplify"* [your lifestyle] as Henry David Thoreau advised.

Don't let budget setbacks get you down.
- We all hit bumps in the road as we progress toward our budget objectives. When unforeseen events knock you off track toward your objectives, revise your budget as needed and develop an action plan to get yourself back on track.
- You have a lifetime ahead of you. Detours in the road toward your objectives won't prevent you from eventually reaching your objectives, they may just slow you down.
- Don't let your emotions run wild in the event of a financial catastrophe, e.g. losing a job or having a stock market meltdown decimate your investment portfolio.
  - o No financial catastrophe, no matter how big, can ruin your life unless you let it.
  - o Remember the old adage "If it doesn't kill you, it will make you stronger."
  - o We can learn from financial "reversals" (a positive-spin euphemism) to make ourselves better financial managers IF we maintain a positive attitude and consider those reversals to be challenges that we will rise up to meet.
  - o We can use the lessons learned from meeting financial challenges to guide us in revising our business plans and budgets in ways that help us minimize the risk of future financial reversals.

Whereas most of us can decrease our expenses faster and easier than we can increase our annual revenue, greater detail about budget management is presented in the following chapter order:
- *Expense management*
  - o *Chapter 12, Playing expense management defense*: minimizing current expenses is probably the fastest way most of us can increase annual bottom line net profit, retire debt, and achieve wealth accumulation objectives. As they say in sports, defense usually wins games. The twin objectives of playing expense management defense are:
    - ▪ Avoid making expensive mistakes.
    - ▪ Prevent anyone or anything from influencing you to spend money you hadn't planned to spend.
  - o *Chapter 13, Playing expense management offense*: the objective of playing expense management offense is to make financially prudent lifestyle choices.
- *Revenue management*
  - o *Chapter 14: Active revenue management* earned from a job.
  - o *Chapter 15: Passive revenue management* from a well-diversified investment portfolio, and other sources of revenue such as social security and a pension.
- *Chapter 16, Budget management within our families*: our loving relationships with family members present so many special considerations for expense and revenue management that these considerations deserve a separate chapter.

Budget terms you need to understand

The meaning of several key financial terms seems to be especially tough for many people to grasp. I know this because I have had to explain these terms to so many people over the years.

Revenue and income: most people in the general public use these two words pretty much interchangeably. However, accounting and finance professionals make a big distinction between revenue and income:

- *Revenue* is the total amount of money you earn each year from wages, salary, interest, dividends, etc. Revenue is the "top line" on a statement of income and expenses.
- *Income* is the revenue you get to keep after paying all your expenses; the "bottom line."
- Revenue and income are differentiated by the expenses that come between them.

The US Individual Income Tax Return Form 1040 contributes to confusing people. The "top line" section of the form in which wages, salary, interest, dividends, etc. are reported (lines 7 –22) is labeled "Income" instead of Revenue.

This book follows suit with general public usage and uses the words revenue and income somewhat interchangeably in order to help make what I say about revenue management sound as familiar as possible to you and to help you digest it.

Gross and net
- *Gross*: think of "gross" as a synonym for the word "before".
  - Gross profit = revenue after direct expenses are subtracted from revenue but <u>before</u> indirect expenses are subtracted
  - Gross price: <u>before</u> purchase discounts and rebates are subtracted.
- *Net*: think of "net" as a synonym for the word "after".
  - Net profit (net income): revenue you get to keep <u>after</u> paying all expenses, including income taxes.
  - Net worth: assets remaining <u>after</u> paying off all liabilities (money you owe to others, e.g. borrowed debt and taxes).
  - Net price: purchase price <u>after</u> subtracting all discounts and rebates.

Owe and own: if you take out a loan to buy a car or a home, you won't "own" that car or home until you have completely repaid the debt that you "owe". *Until a loan that is owed is fully repaid, a borrower is just <u>in the process of buying</u> an asset.*

The differences between revenue and income, gross and net, and owe and own, are critical to understanding budget management. Too many people I talk to in my job as a surety bond agent think that:

- Their gross income a/k/a revenue (a nice fat paycheck) enables them to spend more than they can actually afford. They forget about all of the expenses that a written budget would show them that they have obligated themselves to pay out of their gross income.
- Cash in the bank empowers them to buy whatever they want to buy. They forget about how much of that cash they owe to others that a written budget would show them they owe.

Introduction to Expense Management

Most of us can generate the biggest and fastest improvement to our bottom line net profit by managing our expenses. We can cut back the amount of money we spend much faster than we can increase the revenue we earn from jobs, investments, etc.

"If you are in a financial hole, stop digging."
- Many (if not most) financial holes are dug by a long series of small expenses rather than one really big expense - a "financial hole" being not having enough monthly income to cover monthly expenses and/or having accumulated too much debt.
- "Just say no" to spending a penny more than you absolutely must spend until you can implement a well-reasoned, written budget plan to climb out of whatever financial hole you are in.
- Plug the expense holes in your budget bucket as fast as you can in order to stop as much budget money as you can from leaking out, and use the money that you stop from leaking out to speed up paying off any debt that may have been contributing to digging that hole.

Reducing expenses can be tough.
- It's tough to change spending habits that may have taken a lifetime to develop. Think about all the failed New Year's resolutions and diets.
- "The devil is in the details" of determining exactly which expenses to cut and by how much to cut them.
- We may need to swallow some pride and (a) stop buying some things we would prefer to keep on buying, (b) stop doing some things we would prefer to keep on doing, and/or (c) perhaps do some things we would prefer not to do.

If your current financial position is not dire, and you don't need to make significant spending cuts in order to make an annual net profit, it might be best to give yourself time to ease into changing your spending habits.
- We tend to handle little discomforts a lot better than we do big pains. Keep your life as comfortably enjoyable as possible while you chip away at old spending habits.
- Big spending cuts might cause so much pain that you might stop trying to reduce your expenses. Be careful about trying to make too many big spending cuts all at once, especially if they would alter your lifestyle significantly. Making smaller, more gradual, incremental cuts in spending may be the most effective way to make sustainably significant changes in spending behavior (a little here, and a little there, and over time you have reduced expenses a lot).

Expense management can be made easier if we think of it as a game.
- The act of saving has been a tough self-discipline challenge that people have been facing since antiquity, as evidenced by *Aesop's Fable* about *The Ants and the Grasshopper* that was written some 2,500 years ago. The Fable tells the tale of ants who worked all summer to gather and save up food for the winter, while the grasshopper chose to spend his whole summer playing and singing. When winter came the ants had saved plenty of food to eat and the grasshopper went hungry.
- Using a budget forces us put limits on how much money we spend. That's not fun. Making a game of meeting or beating expense budget objectives can put some fun into the self-denial typically required by budget management. That enjoyment can help us maintain the self-discipline needed to be good expense managers. So go with your human nature. Use your imagination to find ways to make trimming expenses and saving money

immediately satisfying and fun. A few ideas to spur your imagination:
- o Dream up images of the fun you will be able to pay for in the future with the dollars you are saving today (refer back to visualizations in Chapter 5) – perhaps something like seeing yourself on a tropical beach with calendar-photo gorgeous water gently lapping at your feet.
- o Celebrate successes, like substituting one glass of tap water for one soda each day. "Yes! I did it today."
- o You might try making up a game in which the object is to try to find ways to spend less money and save more money (a few ideas are in Chapter 12). If you live with family members try to get your family to play along with you. Put your heads together to come up with game rules, such as:
  - ▪ Make each game one year long with 12 one month long budget planning periods.
  - ▪ Score one point for each dollar (saved and) added to net worth.
  - ▪ Try to hit a new "personal best" score at the end of each one year game for dollars added to net worth.

Good expense management ideas are available from all sorts of sources, such as:
- • Friends and co-workers who have proven to manage their money well.
- • Financial advisors.
- • Self-help books on the subject of personal financial management.
- • Cost cutting tips in magazines, newspapers, and internet websites.
- • Talk shows on radio and television.

Many adages and proverbs provide good expense management advice, for instance:
- • "Watch your pennies and the dollars will take care of themselves."
- • "Every penny counts."
- • To condense and paraphrase: "For want of a nail the horseshoe was lost; for want of a horseshoe the horse was lost; for want of a horse the battle was lost; for want of victory in the battle the kingdom was lost."
- • "A fool and his money are soon parted."
- • "Stop throwing your money away."

Plan to have enough cash available to pay the income taxes that will become due at the end of each year.
- • On the W-2 form you file with your employer, have enough money withheld to pay the income taxes you can reasonably estimate will become due at the end of each year.
- • If your investment portfolio will be generating passive income during the year (interest, dividends, gains on the sale of assets, etc.) set aside enough of that investment income in a cash reserve fund to pay the income tax that will become due at the end of the year.
- • "Deferred taxes": plan to have cash available to pay income taxes that will become due at the end of each year in which you plan to take distributions from your tax deferred savings plans (IRA, 401k, medical savings, etc.). Many people forget to plan for the deferred taxes that will become due on such distributions later in their lives.
- • It might be prudent to seek tax planning advice from a professional tax expert, or, until your budget can afford professional advice, from one or more of your business team members who have the greatest tax expertise.

Introduction to Revenue Management

Revenue drives the budget management bus. You can't spend or save dollars you don't have. You need to plan how to generate all the dollars you are planning to spend and save.

Two ways to generate revenue
- *Actively earned revenue*: money that you work to earn (Chapter 14).
- *Passive income*: money that your investments work to earn for you, and money from other sources such as social security or a pension (Chapter 15).

Chapter 14 overview - active revenue management: revenue generated by working at a job(s).
- Primary job.
- And perhaps a second or third job, such as part time work or turning a hobby into a job, e.g. selling artwork at sidewalk sales, part time teacher or coach, playing a musical instrument or singing in a band.

Total compensation package: seek more than just money as compensation for a job. Seek a total compensation package comprised of *three types of compensation*:
- *Money*: to pay the expenses of the lifestyle you plan to live, and to save for your future financial security and freedom.
- *Job satisfaction*: enjoyment of the work itself.
- *Free time*: personal time away from work to do all the other things you dream of doing in life besides working to earn money, e.g. spiritual life, relationships with family and friends, creative arts, recreation.

"There is more to life than money." *Don't "become a slave to your job"* working until all hours of the night. Don't sacrifice too much of your precious time trying to make every dollar possible.

You have two roles to perform at work:
- *Role 1 - Employee*: this role is scripted by your employer's business plan; in this role you are working to help your employer achieve your employer's objectives.
- *Role 2 - President of your company*: this role is scripted by your personal business plan to "sell" your services to your employer; in this role you are working to achieve your personal business plan and budget objectives.

It is a <u>privilege</u> to have your job, <u>not</u> an inalienable <u>right</u>.

Chapter 15 overview - passive revenue management: revenue generated by your investment portfolio and received from other sources such as social security or a pension.
- A professional financial advisor can be a big help in planning for passive revenue.
- After projecting revenue from a job, social security, a pension, etc. you will know how much investment income you will need in order to achieve the total revenue objectives in your projected annual income statement budgets.
- *Maintain an age appropriate, well diversified investment portfolio.* A diversified mix of investment assets can help you accomplish three objectives:
  - *Preserve capital*: assets that have a low risk of losing value.
  - *Appreciate in value*: assets you could sell at a future date for more than you paid.
  - *Generate passive revenue*: assets that work to earn income for you each year.

Chapter 12. Playing Expense Management Defense

There are two objectives in playing expense management defense:
- Avoid making expensive mistakes.
- Prevent anyone from influencing you to spend money you hadn't planned to spend.

In order to play defense you need to know who and what to defend against. There are many forces that might influence us to spend money we hadn't planned to spend. Those forces can be lumped into two generalized groups:
- *Internal forces*: hormones, emotions and human weaknesses that cause us to spend money we hadn't planned to spend. We each have our own unique combination of hormones, emotions, and human weaknesses that we must learn to defend against.
- *External forces:* the culture of, and the people in, the community and country in which we live.

Internal forces to defend against

All too often we are our own worst enemies when it comes to money. Following are a few of the most common internal forces against which we need to defend ourselves

Hormones and emotions can overpower our rational thinking and lead us to make expensive spending mistakes. When we get angry, depressed, overly excited, etc. we become prone to doing things with our money that we might later wish we hadn't done.

Feeling unhappy can cause some people to try to buy happiness through things such as:
- *Food*, e.g. comfort food and over eating.
- *Escape*, e.g. television and movies, video games, playing expensive sports, or frequent vacations.
- *Vicarious living*, e.g. living a fantasy life through the lives of others, like some super fans of sports teams who spend "excessive" time and money on things related to their team.
- *Alcohol and drugs.*

Feelings of insecurity or inadequacy drive some people to try to compensate by spending money so that they can show off things they bought or brag about things they did.

Feelings of guilt (for which some mothers and some religious institutions are famous for burdening people) can tug at our heart strings and make us spend or give away more money than a well-planned budget could afford on financial support of family members, charities, or religious institutions.

Lapses in self-discipline can lead us to make "just this one little exception" to our budgets which can lead to a whole series of little exceptions that wind up busting our budgets.

Impatience, such as choosing the *immediate gratification* of spending money to buy and do things today rather than choosing the *delayed gratification* of saving that money and having greater financial freedom in the future.

Short attention spans can keep us from paying close enough attention for long enough to gather all the information we should be gathering in order to make well-informed, financially prudent decisions.

Procrastination can lead us to put off spending money today, to do things we should be doing today, that will wind up costing us even more money in the future if and when we do them.

Psychological blinders can prevent us from seeing that we are spending money that a well-planned budget would show us we shouldn't be spending.

Irrational exuberance is healthy enthusiasm taken to an unhealthy extreme. It can:
- Impair people's ability to evaluate the cons as well as the pros of spending decision options.
- Turn some people into lemmings following the crowd in buying or doing what "everybody else" is buying or doing rather than making their own well-informed, well-reasoned decisions about how they should be spending their money.
- Turn some people into "fanatics" or "nuts" who spend too much money on their favorite activities, e.g. golf nut.

Mid-life crisis: a classic financial danger, e.g. the completely impractical little red sports car; a guy trading in a great wife for a sweet young thing; chucking it all and moving to someplace new to find a better life.

Getting spoiled by success can lead some people to make expensive mistakes such as:
- Deluding themselves into thinking they are smarter than they actually are and that they don't need the help from others that they actually do need - "I did this all by myself."
- Thinking they could save money by firing a professional service provider who had helped them "make it" and trying to do the work the professional had been doing for them.
- Firing advisors who had the guts to tell them what the advisors actually thought about what they were doing or not doing, and replacing those good advisors with "yes men" who would gladly accept payment without "making any waves".
- Developing an *"I've got it made" attitude* that causes them to:
  o Get lazy and stop doing all the little things that helped make them successful –they lose their competitive edge in the game of expense management.
  o Drop their defensive guard.
- Advertising to unscrupulous salespeople and con artists that they are so blinded by their own brilliance that they might be gullible enough to get fleeced.

Rising expectations and **the wealth effect** can cause people to lose track of the difference between spending enough money to live a comfortably prudent lifestyle and spending more money than a well-planned budget could afford in order to live a more luxurious lifestyle.

Read some of the books that wise people have written over the years that provide advice about how we can defend ourselves against our human nature. A few suggestions:
- Aesop's Fables
- Book of Proverbs in the Bible
- Sun Tzu's, "The Art of War": 2,400 year old advice intended for generals also offers business management wisdom.
- Books in the self-help, psychology, sociology, and history sections of libraries, bookstores, and websites. Ask librarians and bookstore employees for recommendations.

External forces to defend against

Marketing and advertising culture: *to an ever greater extent marketing and advertising are becoming ingrained in our culture – our lives are being "commercial – ized".*
- We are continuously bombarded with messages created by marketing professionals in attempts to manipulate our spending behavior. There are few places we can go and few things we can do today to escape the reach of marketing professionals; and they keep finding previously empty space into which they can insert advertising - company names and logos on almost everything we wear and use; advertising on everything from buses, to restaurant placemats, to rest room walls; naming rights on buildings and sports facilities; product placements in movies and television shows; sponsorships of everything from sporting events to charity events to public radio and television; etc.
- The marketing and advertising industries employ a workforce of professionals who are well-trained to manipulate our spending behavior; and practice keeps improving their professional expertise. (When I say protect yourself from marketing and advertising professionals, I don't mean to infer that these people have an evil intent to take our money and make us poorer. Their job is simply to influence as many of us as possible to buy the products or services that their clients pay them to market and advertise.)
- Too many people today have been brainwashed by advertising to believe that it is normal to spend money without thinking about the consequences of spending that money – like all those smiling and laughing models and actors in advertisements appear to be doing.

A culture of spending versus saving: over the past few years there have been countless articles written about a spending culture in the United States versus savings cultures in other countries. The articles say US citizens spend too much today and save too little for the future. The silver lining of the Great Recession in the late 2000's may be that more people have learned to decrease their spending and increase their savings. Hopefully in this Information Age we will find ways to lengthen society's collective memory of the pain caused by the Great Recession.

Debt is an obligation to pay back a lender in the future for the use of the lender's money today.

Debt can hurt you in many ways:
- Interest expense: (a) words of wisdom attributed to Henry Ward Beecher are a powerful warning "Interest works night and day, in fair weather and foul. It gnaws at a man's substance with invisible teeth." (b) Interest payments drain away cash that might otherwise be used to grow net worth. (c) Cumulative interest payments on some loans can exceed the loan amount, as in the case of many mortgages.
- Penalties: fees charged if debt payments are made late.
- When you borrow money to buy something:
  o *You owe, you don't own*;
  o You are just in the process of buying.
- When a borrower takes out a loan to buy an asset, the lender typically has a legal right to "repossess" (take back ownership of) that asset if the borrower fails to repay the money in accordance with the terms of the loan agreement. In addition to losing the asset he purchased the borrower would also lose all the money he had sunk into repayments.
- Learn what the terms "security agreement", "personal guaranty", "condition precedent", and "confession of judgment" mean when used in loan agreements.
- If a borrower didn't have enough cash available to make a payment when due, then he would suffer the angst of finding a way to raise that cash. He could be forced to make that payment with money that he had budgeted for necessities such as food, clothing,

medical services, or he could be forced to sell assets he owns.

- Debt has the power to suck a borrower down in a financial death spiral toward bankruptcy if he continues to take on more and more debt to pay for the lifestyle he wants to keep on living. Eventually he would hit economic rock bottom after accumulating so much debt that he could no longer qualify for additional debt and he had outstripped all the financial resources at his disposal to repay his debts. Then he might have no alternative but to declare bankruptcy. And if he did declare bankruptcy the ghost of that bankruptcy would haunt his credit report for years, making future credit much harder to get and more expensive.
- In addition to suffering fiscal harm, debtors often suffer mental and physical anguish when they feel buried by debt.

Debt is especially dangerous because unexpected stuff can happen to drain away cash that a borrower had planned to use to pay off his debt, e.g. loss of his job or a medical emergency.

"Credit culture": following are some personal thoughts about what I perceive to be a credit culture that came into being during the latter half of the 1900's largely as the result of the work of certain lenders, certain influential consumer products companies, and their marketing professionals.

- My perception is that they acted as Pied Pipers of immediate gratification and conspicuous consumption by producing advertising that:
    o Downplayed or omitted altogether the fact that when consumers pay for things with credit cards they are incurring debts that will need to be repaid.
    o Conveyed the message "buy whatever you want, whenever you want it, and don't bother to think about the cash you will need to have available to pay us after your monthly statements arrive."
    o Created an illusion that credit is an easy way for people to buy whatever they want with "easy credit terms".
- Many advertisements feature:
    o Happy, smiling people getting the immediate gratification of all they want in life simply by using the magic of a credit card.
    o Famous celebrities touting "cash back" that a credit card issuer provides to its credit card users on their purchases - but the advertisements make no mention of the far greater amount of cash that credit card users will need to have available each month in order pay back the credit card issuer.
- As the use of credit cards proliferated, <u>too many people did not (and still do not) understand what "credit" is and the mechanics of what is happening when they pay for things with credit cards</u>:
    o Think of "credit" as the right that a credit card issuing company offers to a person to use the credit card issuer's money to buy things - like a pre-approved bank line of credit.
    o When a person uses a credit card to make a purchase, he is not actually paying the merchant. The credit card issuer pays the merchant. The credit card user is incurring an obligation to pay the credit card issuer for the use of the credit card issuer's money.
    o The credit card purchase is in effect a loan from the credit card issuer – the use of "credit" results in "debt".
    o And, to round out the picture, the merchant typically must pay a small percentage of the purchase price to the credit card issuer as a fee for enabling the merchant to sell his merchandise to his customer.

- It seems that certain credit card issuers don't want card users to pay their statement balances in full each month. Rather, it seems they want card users to become "addicted" (strong word, I know) to carrying over unpaid balances from month to month so that those companies can generate predictable monthly revenue from the high interest rates they charge on unpaid balances. I think this every time I see credit card issuers making credit cards way too easy to get for way too many people who don't know how to use a credit card prudently - such as many college freshmen and many airport travelers.

Social pressure: the people in our lives often have significant influence on how much money we spend and how we spend it. Humans are social animals. We developed an instinctive need to belong to social groups in order to assure our survival. Feeling a need to belong leads to feeling pressure to conform to group behavior in order to remain in groups and avoid being ostracized.

Peer group pressure to "keep up with the Joneses": to gain and maintain acceptance in social groups in which they want to belong (e.g. circles of friends, neighborhood cliques, work groups, and social clubs), some people will do what *"everybody else is doing"*. They will:
- Wear the same type clothes.
- Buy the same type foods and drinks, and go to the same restaurants.
- Do the same things for recreation, e.g. golf, swim, ski, play tennis, go to health clubs, go boating or hunting.
- Live in the same neighborhood.

Family pressures present such a special set of money management considerations that Chapter 16 is devoted to Money, Love & Family.

"It's a guy thing" and "It's a girl thing" stereotypes are used all too often when people talk about the spending habits of men and women. Common gender stereotypes include:
- *It's a guy thing* to spend money on the latest and greatest tools and technology.
- *It's a girl thing* to spend money on the most stylish fashion trends in shoes and handbags.

The more that some men and some women hear such gender stereotypes, the more likely they are to believe that the stereotypes are true for all men and all women – as if stereotypical spending patterns are biologically bred into them – and they are often influenced to spend too much money just because "that's what we do". But, spending habits are not biologically bred into us. They are learned behaviors. We each have choices in how we spend our money. Words have great power to shape our thoughts. Don't let society brainwash you into rationalizing stereotypical bad spending habits. When you hear these stereotypes, use them as mental cues to think about your spending budget and your spending discipline. If you have ever joked about these spending stereotypes, refrain from doing it again.

"Predatory lenders": certain lenders get tagged with the name "predatory lender" because so many people think such lenders prey upon borrower victims. Predatory lenders seem to be motivated by greed without much sense of social responsibility. They seem to believe in "buyer beware".

Too much misery is suffered by too many people because too many "predatory" lenders make loans even when they know borrowers have a high risk of defaulting on repayment of their loans. These lenders don't seem to care about the mental duress and financial harm they might be causing for borrowers who don't fully understand the loan terms to which they are committing themselves. Loan terms are often so onerous that a lender might be able to make a greater profit if a borrower defaults than if the borrower makes all payments according to the terms of the loan.

Predatory lenders can make money on just about any loan by using tools such as:
- <u>Collateral</u> in the form of a car title, home, or other assets as security. Learn what the terms "collateral" and "security" mean and how collateral is used by lenders.
- <u>Personal guaranty</u> in which a borrower pledges all of his assets as "security" for a loan - a "blanket filing" against all of his assets. Learn what the terms "personal guaranty" and "blanket filing" mean and how personal guarantees are used by lenders to secure loans.
- <u>Loan terms</u> that make it relatively easy for a lender to take possession of collateral after a borrower defaults on payments as dictated by the terms of the loan.
- <u>Service fees</u> to cover a lender's costs of making a loan, and build a reserve for legal costs they would incur to seize collateral if a borrower defaulted on making payments.
- <u>High interest rates</u> that generate high profits that a lender can use to build up a loan loss reserve fund (learn about "risk premium").

Predatory lending is often associated with:
- "Payday" (cash advance) loans: learn what payday loans are, and why payday loans are considered to be so hazardous by so many people that many states have passed legislation that prohibits payday loans.
- "Title" loans secured by cars that borrowers already own.
- "Sub-prime" loans.
- Advertisements saying things such as "easy cash"; "we can write any loan"; "if you have bad credit, or a low credit score, or a prior debt repayment problems, or a bankruptcy, or you were declined by another lender".

"Usury"
- Learn about usury: what it is, it's history, and laws put in place to regulate it.
- Develop your own working definition of the word usury.

Pushy, dominant personality "Type A" people (like all the pushy salespeople characters you have seen on TV or in the movies – they exist in real life too) who try to pressure others into:
- Buying products and services they are trying to sell - often stuff that people didn't need or didn't really want before they were pushed into buying.
- Investing in things in which they want others to invest.

Natural order of life in a capitalist democracy: money must circulate through a capitalist democracy in order for its economy to remain healthy. All sorts of people in a capitalist democracy compete with each other in order to get you to spend some of your money with them.
- *Companies* need customers like you to buy their products and services so that they can remain in business.
- *Religious and charitable organizations* need contributors like you to fund their operations.
- *Politicians* need financial contributors like you to fund their election campaigns.
- *Governments* need taxes and fees from citizens like you to pay for the services they provide.

Develop mental "radar" to detect spending manipulation attempts

Develop mental radar that detects attempts to manipulate your spending behavior by:
- Pushing your emotional hot buttons to get you to spend money that you hadn't planned to spend.
- Spinning your rational thinking to come around to someone else's way of thinking.

Think of professional marketing, advertising and hard-sell salespeople as enemy agents trying to scramble your brain's radar so that they can get their spending message bombs through your manipulation defense system and score hits on your brain. Their manipulation attempts can be:
- Flagrantly overt - right out in plain sight for your conscious mind to see or hear, e.g. advertising.
- Subtly covert - trying to fly below your radar so that your conscious mind doesn't detect their attempts to manipulate you, e.g. product placements in television shows and movies.

Our spending decisions are influenced to some extent by every piece of information ever taken in by our conscious and subconscious minds - the input we have loaded into our brain computers. We need to detect and filter out as much manipulation junk as possible in order to keep our rational decision making information database as uncontaminated as possible.

Learn how marketing, advertising and sales professionals may try to manipulate you.
- A key strategy for playing defense in any game is to learn as much as possible about what the other side might attempt to do on offense.
- Do as sports teams do, scout the other side. Study the offensive game plans of marketing, advertising and sales professionals. Learn as much as you can about their playbook.
  - Analyze the marketing programs of some major corporations. Who is their target market (demographic group[s] within an entire population who they think are most likely to buy the products or services they are marketing and advertising)? What brand name are they trying to create? What strategies guide their marketing programs – how are they trying to sell people on buying?
  - Study advertisements in the same way that athletes and coaches study "game films". Break down advertisements "frame by frame". Try to identify and learn about the techniques that advertising professionals use – their favorite "moves", e.g. smiling actors enjoying a product; using well known celebrities to attract people's attention and lend credibility to the advertising message; alluring men or women using a product to attract the opposite sex; macho men using guy stuff; sensual women using girl stuff; using words such as luxury and sophisticated.
  - Skim through different TV channels and radio stations at different times of the day and study the different "manipulation games" that advertising pros play with the different demographic audiences that watch and listen to different types of programs at different times of the day.
  - Observe sales people at work. Try to identify the different sales techniques that different salespeople use to sell different types of products.

Study subjects that marketing, advertising and sales professionals typically study.
- Study subjects such as psychology, social psychology, sociology, economics, behavioral economics, behavioral finance, marketing, and advertising.
- Read books they are likely to have read, such as *Scientific Advertising* by Claude Hopkins; *The Father of Spin* by Larry Tye; and *The Medium Is the Massage* by Marshall McLuhan (Author), Quentin Fiore (Author), Shepard Fairey (Illustrator).

Learn techniques marketing and advertising professionals use to identify target market niches such as.

- Demographic analysis of an entire population (e.g. country, state, city, neighborhood) to identify subgroups of people who share common characteristics such as age, income level, gender, and purchase preferences (things they typically buy).
- Use of census data and zip codes to identify income levels, types of homes, etc.
- Organization membership lists, mailing lists, subscription lists.
- Observation of the actual shopping behavior of people in stores.

Learn how they gather information about people in a target market niche using means such as:

- Tracking internet behavior, e.g. websites and webpages that people visit and their online shopping behavior.
- Data mining: identifying spending behavior patterns in things such as the types and quantities of things that people purchase seasonally or prior to weather events that have been forecast, e.g. snow shovels and batteries sold prior to snowstorms.
- Surveys of people who have recently purchased the type of product or service being advertised.
- Focus groups: inviting people to meet in a group to learn what they think about a specific product or service, and what would influence their decisions to buy it.

Learn to differentiate "hard sell" <u>manipulative</u> sales techniques from "soft sell" <u>consultative</u> selling techniques.

Hard sell "manipulative" selling is aimed at emotions more than rational thinking. It is geared to the words "How does it feel?" more than "What do you think?" It will often try to convert you from thinking "I'd like to have that" to "I need to have that". Hard sell techniques include:

- Trying to get you into a buying frame of mind. A salesperson might:
  - o Engage you in small talk and try to maneuver the conversation in such a way that you feel that the two of you think alike and that you can trust him.
  - o Ask you a series of questions intended to get you saying "yes" about things other than the product or service being sold; and then, step by small step, working the conversation around to his "sales pitch" to which he has been programming you to say "yes".
- Offering you the choice between two purchase options ("now, would you like to buy Option A or Option B"), rather than just asking if you want to buy or not.

To use a baseball analogy, hard sell "sales pitchers" won't just throw straight conversational fastballs. They will throw some sales pitch curve balls that deviously drop into your mental strike zone. Like a good baseball batter, learn how to spot sales pitch curve balls.

Soft sell "consultative" selling is aimed at people's rational thinking.

- A salesperson typically will try to learn about you and what you intend to do with whatever you are thinking about buying.
- He will "let the product or service sell itself" by explaining the logical reasons why the purchase might make good business sense for you (or in the best cases of consultative selling, explain why a purchase you had in mind might not make the best business sense for you at that particular time), or perhaps suggest an alternative purchase.

Pay attention to sales presentations you get to observe. Try to identify the different elements of hard sell and soft sell techniques that different sales people use.

You might also use your employer as a case study.

- If your gut instinct is that your company's strategy is to use soft sell techniques, ask the people in your marketing and sales departments for their thoughts about hard sell and soft sell techniques.
- If your gut instinct is that your company's marketing strategy includes use of hard sell techniques, the better part of wisdom might be to just analyze your company's marketing materials, and if possible, observe some sales presentations. If your analysis and observations lead you to conclude that your company's senior management condones the use of hard sell techniques with customers, take that as a warning as to how they might be treating you as their employee.

Shoot up your manipulation radar whenever you hear words or see images meant to:
- *Appeal to your emotions more than your rational thinking.*
  - "How do you feel?" more than "What do you think?"
  - "You'll feel like a king; a queen; a star."
  - "Treat yourself; you deserve it; you've earned it."
  - "Picture yourself using this, wearing this, seeing this in your home."
  - "Be the first in your neighborhood to have one of these."
  - "Trust me" - reputable marketing and sales people typically try to avoid saying these words because of their negative connotation to so many people.
- *Create a sense of urgency.*
  - "On sale for a limited time only; for today only; once in a lifetime."
  - "Limited availability / limited quantity of ..."
  - "Don't wait another minute to get yours; don't miss the boat on this one."
  - "Prices will never again be this low"; "this special offer expires."
- *Create a sense of peer group pressure*
  - "It's what everybody is buying, doing, wearing."
  - "This fashion is sweeping the nation"; "this is the in thing".
  - "Don't get left out."
- *Create the illusion that you can get something for nothing.*
  - "Free trial ..."
  - "At no cost to you."
  - "No money down; easy payments; easy financing terms."
- *Create the illusion that the product will help you attract the opposite sex.*
- *Describe something as the best, the most, or the fastest.*
  - In grammar, these words are called *superlatives*, meaning better than anything that is comparable. Learn about the three levels of "degree of comparison": positive = good; comparative = better; superlative = best.
  - It's awfully tough to be the best, the most, the fastest ... of anything. Think about gunfighters – there is always a faster gun.
  - When you see advertisements declaring that something is "the best" think about exactly who could have determined that whatever is being advertised actually is the best, and how they could have determined that the thing was indeed better than every other thing to which it could be compared.
  - Smart business people who are indeed the best at what they do rarely brag about being the best.
  - It is more prudent to say "one of the best" than it is to say "the best" – but "the ..." must sell better that "one of the ..."

Put on a psychological suit of armor

"Put on a psychological suit of armor" is my way of saying:
- Toughen up your mind to prevent people from "getting into your head" to manipulate your thinking and spending behavior.
- Steel your resistance.
- Don't be a mental "98 pound weakling" that people can push around (a reference to the Charles Atlas body building advertisements in the comic books of my youth).

A business planning and financial budgeting process can help you put on and maintain psychological armor.
- The process of writing a business plan and a projected financial statement budget will help you put on psychological armor.
- Regularly reading your plan and budget will help harden your armor by repeatedly pounding it into your conscious mind (knights' armor was "annealed" – a process that hardened their armor by repeatedly pounding it with a hammer).
- Regularly reading your plan and budget (and revising it as needed) will also help you seal up small cracks that might develop in your armor before those small cracks can grow into holes big enough to let manipulation attempts get into your head.

Get happy. Joy and satisfaction with our lives strengthen our mental resistance to manipulation. Unhappy people tend to be more easily led to believe that they can buy happiness and satisfaction. Marketers, advertisers and salespeople know that one of the best ways to get people to spend money is to create the illusion that buying whatever advertisers are selling will make buyers feel happy – as happy as the smiling and laughing models and actors in advertisements.

Plan to do things that bring you joy and satisfaction.
- The joy and satisfaction you create in life should define who you are, not the things you buy, nor the amount of money you earn, nor the power you wield over other people.
- "Follow your bliss." Develop an action plan that advances you toward your dream objectives. The more steps that you take toward making your dreams come true, the happier you are likely to get.

Get "comfortable in your own skin" - with who you are today.
- Do some introspective naval gazing. Shift your view from what is going on outside your body to what is going on inside your head.
- Don't try to escape from life. Go the other way. Immerse yourself in life, and the joy and satisfaction to be found in it.

Wise elders have been advising countless generations that true love and happiness cannot be bought:
- Think about adages such as "the best things in life are free".
- "Find a higher purpose for your life" – a purpose that gives you an inner glow of satisfaction.
- *Giving of a person's time and talents is a lot cheaper and generates a lot more joy and satisfaction than spending money trying to buy happiness and satisfaction.*

Learn to say "No", politely, and, with conviction. Learning to say "no, thank you" does a great job of toughening a person's resistance to spending unbudgeted money. Practice saying "no, thank you" until it feels comfortable to say it with a courteous smile.

Including a "fair share" objective in your budget for contributions to charitable and religious organizations each year will put a cap on the aggregate amount of contributions your budget can afford and likely help make the tough job of saying "no" to these good people a little easier.

- *Think of yourself as the "golden goose."* You will need to maintain good financial health if you are to continue providing financial support to charitable and religious organizations throughout the course of a long and satisfying life.
- From a strictly financial perspective, your fair share should be enough money to make you feel good about how much you plan to give each year.
- As you plan your long term and ultra-long term budgets, feel good about how much more money you will be able to contribute each year as your income and your wealth increase.
- Re-examine your beliefs about money, particularly any belief along the lines of "money is the root of all evil". Make sure that your thoughts about giving are not motivated by a feeling of guilt.
- It might be helpful to discuss the idea of a "fair share" limit on giving with at least one confidant on your business team who you think lives a good life and manages his money well, and perhaps a professional financial advisor.

Play a "*Star Wars*" game in your head to put a lighter side spin on the heavy duty subject of manipulation attempts made by marketing and advertising professionals. Think of money as "The Force" (the *Star Wars* movies offer some good life lessons. Learn what sources influenced George Lucas as he wrote the scripts).

- In this game think of The Dark Side of The Money Force as its power to influence our minds to spend money we had not planned to spend. Imagine marketing and advertising professionals as the Emperor, Darth Vader, and their henchmen. Imagine these characters trying to use the Dark Side of The Money Force to gain control of your mind and get you to spend your money the way they want you to spend it.
- Think of the good side of The Money Force as its power to help you lead a happy and satisfying life and provide you financial security. Imagine financial advisors and other professional service providers on your team as being Yoda or Obi Wan Kanobe training you to use The Money Force to do good and satisfying things in your life, and to resist the efforts of the Dark Side to get you to spend your money the way they want you to spend it.
- Remember that Darth Vader started out as a good-guy Jedi Knight. In this game think of marketing and advertising professionals as good guys who succumbed to the power of the Dark Side of The Money Force. (To my friends in the marketing and advertising businesses - <u>this is just a mind game</u>. I know most of you are good people who have good social consciences and are just doing your jobs.)

Making up games to play with advertisements is another way to help harden your psychological armor. If you live with family, make these family games. Following are a few game ideas to spur your imagination.

What's in there? Analyze advertisements that catch your attention.

- What grabbed your attention? Was the advertisement designed to appeal to your conscious mind? Your subconscious mind? Both? How did they try to do it?
- What's the "buy" message the advertisement is trying to convey? What reason(s) does the advertisement give you to buy? What need or want will be satisfied with a purchase?
- Is the product being advertised as a practical item to satisfy a need? A luxury item to satisfy a want?

- Context: why was the advertisement placed in the medium in which you saw it or heard it, e.g. TV, magazine, internet, radio? Why the place, location, or time in the medium?
- Target market audience demographic group(s)? Given that the ad caught your attention, in what demographic group(s) do you think advertising people would place you?
- Identify component elements in the ad and why they were chosen, such as:
  o People: age group? Male or female? Tone of voice? Speed of speaking? Why are they smiling, or looking sexy, or doing whatever they are doing?
  o Why were specific words, images, and colors chosen?
  o Lighting: bright and sunny; dark and dramatic?
  o Type and volume of music?
- What might you have done differently to make the ad more effective?

What's the catch? No successful business would pay money to advertise that they are selling their products or services at deeply discounted prices or giving away "free" products or services unless they had a plan to generate revenue in some way from their "largesse" (means giving things away - good word to know). Find the "catch" that will allow the seller to make a profit. Examples:
- A "loss leader" to get you into a store or onto a website to buy other merchandise.
- A "teaser" intended to get you hooked on buying more of the product at regular prices.
- A product that requires you to buy something else in order to use the cheap or free product. A classic example is the old Kodak film cameras. Kodak sold Brownie cameras at the lowest price they could in order to lock people into buying film and getting that film processed into photographs. A modern variant might be selling electronic devices at the lowest price possible in order to sell software applications, games, music, etc.
- Free subscriptions that automatically convert to paid subscriptions at the end of a trial period, and then keep on renewing automatically until you cancel the subscription; and the cancellation process is often a pain.
- "Sweat shop" labor that you would find reprehensible was used to make cheap products.

Mental keep-away: each time you see a point-of-purchase (point-of-sale) advertising display in a store (a display designed to get you to make a spur of the moment purchase) pretend a marketing professional is trying to grab money out of your wallet. Imagine a person's hand is reaching out to grab your wallet and then tap that wallet or handbag lightly to swat away the imaginary hand.

Surrounding yourself with good people will help minimize peer group pressure that could cause a crack in your psychological armor. Surround yourself with people who:
- Live comfortably prudent lifestyles practicing good budget management.
- Don't care how much money you have.
- Don't make you feel like you need to spend money the way they spend money.
- Like you just the way you are and make you feel good about yourself.

Ask your business team members to help you keep your psychological armor in good shape by telling you whenever they notice a small crack developing in your armor. "A stitch in time saves nine" type of maintenance work can help prevent repeated manipulation attempts from creating small cracks in your psychological armor and then gradually widening those cracks enough to let manipulation attempts get into your head. Ask your business team members to:
- Observe your spending behavior.
- Monitor the way you talk about money.
- Tell you as soon as they notice a crack developing in your armor.

General thoughts on playing expense management defense

Our game plans for playing expense management defense should be an integral part of the behavioral control system that we use to manage our daily lives.
- The more issues you have had with controlling your spending behavior, the more ideas in this book you might consider in developing your spending behavior control system.
- *Find a financially prudent middle ground between "free spending" and obsessive micro-control – between a luxury level lifestyle and a survival existence lifestyle.*

Monitor your actual spending versus your expense budget objectives. Suggestions:
- *Prepare a statement of income and expenses on a regular basis, perhaps monthly until sticking to your budget becomes a well ingrained habit* (a suggested five column spreadsheet format is on the Your Money Is Your Business website (www.ymiyb.com).
   - o Preparing monthly statements can help you:
      - Maintain awareness of how you have been spending your money.
      - Determine if you are on track to achieve your year end objectives if you keep spending at the same rate as you have been during the year to date.
   - o In the first column, copy your projected statement of income and expense budget objectives for the next one year planning period.
   - o In the second column, write budget objectives for the next one month period.
      - Monthly objectives will give you milepost objectives that lay out a path toward achievement of your year end objectives.
      - For the first year that you use this projected expense budget tool, just divide each annual objective by twelve. Don't drive yourself nuts trying to come up with an exact monthly budget number for each item.
         - o Month to month revenue and expenses will vary: monthly revenue will depend upon when you receive compensation from your employer (e.g. weekly, bi-weekly, or monthly salary or wages; bonuses), and certain expenses will vary with the seasons during the year (e.g. seasonal clothes for school or work, summer air conditioning, winter heating).
         - o The more years that you keep historical records of your monthly revenue and expenses, the more data you will have available to use in projecting more accurate monthly objectives in the future.
   - o In the third column, write your actual revenue, expenses, and profit for the month.
   - o In the fourth column, write the totals of your actual revenue, expenses, and profit for the "year to date".
   - o In the fifth column, "extrapolate" your actual revenue and expenses year to date out to the end of the year to see if you are on track to achieve your year-end objectives (extrapolate means project your future spending based upon the rate you have been spending your money year to date - learn how to extrapolate).
- Ask for a receipt for each purchase you make. Use these receipts to maintain a log of the aggregate amount of money you have spent in each expense category each month so that you can plug those numbers into your statement of income and expenses.
- Keeping track of aggregate discretionary expenses each month is especially important because by definition specific discretionary expenses items aren't planned expenses.
   - o You might try carrying a piece of paper and a pen with you (or a comparable hand held electronic device) to make note of the amount of each purchase each day that you would categorize as a discretionary expense.

- o At home each night, add your discretionary purchases for the day to a running total list for the month. Subtracting your running total of actual discretionary purchases for the month from your discretionary spending budget for that month will tell you how much money you have remaining to spend on discretionary purchases for the rest of the month.
- Use a checkbook register or whatever electronic equivalent tools your bank provides.
  - o Make note of each check you write and each cash withdrawal (include fees for using automated teller machines - ATM's).
  - o Reconcile your checkbook register with the monthly statements you receive from your bank.
- Learn how to use the online expense monitoring tools offered by the banks and credit card issuing companies with which you do business.
- Inject an element of fun into monitoring your expenses. Make it a game to try to generate the biggest profit you can each month, each quarter, each year.

Surround yourself with good people who can and will help you defend yourself against spending money you hadn't planned to spend.
- Choose your business team members wisely.
  - o People who share your business strategies, e.g. live below their means; make well-informed, well-reasoned spending decisions.
  - o People who have good "business smarts" and enough concern for your well-being to speak their minds if they see you doing or planning to do things that they think you shouldn't do with your money.
  - o Avoid "yes-men" who would agree with everything you want to buy or do, even if they thought it might not be wise for you to spend that money.
  - o Include at least one person with whom you can talk confidentially about your financial affairs.
- Choose friends who:
  - o Manage their money prudently.
  - o Will not burden you with peer pressure to keep up with their spending.
  - o Value you for your inner qualities, rather than as a playmate for expensive recreation, sports and hobbies.
- Make prudent decisions about the neighborhood in which you live, social clubs you join, sports you play, etc. Try to avoid putting yourself in social situations in which people might make you feel a need to spend more money than your budget could afford.
- Choose a life partner wisely.

Beware the insidious creep of "just this one little exception".
- "Oh, just this one little exception won't hurt" is famous for leading to "just this second little exception", which leads to another little exception, and on, and on, until a person's budget is "busted" (objectives are not achieved).
- Think about your budget as a spending diet. What often happens to food diets after a dieter sneaks in just one little chocolate bar? First, he thinks that one little exception isn't such a big deal. Then, that first exception lessens his will power to resist the temptation of a second little sweet treat exception, which lessens his will power to make more and more little exceptions until exceptions become the rule, and there goes the diet.
- Have you ever seen a cartoon in which a devil is sitting on a person's shoulder saying "oh, go ahead and do it" while an angel is sitting on the other shoulder saying "oh no, don't do it; that wouldn't be right"? *Picture a cartoon angel and devil sitting on your shoulders. Listen to the angel.*

The above said, plan for budget exceptions. Whereas we are all prone to have lapses in our self-discipline (e.g. just this one bowl of ice cream, just this one great new golf club) we should plan for them. One good way to plan for budget exceptions is to build up a cash reserve fund ("mad money" in a "rainy day fund") to pay for unplanned, spur-of-the-moment purchases. Make the build-up of a rainy day fund an objective in your projected statement of income and expenses budget and projected balance sheet budget.

Choose payment methods that are likely to work best to protect you from yourself.
- Automatic electronic payments: setting up automatic electronic payments from your bank account for regularly scheduled bills (e.g. credit cards, utilities, mortgage) will help you avoid forgetting to pay a bill and then incurring a late payment penalty expense.
- Credit card: use a credit card only if you have enough self-discipline to keep track of your purchases each month and not exceed your expense budget objectives.
- Debit card: will limit your spending to the amount of cash in your bank account. But, as with a credit card, use a debit card only if you have the self-discipline to closely monitor your purchases and not exceed your monthly expense budget objectives.
- Checks: writing a check can have two benefits:
  - o Give you a moment to take a quick run through the steps of your decision making process to make a reasoned decision about spending the money.
  - o Using a checkbook register will help you track cash spent and available to spend.
- Cash: paying cash will enable you to physically observe dollar bills leaving your wallet. When that cash is gone, it's gone. You can't spend what you don't have.

Remove the temptation to spend. Move your money "out of sight, out of mind". A few suggestions to consider:
- *"Pay yourself first".*
  - o If possible, have your paycheck deposited directly into a bank checking account.
  - o Then arrange an electronic transfer of a pre-established amount of each paycheck from your checking account into a savings account; or do the transfer manually if you can't arrange an electronic transfer. You can call these transfers a "cash reserve expense" on your projected income statement budget and "cash reserve account" on your projected balance sheet budget.
  - o If you get paid every two weeks (26 paychecks per year), prepare monthly budgets based upon 2 paychecks per month (24 paychecks) and deposit the 2 "extra" paychecks into your cash reserve savings account.
  - o After you have achieved your cash reserve savings objective, start transferring excess cash into your investment account.
- *Limit "pocket money".* The less cash a person has in his pocket the easier it is likely to be to manage discretionary spending.
  - o Cash can "burn a hole in your pocket".
  - o Some people can almost hear cash in their pockets calling out "spend me".
  - o If you are not paid weekly, you might set a limit on the amount of money you spend out of each paycheck on discretionary purchases, and start out each week with just a fractional amount of that money as cash in your pocket.
  - o Limit the number of times you withdraw cash from automated teller machines (ATM's). Many people seem to have a mental disconnect between the cash they withdraw from ATM's and the cash remaining in their bank accounts. Each time you make a withdrawal from an ATM:
    - Check the cash balance remaining in your account.
    - Take a moment to think about how much of your discretionary expense

> budget you have remaining to spend for the rest of the month.
> - o To help keep track of how much cash you have remaining in your pocket, you might keep the paper money you carry in denomination order - ones, fives, tens, twenties, etc. After each cash purchase, put the change you receive as paper bills back into your pocket with your other cash in denomination order. This will give you an opportunity to count your remaining cash.
> - o Make a game of saving loose change - "a penny saved, is a penny earned."
>   - ▪ The act of taking loose change out of your pocket and saving it in a "penny jar" (my mother used an old mayonnaise jar) or piggybank will serve as a reminder to think about every penny you spend.
>   - ▪ And, it will provide a visual reminder of how small amounts of money that are saved can add up to much larger amounts over time.
>   - ▪ Plus, it's fun to watch a pile of cash grow.
- Whenever you see a penny on the ground (or any other coin), pick it up. I know some wealthy people who do this religiously (and, yes, my mother did this too). Then put that penny in your penny jar when you get home. Besides having another penny to put in your penny jar, there are other benefits:
  - o A cautionary reminder that somebody lost some of his money and you should defend yourself from losing any of your money.
  - o From a metaphysical perspective, it can be a reminder that the world provides us with all sorts of opportunities to bring money into our lives if we keep our eyes open and recognize opportunities when they occur.
  - o Bending down is exercise.
- If you receive money unexpectedly, money that you hadn't budgeted to be a part of your annual revenue (e.g. tax refund, bonus paid by your employer, an inheritance), deposit most/all of that money in your cash reserve savings account – just don't blow it all.

Identify "emotional spending soft spots" in your "psychological armor" - "hot buttons" that might get you to spend money you hadn't planned to spend if they got pushed. To help identify your emotional spending soft spots you might ask yourself questions such as:
- Why did I choose to live where I live? Why do I dress the way I dress?
- Why do I do certain things I know aren't good for me, e.g. go off on spending sprees, spend money on a nice car that I drive too fast, eat unhealthy foods, etc.?
- Do I tend to buy higher priced name brand products rather than a less expensive generic or house brand products that would provide me equal quality, e.g. clothes, food? Why?
- Do I try to buy my way into people's hearts?
- Are there any parts of my life with which I not happy?

Unhappiness is emotional spending soft spot for many people. People try to buy themselves greater happiness in many different ways, such as:
- Escape – trying to get away from it all: spending more money than a prudent budget could afford on sports, hobbies, vacations, expensive entertainments, etc.
- Treating themselves to psychological "comfort food".
- Trying to attract the opposite sex by buying things that advertising professionals want people to believe will attract the opposite sex, e.g. an impressive car, the latest clothing styles (which clothing sellers continuously change to keep people buying), the right beer or alcohol to drink (or be seen buying in a bar), men's body sprays, women's make-up.
- Living vicariously (living through the lives of others), e.g. mega-fans who spend more money than a prudent budget could afford on team merchandise or celebrity magazines.

To help minimize feelings of social pressure to spend money, keep in mind that things are not always what they appear to be.
- It is likely that some people in your neighborhood are living beyond their means. They may be putting on an appearance of having plenty of money, but, in reality, they are spending every dime of their income, and perhaps going into debt to finance their lifestyles.
- Keep reminding yourself that the people we see living expensive lifestyles in TV shows and movies are just actors playing fictitious characters in make believe stories. Watching fictional characters living expensive lifestyles over extended periods of time can subtly influence the spending behavior of some audience members.

Practice preventive maintenance to minimize repair and replacement expenses. Remember what your parents and elders taught you about taking care of things.
- "An ounce of prevention is worth a pound of cure."
- "A place for everything and everything in its place."

The best run businesses tend to take the best care of their property, equipment, and vehicles. Follow their example with things you own such as your:
- Car, e.g. regularly change the oil and rotate the tires.
- Home, e.g. have seasonal inspections of your heating and air conditioning systems, clean out rain gutters, and periodically paint the exterior.

If you have children, keep in mind that kids can be big drains on cash until they learn to be responsible stewards of their toys, bikes, sports gear, and "our" home and its furnishings.

Create your own expense cutting games. A few game ideas to spur your imagination:
- Lunch chef: have fun saving money on food by learning how to make delicious, nutritious low cost lunches to bring to work rather than buying lunch at work. You might get co-worker friends to play along with you and share lunch ideas with each other.
- Barista: instead of buying an expensive cup of coffee on your way to work, see how good a cup of coffee you can make at home each morning; maybe cut back to buying coffee every other day.
- Connect-a-place: when you need to use your car to run multiple errands on any given day, try to combine as many stops as possible into one trip and plan the shortest, most fuel efficient route between stops in order to minimize gasoline consumption.
- Hyper-miling: a gasoline saving game that became popular during the gasoline price explosion in the late 2000's. The objective is to get as much mileage as possible from each gallon of gas by means of coasting into stop lights, accelerating slowly, etc.
- Bargain hunting: search out sales, second hand stores, etc. – but, don't buy cheap.
- Coupon clipper: see how much money you can save each month using coupons.
- How low can you go: seek ways to minimize the money you spend each month on the daily living expense items in your budget. Monthly statements of income and expenses will help you keep score.
- What does it cost them: try to figure out the sellers' costs for things you buy, and how much profit they are making off of you. Thinking about how much of your money would become other people's profits might help dampen your enthusiasm to spend your money, and perhaps motivate you to try to negotiate lower prices.

- Discover or re-discover the joy and satisfaction of low cost entertainments such as family game nights, leisurely walks, hiking, or going to local high school plays and community theatre productions.

To help defend against "rising expectations" and "the wealth effect":
- Re-read Chapter 6 of this book on a regular basis, and use the suggested ten point wealth and success management system.
- Each year as you preparing your projected financial statement budget for the next one year planning period:
    - o Review the year-end financial statements you prepared for prior years.
    - o Identify expense items on which your spending has been increasing from year to year.
    - o Analyze why your spending has been increasing: increasing prices of the exact same things you have been buying year to year, spending more money on more expensive versions of the same type items, spending money on new things?
    - o Do the reasons for increased spending make good business sense to you?
    - o Ask yourself "given my current income, net worth, and current position in life, how much of my total annual revenue could I spend this year before a comfortably prudent lifestyle would start stretching out into a luxury level lifestyle?"

To help change spending habits that you want to change:
- Learn about cognitive behavioral therapy (changing the way we think can help us change the way we behave – e.g. the idea behind thinking of your money as your business).
- Learn how various professionals suggest we go about changing our habits.
- Get some practical tips on kicking bad spending habits by learning how people have successfully kicked other bad habits, e.g. smoking, drinking too much, eating too much, and not exercising enough.
- Understand that behavior modification is tough work, and that the longer a person has had a bad spending habit the tougher it is likely to be to change that habit.
    - o Don't get frustrated or upset if a habit doesn't change overnight. Be patient with yourself and just keep working at the change you want to make.
    - o Congratulate yourself on each step you take toward changing a spending habit.

Consider focusing your attention on minimizing your largest expense items first. On your projected income statement budget, focus your attention on minimizing your largest expense items first. These expense items might include:
- Taxes
- Housing
- Food and drink
- Clothing
- Medical and dental healthcare
- Transportation
- Charitable contributions
- Recreation: hobbies, sports, boats and other recreational vehicles
- Maintenance, repair and replacement of a car, home, furniture, or boat.

Defending against tax expenses

Defer, minimize, pay - three key words for income tax management.
- *Defer* tax payments as long as prudently reasonable. You might consider:
    o   Maximizing contributions to tax deferred savings accounts.
    o   Holding investments long enough to qualify for long term capital gains treatment.
- *Minimize* tax expenses as much as tax codes allow. You might consider:
    o   Asking a financial advisor or professional tax expert for advice.
    o   Taking advantage of non-taxable employee benefits provided by your employer.
- *Pay* income taxes you owe.
    o   Do NOT play tax avoidance games with the Internal Revenue Service. Failure to pay taxes that are legitimately owed can lead to serious financial harm to tax cheats after IRS tax auditors eventually catch them.
    o   Declare all the revenue you earn.
    o   Do not fake expenses or fudge actual expenses upward.
    o   Have documentation for your deductible expenses.

Two of the best ways to defend against taxes:
- Hire a professional tax expert to get expert advice.
- Get involved in the political process that determines the taxes you pay.

Hire a tax accounting professional as soon as your budget can afford it ("afford" being a highly relative term). Smart business managers hire income tax experts to help them minimize their tax expenses. Follow their example.

A good tax professional is likely to more than cover the cost of his services by saving you:
- *Lost opportunity cost of the time* that you could have spent doing things that would have generated far more joy and satisfaction in your life.
- *Headache and heartache* of completing tax return forms.
- *Tax dollars*: good tax accounting professionals know how to use the income tax code (regulations) to their clients' best advantage, e.g. tax credits available, allowable deductions, timing of when to recognize income, use of tax deferred savings plans, etc.

Until such time as your budget can afford hiring a tax accounting professional:
- Consider buying and using one of the tax preparation software packages available for home use.
- Seek advice from your business team members who have the greatest tax expertise.

Think of your federal, state, and local governments as service businesses.
- Think of your elected government representatives as government service providers that you hire and pay, e.g. mayor, county executive, congressperson, senator, president.
- You hire them with your votes. You pay their salaries with your tax dollars.
- Their business is to provide you with government services.
- They are your public service employees (a/k/a "public servants" - an old fashioned term that isn't used much today).
- *As a society we often elevate our elected representatives to celebrity status. We forget that they work for us.*

Get involved in the political process that determines the taxes you pay.
- Speak up for yourself as convincingly as your personality allows.
- Call, write, and visit your elected government representatives. Tell them about the tax policies you think they should adopt, and how you think they should spend your tax dollars. Otherwise, you could wind up paying more than you think is your fair share of government tax revenue and getting back less than you think is your fair share of government services. <u>Your opinions must be heard if they are to be considered</u>.
- Each of your government representatives has a staff that helps him formulate positions on tax and spend issues. Staff people have a huge influence on your money. Call, write, and visit them too. Get to know them, and get them to know you as a level headed, fiscally prudent constituent who carefully thinks through your positions on tax and spend issues.
- Tell them that you vote, and that you have family and friends who you will be encouraging to vote the way you recommend they vote - your voice is multiplied through the people you know.
- Too few people communicate with their elected officials. Individual citizens are likely to have a lot more influence than they think they have.
- Don't wait for the election season to speak up. Politicians and their staffs tend to be more responsive to input from constituents before they get into the heat of election campaigns.
- Politicians typically pay the most attention to the people who provide the most help to get them elected or re-elected by means of voting, financial support, and volunteer work.
- Adopt a positive attitude about paying your taxes. This will help you project a <u>solutions-oriented business attitude</u> as you get involved in the political process.
  - *Think about taxes as the dues you pay to live where you live.*
  - Be thankful you have the income on which to pay taxes.
- *VOTE – "walk the talk".* Use your right to vote to "hire" the politicians who are most likely to work on your behalf to get done what you want done in regard to:
  - The tax dollars you pay.
  - How your tax dollars are spent – government services you get for the money you pay.

Apathy can cost you big bucks.
- If you decide to sit on the sidelines of the political game you will be allowing other people to determine how much of your money your local, state, and federal governments take away from you in the form of taxes and how they spend your money.
- "If you are not a part of the solution, you are a part of the problem."

Learn how the political process is supposed to work in theory, how it often works in reality, and the difference that one politically involved person can make.
- All too often there is a big gap between the way the election process and government operations are <u>supposed to work</u> in theory and the way they <u>actually work</u> in practice. To paraphrase Prince Otto von Bismarck, "the making of sausages and laws are both such messy processes that some people may not have the stomach to watch them being made".
- Learn:
  - How politicians are supposed to get nominated and elected.
  - How the legislative process is supposed to work - creating, amending, and repealing laws.
  - How regulatory authorities are supposed to regulate.
- *Learn about the <u>importance of political compromise to</u> the governance of a <u>sustainable democracy</u>.* The politicians we elect who have gravitated toward the "liberal left" end of the political spectrum and politicians who have gravitated toward the "conservative right"

end must be able to find ways work together and reach comprises that help us manage the serious financial challenges that we all face together as a nation. Meeting these financial challenges will require financially savvy government leadership and mind-boggling amounts of money (a few of our financial challenges are listed back on pages 2 and 3).

- Learn about "gerrymandering" and how it influences who gets elected (re-drawing of electoral districts on a map by the political party in power in order to include as many voters as possible who are likely to vote for their candidates).
- *Learn how "big money" influences the taxes you pay*, e.g. *big financial contributors and special interest groups.*
- Watch the movie *Mr. Smith Goes to Washington* for inspiration as to the difference one person can make.

Study the financial management of governments from a business perspective. Learn enough about the business of government to become a well-educated voter and convey that you know what you are talking about when you talk to your legislators about governing. Learn:
- How budgets are supposed to be prepared at local, state, and federal government levels.
- How governments can generate revenue: (a) taxes, e.g. income, Social Security, Medicare, sales, excise (specific sale items, e.g. gasoline, tobacco, alcohol), and property; (b) fees, e.g. for licenses and permits, use of parks and other government facilities.
- How tax codes come to be written; how courts interpret the meanings of tax code provisions as those provisions are applied in real world situations; and how "bureaucratic inertia" can impede making changes to tax codes that have become entrenched in society over time.
- How taxes are collected: Internal Revenue Service operations, income tax returns, etc.
- How government personnel and government service programs are managed.
- How expense dollars get allocated to spending programs.
- How government spending programs can "take on lives of their own" over time as they become ingrained in the lives and future plans of citizens, government employees, private sector companies, and non-profit organizations.

Learn about the pros and cons of using different types of taxes and tax rates to fund government operations:
- Income taxes
  - *Progressive tax rates*: sliding scale tax rates - tax rates increase as tax payer incomes increase - high income earners are supposed to pay higher rates than low income earners.
  - *Flat tax rate*: the same tax rate is assessed on each dollar of income, no matter the amount of each tax payer's annual income (everybody pays the same rate).
- Sales taxes, real estate taxes, and other special purpose taxes (e.g. gasoline and alcohol).

Learn how tax policies can impact the vibrancy of the local economy in which you live and work - especially in relation to the economic vibrancy of "economic competitor" states and countries.
- Government tax policies are a major factor in economic vibrancy, e.g. where companies locate their operations, where jobs are created, and where jobs are lost.
- Low to moderate tax rates can help foster the growth of an economy by encouraging companies to locate facilities in a particular area, invest money in those facilities, and provide jobs for people who live in the area.
- "Heavy" taxes can discourage economic vibrancy by motivating both employers and prospective employees (residents) to move away from a city, state or country.

Learn about the tax policies and government management practices of the countries that have the most vibrant economies in the global marketplace and the states that have the most vibrant economies in the national marketplace.
- What countries and states have had the largest budget surpluses (profits) year after year?
- What commonalities in tax policies do these countries and states share?
- What commonalities in government management practices do they share?
- What tax policies and government management practices might provide the most vibrant, sustainable economy for you?

Do a "compare and contrast" study of the business management practices of government entities and private sector companies. Things you might study:
- How government entities and private sector companies use a planning and budgeting process to manage their respective operations.
- How government entities and private companies coordinate the activities of various departments to maximize operational and cost efficiencies in delivering services.
- How government entities and private companies use cost-benefit analyses.
- How direct expenses and overhead expenses are managed in government and in business.
- How customer satisfaction is measured in private companies, and how taxpayer satisfaction is measured in the delivery of government service programs?
- How employee productivity is measured in government entities and in private sector companies. Has the productivity of government employees been keeping pace with the increase in productivity of private sector employees?
- How employee performance reviews are used in government entities and in private companies, from entry level employees on up to the highest level senior executives.
  - o Are employees who do the best work in the most efficient manner typically rewarded with the best pay increases and promotions?
  - o Are employees who do the lowest quality work in the least efficient manner typically "weeded out" and replaced over time?
- How well would management consultants say that your elected government officials have been managing the operations of your local, state, and federal government entities?
- Why did the phrases "bureaucratic waste" and "corporate inefficiency" come into being?

Develop your own opinions about how the business of your local, state, and federal government entities should be conducted.
- What should be the mission of each level of government? What do you think about:
  - o Puritan work ethic - what should individual citizens do for themselves and what should government do for them?
  - o Henry David Thoreau's comment "That government is best which governs least"?
- How should revenue be generated at each level of government - local, state, federal: income tax, sales tax, real estate tax, other special purpose taxes, fees?
- What services should be provided at each level of government?
- How should each government entity finance its business operations:
  - o Cash flow financing: revenue equal to or greater than expenses each year?
  - o Equity financing: generate a budget surplus each year and build a cash reserve ("rainy day" fund) to finance dips in annual revenue and emergency cash needs?
  - o Debt financing? How much debt would be too much debt?
- What percentage of each tax dollar should be spent on which government services?
- How could / should the cost of government operations be reduced:

- o Direct costs of specific services (government programs) provided?
- o Overhead costs, e.g. salaries, employee benefits, office space?
- *Degree of social responsibility* necessary for a society to maintain social order, and avoid civil unrest - violent demonstrations, riots, economy crippling strikes, etc.? To maintain the viability of an economy, must each citizen be guided by "benevolent self-interest"?
- *Redistribution of wealth*: taxing higher income citizens in order to provide government services and economic advancement opportunities for lower income citizens?
- *Should each government entity publish its "comprehensive annual financial report" in a user friendly, easy to understand format similar to the annual report to stockholders published by publicly owned companies - a report that would enable the average taxpayer to evaluate how efficiently the government business is operating?*
  - o Executive letter (from president, governor, etc.) to taxpayers summarizing government operating results for the past year, challenges faced by the government and objectives, strategies and action plans to meet those challenges.
  - o Income statement ("statement of activities") that helps taxpayers understand:
    - How revenue was generated during the year (taxes, fees, etc.).
    - How expense dollars were allocated to major departments and agencies.
    - Annual operating profit or loss – surplus or deficit.
  - o User friendly balance sheet ("statement of net position") that summarizes assets owned by the government entity, liabilities owed, and net worth ("net position").
- *Should each government entity publish its annual budget in a user friendly format?*

If you think an income tax is a good way to fund government operations:
- What percent of your annual income do you think you should pay as income tax? What would be your "fair share" percentage of your income to pay to as income tax?
- Should you pay the same percent of your income as the retired lady down the block who is living on a fixed income, or the young couple next door who are financially strapped with a new baby, or the highly compensated senior officers of big companies?
- What percent of their annual incomes should companies pay?

Minimize your potential for future regret.
- Understand that our thinking about taxes and government spending tends to evolve as we age and as our income and wealth rise.
  - o As many people age they tend to get more protective of their money and to get more conservative about taxes and government spending.
  - o It's likely that your positions on tax and spend issues will change as you age and your financial position improves.
- Understand that the outcomes of government tax policies and government spending programs typically play out over periods of years, often many, many years (as with funding social security payments).
- Consider your long term and ultra-long term business plans as you develop your opinions and political positions on tax and spend issues, and as you make decisions about politicians for whom you will vote. Project how the positions you favor today and the voting decisions you make today are likely to impact the world in which you will be living in the future – in particular the impact on your lifestyle and your money.
  - o Are the tax policies and government service programs that you support today likely to lead to a sustainably vibrant economy in 10, 20, 30, or more years?
  - o How are tax and spend policies that you support today likely to impact your annual income and your investment portfolio years out into the future?

Defending against debt

Practice the principles of risk management
- *Avoid* as much debt as a professional financial advisor would advise avoiding. Consider using cash flow and equity financing to finance your life to the greatest extent possible.
- *Transfer the risk of default on debt*. Consider buying long term disability [and accident] insurance to help make home mortgage or automobile loan payments in the event of an interruption to your stream of income.
- *Manage the risk of debt you decide to accept*.
  - o Learn all you can about the prudent use of debt financing. Debt can be a prudent financial management tool if it is used as cautiously as any other potentially dangerous tool such as a chain saw is used. Learn how to use the tool of debt before you pick it up.
  - o Use a projected financial statement budget to put a prudent limit on the amount of debt you accept, e.g. relative to the amount and predictability of your future income, current cash reserves and other liquid assets, and your liabilities.

BEFORE borrowing money, do enough homework to make a well-informed, well-reasoned decision as to whether a loan would make good business sense.
- The more you feel a need to borrow money, the greater the risk that your emotions might interfere with your rational thinking, and the more important it might be to discuss a decision about a loan with a confidant you think has a good business mind. Discuss:
  - o Why you think you need the loan.
  - o What additional need for borrowed debt you might have prior to repaying this loan in full, e.g. student loan, car, home purchase or repair.
  - o How the loan would fit into your projected financial statement budget.
- If you decide that a loan makes good business sense, then seek a lender that has earned a good reputation for being *a "socially responsible" lender* – a bank, credit union, savings and loan, etc.
  - o Socially responsible means that the lender cares for the financial well-being of its clients, and the economic and social health of the community in which it does business.
  - o Socially responsible lenders seek to make loans that make good business sense for their borrowers.
- Ask the lender to help you do your homework by "pre-qualifying" you for a loan.
  - o "Pre-qualify" means the lender will determine if a loan makes good business sense for you from their perspective.
  - o During the pre-qualification process, a good lender will try to get to know you, what you plan to do with the money, and the details of your current financial position. They will analyze this information and discuss with you the reasons why or why not they think the loan would make good business sense for you.
  - o As you go through this loan pre-qualification process keep in mind:
    - The business of lenders is to make as many prudent loans as they can.
    - A key business strategy of socially responsible lenders is to develop long term customer relationships that generate repeat business and referrals from satisfied customers.

If a socially responsible lender didn't think that a loan made good business sense for you at the time, the lender would decline to make the loan.
- When a lender declines a loan the lender is supposed to tell the loan applicant the reasons

why the loan was declined.

- *Accept a loan declination as valuable financial planning advice* (of course if you don't agree with that lender's decision, it might be wise to get a second opinion from a second socially responsible lender).
- A prudent borrower can then start taking action to resolve whatever issues caused the lender to decline the loan. Good lenders will often advise a declined borrower as to what he can do to qualify for a loan in the future.
- A loan declination can help a prospective borrower defend himself against:
  - o Taking on the obligation of loan payments that a professional lender thinks the borrower would have too much difficulty making.
  - o Payment obligations that might cause the borrower to have sleepless nights.
  - o Risk of a default that could trigger all sorts of bad outcomes for the borrower.

Understand that even if today your projected financial statement budget indicates you have a predictable stream of annual revenue to cover your regularly scheduled loan payments, you might not have that money tomorrow. Unexpected stuff can happen and cut off or significantly reduce a stream of revenue, such as:

- Losing a job if an employer eliminates a job position, has a reduction in force to cut overhead expenses, moves out of town, etc.
- Serious accident or medical condition that impairs a person's ability to do his job.

A few suggested borrowing guidelines:
- <u>Borrow money only to satisfy a genuine need not to satisfy a want</u>.
- Save up as much cash as possible to maximize your down payment. The larger the down payment, the less the amount of money you will need to borrow and the lower the interest rate you might be able to get.
- Make sure that the proposed debt repayment terms fit comfortably into your projected income statement budgets for the next one year and for the full term of the loan.
- The longer the term of a prospective loan and the less predictable your future stream of annual revenue (job security, interest rate risk on passive income, etc.) the more caution you should take in planning to borrow the money.

If you have current debt:
- Consider paying off your debt as fast as prudently possible to help minimize interest expense (assuming no prepayment penalties). Consider asking a professional financial advisor for advice about developing a prudent debt repayment plan.
- Consider paying off the debt that charges the highest interest rate first, e.g. credit card balances that have carried over from month to month.
- If you have high interest debt that you can't pay off in the short term, and you own real estate, you might consider replacing high interest debt with lower interest debt, e.g. refinancing a home, second mortgage, home equity line of credit. Consider seeking advice from a socially responsible lender, a confidant you think has a good business mind, and perhaps a professional financial advisor.
- To minimize the risk of incurring late payment fees, set up automatic electronic payments from your bank account to help assure your monthly payments are made as scheduled.

Paying off debt as fast as possible is just a general rule of thumb. Exceptions might include:
- Home mortgage – considerations to evaluate include:
  - o Mortgages typically have low interest rates.
  - o Investment portfolio generating an annual return greater than interest expense.

  o   Interest and real estate tax payments deductions on income tax returns.
- Car loan: if a dealer provided a sales promotion at an extremely low interest rate, or in some cases no interest at all.

Credit card debt: the major danger of using a credit card is the risk of accumulating debt that your budget couldn't afford to repay in full each month.
- Technically speaking the word "credit" means the right that a credit card issuing company provides to a person to use the company's money. But after using that credit the credit card user becomes indebted to the credit card issuing company.
- A credit card user isn't actually paying a merchant when he makes a purchase. The credit card issuing company is the one who actually pays the merchant. The credit card user is incurring a debt to repay the credit card issuer.
- The credit card issuer sends the card user a statement each month itemizing the money the card issuer paid to merchants on the behalf of the card user, the total amount of debt that the card user owes to the card issuer, and the minimum amount of debt the card user must repay that month.
- Credit card issuers typically generate revenue in three ways:
  o   Interest paid by credit card users on debt balances that are carried over from month to month. If a card user doesn't pay the total debt in full each month, the card issuer charges interest on the unpaid amount that is carried over to the next month. These interest rates typically are among the highest interest rates most people will ever become obligated to pay.
  o   Annual fees charged to credit card users, late payment penalties, etc.
  o   Fees paid to them by merchants: merchants who accept credit cards pay credit card companies a fee (a small percentage of each sales dollar) in exchange for their ability to make sales to customers who want to use credit cards. This requirement to pay fees is why some merchants won't accept credit cards (certain cards or all cards) – these merchants want to be paid by cash or check so that they can keep every penny of every sales dollar.

Defensive measures to consider include:
- Use a credit card only if you have the self-discipline to use it prudently.
- Use a credit card as a convenient way to make only those purchases that fit into your budget.
- Maintaining a running total log of the aggregate amount of your credit card purchases each month will tell you how much cash you will need to have available to pay the full balance each month and help you stay in line with your monthly expense budget.
  o   Ask for a receipt for each purchase. Use those receipts to maintain the running total list - like a checkbook register.
  o   Use online account management tools offered by your credit card company(s).
- If you have been carrying over a credit card balance from month to month, develop a plan to pay off the full balance due as soon as prudently possible. It might be wise to discuss your plan with the most financially astute confidant on your business team or with a professional advisor well practiced in helping people "get out of" credit card debt.
- Limit the number of cards you have in order to minimize your temptation to use them.
- To help defend yourself against the influence of credit card commercials on your spending behavior, you might program your brain to think of "catchy, breezy" credit card commercials and advertisements as insults to your financial intelligence.

Home mortgage loans: use of a home mortgage loan is generally thought to be a good use of debt when a well-informed, well-reasoned decision is made to use it. However, debt is debt, and debt carries significant financial risk, i.e. if you didn't make payments as agreed it is possible that you could lose your home in addition to all the money you had invested in it. Following are some things to consider and perhaps discuss with at least one business team member whose business judgment you trust and/or a professional financial advisor.

Before beginning to shop for a home, do your homework. A few suggestions to consider:
- Write a list of the pros and cons of home ownership.
    - o The idea of "home" is loaded with emotion.
    - o Writing this list will help you think about the sobering cons as well as the exciting pros – a good emotional control measure.
- Compute the maximum monthly loan payment that your budget could afford during your next one year planning period.
- Research socially responsible lenders from which you could choose to borrow. Consider talking to one or two of these lenders to get their professional opinions about:
    - o Prequalifying you for a loan that your budget could "comfortably" afford.
    - o The pros and cons of each of the various types of mortgage loans available, e.g. fixed rate loans, adjustable rate loans (ARM's), and "balloon" loans (payments of interest only until the end of the loan's term when a final "balloon" payment of the principal amount s paid).
    - o Costs of each type of mortgage available, e.g. interest rates and closing costs.
- Compute a maximum home purchase price based upon the maximum monthly payment your budget could afford, loan closing costs, etc.
- Research homes available for purchase that your budget could afford - types, sizes, and prices of homes in neighborhoods in which you might like to live.
- Seek referrals to professional realtors from people on your business team whose business judgment you trust; interview each prospective realtor; and decide upon a realtor with whom you would like to work.

After you have done your homework, then engage a professional realtor and begin your home shopping in earnest. Caution: beware talk about "growing into a loan" (projecting your future income and how loan payments would fit into a future budget). This is dangerous stuff. Projected future income doesn't always materialize. If the realtor seems to be forgetting the maximum price you told him your budget could afford and he is pushing you to buy the most expensive home for which he could help you get a loan approved, consider getting another realtor.

Car loans
- Save up a cash reserve and make the largest possible down payment.
- Comparison shop to find the vehicle that provides the "best value" for your money.
- Then shop for the best price and best loan terms available.
- To help minimize the amount of a car loan you might need, research advice available about how to get the lowest price on the car of your choice, e.g. buy at the end of a model year, consider buying a well maintained used car (cars tend to have their greatest depreciation in value during their first two or three years).

Student loans
- Before taking on student loan debt a student should plan how he would repay his debt.
- To determine a maximum affordable loan amount, the student should prepare a projected statement of income and expenses budget that factors in repayment of the loan while also

paying all his other expenses during the term of the loan.
- He should have a career path plan in mind to get a job that has reasonable potential to generate the annual revenue that would be needed to repay the loan as well as pay all his other expenses during the term of the loan.

Suggestions that might help minimize student loan expenses:
- Take pre-requisite classes at a lower cost, local community college, and then transfer to a college of choice to get a desired bachelor's degree.
- Attend a public, in-state college instead of a private school or out-of-state college.
- Continue to live at home while going to school.

Payday loans and car title loans are D-A-N-G-E-R-O-U-S.
- *Payday loans (cash advance loans)* can be so hazardous to the financial well-being of consumers that a number of states have passed laws that prohibit them. Learn why.
- *A car title loan* gives a lender a right to take a borrower's car if the borrower defaults on repayment.

BEWARE lenders who advertise with words such as "easy credit" or "we will find a way to lend you the money you need no matter what your credit history". These advertisers often turn out to be the type of predatory lenders we discussed earlier. A rule of thumb: the higher the interest rate a lender charges, the more careful a person should be about borrowing from that lender.

The more a person felt he was in such dire financial straits that he had no alternative but to resort to one of these loans, the more important it would be to seek advice from at least one financially savvy confidant about how to manage whatever financial problem(s) were making him feel the need to borrow. Possible sources of advice include: a successful business person that the person knows and trusts, a local government assistance program, certain religious leaders who have experience working with congregation members who have considered or used such loans with some regularity, Consumer Financial Protection Bureau (CFPB).

Stock purchase "margin" loans are EXTREMELY risky. Learn about margin loans (and margin calls), their risks, and the agony these loans have caused so many people who couldn't repay their loans after stock market values dropped significantly, as they periodically do.

Maximize your credit score to help minimize the interest rates you will be charged for any future debt you decide to take on. Learn about:
- Fair Credit Reporting Act (FRCA).
- How a credit score is computed, and factors that go into computing a credit score (e.g. current amount of debt, credit cards owned and used, debt repayment history)

Research ways to maximize your credit score. Suggestions I have heard include:
- Pay bills promptly. Use automatic bill payments when possible to lessen the chances of forgetting to make a payment.
- Limit the number of credit cards you have. Learn about the impact that the act of signing up for a new credit card can have on your credit score.
- FRCA entitles you to a free copy of the credit report issued each year by each of the three credit reporting agencies (Experian, TransUnion, and Equifax). Considering ordering a report from a different agency every four months at (annualcreditreport.com) to monitor your credit history and correct any errors. Credit scores are not on these reports – only credit history. But, your credit history is a major factor in computing your credit score.

Defensive Shopping

"Caveat emptor" (buyer beware) has been such good advice for so long that it comes down to us in the old Latin language.

Buy "best value". In this book best value means that combination of price paid and utility gained (e.g. practical use, joy, satisfaction) that provides a buyer an optimal return on money spent.
- Components of best value for products might include:
    - Competitive pricing in a price range your budget can afford.
    - Personal satisfaction derived from the product's use or appearance.
    - Better operating performance than comparable products.
    - Lower maintenance and repair expense than comparable products.
    - Longer useful life expectancy.
- Components of best value for services might include:
    - Competitive pricing in a price range your budget can afford.
    - Top quality expertise and experience.
    - "Sleep insurance" - a feeling of comfort that you are being well served.
    - "Value added" services in addition to the basic services you planned to buy:
        - *Advice that helps protect you from yourself.*
            - *Good* advisors will tell you things you need to hear, not just things you want to hear.
            - Advice to (a) do things that you should do that you may not want to do, and (b) not do things that you want to do if those things aren't a good fit with your plan and budget.
        - Proactive planning advice. After a professional gets to know you he can offer you helpful advice that you hadn't specifically requested.
        - Referrals to other best value service provider professionals as their services are needed.

Do NOT assume a direct relationship between price and quality.
- Higher price doesn't necessarily equate with higher quality. Professional marketers know that most consumers tend to associate higher prices with higher quality. Therefore, prices of products and services are often inflated to create the perception of higher quality. Do some research to determine if a higher price is based upon actual higher quality or just the perception of higher quality created by a higher price. Two examples:
    - Consumer products: there is an urban legend that that certain shampoo manufacturers put a batch of shampoo in a plain looking bottle and sell it at a low to moderate price; and then add some fancy scent to that same shampoo formula, put it in a fancier bottle, and sell it at a higher price.
    - Professional services (e.g. accounting, legal counsel, and haircutters): during my career I have observed that many high priced professionals don't provide services as valuable as the services provided by more moderately priced professionals.
- Lower cost doesn't necessarily equate with lower quality.
- Cheapest is rarely best value. Don't be "penny wise and pound foolish."
- *Best value is usually somewhere in the middle* between highest and lowest prices of comparable products or services. I have heard many successful people say "throw out the highest price and the lowest price, and consider one of the options in the middle".

Store brand products (e.g. cereal, peanut butter, milk) are often best value choices. Certain stores have earned well-deserved reputations for selling store brand products that deliver quality that is equal to or greater than the quality of comparable name brand products at lower prices than the name brand products. And, similar to the example of shampoo above, I have heard stories about vegetable canneries putting half of the vegetables from a harvest into cans bearing store brand labels that are sold at lower prices and putting the other half into cans bearing name brand labels that are sold at higher prices.

Become an "educated consumer".
- The greater the purchase price, the more time and resources it would be prudent to invest in doing research as to best value prior to making a purchase decision.
- The internet offers a wealth of information about most products and services.
- Do some comparison shopping with different sellers to gather information on the prices and quality of comparable products or services
- Ask people who may have already purchased a product or service of the type you want to buy for their opinions about the prices and benefits of comparable products or services.

A few suggestions for making best value purchase decisions.
- Determine a price range that your budget could afford for the item to be purchased.
- Do a cost versus benefit (cost-benefit) analysis. Will the benefit you gain from spending the money be worth the cost?
- Evaluate your lost opportunity cost. Is there anything else you could do with that money that might generate a greater value for you (e.g. practical use, joy, satisfaction)?
- The greater the purchase price, the more beneficial it might be to discuss your cost-benefit analysis with a business-savvy member of your business team to get an objective evaluation of your analysis, and to get his advice and recommendations.

Pre-qualify the stores in which you shop, both brick and mortar and online stores.
- Ask people in your network of business contacts for recommendations of stores that have provided them with best value shopping experiences.
- Comparison shop to help determine the pricing strategies of stores.
- Use the internet to research store reputations for the value they deliver.
- Analyze the marketing strategy of each store.
  - o Does the content of their advertising, and the media in which they choose to deliver it, seem to be targeted at people who are seeking to become "educated consumers" so that those people can buy best value?
  - o Does it seem that they are trying to develop long term relationships with well-satisfied customers in order to generate repeat business sales and referrals?
- Visit the brick and mortar stores and online stores you are pre-qualifying.
  - o Do the pricing and quality of products in each store's product mix appear to be intended to offer best value to customers?
  - o On visits to brick and mortar stores:
    - Observe sales staff. Do they seem knowledgeable about products offered for sale in the store and where products are located in the store?
    - Are stores shopper-friendly, e.g. physical layouts, appearance, parking?
    - You might ask other shoppers what led them to this particular store, and what other stores they may research.

If an online store advertises that it can offer lower prices because they "cut out the cost of the middleman" (middleman being a "retail" store that provides the services of salespeople, customer service representatives, etc.) (a) Learn about the services typically provided by reputable retail stores, and (b) determine what services you might not get from the online store.

Be especially cautious if you are considering shopping for professional services online.
- Delivery of professional services via the internet without any human interaction reduces or removes altogether the human touch that can make professional services so valuable.
- A good professional who has good expertise and good experience can pro-actively ask you questions intended to help him learn about you, exactly what you think you need or want, and what you don't know that you should know in order to make a well-informed purchase decision. The professional can then offer advice and services tailored to your specific needs and wants.
- *Keep in mind that you don't know what you don't know about the professional service you are seeking to buy. If you don't know what a good professional service provider is supposed to know and what he is supposed to do, it will be tough to determine if you will be buying a best value deal or just a cheaper deal.*

Shopping for higher priced, "big ticket" products
- Comparison shop. Get proposals from multiple sellers.
- Talk to salespeople.
  - Try to get them on your side by connecting with their human nature.
    - Be nice.
    - Be empathetic. Be understanding of salespeople's working conditions and pressure they might be getting from their employers to make sales.
    - Ask for their help. Ask what they would do if they were you.
  - Seek salespeople who use "soft sell" consultative sales techniques – people who try to get to know you, your needs and wants, and then clearly explain why their products and customer service can provide you best value.
  - Tell them that you are comparison shopping to get the best value for your money. Ask them to explain why their products and customer service offer you better value for your money than the products and service their competitors offer.
  - *Ask for the best deal.* Ask if they can add any additional benefits to their proposal, or if there are any unadvertised discounts, or if they can lower their prices any further. Sometimes a better deal can be had just by asking for it.
- *Look and act like you know what you are doing.* Time and again I hear stories about how customers who appear to be educated consumers and carry themselves in a confidant, business-like manner are able to negotiate the best deals.
- *Consider the long term maintenance costs and eventual replacement cost of "capital goods"* (products intended to last a long time like a car or home appliance). The greater the purchase price of capital goods, the more you should consider long term maintenance costs and eventual replacement cost. A product that costs twice as much as a comparable product, but lasts more than two times longer, with less maintenance cost, might provide the best value.
- Review the proposed sales agreement (sales contract) with the salesperson prior to finalizing a purchase. Make sure you understand the terms of the agreement.

Be prepared to walk away from your initial contact with a salesperson.
- Walking away can be a great negotiating tool. It demonstrates that a prospective buyer doesn't feel an emotional need to buy immediately.
- Socially responsible "soft sell" salespeople will take your willingness to walk away as a signal that you want to digest what they have said and what you saw, and that you are doing prudent shopping to get a best value deal. They will do their best to make sure you walk away with all the decision making information they can provide, that they have answered all your questions, and that they have offered you their best deal.

- When dealing with pushy, "hard sell" salespeople, especially those who are hyping "special deals", walking away gets you away from them and gives you an opportunity to research better places to shop.

"Sleep on it".
- It's amazing how a decision option can seem so right one day and then seem so wrong the next morning.
- The higher the price of an item, the more important it is to take enough time to do a thorough cost-benefit analysis
- The more that the price of an item would exceed your expense budget, the more important it would be to take the time needed to determine if you could revise your budget to fit in the purchase price of that item.

Wait for sales.
- Try to plan ahead for seasonal sales and sales events that certain stores have periodically.
- Certain stores offer "limited time" sales on a rotating basis on a portion of the items they sell. Wait for the next "limited time sale" to come around on an item you want to buy.
- Avoid buying in a rush when possible.

The above said about waiting for sales, be aware that sale prices are often "loss leaders" that are used to lure shoppers in to a store in the hope that shoppers also will buy more profitable items they see in the store. Some great bargains can be had if you have the discipline to walk in to a store and buy only the sale price item(s) you went in to buy.

Defend yourself against spur-of-the-moment "impulse" purchases (buying things that you hadn't planned to buy). The more difficulty you have had resisting impulse purchases, the more you should consciously think about the following:
- *Prepare a shopping list* before walking into a store and buy only the things on your list.
- Merchandise typically is arranged within stores where store managers think the arrangement will lead shoppers to spend the most money during each visit, while concurrently making the shopping experience easy enough and enjoyable enough to motivate shoppers to come back over and over again.
  - o A common example I hear people talk about is grocery stores that typically spread out the locations of their best selling items (e.g. meat, milk, bread, produce) in order to get shoppers to walk by as many other items as possible.
  - o Some stores periodically change locations of certain items in order to get shoppers to walk by items that they may not have noticed or tried before.
  - o *Point-of-sale displays* place products in strategic locations within stores to catch shoppers' attention (and the attention of their children) and motivate spur-of-the- moment "impulse" purchases. Classic point-of-sale displays are candy and magazines at check-out counters.
  - o *Make a game of figuring out why merchandise is placed where it is in each store in order to motivate shoppers to buy things they hadn't planned to buy.*
- Each time you catch yourself with an impulse to buy something you hadn't previously planned to buy, take a moment to think about how much of your discretionary expense budget for the month that you have already spent (a good reason to maintain a running total list of your discretionary purchases each month), how much money you have remaining in your discretionary expense budget to spend during the remainder of the month, and what else you might want to buy with that money prior to the end of the month (your lost opportunity cost).

To minimize the prices you will need to pay for things in the future, consider making purchase decisions that contribute to a "<u>sustainable economy</u>".
- Learn how experts in various fields define "sustainable economy", and what they say each of us can do to help foster a sustainable economy.
- Learn how forward thinking companies define:
  o Sustainable living.
  o Corporate sustainability programs.
  o Sustainable supply chains.
- To me, a sustainable economy is one in which enough of us do enough of the "right thing" today so that the supply of things we will want to continue buying in the future will remain available at affordable prices as far out into the future as we can reasonable project – be that 10 years, 30 years, 50 years, or 100 years.
- <u>A sustainable "domestic" economy requires a sustainable "global" economy</u> in which enough people <u>in each country</u> are satisfied enough with their economic lots-in-life that they want to maintain political stability and avoid the type of political instability that could lead unhappy people to risk going to war to get what they want - be that an internal civil war, an international economic war, or an international military war.
  o Political stability requires that enough socially responsible domestic and global employers provide enough well-paying jobs for enough people.
  o Consider the long term benefit of paying a little more money to buy from socially responsible employers who take good care of their employees.
  o Consider the economic value of "benevolent self-interest" – "benevolent" meaning good for others, and "self-interest" meaning good for you.
- A sustainable economy requires a sustainable, ecologically healthy, natural environment.
  o <u>Learn about, and consider the economic value of practicing, Native American teachings about The Honorable Harvest and Seventh Generation stewardship.</u>
  o Learn how taking good care of our home here on Planet Earth can help us minimize the prices we pay for things in the future.
  o Learn about the economic importance of healthy ecosystems in our biosphere.
  o Learn about the likely impacts on a sustainable economy of factors such as:
    ▪ Our use of, and pollution of, our air, land, and water resources.
    ▪ The role our human actions may be playing in climate change.
  o Develop a personal opinion about the following statement, "the more we foul our nest today, the greater the price we are likely to pay for our actions in the future".

As you make your purchase decisions keep in mind how supply and demand will govern prices you pay in the future.
- Regarding supply, keep in mind that here in the biosphere of our home on Planet Earth:
  o There is a limited supply of fertile land that can be used for farming. To help maximize the supply of food that can be produced in the future, consider buying food produced by farmers who make a concerted effort to farm their land sustainably.
  o There is a limited supply of fish in the sea. Overfishing has significantly depleted stocks of fish worldwide. To help maximize the supply of seafood available in the future, consider buying seafood that has been farmed sustainably or caught by commercial fishers who fish sustainably.
  o There is a limited supply of certain "non-renewable" natural resources. After we use up the limited supply of a non-renewable resource we won't be able to get any more of it (at least until such time as affordable alternatives are found or ways to manufacture new supplies are discovered). Keep this in mind as you plan

your purchase of items that are made with currently non-renewable resources.

- o *Consider paying more today for "sustainably sourced" products in order to assure the greatest possible supply of those products in the future.*
- Regarding demand, plan for prices that are likely to increase (or even escalate) as global demand increases for most of the things that you buy regularly.
  - o Global population is growing fast. It is said that there will be at least 50% more people on this planet in the not too distant future.
  - o Rapidly growing economies in many countries will enable a great many more people to earn a great deal more money to buy a great many more of the things they see and hear about through the global telecommunications network.
- "Waste not, want not." "Use it up, wear it out, make it do, or do without."

Consider the long term economic benefits of buying higher priced, locally produced products versus buying less expensive products produced by regional, national and international businesses and delivered to you over some distance.

- Paying higher prices today for products that are produced locally in an economically sustainable way is likely to help maximize future supply of those products and help minimize the future prices you will need to pay for those products.
- Spending money with locally owned and operated businesses will help them operate profitably, and profitable local businesses can in turn:
  - o Provide jobs for your family, local community members (and maybe even you at some time in the future).
  - o Help optimize the vibrancy of your local economy, thereby increasing the value of your home and any other local real estate you may own.
  - o Generate local tax revenue that:
    - ▪ Takes some the local tax burden off your shoulders and minimizes your future tax expenses.
    - ▪ Provides funding for local governments to invest in schools, fire departments, police, libraries, recreational facilities, etc. that contribute to your community becoming what you dream about it becoming.
  - o Help protect you from the risks of an oligarchy of national and international suppliers, e.g. higher prices; quality of products and services sacrificed in order to boost quantity of sales; discontinuance of products that you have grown to love over the years if those products don't have enough "mass market appeal" to a national market.
- Buying locally grown fruits, vegetables, meats, and other food products (perhaps organic) might also help you reduce your future medical expenses by:
  - o Providing greater nutritional value for each dollar you spend on food.
  - o Helping local farmers preserve the open space and biodiversity that are essential for preserving the type of ecologically healthy environment that we humans need in order to optimize our physical health.

By setting a good example as a shopper you will help influence other people to become wiser shoppers, thereby multiplying the impact of your shopping behavior today on the prices you will be paying in the future.

Chapter 13. Playing Expense Management Offense

The objective of playing expense management offense is to make financially prudent lifestyle choices that enable us to achieve our projected financial statement budget objectives while enjoying happy, satisfying lives. To inspire your thinking about your lifestyle choice decisions:

- Choose <u>aspirational long term objectives</u> that lead toward living the happy, satisfying, and financially prosperous life you dream of living.
- Choose lifestyle <u>strategies</u> that are likely to guide you toward making financially prudent lifestyle choice decisions.
- Read biographies of people you think have led good and satisfying lives and learn from the lifestyle choices they made in their lives (you might ask a reference librarian or bookstore employee for suggestions).

Think of lifestyle choices as being on a continuum.

- *Survival existence lifestyle choices* at one end of the continuum would have you spend the bare minimum amount of your annual income needed to stay alive and do the job your employer pays you to do - no frills.
- *Luxury lifestyle choices* at the opposite end would have you spend every penny you earn, and perhaps go into debt, trying to live the "high life".
- *Comfortably prudent lifestyle choices* somewhere in the vast middle that allow you to live a happy, satisfying life while achieving your projected financial statement budget objectives each year.

Like Goldilocks, make economically sustainable lifestyle choices that are not too cheap, not too expensive, but just right for your budget.

The dollar amounts of what people would consider to be survival lifestyle, comfortably prudent lifestyle, and luxury lifestyle choices tend to shift upward as they earn more annual income and accumulate more net worth. There are two major causes of these upward shifts:

- *Rising expectations* that convert wants into needs.
  - People tend to expect more as they can afford more.
  - People tend to desire to "move on up" in lifestyle as they move on up the income and wealth ladder.
  - As people's economic situations improve, things that were wants when people couldn't afford them tend to morph into needs after they have become accustomed to having those things - luxuries become necessities.
- *Wealth effect*: the greater a person's annual income and wealth become, the more comfortable she is likely to become with spending her money.

Making financially prudent lifestyle choices requires that we understand:

- We don't have limitless amounts of money to spend on whatever our hearts desire.
- We can't spend the same dollar on two different things - we must evaluate our <u>lost opportunity costs</u> - if we choose to spend money on one thing we lose the opportunity to spend that money on something else.
- We can't save money we have already spent.
- We need to arrange the things we value in life in a priority order.
- *We must "trade-off" getting things we value more for the loss of the opportunity to get things we value less.*

Two suggestions that are likely to help you make financially prudent lifestyle choices:
- Develop and use a written business plan and projected financial statement budget (see Chapter 4). As you plan, consider:
  - Placing a higher priority on those aspects of life that are either free or relatively inexpensive, e.g. human relationships, walking and jogging, enjoyment of nature, spiritual life.
  - Placing a lower priority on those aspects of life that are relatively expensive, e.g. living in "high rent" neighborhoods, wearing designer clothes, eating in fancy restaurants, playing expensive sports.
- Develop a formal decision making process (see Chapter 7) and make decisions that are guided by your business plan and projected financial statement budget.

You might try writing down the expense items in the projected statement of income and expenses part of your budget on a separate sheet of paper (or computer page) in dollar size order from the biggest expense item down to the smallest expense item.
- Seeing your expenses listed in dollar size order will help focus your attention on lifestyle choice decisions that are likely to have the greatest impact on minimizing your expenses.
- Think about more "expense efficient" lifestyle choices you could make - expense efficient meaning less expensive choices that are likely to provide equal or greater satisfaction.

A list of expense items might look something like this:
- Housing
- Taxes
- Food and drink
- Clothing
- Medical and dental healthcare
- Transportation
- Education
- Charitable contributions
- Recreation: hobbies, sports, boats and other recreational vehicles
- Maintenance, repair and replacement of a car, home, furniture, or boat.
- Interest expense

On the following pages are some suggestions you might consider using in making expense efficient lifestyle choices.

Housing expenses

We humans need housing as protective shelter from nature's elements, e.g. freezing cold, burning sun, bone chilling rain, lightning, and blizzards. Different people living in different geographic areas have different needs for different types of shelter based upon the temperature ranges and weather patterns where they live.

Think of housing choices as being on a "shelter continuum":
- At one end of this continuum - "needs" satisfaction: at this end would be finding just enough shelter to stay alive, be that out in the "wilds" of nature, on the streets in the city, or in shacks that have no electricity, indoor plumbing, or other modern "conveniences".
- At the opposite end of this continuum - "wants" satisfaction, such as choosing to live in a huge "McMansion" or a luxury penthouse condo.

Consider housing choices somewhere in the comfortably prudent mid-range that satisfy your shelter needs and as many of your housing wants as a well-reasoned budget can afford.

"Location, location, location" - the geographic location in which you choose to live is perhaps the most significant factor in determining your housing expenses, as well as many of your other expenses too.
- Home prices and rents for the same types and sizes of housing can vary widely from one location to another – from neighborhood to neighborhood, city to city, and state to state.
- Heating and cooling expenses: the average seasonal temperatures in the location of your home are major determinants of home heating and cooling expenses.
- Commuting: the location of your home in relation to your workplace is a major factor in the cost of getting to work.

"Cost of living" is a measure of how much it costs to live in a specific geographic location.
- Costs of living are higher in certain locations (e.g. New York City) and lower in other locations (e.g. Buffalo, New York).
- The local cost of living typically varies as a function of factors such as:
  o Vibrancy of the local economy, the types and number of jobs available, and the compensation employers are paying for those jobs.
  o Demand for housing created by desirability of a location as a place to live.
  o Prices that merchants and professional service providers think that local residents can afford and will pay for their products and services, e.g. food, gasoline, haircuts. Sellers located in "high rent districts" tend to charge higher prices.
- Some employers pay "cost of living" adjustments to employees in order to cover the higher costs of living in certain locations.

One option for decreasing your housing expenses might be to move to a location that has a lower cost of living. If you want to consider a decision to move, consider factors such as:
- Impact on: your plan and budget; the lives of your family members; your personal relationships; all your connections to your community; etc.
- State and local taxes you would need to pay, and the type and quality of government services you would be likely to receive in return.
- Findings of research visits you are able make to prospective new locations:
  o Type and size of homes and desirability of neighborhoods your budget could afford.
  o Local living conditions at different times of day, e.g. morning rush hour and weekend

traffic, night time noise.
  o Opinions of local residents about quality of life issues such as their schools, public safety, police, fire, medical services, garbage collection, street maintenance (potholes and snow plowing), public parks, library, and other community amenities.
- Your ability to lock in a job BEFORE moving that would enable you to achieve your short term milestone objectives as you advance toward your longer term objectives.
- *Contingency plan for what you could do if the new location didn't work out as planned.*

Type of housing (apartment, condominium, townhouse, or detached single family house) can have a significant impact on housing expenses. Write a list of the pros and cons of each type of housing to stimulate your thinking about the type of housing to choose.

Size of a home also has a significant impact on housing expenses.
- If you are thinking about buying a home *"don't buy more house than you need."*
- If you already own a home and your life circumstances are such that you could "down-size" (move to a smaller home), you might be able to lower your annual expenses.

A suggested priority order of considerations for a housing purchase decision:
- First priority - buy housing to be your home.
- Second priority - buy housing to be an investment.

When considering the potential investment value of a home, keep in mind:
- Real estate usually increases in value over the long term (but not always), but it typically goes through a <u>cycle of increases and decreases in value on its way up to long term increases. Make well informed projections of (a) when you might want to sell your home</u> and (b) lowest market value you can reasonably expect at the time you sell.
- The principles of investment diversification and risk management spread of risk - decide what percentage of your net worth would be prudent to have tied up in real estate.

Mortgage loan expense.
- *This book can only scratch the surface of all the factors you should consider in regard to using a mortgage loan to help finance a home purchase* (see also Chapter 12).
- Consider limiting mortgage expense to amounts your short term and mid-term projected income statement budgets could comfortably afford; don't "stretch your budgets too far".
- Learn enough about the pros and cons of mortgage loans to avoid getting lured into the biggest loan for which you could qualify just because (a) interest is tax deductible, and (b) "the government will help you pay for the home".
- Consult with a professional realtor after doing your own independent research.

Weigh the potential dangers of mortgage debt against the benefits of owning a home.
- *Potential dangers include*
  o You wouldn't own a home until you finished repaying the mortgage. If you couldn't repay all the money you owed according to the terms of the loan, you could lose all the money you had repaid plus all the money you had sunk into the home for maintenance and improvements. Learn about a lender's right to "repossess" a home.
  o Property values can go down as well as up for many reasons.
    ▪ After the Great Recession began in 2008 many people were stuck "under water" with homes worth less than their mortgage amounts.
    ▪ Local job markets typically have a big impact on home prices. If one or

> > more large employers were to leave an area, local home prices could drop, e.g. research home prices in the Detroit area over the past 50 years.
> - o Real estate taxes typically increase as property values increase. When local property values increase significantly, real estate taxes can shoot up. "Gentrification" of city neighborhoods is a classic example. Gentrification occurs when older neighborhoods rapidly become highly desirable to higher income earners, who begin buying homes in the neighborhood, which drives up property values and "property tax assessments" and annual real estate tax payments.
- *Potential benefits include*:
  - o A fixed rate mortgage can lock in principal and interest payments for 15, 20 or 30 years. This typically provides greater control of housing expenses than renting.
  - o A mortgage can also help provide greater control over the location of where you live than a rental property. Owning a home means there is no landlord who could force you out by increasing your rent to an unaffordable price, converting apartments to condominiums, or selling the building.
  - o Current income tax regulations allow interest to be deducted from taxable income on tax returns (but keep in mind that tax regulations could change during the term of a 15 or 30 year mortgage loan – that's a long time, and economies do evolve).
  - o A home can also serve as an investment that *might* increase in value.

Utility expenses, e.g. electricity, gas, water.
- Typically, the larger the home the greater the utility expenses.
  - o Single family homes tend to require the highest utility expenses.
  - o Comparably sized town homes, especially interior units, tend to require lower utility expenses.
  - o Condominiums and apartments tend to require the lowest utility expenses.
- There are many sources of advice and recommendations about choices we can make to minimize our utility expenses. A few classic pieces of advice:
  - o Electricity: turn off the lights when you leave a room.
  - o Heating and air conditioning: follow President Jimmy Carter's recommendations to set the thermostat at 68 degrees for heating and 78 degrees for cooling (made during the energy crisis of the 1970's). That's only a 10 degree swing. Make it a game to see how low a home temperature you can live in during the winter and how high a temperature you can tolerate in the summer.
  - o Water: take shorter showers, turn off the water faucet while brushing your teeth, and plant a landscape that requires less watering.

Maintenance, repair, and replacement expenses: all homes require periodic maintenance and repair, and at some point in time replacement of expensive items such as heating and air conditioning equipment, roofs, and major appliances.
- When making a home purchase decision, factor in long term maintenance, repair, and replacement expenses
  - o Homes can become "money pits" into which homeowners must keep dumping money.
  - o Significant factors to consider include the home builder's reputation for quality construction; type, size, and age of home; types of siding and roofing materials.
- Choose to invest in preventative maintenance in order to minimize the risk of large, unplanned repair and replacement expenses.
- Make "best value" choices when buying maintenance and repair services and buying replacement products. Buying cheap typically winds up costing more in the long run.

Tax expenses

Two lifestyle choices can have significant impact on a person's tax expenses:
- *Geographic location of a home* determines types and amounts of state and local taxes.
- *Degree of personal involvement in the political process.*

State and local governments vary widely as to taxes they assess residents. One way you might be able to lower your tax expenses would be to move to a different location. If you have the flexibility to consider a decision about moving to a new location be sure to consider:
- ALL the taxes you would have to pay in that new location, e.g. income taxes, sales taxes, property taxes, and other special purpose taxes. For example, a different state might have lower income tax rates but have higher sales tax and/or property tax rates.
- The "spend" side of the government "tax and spend" equation. How would state and local governments spend the taxes you paid?
  - o What government services would you receive in return for the taxes you paid?
  - o Typically, the higher the tax rates, the better the quality of government services that <u>might be</u> provided. But, higher tax rates don't guarantee better quality government services <u>will be</u> provided.
- How the local cost of living in that new location would impact all of your other expenses besides taxes.
- The impact a move would have on the lives of you and your family.

Choose to get active in the political process that determines your tax expenses.
- Tell your elected federal, state and local government officials your opinions about:
  - o Taxes and tax rates that should be used to finance government operations.
  - o The percentage of your income you think would be your fair share of tax revenue - the tax rates you think would be fair for you and everyone else to pay.
  - o How your money should be spent:
    - ▪ Services/programs that should be provided by each level of government.
    - ▪ Percentage of annual budget money that should be allocated to each government department/agency to provide those services/programs – which should get more money to spend and which should get less.
  - o How government could operate more efficiently in order to provide you "best value" in government services for the taxes you pay.
- Help elect politicians who profess to support your positions on tax and spend issues.
- VOTE.

As your budget can afford it, consider hiring a professional tax expert or financial advisor to advise you about tax planning matters such as:
- Tax deductions and tax credits available to you.
- Paying off a mortgage versus continuing to make mortgage payments and deducting the interest on your tax returns.
- Minimizing current and future taxable income:
  - o Tax advantaged investments, e.g. retirement and medical savings accounts.
  - o Planning for a predictable stream of revenue from dividends, and sales of assets held long enough to generate capital gain income rather than ordinary income.

Food and drink expenses

Think first of food and drink as nutrients and second as enjoyable taste treats.
- We each need to consume certain amounts of nutrients and water in order to survive. Learn about:
    - "Minimum daily requirements" of essential nutrients and the amount of water that doctors and nutritionists recommend we feed our bodies.
    - Lowest cost sources of those nutrients and water.
- Nutrients and water come in all sorts of foods and drinks at all sorts of prices. We can reduce our expenses if we think more about the nutrition we receive for the money we spend, and less about the taste and convenience of our food and drink choices.
    - Build a diet based upon low cost sources of essential nutrients and water - a diet that allows you to maintain peak physical health at the lowest possible cost.
    - Then add in more expensive sources of nutrients as your budget can afford them.

Think of food and drink choices as being on a continuum:
- At one end of this continuum, a survival lifestyle of nutrition "need" satisfaction: at this end people would spend as little as possible on food and drink while consuming the minimum amounts of nutrients and water needed to keep themselves alive and healthy.
- At the other end, a luxury lifestyle of "want" satisfaction: at this end people would eat "gourmet" foods, shop in trendy high end food stores, buy fancy bottled water from select springs around the world, and eat in expensive restaurants.

Many people whose budgets would enable them to eat and drink pretty much anything they so desire might do well to remember what they ate and drank when they first began to live independently on their own and pay for their own food. They might also do well to think about how much healthier a lower cost diet might be (perhaps with staples such as brown rice and beans) and how much more money they could be saving for future financial security and freedom.

Lifestyle choices that could help us minimize our food and drink expenses include:
- Cooking more meals at home from scratch.
- Decreasing the number of times we eat out at restaurants and buy take-out food.
- Buying more of the lower cost store brand products and less of the more expensive name brand products.
- Drinking more tap water from a home faucet and less bottled water and other bottled drinks.
    - Publicly regulated water companies typically provide tap water that is monitored to assure healthy drinkability – however, if you live in an older home in an older community it would be wise to ask specifically about the possibility of lead contaminating the water supplied to your home. If you so desire, there are all sorts of water filtering systems you can buy to further filter the tap water in your home.
    - Consuming bottled water, or water as a component of other drinks (e.g. bottled soft drinks) ratchets up the cost of water significantly.
- Growing some of our own herbs, vegetables, and fruits in containers on patios, backyards, or community gardens. Learn about the "victory gardens" that people were encouraged to grow during World Wars I and II in order to provide some of their own food.

Clothing expenses

Think of clothing choices as being on a continuum.
- At one end of this continuum, a survival lifestyle of clothing "need" satisfaction: at this end people would wear the bare minimum clothing needed to protect the body from weather elements and to cover the body well enough in public places to satisfy modesty and sanitary requirements mandated by law, e.g. public decency laws, health department requirements for clothing to be worn in restaurants.
- At other end, a luxury lifestyle of clothing "want" satisfaction: at this end people might buy expensive, fashionable clothes and shoes each season, have closets full of clothes that they just don't find stylish enough to wear anymore, and pay small fortunes in dry cleaning bills.

Choose each piece of clothing for its utility value (e.g. warmth, social modesty) more than for its ornamental value (e.g. style, social prestige). To help stimulate your thinking about your clothing choices:
- Research how clothing styles have changed over the past fifty years.
  - Look at clothing people have worn through the years in movies and TV shows.
  - Look at clothing advertisements in magazines and newspapers over the years.
  - Notice how some styles have come and gone and come again.
  - Ask older folks about all the clothing styles they have seen come and go (and often come back again) during their lifetimes – and clothing choices they think might "stand the test of time" while providing you optimum utility value.
- Learn about the clothing choices of indigenous people living in different climate zones (e.g. polar, temperate, tropical) and what led them to make their choices, perhaps factors such as temperature and weather conditions with which they had to deal and raw materials they had available to make into clothing.

Innumerable sources offer suggestions about how to assemble a good looking wardrobe without busting a clothing budget. A few suggestions to consider:
- Develop your own "timeless" style so that you can wear clothes for longer periods of time rather than shorter periods of time. Project the inner you.
- Develop a style that fits your budget, and learn to love what your budget can afford.
- Don't try to keep your entire wardrobe up to date with current fashion styles. Rather, you might choose to add one or two stylish pieces each season.
- Let the clothes in your closet evolve. Gradually swap out older pieces of clothing for newer pieces.
- Buy classic clothing that will age well. Be guided by the old folk wisdom about buying "sensible" shoes, a sensible wool coat, and other sensible clothes that you can wear as the core of your wardrobe for years to come.
- Think of well-worn clothing as gaining patina as it ages.

To minimize clothing care and maintenance expenses:
- Buy clothes that you can wash and iron yourself, rather than paying a laundry to clean and press clothes for you. If you never learned how to wash and iron, then learn now.
- Consider some "old school" ways to extend the lives of clothes - ways that many (if not most) people used to extend the lives of their clothes until not too long ago, e.g. mending socks, patching knees and elbows, turning frayed collars, and re-soling shoes.

Medical and dental healthcare expenses

The earlier in life we begin making healthy lifestyle choices, the more we can minimize our healthcare expenses as we age.

Play the genetic cards that you were dealt at birth to the best of your ability. Adopt healthcare practices recommended by medical and dental professionals, such as:
- Eat a healthy diet.
- Get plenty of exercise.
- Get enough sleep.
- Brush and floss your teeth at least twice a day.
- Follow recommended guidelines for consumption of alcohol and prescription drugs.
- Avoid use of tobacco products.
- Protect your skin from sun damage and skin cancer.
  - Minimize exposure to the mid-day sun.
  - Use a high SPF sunscreen.
  - Wear a wide brimmed hat and sun protective clothing.
- Minimize exposure to carcinogenic substances and other hazardous materials in your diet, in your home, and in your workplace.
- Make lifestyle choices that minimize the stress in your life.

Follow the age old advice for making healthy lifestyle choices "*all things in moderation*".

Healthcare expenses tend to increase as we age.
- The older our bodies get, the more they wear out.
- The older we get the more likely it is that we will have to pay for not having taken as good care of ourselvelves as we could have taken when we were younger – "paying for the sins of our youth". For instance:
  - Tobacco smokers and chewers often pay for lung and mouth cancers.
  - Sun lovers often pay for skin cancer.
  - People who didn't brush and floss their teeth well enough often pay for more fillings, root canals, crowns, and dental implants.
- Youthful athletes and middle age weekend warriors who have repeatedly strained muscles, broken bones, torn ligaments and/or cartilage, or sustained head traumas often pay for all sorts of expensive aches, pains, and disabilities.

As president of your company, establish an "employee wellness" program for yourself and your family members. Learn how employers use employee wellness programs to:
- Minimize healthcare insurance expenses.
- Reduce the number of employee sick days.
- Improve the health of employees as a means to help improve their mental acuity and physical productivity.

Elements of employee wellness programs that you might consider including in your family wellness program include:
- Be a role model for healthy lifestyle choices.
- Encourage family members to practice preventive healthcare:
  - To think of healthy lifestyle choices as preventive maintenance for their bodies that can significantly decrease their healthcare expenses.

- o To visit a doctor and dentist for regular check-ups and preventive healthcare that helps avoid the future cost of disease or bodily harm - heeding the old adage *"pay me now or pay me more later"*.
- Encourage family members to learn about the elements of good healthcare.
- Buy healthy food for family members to eat in your home.
- Encourage people to exercise daily.
- Encourage participation in a weight loss or stop-smoking support group if needed.
- Provide medical and dental insurance that provides coverage for check-ups and preventive healthcare – if available and affordable.

Transportation expenses

Think of your transportation choices as being on a continuum:
- At one end of this continuum, transportation "need" satisfaction: at this end people would try to find the lowest cost, most reliable form of transportation to get to a job, shop for the basic necessities of life, and get to other places they need to go.
- At the other end, transportation "want" satisfaction: at this end people would have little concern for the cost of transportation; people might buy multiple luxury brand cars for different purposes – a Porsche Carrera sports car for fun, a Land Rover sport utility vehicle to transport family and friends, and a BMW sedan for commuting.

Lifestyle choices that might help minimize your transportation expenses include:
- Walk or ride a bicycle whenever possible.
- Find a new home closer to the places where you travel most frequently, e.g. work, stores, homes of relatives. Some people try to find homes where they can walk, ride a bicycle, or take mass transportation to most of the places they travel most frequently.
- Find a new job closer to home.

If you choose to own an automobile, you might consider:
- Accelerating repayment of any car loan you currently have, if your budget would allow you to do so and you wouldn't incur a prepayment penalty.
    - You would save whatever interest expense remained to be paid.
    - If you did choose to pay off your loan ahead of schedule, you might consider continuing to make the same monthly payment but make it to yourself in the form of a deposit into your cash reserve account. This would enable you to maximize the down payment on the replacement car you will eventually need to buy, or perhaps even pay cash for that next vehicle, thereby minimizing or eliminating altogether future interest expense.
- Trading in an old car for a newer, more fuel efficient car before the old car starts to rack up increasing repair and maintenance costs.
- Planning ahead in order to minimize one-stop car trips.
    - Make a list of all the places you need to go during any given day that require the use of your car, and then plot the shortest route connecting those places.
    - Plan errands you can run while on the way to work or home from work.

If you will be making an automobile purchase decision:
- *Identify the factors that will carry the most weight in your decision:*
    - Functional utility: how you plan to use the vehicle – to move yourself and/or other people and/or things from one place to another. For instance:
        - Commuting to work.
        - Shopping for food, clothing, household needs.
        - Ferrying kids to and from school and after school activities.
        - Freedom to travel wherever you want.
    - Appearance to other people, e.g. friends, neighbors, the opposite sex.
    - Enjoyment: the pure fun of driving an expensive toy.
- Consider placing more weight on a vehicle's functional utility as safe, reliable transportation than on its stylish appearance and value as an expensive toy.
- Consider ALL the expenses associated with each vehicle you are considering:
    - Purchase price
        - Consider buying a less expensive, but just as dependable car.

- Consider a two or three year old used car that has low mileage on it. Depreciation in price typically is greatest during a car's first few years.
  - o State and/or local taxes you might be required to pay.
  - o Operating expenses, particularly gasoline: use of regular grade gasoline rather than premium grade; mileage per gallon; future price per gallon.
  - o Routine maintenance expenses over the life of the vehicle, e.g. oil changes, tire rotation, brake systems.
  - o Repair expenses: track record of mechanical reliability.
  - o Insurance expense: "sensible", reliable, low to mid-priced cars typically cost less to insure than sports cars and luxury vehicles.
  - o Interest expense on a car loan, if a loan would be needed to help finance the purchase.
- A thought progression for a vehicle purchase decision might be along the lines of:
  - o Determine a <u>purchase price range</u> that your projected financial statement budget could afford.
  - o Determine which type of vehicle (e.g. bicycle, motorcycle, sedan, sport utility vehicle, truck) in that purchase price range would provide the best <u>utility value</u> – the vehicle best suited to the primary use you are planning.
  - o Determine which makes and models of the type vehicle that would provide the best utility value would provide the best <u>economic value</u>:
    - Purchase price
    - Lowest operating expenses (e.g. gasoline mileage, grade of gasoline) and maintenance expenses during the time you plan to own the vehicle
    - Best track record of operating reliability – require the fewest repairs.
  - o Then choose the vehicle that you think would provide you an optimum combination of:
    - Economic value.
    - Utility value.
    - Joy and satisfaction:
      - Most comfortable for you to sit in.
      - Best handling "feel" to drive, e.g. smoothness of ride, acceleration, turning.
      - The vehicle you think looks best.

Education expenses

Identify the benefits you desire to gain from attending a school, and prospective schools that offer the best combinations of those benefits.
- Gain an education that will help you get jobs along the career path you are planning?
- Specific classes offered by specific schools, perhaps taught by specific teachers?
- Expand your network of contacts who might be able to help you succeed in the career path you are planning, and achieve your plan and budget objectives?
- Gain the prestige of attending a certain school?
- Pure scholarship - the joy of learning?
- Enjoyment of the "college experience"; to be able to say later in life that "those were some of the best years of my life"?
- And for some people, postpone the time at which they must begin to deal with the real world out on their own, i.e. get a full time job and pay their own expenses?

Prepare a projected statement of income and expense budget for each year you are planning to attend each prospective school.
- Identify ALL the expenses of going to each school, e.g. tuition, housing, food, books, fees, transportation to and from school, etc.
- Determine how you would generate the revenue that would be needed to pay the expenses of going to each school, e.g. parents, job, scholarship, financial assistance program, loan.
- As early as possible in the process of deciding upon a school to attend research scholarships and financial assistance that might be available.
    - Talk to professionals whose job it is to help students and their families identify sources of financial assistance for which you could qualify.
    - Ask other people for their advice, perhaps current classmates, students at prospective schools, or recent graduates.
- <u>If you would need to take out a student loan</u>, prepare a projected statement of income and expenses budget for repaying the loan within a reasonable period of time after graduation (perhaps 5 or 10 years), and a career path plan for jobs that have reasonable potential to pay the money you would need to in order to repay the loan while also paying all of your other living expenses during the term of the loan.

Then do a cost-benefit analysis of attending each prospective school – would the cost of attending a school outweigh the benefit you would gain from attending the school? Would the choice of a school be worth the money you would have to pay to go there?

Choices that might help minimize college education expenses include:
- In-state public colleges typically cost less than private schools and out-of-state colleges.
- Community colleges: some people seeking a bachelor's degree save money by taking a two-step approach.
    - Taking certain required classes at a lower cost community college.
    - And then transferring to a higher cost college that would accept transfer-credit hours and could confer the desired bachelor's degree.
- Choosing to work hard in high school in order to qualify for whatever scholarships may be available.
- Choosing a school close to home to help save transportation expenses.
- Choosing to continue living at home to help save room and board expenses.

Charitable and religious institution contribution expenses

Contributions to charities and religious institutions can be emotionally loaded choices:
- There are countless charities and religious institutions doing good works that could use some of our money, but, we each have only a limited annual income and a limited amount of net worth.
- It is impossible to contribute to all the organizations that would be worthy to receive some of our money.
- <u>We must on occasion make decisions to say no to some good causes if we are to maintain our own good fiscal health</u>.
- But deciding to say "no" to a good cause can be a gut wrenching experience for a person with a good heart.

We must learn how to say "no", and to say it graciously.
- First we must understand that we can't afford to "kill the golden goose" by bleeding it to death - the golden goose being our financial resources – our annual income and net worth.
  - o For the sake of financial health, we must put a limit on the amount of money we contribute to charities and religious institutions.
  - o There are so many charities and religious institutions that could use our money that we could give away all of our money and then have no money left to pay our own expenses.
  - o Then we too might need financial assistance from charities and religious organizations.
- Then we can use a planning and budgeting process to establish a "<u>fair share</u>" contribution expense objective in our annual projected statement of income and expense budgets.
- A formal planning and budgeting process can help you:
  - o Get in touch with your deepest humanitarian and spiritual beliefs about how you should spend your money
  - o Determine a dollar amount that your budget could afford as a fair share giving expense, while still enabling you to achieve your other expense and savings objectives for the year.
  - o Ease your conscience about putting a limit on your contributions during the next one year planning period by means of establishing progressively greater objectives in your budgets for your mid-term and long term planning periods (i.e. increase contributions as your annual income and net worth increase).
  - o Allow you to feel good in your soul and sleep in peace each night knowing that you will be spending all the money you can reasonably afford to spend to help others and make the world a better place.
  - o Identify the charities and religious organizations whose good works you have the greatest desire to fund with your money.
  - o Generate the greatest personal satisfaction from your expense budget dollars.

If you feel a need to increase your fair share level of giving during shorter term budget planning periods, you can use your planning and budgeting process to guide an analysis of your expenses, and help you identify expenses you could trim back in order to free up more money for contributions. You might ask yourself questions such as:
- Can I trim back the amount of food I eat in restaurants so that I can help people who don't have enough to eat?
- Can I cut back my thermostat a few degrees in the winter so that I can contribute to a fuel

fund for others who might otherwise be cold?
- Can I do without that new suit I would like to buy so that I could help a child have nice clothes to wear to school?

Consider contributing your time to augment the dollar contributions your budget can afford. This suggestion is rooted in my experience as a paid employee of the Boy Scouts of America and my subsequent experience as a volunteer leader in many non-profit organizations.
- Your time may be more valuable than your dollars to charitable and religious institutions.
- Most non-profit organizations rely upon volunteers to do a significant amount (if not most) of the work needed to accomplish their missions.
- Charitable and religious institutions typically can't raise enough money each year to hire all the paid employees they would need in order to do all the good deeds they would like to do.
- Many times volunteers have special skills and abilities that paid employees of charitable and religious institutions don't have. The special skills and abilities of volunteers often become highly valuable contributions to the capabilities of non-profit organizations to do the good works they aspire to do.
- Therefore the time that volunteers contribute can have great economic utility for charitable and religious institutions.

Plus, there is a huge personal benefit that comes with spending time helping others – it feels great! Time and time again I hear volunteers say things such as:
- Volunteer work is one of the most rewarding things they have ever done.
- Spending their precious time is far more satisfying than spending their money.

Recreation expenses

Make a list of the forms of recreation you have been choosing to include in your lifestyle - hobbies, sports, creative arts, etc.

Identify why you have been choosing each form of recreation.
- Because you truly love it - it brings you joy, satisfaction, peace of mind, etc.?
- Socialize with old friends?
- Meet and develop relationships with new friends?
- Networking opportunities to meet and develop relationships with people who can help you succeed in your career?
- Force of habit doing something you had loved at one point in your life, but no longer enjoy nearly as much?
- Parents pushed you into it and you don't want to disappoint them?
- Escape from other areas of your life, e.g. work you don't enjoy, unhappy social life?

Beware escapism.
- Some people "bury themselves in their work" to escape from parts of their lives that they don't like, and some people spend "too much" money on recreation for the same reason (I have known men who play golf mostly because it gets them out of the house for a big chunk of the day).
- People who try to escape life through recreation might do well to gear their planning toward improving those parts of their lives from which they are seeking escape, and seek ways to trim the expenses of whatever form of recreation they are using as an escape vehicle.

Arrange your list of forms of recreation in a priority order – from the forms of recreation you love most down to the forms of recreation you care about least.

Identify the cost of each form of recreation in which you have been engaging. Be sure to identify ALL the expenses connected with each of those forms of recreation, such as:
- Equipment; special clothing or shoes.
- Participation fees, tickets, etc.
- Club memberships and dues.
- Transportation to and from recreation sites.

Try to identify ways you could minimize the expenses of each of those forms of recreation.

Then choose a combination of forms of recreation that provides an optimal amount of joy, satisfaction, and peace of mind at a dollar cost that your budget can afford.
- First, allocate budget dollars to those forms of recreation that you love most.
- Second, allocate remaining budget money to forms of recreation you care about least.

Chapter 14. Active Revenue Management

Managing income from your job

In this book about money, I implore you to work for more than just money! Just as there is more to life than money, there should be more to a job than just money. Seek a job that provides *three types of compensation that combine to form an optimal "total compensation package"*.

- *Money* enough to achieve the annual revenue objective in your projected financial statement budget.
  - o Paycheck (salary or wages).
  - o Performance bonuses, profit sharing, tips.
  - o Employer's matching contributions to a retirement savings plan, e.g. 401(k) plan.
  - o Subsidies for insurance programs: medical, dental, eye care, life, disability.
  - o Other financial benefits: free parking, parking allowance, daycare, exercise facilities, etc.
- *Satisfaction* enough to achieve your job related business plan objectives.
  - o Job satisfaction; enjoyment of your work; opportunity to "be all you can be".
  - o Social satisfaction: enjoyment of the time you spend with people at work.
- *Free time* enough away from work to achieve as many of your other personal objectives as possible - to do all the other things besides work that make life good and satisfying, e.g. attend to spiritual life, build and maintain relationships with family and friends, savor peace of mind, experience the joys of recreation and creative hobbies.
  - o Reasonable work hours.
  - o Flexible work hours that enable you to help decide when you work.
  - o Vacation, holidays, personal days, maternity/paternity leave, etc.

You have two roles to play at work – employee of your employer and president of your company. Play both roles concurrently, and play them both well.
- *Role 1. Employee*: scripted by your employer's business plan and your job description.
- *Role 2. President of your company*: scripted by your personal business plan to "sell" your services to your employer as a means to achieve your objectives.

The "right job" is crucial for optimizing your total compensation package. What is the right job for you?
- The better that the total compensation package you desire matches the total compensation package that your employer can and will provide, the better the job.
- The fewer the trade-offs you must make between maximizing income and maximizing job satisfaction and free time, the better the job.
- The more that a job fills you with enthusiasm, the better the job. A dream job would have you jumping out of bed each morning with the anticipation of getting to your workplace.
- The more that a job fills you with joy, the better the job. A dream job would pay you all the money you desire for doing what you would gladly do for free.
- The more that a job feels like it is your "calling in life" to do it, the better the job.
- The better that your personal business plan objectives, strategies and action plan match up with your employer's objectives, strategies and action plan, the better the job.
- The better that your skills and abilities match up with the skills and abilities your employer wants to buy, the better the job.
- The more care and concern your employer has for the well-being and job satisfaction of employees, the better the job.

Keep in mind that:
- There are no perfect jobs. Every dream job is likely to have at least some imperfections.
- There are many, many good jobs that people can proactively work to make even better.
- There are no perfect employers. Employers are just groups of us imperfect humans.
- There are many, many good employers.

A job is a privilege, not a right!
- Some people seem to think that they have a right to their jobs. They don't. No one has an inalienable right to his job.
- An employer has no obligation to retain any employee beyond a legal obligation to obey statutory employment laws and to comply with the terms of any employment contract.
- As so many parents have said "*the world doesn't owe you a living.*"

Some people also seem to think that they are irreplaceable. They act as though they couldn't possibly be replaced by other people who could do their jobs. *Nobody is irreplaceable.*

Learn what experts in various fields of study have to say about how to succeed in life - experts in business management, career counseling, psychology, sports psychology, sports team coaching, etc. Seek lessons that you can apply to succeeding in your job, optimizing your total compensation package, and planning a satisfying career path.

Students – if you have been thinking about dropping out of school:
- If your thoughts have been about going to work to make money rather than just sit in class, don't be short sighted about the money you might be able to earn today if you dropped out. Many people who dropped out of school without having a dire need to start earning money have said later in life that the money they thought looked so good at the time they dropped out didn't look nearly so good years later after they realized how much more money they *could have* been making on jobs for which they *could have* qualified if they had stayed in school and graduated.
- Graduation from high school, trade school, or college is likely to be one of the qualifications you will need in order to get at least one of the jobs you would like to get as you progress along your career path. Research the typical education requirements for jobs that you think might interest you.
- If you work hard to get the best grades you can, those good grades will help separate you from your future competitors for jobs you want to get.
- If you work hard to learn and retain as much knowledge as you can, that knowledge is likely to prove valuable down the road in optimizing:
  - The quality of the work you do for your employer and the compensation you are paid to do it; and
  - Your success as president of your personal financial management business.
- *There is a big difference between grades earned and lessons learned.*

Plan a career path

Start your career path planning by writing descriptions of your dream job, dream compensation, and dream job location. These descriptions will serve as aspirational long term objectives that guide your career path planning.

- *Dream job*: use your list of things you love to do to stimulate your thinking. Incorporate as many of the things you love to do as possible in your job description. Be as specific as you can, while being as general as you need to be in order to get an initial description written. This dream job should become a long term objective in your business plan.
- *Dream compensation*: write the details of a dream total compensation package. The money part of this total compensation package should become a long term revenue objective in your projected financial statement budget.
- *Dream job location*: the community in which you now live? The place where you grew up? A place you have always dreamed about living?

If you don't yet have a dream job in mind, write a list of the component elements you would like to be a part of your dream job. Use this list to guide your creative thinking as you plan a dream job for yourself. To stimulate your thinking, you might ask yourself if you would like to:

- Make a difference in the world - make it a better place for you having been in it?
- Do work related to a favorite interest or form of recreation?
- Meet interesting people and develop enjoyable relationships with them?
- Manage people, or be a hands-on technician doing work you love to do?
- Make big picture decisions with potentially wide ranging impact on the lives of many people and the success or failure of your employer's business, or do fairly routine, relatively stress free work after which you go home feeling great about your day?
- "Left brain" analysis of business challenges, "right brain" creative thinking, or both?
- Fixed work hours (e.g. 9:00 to 5:00) or flexible work hours that allow you to set your own schedule?
- Work inside, work outside, or spend parts of each day inside and outside?
- Travel to fun and interesting places?

Another way to stimulate your thinking about a dream job might be to write two lists (in the inventory section of your business plan):

- *Things you love to do*: hobbies, sports, travel, etc. - ways you would spend your precious time if you could do whatever you wanted to do.
- *Industries in which you think good and satisfying work is being done.*

Then plan a career path that leads from where you are today <u>toward</u> your dream job.

- Plan a career path of progressively more desirable jobs that lead from where you are today toward your dream job.
- Keep in mind that planning is a continuous process. You can revise and refine your dream job description and your career path toward that dream job as you progress along your career path, gain experience in life, and learn more about yourself.
- Be prepared for your career path plan to evolve. As we age our dreams about what we want to do in life are likely to change. Think about how over the course of just one year a child may want to be a policeman, a pilot, a construction machine operator, and a professional athlete.
- Be prepared to segue into career opportunities you had no idea existed when you began your career path planning. You can't know today what you might learn tomorrow about a

career path opportunity that would stoke your passion to do it.

- Be prepared to discover that as you progress along your career path and get closer to what you thought was a dream job you might begin to see that it doesn't look nearly as good up closer as it looked from farther away. For example, many people dream about becoming managers and then after they become managers they discover that they don't like dealing with the headaches that can come with being a manager, e.g. dealing with employees' personal problems, bickering among employees, corporate bureaucracy, etc.
- If you can't get to your dream job today because you lack certain qualifications (e.g. skills, abilities, experience, education, professional license) plan to acquire those qualifications you lack as you progress along your career path.

Let your planning be guided by these wise sayings:

- *"Follow your bliss."* Learn why Joseph Campbell taught this valuable lesson.
- *"If you love what you do, you will never work a day in your life."*
- "Work to live. Don't live to work."

Be an "optimistic pragmatist" as you plan.

- The optimistic part of "optimistic pragmatist" is:
  - o Having a firm belief that good things tend to come to good people who think positively and seek to do good things.
  - o *Understanding that you can accomplish just about any career objective you set for yourself:*
    - ▪ <u>IF you have enough time</u> to gain the expertise and experience you would need to have, to meet the people you would need to know, etc., <u>and</u>
    - ▪ <u>IF you use your career path planning process with enough diligence</u>.
- The pragmatist part is understanding that:
  - o We each get only a limited number of days to live our lives. Many of us just won't have enough time in life to reach our <u>dream</u> jobs.
  - o If we diligently use a career path planning process we will gain peace of mind knowing that we are advancing toward the best possible jobs for ourselves.
  - o *The earlier in life we begin using a career path planning process:*
    - ▪ *The better the odds we give ourselves to get to the right jobs for us; and*
    - ▪ *The closer we are likely to get to our dream jobs.*

Be a realistic dreamer.

- *Reach high, but be careful not to over-reach the expertise and experience you* bring to each successive job along your career path. Over-reaching often leads to tripping and falling flat on one's face. Be mindful of The Peter Principle. As the old adage cautions "the longer the leap, the less the likelihood of making the leap successfully".
- *Temper your "can do" spirit with a practical dose of self-honesty as to what you are likely to be able to do* in the next job along your career path.
- Plan to take a prudent amount of time to prepare yourself to succeed in each successive job along your career path.

The <u>right job</u> for you is likely to have a great deal of what you desire to have in your dream job, but not everything. This will require you to make <u>trade-off decisions</u> between money, job satisfaction, free time, and location as you decide whether or not a job is the right job for you. For instance, the right job for you might:

- Pay enough of the money you dream of earning, and offer enough of the free time you dream of having, but require you to do some job duties you wouldn't enjoy doing.

- Pay enough of the money you dream of earning, but require you to work so many hours that you wouldn't have enough free time to do enough of the other things you would like to do in your dream lifestyle.
- Provide an opportunity to do work that you love to do, but not pay all the money you dream of earning or not be located in a dream location.

Writing a prioritized list of the things you value most in life will help you make these trade-off decisions (maintain this list in the inventory section of your business plan). Many happy, successful business people prioritize their lives along these lines:

1. Spiritual life.
2. Family life.
3. Physical and mental health.
4. Self-fulfillment - job satisfaction; a comfortable feeling that they are living good lives.
5. Money and the material things that money can buy.

Plan for an optimum total compensation package in each successive job along your career path:
- *Enough money* to achieve the revenue objective in your short term budget.
- *Enough job satisfaction* to keep your heart light.
- *Enough free time* to maintain your personal relationships, enjoy your favorite recreation activities, and do all the other non-work things you desire to do.

If your career path plan is to move up the "corporate ladder" to positions that provide a progressively better total compensation package and <u>greater authority of position to manage people,</u> keep in mind the principle of "risk – reward" - *the greater the potential reward of a job, the greater the risk is likely to be.*
- Promotions carry the risk of The Peter Principle – rising to a level at which a person doesn't have the ability to do the job well.
  - o For most of us, if we were to get promoted through successively higher positions in our employers' organizations, it is likely that we would eventually rise to a position at which we didn't have ALL the skills and abilities needed to do the job successfully (if you know anything about football, think about all the great offensive and defensive coordinators who bombed out as head coaches).
  - o Prepare yourself to succeed as well as you can before accepting a promotion.
- More authority as a manager means more responsibility for the performance of other people. *The higher you rise, the more you become "the man" – responsible for all that happens, and all that doesn't happen, under your leadership – other people's failures as well as their successes.*
- The higher you rise through your employer's organization, the more visible you become to more people, and the easier it becomes for those people to see your mistakes and failures, to see what you are good at doing and what you are not so good at doing.

"Sometimes the best jobs are the ones we don't get." The older you get, and the more work experience you accumulate, the more this saying is likely to mean to you.
- Sometimes people would have been better off if they hadn't taken jobs that "beat them up" mentally and damaged their reputations as top performers.
- Sometimes there is greater job satisfaction in being a talented worker bee than there is in being the queen bee.

Do "<u>market intelligence</u>" research on the entire universe of jobs available to you.
- Jobs within your employer's organization, with other companies in your industry, and in

other industries in which you think good and satisfying work is being done.
- Jobs within the geographic area in which you currently live, locations where you would be willing to live in order to advance along your career path, and in prospective dream locations.

Networking may be the single best way to research the universe of desirable jobs available to you (and perhaps meet someone who can get you on an "inside track" to one of those desirable jobs).
- *Many of the best jobs with the best employers are not advertised*. They are obtained through personal referrals and word-of-mouth recommendations.
- Ask the members of your business team who know you best:
  o For their thoughts about types of work and industries that might provide the best career path opportunities for you.
  o If they can refer you to someone who might be able to help you get a desirable job along a desirable career path.
- Pick the brains of as many people as you can to get their thoughts about great industries in which to work, great employers, great jobs, and to whom they might be able to refer you to get more information about industries, employers, or jobs that interest you.
  o Attend trade association meetings and continuing education seminars.
  o Attend job fairs. Browse around and gather information about employers and jobs that you find attractive.
  o Get active with one or more community service groups to meet people who work in a wide range of industries and jobs.
- Talk to career planning professionals: guidance counselors, college career counselors, student placement offices, human relations personnel in companies, employment agencies, recruiters, etc.
- Take advantage of college alumni organizations and career networking groups.
- Ask librarians for their advice about career path planning resources.

A few job market research questions to consider asking people (in your own words):
- What industries and jobs do you think offer the best career opportunities?
- What are your favorite parts of your job?
- What career path did you take to get to your job?
- Have any companies in your industry earned reputations as "employers of choice" - places where everybody in the industry would like to work? If so:
  o Which companies?
  o What did those companies do to earn their reputation??
- What is your dream job?

Other job market research ideas include:
- Your experience in life discovering what you love to do, what you don't like to do, and what you daydream about doing.
- Keep your eyes and ears open to identify desirable jobs that you see people doing or hear people talking about.
- Monitor industries you find interesting:
  o Read the "trade press" of trade associations in those industries, e.g. magazines, websites, blogs.
  o Stay alert for stories in the news about those industries.
  o Visit companies in those industries and talk with people in those companies.
  o Attend trade association meetings in those industries.

- Read help wanted advertisements and job message boards, and then research the types of jobs and the industries that appear to be interesting. Keep in mind that many of the most desirable jobs are not advertised. While planning your career path, help wanted ads are likely to be more useful as a generalized job market research tool than as a source of leads to specific desirable jobs.

Consider the economics of supply and demand in your planning. The compensation an employer will provide you for your business services in large part will be a function of:
- Supply:
  - o *What you can supply to an employer*:
    - ▪ *Quantity* (types) of skills, abilities, and resources you can supply.
    - ▪ *Quality* of skills, abilities, and resources you can supply relative to skills, abilities, and resources your job seeking competitors can supply.
  - o *Competition*: number of job seeking competitors from whom an employer can choose to supply skills, abilities, and resources comparable to yours.
- *Demand*: how much an employer needs or wants you specifically and your particular skills, abilities, and resources, rather than just someone to fill a position.

Regarding supply: maintain an inventory list of all the valuable things you can supply to an employer. Be honest with yourself. Do NOT kid yourself about what you can supply.
- Skills and abilities, and level of expertise in each.
- Experience: job specific experience with your employer or a previous employer, or personal life experience that applies to a prospective job.
- Education and training: high school, college, trade school, apprenticeship program, etc.
- License or certification required by law to do a job; professional designation.
- Value added skills and abilities such as:
  - o Computer skills to keep a computer system updated and operating efficiently.
  - o Athletic skills that could help with marketing, e.g. golf.
  - o Leadership ability.
  - o Ability to assess situations and successfully manage workplace challenges, and develop creative ideas for improving operating efficiencies (i.e. increase profits).
  - o "Goodwill" value of your personal reputation in the industry and/or community.
- Personality traits that good employers typically seek, such as:
  - o Passion to succeed.
  - o Enthusiasm - highly contagious, and highly valuable.
  - o Initiative - to do superior work without close supervision.
  - o Team player who helps people work well together as a team.
  - o Business smarts and common sense needed to make prudent decisions.
  - o A curious mind coupled with a desire to become a progressively more knowledgeable and valuable employee.
- Network of business relationships: current customers, prospective new customers, suppliers, subcontractors, etc.
- Market intelligence: knowledge of more efficient and profitable operating systems and procedures; knowledge of which competitors are doing what.

Compare the quantity and quality of the skills and abilities you can supply to the quantity and quality of skills and abilities that your job seeking competitors can supply.
- How good are you at doing your work in comparison to your competitors? Are you better than anyone else available to your employer to do your job; about average when compared to other people who do jobs like yours; or, not so hot?

- What about you is likely to increase your desirability to an employer versus the desirability of anybody else the employer could choose to hire?

To the best of your ability, anticipate and acquire the qualifications you expect you will need for each successive job along your career path. *The closer that you get to each job, the more clearly you will be able to identify the qualifications you are likely to need for that job*, such as:

- Education: high school; college degree in a specific field of study; technical training.
- Trade or professional certification.
- Job skills expertise.
- Work experience, both type of experience and years of experience needed.

Regarding demand: make sure you understand exactly what skills, abilities, and business services an employer wants to buy from you, and degree of need they have for you.

- *Formal demand* - objective factors.
  - *Job description*: a written description of the work an employee is expected to do.
  - *Qualifications* that an employee in a job position is expected to have, e.g. education requirements; specific skills and abilities expertise; specific types of experience; license or certification required to do the job.
- *Informal demand* - subjective factors such as:
  - Personality traits the employer values.
  - Employer's perception of you, your personality, and the image you project.
  - Value added skills and abilities that are not stated as qualifications for a job.

Where would you fit on a continuum of employer demand?

- High demand end of the continuum:
  - Employer would have a strong need for you and your particular skills, abilities, experience, business contacts, market intelligence, etc.
  - Employer's business model: each employee is a carefully selected investment in human capital who could not be replaced easily; employer does all they can (within reason) to retain each highly valued "team member".
- Low demand end of the continuum:
  - Employer would have negligible demand for you as the unique person you are.
  - Employer's business model: employees are interchangeable cogs in the organizational machinery; prospective replacement employees are a plentiful "commodity" that can be purchased inexpensively in a short period of time; employees just like you are "a dime a dozen".

Competition: wise business people and military leaders identify and keep track of their competitors. "Keep your friends close and your enemies closer" has been attributed to Sun Tzu, author of the *The Art of War* some 2,500 years ago, and spoken as dialogue by Michael Corleone in the movie *The Godfather Part II* in 1974.

- How many job seeking competitors can supply the same things you can supply?
- How many people would like to have the job you have now and the jobs you aspire to get as you progress along the career path you are planning?
  - Internal competitors: people within your employer's organization who could do your job today, or do it tomorrow with little training?
  - External competitors: people outside your employer's organization?
- A scarce supply of qualified competitors would increase your negotiating leverage for an optimum total compensation package and jobs you aspire to get along your career path.
- A plentiful supply of competitors would decrease your negotiating leverage.

- The more competitors you have:
    - o The less compensation an employer might to need to provide to you in your current job and in the jobs you aspire to get along your career path.
    - o The better your job performance will need to be in order to retain your job, earn compensation package improvements, and advance along your career path.

Consider taking a career "road less traveled" into one of the less glamorous "mature" industries in which there is likely to be high employer demand and a relatively scarce supply of qualified job seekers. "Mature" means industries that have been around for years, such as:
- Surety and insurance (OK, so I plug my own industry, but only because there are so many good jobs that so many people don't know exist, and there is such high demand for good people to fill those jobs).
- Banking.
- Construction.
- Engineering.

There is a continuous demand for people to fill all sorts of good jobs in many mature industries, and over the past few years there has been a shortage in the supply of people seeking those good jobs. Too many people overlook these industries because they just don't know much about them and they mistakenly assume (a) jobs in these industries aren't interesting, and (b) compensation isn't good (learn what the old business adage says happens when people "assume"). If you explore some mature industries you may find that there are all sorts of good jobs that you never knew existed. "Don't miss the boat." You might be able to "catch a gravy train."

Engineering is a classic example of a career path that is screaming *"high demand – short supply"* off the pages of countless news articles as this book is being written because there is such a shortage of students choosing engineering as a college major and career path. There is a big push to get students to study science, technology, engineering, and mathematics (S.T.E.M.) in order to fill the demand for qualified employees.

For younger readers especially, think long and hard about a career in whatever type of engineering interests you most, perhaps:
- Design of the electronic systems that run everything – computers, telecommunications, "the internet of things", robotics, automobiles, aerospace, etc.
- Design and construction of beautiful buildings, transportation systems, ...
- Generation, storage, and transmission of "green" electricity, e.g. solar, wind, tidal turbines; development of biomass fuel from sources such as algae, etc.

Seek "employers of choice" – employers with whom people have the greatest desire to work - employers who have earned the best reputations in their industries and their local communities.
- The best employers seek to be the "employer of choice" for the best people in their industries because they know that the best people create the most successful companies in their industries.
- Therefore, they typically offer the best total compensation packages in their industries in order to attract and retain the best people and minimize the risk of losing their highly valued employees to competitors.

Two career path planning strategies to consider (and sometimes evolve from one to the other):
- *Type of work strategy.*
- *Industry strategy.*

"Type of work" strategy: if you decided to use this strategy your first action plan item would be to get a job doing a type of work you enjoy.
- Many types of work are "transferable" to many industries - sales, marketing, accounting, human resource management, etc.
- Finding a job doing a type of work you enjoy would provide you an opportunity to research career paths doing that type work while you are:
  - Gaining valuable expertise and experience doing that type of work.
  - Working with your supervisor and perhaps other managers to craft a career path toward the right job for you within your employer's organization.
  - Developing a network of business contacts who can provide career path advice, and perhaps referrals to "next" jobs that advance you along your career path.
- For example, if you enjoy working with numbers, an entry level job as an accounting clerk could help you plan a career path in the financial management field, perhaps from accounts payable clerk, to bookkeeper, to controller, to chief financial officer.

"Industry" strategy: if you decided to use this strategy your first action plan item would be to get a job in an industry in which you think good and satisfying work is being done.
- A "toe-hold" job in the industry would provide you a vantage point from which to:
  - Scout the industry from the inside to identify:
    - Types of jobs available in the industry that you think you would enjoy, perhaps even a dream job that you had no clue existed before you started to work in the industry.
    - Employers of choice in the industry, and a job that you think you would enjoy that is available with one of those employers.
  - Get ideas about a dream job you might create for yourself.
- For example, if you enjoy watching buildings being built, an entry level job in the construction industry (perhaps as a summer job) could provide you a vantage point from which to research all the different career path opportunities available within the industry, e. g. architect or engineer who helps design buildings, craftsperson who does the actual construction work, project manager who manages building construction, entrepreneur running your own company.

Career path starting points:
- Never had a full time job.
- Currently unemployed after having had a job.
- Have a current job.

If you have never had a full time job, use this book as you see fit to help plan a career path.

If you are currently unemployed after having had a job:
- Analyze why you are now unemployed.
  - Because you quit your previous job? If so, did you have good reasons that prompted you to quit that would sound reasonable to a new employer?
  - Because of circumstances beyond your control, e.g. employer eliminating positions or laying off employees in a tough economy; the entire industry slowly dying?
  - Because of circumstances you could have controlled but did not? What lessons can you learn / have you learned from the experience?
  - If you were let go because of something you did or didn't do, you might try to talk to your prior employer. If you do talk to your prior employer, you might start

out by tactfully saying you are sorry your employment didn't work out, and ask for an "exit interview" to learn why you were let go, and get advice and recommendations about what you might do differently with a new employer.

- Prepare to explain to a prospective new employer why you are now unemployed, lessons learned from your experience working for your previous employer, and why you will be a good, long term employee for a new employer.
- If your employer had terminated your employment, allow yourself a short period of time to grieve for the loss of your job. But, get over it. Fast. Get back into a positive thinking frame of mind. Don't allow yourself to get stuck in a negative mindset feeling sorry for yourself. Negative thinking will hinder your ability to get a good new job. The type of good employer with whom you should be seeking employment will be seeking to hire happy, positive thinking people. *Get out of your house and back into the world with a smile on your face.*
- *If you have been unemployed for a significant period of time, find a job, any job.* Don't be picky while you are hunting for a more desirable job.
  - o *It's easier to get a better job when you already have a job.*
  - o The longer you are unemployed, the more that a prospective new employer might question your desirability as an employee.
- Consider taking a less desirable position with a desirable employer to get your toe in the door and an opportunity to demonstrate how valuable an employee you could become.
- Consider offering your services to an employer as an unpaid volunteer or intern to demonstrate your job skills and your potential to become a valuable employee.
- *Focus on networking* to connect with prospective employers and jobs that fit your personality, level of skills expertise, abilities, and career path plan. Consider using some of the networking ideas suggested in this book.
- Write a resume that sells you (see the Marketing Plan section later in this chapter).

If you have a job:
- If you like your job, seek ways to make it even better – to make it the right job for you.
- If you don't like your job as it is today, learn to like it as much as you can, and work to make it as good as you can while you are proactively working toward making it the right job for you. If you put your mind to learning to like your job and you proactively do all you can do to make your job better, you just might surprise yourself by turning it into a job you wind up liking. To help you learn to like your job more:
  - o Start by being thankful you have the job and the compensation it provides. It's likely that many people would like to have your job.
  - o Identify aspects of the job you like and build on those things, perhaps:
    - Nice people with whom you work.
    - Your ability to do your work well.
    - An opportunity to suggest ways to make your work more enjoyable for you and more profitable for your employer.
  - o Keep in mind the advice Mary Poppins gave us in the song "A Spoonful of Sugar" in The Walt Disney Company's classic 1964 movie *Mary Poppins* "In every job that must be done, there is an element of fun. You find the fun, and – snap – the job's a game."
- Please see the next section for suggestions to consider for use in pro-actively working to make your job more satisfying and enjoyable as you advance along your career path.

If you have a job

Your degree of satisfaction with your <u>employer</u>, your <u>job</u>, and your <u>compensation</u> should dictate:
- The time and effort you invest in career path planning.
- The urgency you place on taking action on your career path plan.

Key decisions to make include:
- How satisfied are you with your <u>employer</u>?
    o Do your employer's actions demonstrate that they consider you and your co-workers to be valuable investments in human capital?
    o How much care and concern does your employer demonstrate for your well-being and the well-being of your co-workers?
    o Do you have a satisfactory opportunity within your employer's organization to advance along a career path from your current job toward your dream job?
- Are you satisfied with your job? How much do you enjoy your work?
- How satisfied are you with your total <u>compensation</u> package – with the investment return on the "sweat equity" of time, talent and energy you are investing in your job?
- *<u>Can you talk openly and honestly about your career path aspirations with your supervisor and any other senior manager(s) with whom you might need to talk about your career</u>*? If you can't talk with them, you can't plan with them.
    o When you hear these people talk, and when you observe them during their daily activities, do they seem open minded and genuinely interested in helping others?
    o If in the past you asked for help with something, how did they respond?
    o Do your co-workers think they can talk openly and honestly with their supervisors and other senior managers?

Keep in mind that:
- *Many people don't know how good they have it with their employer and their job* -especially those people who don't have much to compare it to – people who don't have much in the way of work experience, market intelligence about other employers, etc.
- *Our emotions and experience in life to date can put "subjective blinders" on us and make it hard to evaluate our jobs and employers in a coolly rational and objective manner.* This is especially true of people who have lived a relatively pampered life in which they haven't had to conform to a disciplined behavior structure such as the workplace can impose, nor been held strictly accountable for their performance by anyone.
- The less experience you have in your industry and in the business world in general, the more important it might be to ask other people for their perceptions of your employer and your job, perhaps co-workers, outside parties who work with your employer (suppliers, subcontractors, professional service providers), and people on your business team who have enough knowledge of your employer and your job to offer well-reasoned opinions.

Conduct continuous "market intelligence" research on the job market. Knowledge of other jobs and other employers is of critical importance in making well-informed decisions as to how good your job is, how good your employer is, and how good your career path opportunities are with your employer relative to opportunities that might be available with other employers.

Market intelligence research will help you learn how good your employer is considered to be by other people in your industry and in your local community.
- Do people think your employer is a good employer, perhaps even an "employer of

choice" where "those in the know" want to work? Is "to know them to love them?"

- Is your employer known for trying to attract and retain the best people in your industry?
- Do other people think your employer provides good compensation packages (the best?) in comparison to other employers in your industry and in your community?
- Is your employer thought to have a track record of:
  o Offering employees opportunities to develop their skills and abilities, and advance along satisfying career paths?
  o Promoting people within their organization to fill desirable positions ("growing their own") or frequently reaching outside the company to fill those positions?
- How good is your employer's reputation:
  o In your industry for fair dealings with suppliers, subcontractors, service providers, customers? Are they thought to treat people well?
  o In your community? Are they thought to be a good "corporate citizen"?
  o In comparison to other employers in your industry and in your local community?

Market intelligence research will also help you:
- Learn the compensation and management practices of different employers in your industry and in different industries, which you can then use as benchmarks in evaluating your employer's compensation and management practices.
- Identify:
  o Other industries in which good and perhaps more satisfying work is being done.
  o Employers of choice in your industry and other industries.
  o Jobs that might provide greater opportunities to achieve your objectives.
  o Prospective career paths that might offer greater opportunity to advance toward your dream job.
- Discover a type of work, job, employer, or career path that you had not known existed.
- Monitor how well your employer and your entire industry are doing in the marketplace - prospering and growing or becoming less profitable and gradually dying?
- Develop a career path "Plan B" (more on Plan B careers in a few pages).

Determine what financial compensation package your employer has the <u>capability</u> to provide to a person in your current job and in future jobs along a satisfying career path? If your employer doesn't have the capability to provide a compensation package that would enable you to achieve your projected financial statement budget objectives, "you can't squeeze blood from a stone". A desirable financial compensation package might include things such as:
- Salary or wages.
- Bonuses based upon individual performance and/or company profit sharing.
- Insurance plans, e.g. medical, prescription drug, dental, vision, life, long term disability.
- Retirement plan, e.g. 401(k) type retirement savings plan (preferably with "matching fund" employer contributions), or employer funded "defined benefit "pension plan.
- Medical savings account.
- Paid vacation and holidays.
- Free or reduced rate parking; reimbursement of other commuting expenses.
- Subsidized meals in a company cafeteria.
- Use of a company vehicle, or personal vehicle use allowance.
- Childcare or other "fringe" benefits that would otherwise cost you money.

When evaluating financial compensation, be sure to consider the impact of income taxes.
- Some financial benefits provided by employers are immediately taxable in the year

earned (e.g. salary, wages), some might be tax-deferred (e.g. 401k retirement plan, employer's matching contributions to a 401k plan), and some might not be taxed at all (e.g. parking on company property, subsidized prices in a cafeteria, exercise facilities).
- Tax deferred and non-taxed benefits can make one employer's financial compensation packages more attractive than another employer's.

Internal factors affecting financial compensation that an employer can provide might include:
- Budget: an employer's annual expense budget typically contains a specific aggregate amount of money available to pay all employees.
  - o This limited pool of dollars must be allocated among all employees in such a way as to optimize the employer's net return on the money spent.
  - o No employer has a bottomless pot of money that they could use to pay you and all your co-workers all the money that each of you dream about earning.
- Written compensation guidelines:
  - o Many, if not most, companies have formal financial compensation guidelines for each position within their organizations.
  - o Salaries are often managed by means of a "matrix", that factors in elements such as salary grade level, years of employment (time in grade), performance review rating (compared to other employees in same grade), and local cost of living (for employers having facilities in multiple geographic locations).

External factors affecting financial compensation that an employer can provide might include:
- "Local cost of living": the employer's other costs of doing business in the local economy, e.g. taxes, rent, utilities, costs of goods and services they must buy locally, etc.
- Compensation paid by competitors: employers must take into account prices charged by competitors when pricing their own products and services, and the expense of employee compensation typically is a significant component of pricing. If an employer's competitors are holding down their prices by paying people significantly less money, then, in order to keep their products and services priced competitively, the employer might not be able to pay its employees all the money the employer would prefer to pay.
- Union wage scales.

Determine what financial compensation and benefits packages your employer has the willingness to provide to employees?
- What is your employer's business model?
- What is your employer's compensation strategy?

Business Model A - maximize long term profit.
- Compensation strategy: offer excellent compensation packages that enable the employer to attract and retain a team of the best people in the industry in order to provide the best value in products and services available to their customers; employees are considered to be "human capital" – each employee is considered to be a highly valued investment.
- "Share the wealth" (wealth being company profits) through salary, wages, profit sharing plans, performance bonuses, etc.
- Maximize long term profit rather than make a "quick buck" today.

Business Model B - minimize current expense
- Compensation strategy: pay as little as possible to interchangeable "individuals" who do acceptably competent work; employees are considered to be readily replaceable commodities who are "a dime a dozen".

- Save every penny possible, even if that might mean making decisions to sacrifice the quality of products they sell, e.g. "shaving off" a little bit here and a tiny amount there and hope customers either don't notice or don't "make a big deal" of it.
- Maximize profit today, and "let the future take care of itself", even if that means not making the investments in the human resources that would be necessary to continue generating the future profit needed to maintain company viability over the long term, e.g. senior executives doing what they can today to maximize retirement compensation and/ or "golden parachute" severance packages when/if they depart in a few years.

Social environment - do you enjoy the company of the people with whom you spend so much of your life?
- Is it a happy workplace?
  - o Do you see lots of smiles and hear an amount of laughter appropriate in a workplace setting?
  - o Is there minimal griping "in the lunch room" or "around the water cooler"?
- Do your co-workers seem to have positive, optimistic attitudes?

Physical environment of your workplace - do you enjoy the physical environment of your workplace?
- Is it a nice place in which to work?
- Good employers understand that an enjoyable physical environment fosters contented employees, and contented employees tend to be more productive employees.
  - o Does it seem that the physical environment of your workplace is intended to foster contented employees?
  - o Does it seem that senior officers conspicuously spend far more money creating luxurious executive offices for themselves than they spend on a safe, comfortable, enjoyable work environment for you and your co-workers?

Location of your workplace.
- Is your workplace in a desirable location?
- How much of your valuable time is consumed by commuting to and from work?
- Could you negotiate doing some of your work remotely from home, e.g. telecommuting?
- Does your employer have another location where you could work; a location that might provide you greater opportunity to achieve your personal business plan and budget objectives – perhaps even a dream location?

If you decide you have the <u>right employer</u>, then decide if you have the <u>right job</u> within your employer's organization. Keep in mind that no employer is perfect, and no job is perfect - even "dream" jobs are likely to have some imperfections.
- Does your job enable you to achieve your short term career path, business plan and projected financial statement budget objectives?
- Does your total compensation package provide a satisfactory return on your "sweat equity" - sweat equity being the time, talent and energy that you are investing?
- Do you think you could remain in your current job for your entire career and achieve your long term objectives - perhaps with enhancements to your job responsibilities, duties and compensation? If so, count your blessings.
- How well does the supply of skills and abilities that you have available to sell match up with the demand that your employer has for those business services?
  - o If you can't yet supply all the services your employer wants to buy, can you develop a plan that will enable you to supply those services in the future?

- o If you can't plan a way to supply the services your employer wants to buy from a person in your job position, then you would be a "square peg a round hole", and it is not likely that your job could become the right job for you.
- Use your performance reviews to help determine if your job is the right job for you today, and if it is not, the likelihood that you could turn it into the right job for you in the future.
- *Acid test of the right job – are you happy with where you are in your career?*

Many people already have jobs that they consider to be the right job for themselves, and they lead happy, comfortable lives. These people might just continue proactively managing their jobs in order to nudge them as close as possible to becoming dream jobs.

And a number of people who have "created their own good luck" already have advanced along career paths to their dream jobs. These people should count their blessings and continue doing all they can to keep on creating good luck for themselves in the future.

If you decide that you don't yet have the right job, can you work proactively to turn your job into the right job for you?
- If you think you can talk openly and honestly with your supervisor, consider asking him for any thoughts he might have about what you might be able to do to become a more valuable employee for him - make the conversation about him to start.
- *Carefully read your supervisor's receptivity to your request for his thoughts*. If he appears to be receptive, you might consider asking follow up questions - in your own words - that bring the conversation around to you and your career:
  - o How can we work together to enrich my job in ways that would make me a more valuable employee for you and make it more satisfying and enjoyable for me?
  - o What new things can I do that would help you and challenge me?
  - o What can I do to improve my total compensation package?
  - o What career path do you think I can plan within the company?
  - o What would you do if you were me?

BE CAREFUL!
- Let me say this again - when deciding if it would be safe to talk openly and honestly with your supervisor about your career aspirations, be sure to consider the ways that your supervisor and other more senior managers have treated you and your co-workers in the past. Become as sure as you can be that talking with your supervisor or more senior managers won't backfire and come back to hurt you.
- If you have a shadow of doubt about how your supervisor or more senior managers might react, you might try sending up one or two "trial balloons" in conversations with them - learn about trial balloons and how to use them. Don't just blurt out what is on your mind until you can be as sure as possible about how what you say will be received.
- Use discretion, tact, and good common sense.
- Have empathy. Put yourself in your employer's shoes. Your employer might have constraints on their ability to provide you with the compensation or career advancement you desire in the near term future:
  - o Employee compensation budget that must be allocated among all employees (more money for you might leave less money for similarly well qualified co-workers).
  - o A salary matrix for all employees such that it would be unfair to others to give you special consideration.
  - o Temporary budget crunch conditions that limit the money immediately available

for a raise.
  o Temporary bottleneck of too many people already in positions to which you would like to be promoted.
- Have sympathy for your supervisor's position. Try to not let your career aspirations:
  o "Upset the apple-cart" of a supervisor who may not want to "lose" you through promotion or transfer.
  o Be perceived as a possible threat to take your supervisor's job someday.
  o Embarrass a supervisor who is not as motivated to advance along a career path as you are.
- Try to help your supervisor see your situation from your perspective, and to understand that you are only doing what every prudent businessperson should do – that is working to achieve your career path objectives.
- Do your absolute best "to not burn any bridges" with your supervisor.

<u>If you decide that it would be safe to talk openly and honestly with your supervisor about your career aspirations, also give a lot of thought to how your supervisor might react to your job market research if you told him about it.</u> Be aware that there is both a powerful upside and a potentially dangerous downside to using job market intelligence when negotiating job enhancements, compensation package enhancements, and career path advancement. Be careful not to antagonize your employer.
- *Powerful upside*
  o Good employers who have demonstrated that they seek to attract and retain the best people in their industry typically employ supervisors who are likely to have open minds and a willingness to have an intelligent conversation about the facts of the local marketplace. Good supervisors typically appreciate and respect:
    ▪ The business smarts it takes for an employee to do job market research.
    ▪ The kind of honesty and guts it takes for an employee to speak up.
  o Few things other than exceptional performance can motivate a good employer to sweeten the compensation package of a valued employee more than the risk of losing that valued employee to another employer.
  o Good employers typically try to take the best possible care of their good employees given their current budget constraints. However, good employers have been known to tweak their budgets to free up additional compensation, or put a person in line for a promotion, after a valued employee told them about better compensation or a more desirable job available with another company.
- *Potentially dangerous downside*
  o Telling a supervisor who is not an open minded "people person" about your research into the management and compensation practices of other employers might cause him to shift him from thinking and acting rationally to thinking and acting emotionally as a hurt, angered, or resentful person. If you stay, you might damage your long term relationship.
  o If your employer has communicated through their words and actions that they think of employees as commodities who are readily replaceable, they may react along the lines of "we don't care what you think, if you don't like your job you can leave anytime you want and we'll get somebody else to do it."
  o Be especially careful about mentioning a job offer you may have received from another employer. You might goad your employer into saying something like "OK, get out of here now and take that job."

If you think you have tried your hardest to work with your employer to (a) turn your job into the right job for you, and/or (b) plan a satisfying career path toward the right job for you, but you are unsatisfied with the results of your efforts:

Take a long hard look at yourself:
- *The issue may be you, not your employer.*
- Make sure you have been "making the best of what you've got". Are you sure you tried your hardest to work with your employer to enrich your job, to optimize your total compensation package, and to plan a satisfying career path?
- Try to see yourself through your supervisor's eyes - what does your employer see or not see in you as an employee? Go back over your performance reviews.
- Remember - "whenever you point a finger of responsibility at anyone else, you have three fingers pointing back at you".

Discuss your situation with at least one confidant whose business judgment you trust – preferably someone who knows you well enough to provide an <u>objective, constructive critique of your thinking</u> about <u>your employer and your career path plan</u>. You might discuss things such as:
- Your employer's reputation in the local community, general news media, and trade press.
- If your business plan is a good match with your employer's business plan.
- An evaluation of your current skills, abilities, work habits, and diligence in working at a well-reasoned career path plan.
- Your prospects for being hired by a new employer for a more desirable job exactly as you are today - without working to improve any of your current skills and abilities, gaining any new skills or abilities, or changing any of your personal or work behavior habits.

If you ultimately decide you will need to find a new job with a new employer in order to achieve your objectives:
- *Do NOT quit immediately after making a decision that you will need to leave.*
- Make the best of your situation while you are taking whatever time you need to develop a well-reasoned career path action plan to secure a new job with a new employer, and secure that new job.
- Observe the conditions of any employment contract or non-compete agreement you may have signed.

No matter how happy you are with your employer and your job, consider developing a Plan B career path plan - a "back-up job" you could move to quickly in the event of scenarios such as:
- Your job being eliminated after:
  - o Economic hard times led to a corporate reorganization.
  - o Your employer was acquired by another company.
- New technology making obsolete your job, your company, or your entire industry.
- A good supervisor being promoted or retiring and being replaced by a not so good supervisor who makes a previously satisfying job decidedly less so.
- The corporate culture of your company changing after a change in senior management, e.g. changing from street smart business executives to people who lack the street smarts needed to continue managing the company as successfully as it had been managed; changing hands from good managers who care for employees as valued human resources to managers who care more for their own well-being and less about "the little people" who make them their money.

<u>Thoughts about planning for a new job with a new employer</u>

<u>Don't quit your old job</u>! It's easier to get a new job when you already have a job.
- Having a job gives a person negotiating leverage with a new employer.
    - o The better a person's job would appear to be to another employer, the less the person's need for a new job might be perceived by that prospective employer, and the better the compensation that might be offered in order to hire the person.
    - o A current employer gives a person an implied performance reference by virtue of retaining that person as an employee.
- Even if you started to think "I hate this job and I can't take it another day", almost undoubtedly you could take it for another day and even more days if prudent planning necessitated it. "Suck it up" and "stick it out" until you can get a better job.
- Live for today, plan for a better tomorrow - make the best of each day.
    - o "Live in the moment" and find joy in planning for your future. The past is gone. The future may never come. Today is the only day you have to experience the joy and satisfaction that will result in fond memories of a life well lived.
    - o Listen to the lyrics in Jimmy Buffett's song "It's My Job".
    - o As Stephen Stills said in a song "Love The One You're With".
- Continue working to improve the conditions of your current job or get a new job within your employer's organization that you think you would enjoy more. One never knows when a "miracle" may happen as the result of diligent use of a business planning process.
- *<u>Don't quit your old job until you are sure you have locked in a new job</u>*. If possible, get a written and signed employment contract/agreement with your new employer, not just an oral offer.

Take all the time you need to (a) fully research a prospective new job with a new employer and (b) make a well-informed, well-reasoned decision about taking that job.
- Work your career path planning process as fast as prudently reasonable – but, don't rush too fast and risk making a big mistake because you didn't take enough time to do enough due diligence research.
- Because so many people have been prone to acting rashly since the time our ancient ancestors began passing down advice from one generation to the next, a great deal of folk wisdom has accumulated regarding taking action too quickly based upon emotion:
    - o *"Don't jump from the frying pan into the fire".*
    - o "Look before you leap."
    - o "The grass looks greener on the other side of the fence."
    - o "The devil you know may be better than the devil you don't know."
- The looks of a bright and shiny prospective new job can be deceiving. From your perspective on the outside of a prospective employer's organization a job might look like it offers a better future, but that might not be the case. In actuality, it might not be better, and it might be even worse.
- *False impressions are sometimes created by employers during the hiring process.* Employers have been known to lure in new employees with "sweet talk" about how great the company and the job are - *"they promise the Earth, moon and stars."* Then after new hires report for duty the new hires sadly discover that things are not what those people were led to believe that they would be.

As part of your research, ask people you know for their thoughts about a prospective new employer:
- *People who have had first-hand experience working with a prospective new employer* in

capacities such as:
- o Current or former employee (to get the most honest answers from a current employee, try to talk to the person away from the workplace).
- o Customer, supplier, or professional service provider.
- Second hand reports from people who "have heard such and such" about a prospective new employer.
  - o People who have heard things from friends or co-workers.
  - o Reports they have read or heard about in the news.
- First hand reports based upon actual experience are preferable to second hand reports based upon hearsay. Be cautious about relying upon second hand reports.

Two suggestions:
- Write a list of all the pros and cons that you can think of regarding a prospective new employer and a prospective new job.
- Ask at least one confidant whose business judgment you trust to critique your analysis of the pros on your list, talk through the possible ramifications of the cons, and provide you any additional pros or cons he can think of.

Consider getting a second job as a means to:
- Generate additional income while you are pursuing a more desirable new job.
- Research an industry in which you think good and satisfying work is being done from the perspective of an "industry insider".
- Gain valuable expertise and work experience that would help you qualify for the next job you are planning to get as you advance along your career path.
- Explore turning a hobby into your primary job, e.g. photographer, musician, writer.

If another employer in your industry seems to pay employees significantly more than your employer pays, find out why.
- Has that employer adopted a business model based upon building a team of the best people in their industry so that they can outperform their competitors over the long haul?
- Or, could it be that the employer runs such a "meat grinder" workplace that the employer must pay employees more money than other employers in order to prevent people from "jumping ship" to take jobs with their competitors?
- What trade-offs in job satisfaction or free time might employees have to make in order to earn that higher pay? Is the employer paying more money in order to compensate employees for putting them under greater stress, or offering lower levels of job satisfaction, or requiring that employees spend a greater amount of time on the job?
- Keep in mind the adage "If it sounds too good to be true, it probably is."

Geographic location: if a prospective new job would require you to move to a new geographic location, think long and hard about the significant impact that such a move might have on you and your family BEFORE you commit to moving – be it across town, to a different city, or to a different state.
- Could a new employer in another geographic location really provide you a better opportunity to achieve your career path, business plan, and budget objectives?
- Implications of uprooting yourself and your family from your current home, your community, and your friends?
- Research local living conditions, e.g. cost of living, housing, commute to and from work?
- *What would be your Plan B if you didn't like the new job or living in the new location*?

Don't "job hop" from one employer to another, to another, ... Many employers screen out the resumes of job applicants who appear to be "job hoppers".

- *Good employers think of hiring a new employee as investing in a human resource* – an addition to their human capital. And an investment in a new employee can be expensive. It is often unprofitable for an employer to be just another temporary stopping place along the way of a job hopper. An employer's cost of hiring a new employee includes:
  - o The hiring process.
  - o Training costs.
  - o Lower productivity of the new employee while he is learning the employer's operating systems and procedures ("how we do things around here").
  - o Drain on the productivity of co-workers and supervisors as they help train the new person and integrate him into their work team.
- Job hopping can be a warning signal to employers that:
  - o A series of prior employers might have thought that the job hopper's performance was unsatisfactory.
  - o The job hopper might have poor planning and decision making skills - he hasn't been able to pick a job with a good employer that provides a good fit with his personality, skills, abilities, and career path plan.
  - o The job hopper might have personal problems that impact his work or relationships with people, e.g. uncooperative personality or substance abuse.

The above said, most people will change jobs at least once in their careers.
- Most employers have come to accept that the old business model of an employee staying with one employer for life may be fading into obsolescence.
- If you have had multiple jobs in the past, prepare answers to prospective employer questions such as "what is your career path plan" and "how does this job with my company fit into your plan".

Try to make your first contact in the hiring process with a person who would have a vested interest in hiring you, e.g. your prospective new supervisor or a senior manager further up the employer's "chain of command".
- When an employer is sifting through a stack of resumes and employment applications, it is difficult for one job seeker to stand out from a whole crowd of job seeking competitors.
- *Being able to put your face and personality together with your resume and application can have a huge influence on a person making a hiring decision.*
- If you are referred to an employer by someone you know, ask that person if he could arrange a meeting for you with a person who would have a say in hiring you.
- If you learn about a job from an advertisement or an employment agency, ask people in your network of business contacts if they have any contacts within the prospective employer's organization to whom they could refer you.
- Try to bypass the bureaucracy of an employer's human relations (HR) department to the greatest extent possible during the hiring process. HR departments are infamous within certain business circles for being quagmires in which prospective new hires can get stuck for a lot longer than the managers who want to hire new employees would like them to be stuck – and from which some prospective new hires never get out.
- The larger (and more bureaucratic) a prospective employer's organization, the more beneficial a face to face meeting might be with a person who has a vested interest in getting you hired. A flesh and blood person can escort you through the bureaucracy of an HR department and the hiring processes that HR departments dictate within many large employers' organizations.

- If "your file" makes its way to an HR department, politely try to get the name of an HR employee with whom you can maintain contact for status updates on your "paperwork" and the hiring process (interviews, drug test, etc.). *Seek as much human contact as you can in order to humanize the "human relations" process.*

Prepare for a job interview the way a good salesperson would prepare for a sales meeting.
- Research the prospective employer's business plan, products or services sold, target markets, advertising, etc. Identify specific things that interest you about the employer and the job for which you will be interviewing.
- If possible, try to get the name of the person who will be interviewing you and do some research on that person's background, e.g. schools attended, family, community service work, favorite sports, personal and professional accomplishments. This type information can help you build a personal bond with the interviewer during the interview.
- Use your resume as an outline of "talking points" for a sales presentation that highlights the things about you that set you apart from your job seeking competitors, and would make you the best choice for the employer to hire.
- Prepare to answer questions.
  - Write down questions you can reasonably expect to be asked along with answers to those questions.
  - Answer questions in a succinct, businesslike manner.
  - Be careful about volunteering too much information that is not directly related to answering the question (learn what some attorneys advise clients about the risk of volunteering information) - don't get nervous and ramble on.
  - Be ready to go off-script and improvise answers to follow up questions the interviewer might ask based upon the course of the conversation and how well your two personalities seem to be clicking.
- Prepare to ask questions.
  - Interviewers usually ask "do you have any questions you would like to ask me?" Prepare at least two questions you can ask about things you want to be sure you understand about the job and the employer, e.g. job duties, career advancement opportunities, total compensation package, employer's business plan.
  - If you aren't specifically asked if you have any questions, try to work your questions into the conversation.
  - The quality of your questions will be of interest to a good interviewer. Well thought questions typically demonstrate that a job applicant has the business smarts that are needed to ask good questions.
  - Good questions can help distinguish you from your job seeking competitors.
  - Questions can also help you build a bond with the interviewer if you ask questions that get him to talk about his employer, his job, and perhaps himself.
- Ask a confidant on your business team to help you rehearse for your interview.
  - The less experience you have with job interviews or sales presentations, the more beneficial it will be to rehearse.
  - Have the person ask you the questions that you think you are likely to be asked.
  - Also have him ask you some questions he makes up so that you can practice going off script to answer unexpected questions.

During job interviews:
- "First impressions count" – they typically have a big impact on hiring decisions.
  - Many job applicants never recover from a less than optimal first impression.
  - Dress the way you think your interviewer would expect the successful job

applicant to dress (skip ahead a few pages and read about dressing for success).
- o *Practice a firm handshake*. This goes for men and women. A good handshake projects the self–confident and humbly assertive personality that most good employers associate with their best employees.
- o Smile!
- *Be yourself.*
  - o Don't pretend to be the type of person you think the employer is seeking.
  - o If your personality, skills, and abilities are not a good match with a prospective job and employer, it would be better to find that out before wasting any of your precious time pretending to be something that you are not.
  - o If you did pretend to be something that you are not, it is likely that over time the employer would learn that you are not what you pretended to be. This discovery would likely make the employer unhappy, and your career could suffer the repercussions of an unhappy employer who felt he was deceived.
- Project the image of a positive thinking, self-confident person who knows in his heart that he would do this job well.
- Convey how good you are at doing what your resume says you are good at doing - but don't brag.
- Present your accomplishments in a humble manner befitting a soon-to-be colleague with whom the interviewer would enjoy working.
- Sit straight. Don't fidget.
- Look the interviewer in the eye. Eye contact displays self-confidence and it helps to build a human interaction bond with the interviewer. Do NOT look down at your shoes.
- Show enthusiasm to get the job.
- Do NOT let yourself feel intimidated by anyone with whom you talk. Keep in mind that even if the person who interviews you has an important sounding title (and perhaps is many years older and has an imposing demeanor) he is no better than you are as a person. YOU ARE PRESIDENT of your own company!
- "Read" the interviewer as your conversation progresses.
  - o Try to gauge his reaction to what you are saying and his level of interest in you. This is valuable information to have during any negotiating you might do relative to job duties, compensation, etc.
  - o Be an active listener to what he says and a keen observer of his body language.
  - o Ask your questions and make your comments according to how your senses tell you that they are likely to be received.

As president of your company, <u>you also should be interviewing the employer</u> as a prospective client for your business services.
- A job interview provides an excellent opportunity to gather information to use in making a decision about accepting a job offer (if an offer is made).
- Ask the questions you prepared in advance - about the job, the employer, and the potential for advancement along your career path. Learn as much as you can. Minimize the risk of discovering after you had started to work for the employer that you had made mistake.
- Interviewers tend to be good reflections of their employers. Good employers typically do not have poor interviewers talk to prospective new employees. If an interviewer comes across as having little passion for his job, for his employer, and/or for the job for which he is interviewing you, take that as a warning to think long and hard about that employer as a good employer for you.

Develop a marketing plan to sell your business services

As president of your company, develop a marketing plan to sell your business services to your employer as your client. Your personality and all that you can offer an employer should dictate your marketing plan - an introvert should not try to sell himself in the same way that an extrovert would sell himself.

Create a "brand name" that sells you. A brand name is the "good name" a person creates for himself. Your brand name is a function of:
- *The promise of the quality of the business services you are selling* - your job skills expertise, ability to develop good working relationships, passion to succeed, etc.
- *A past performance track record that validates you can deliver on your promise - your reputation.*
- If you don't yet have work experience in a job, create a past performance track record of accomplishments in your personal life and school life.

Your brand name should:
- Conjure up images in employers' minds of what they want to see in their best compensated employees - expertise, experience, passion to succeed, integrity, etc.
- Convey that you are deserving of great jobs and excellent compensation.
- *Differentiate you from your promotion seeking and compensation seeking competition*:
  - o For job enrichment opportunities and promotions.
  - o For the limited compensation dollars that your employer has budgeted to allocate among all employees.

Give people good things to say about your past performance and your potential for the future.
- Think of the office gossip you hear when people talk about other people who aren't in the room. When you aren't there, it's a pretty good bet people talk about you. Give them a steady diet of good things to say.
- Each time you perform a task well, or help a co-worker, or do something kind for someone, or do something that helps your entire work group succeed, you will be building the brand name image of "now that's a good guy who is going places" that is likely to pop into people's minds when they think of you.

Allow your reputation to speak for itself.
- "Word of mouth" is the best form of advertising - when the words come from other people's mouths.
- Don't brag about how good you are. Nobody likes braggarts.
- However, you may need to find diplomatically tactful ways to get your name and reputation in front of decision makers who do not yet know about you and your brand name (see comments about using "psychological operations" a few pages onward).

Target your marketing. A key marketing principle is to (a) identify the "decision maker" who makes the final decision about a purchase and the people who influence that decision maker's decisions, and (b) target a marketing campaign at those people. Research your employer's organization to identify the person who makes the ultimate decisions about your compensation and career advancement and the people who influence that decision maker's decisions.
- Your supervisor who does your performance reviews may not be the ultimate decision maker who makes the decisions about your compensation or promotions.

- Your supervisor may be making recommendations to the actual decision maker who is one or more rungs up the organization chart, e.g. your immediate supervisor's supervisor, a department head, or even the president.

Keep in mind that within every organization there are formal and informal leadership power structures (an important reason to study sociology). Seek to identify your employer's:
- *Formal leadership structure*: formal leaders in your employer's "chain of command" who have clearly delineated authority and responsibility to make recommendations and/or decisions about your compensation and career advancement.
- *Informal leadership structure*: informal group leaders assume leadership positions in informal groups based upon their personality, expertise, personal relationships, and people's perceptions of them. An informal leader might significantly influence the decisions of the formal leader who makes the decisions about your future.

Also keep in mind that other people might also influence the decision maker:
- Other managers (his buddies) who either know you personally or hear about you from others might be providing their opinions about you and your value to the organization.
- Spouses of decision makers sometimes provide significant input based upon their perceptions of what they hear at home about employees, what they hear from other spouses, and what they may observe at company functions they attend. Spousal input might be based upon such things as liking or disliking an employee, perceiving the employee to be a threat to the decision maker's job (and therefore the spouse's income), or to be a rival for the affections of the decision maker (beware actual office romances and the perception of romances).

Learn about your target market audience. What makes your supervisor, his manager, and their manager(s) tick? In school you might have known this as *"psyching out the teacher."*
- What are their business objectives and strategies?
- Do they think of employees as human resources who should be nurtured to grow in value? How essential do they think your job is to company operations?
- What budget pressures might they be feeling to control their expenses?
- What motivates them most in doing their jobs? Money? Benevolent self-interest - doing well personally by helping others do well?
- What are their personal backgrounds that formed their frame of reference for evaluating you and the work you do, e.g. where they grew up, where they went to school?
- What are their favorite interests, e.g. family, sports, gardening?

Seek people who can help you sell yourself. It's easier to climb a corporate ladder when people are giving you a helping hand. Three ways people might give you a helping hand are:
- *A champion* who can pull you up the corporate ladder, as in "championing your cause".
  - A champion might be:
    - Your direct supervisor.
    - Your supervisor's supervisor, or a trusted advisor of your supervisor.
    - Someone as high up your company's organization as the president. Some senior managers enjoy the game of identifying and bringing along top performers in their organizations.
  - A champion might be motivated by:
    - Benevolent self-interest - helping people who the champion thinks can help him succeed over the long run.
    - Altruism - the good feeling of helping another person succeed.

- o Caution: be a tactful office politician. Be careful not to offend or antagonize your direct supervisor if you should happen to develop a relationship with a person who outranks him. Try to avoid a situation that your supervisor might perceive as an attempt to "go over his head".
- *A mentor*: in days gone by the "master and apprentice" business model was the primary way that job skills were passed down from generation to generation. Today, mentors are akin to masters. Seek a mentor who can "take you under his wing" as an apprentice to:
  - o Show you the "company way" to do your job well.
  - o Coach you in how to succeed "in this business". Give you tips based upon his experience and knowledge of your employer's organization (perhaps gained from days gone by when he may have been in a position similar to yours)
  - o Help you improve your current job skills and perhaps learn new skills.
- *A closer* who can "close a deal for you", that is, influence a decision maker to make a decision in your favor. Smart salespeople try to determine who they know who is likely to have the most influence on a prospective customer's decision to buy, and then seek that person's help in making a sales pitch to the customer. After you identify the decision maker who makes the decisions about your future, determine if anyone you know might be able to help you influence the decision maker to make decisions in your favor.

An old adage says "It's not what you know, but who you know."
- This is true to the extent that playing office politics sometimes helps less qualified employees get opportunities that should have gone to more qualified employees.
- A more useful corollary might be *"It's how well people know you, and how much they respect your past performance track record"*. It sure helps to have an impressive performance track record to go along with political connections.

Act like a member of your company's sales team. *Every person in every company is responsible to some extent for company sales.*

The most profitable sales typically are generated by:
- Repeat business from satisfied customers.
- New customers referred by satisfied customers.
- Word-of-mouth advertising from people with whom employees have regular business contact, e.g. their employer's subcontractors, suppliers, and service providers.
- A company's good reputation (a good brand name) that every employee helps the company earn by contributing to the quality of products or services the company sells.

No matter your position, help your company generate these profitable sales.
- Do your job as well you can do it so that your work contributes to providing your company's customers with the best products or services that your company can provide.
- Be enthusiastic about what you do. Your enthusiasm will help motivate your co-workers.
- Generate positive "vibes" for your employer that emanate out to everyone who has contact with you through your attitude, enthusiasm, words, actions, etc.

Speak up.
- The more shy you are, the more effort you should make to market yourself. Let the decisions makers know who you are, what you are doing for them now, what you can do for them in the future, and the compensation and career advancement you desire in return.
- "Toot your own horn", in a confidently humble manner.
- There can be a pretty fine line between being outspoken in a confidently humble manner

and in an offensively brash manner. Stay on the confidently humble side of the line.

Business meetings are opportunities to shine. Meetings offer you opportunities to stand out from the crowd and demonstrate why you deserve a pay increase or a promotion.

Before meetings, *do your homework*. Come prepared to shine.
- Find out what is on the agenda and study up on agenda items as your time permits and the significance of agenda items dictate.
- Find out who is scheduled to attend. If key senior managers, why will they be attending? What might they want to take away from the meeting? What good take-aways can you give them?
- If you are scheduled to talk, prepare a written outline of what you will say. Keep your words "short and sweet" and "on point". Don't ramble. Talking too much can risk annoying busy people who want to get out of the meeting as soon as possible in order to take care of their other business.
- Prepare some questions, observations, ideas, and/or suggestions that you could offer during the meeting if opportunities present themselves.

At meetings, "*carpe diem*" (seize the day).
- Be early. It demonstrates interest and respect. Do NOT be late! Lateness demonstrates poor time management or a lack of care, and everybody notices who walks in late.
- Be visible. The first people in the meeting room get to choose the most visible seats. Sit up front where you can be seen, not in the back. Don't be a wall flower.
- Pay attention. Look interested in what speakers have to say. Try to make eye contact to connect with speakers. Do NOT fall asleep. Nap time does not send a good message to managers.
- Bring a pen and paper, and take notes – of things to remember and questions to ask.
- Try to ask at least one meaningful question.
  - o Asking a question will get you noticed.
  - o Good questions demonstrate that you have been paying attention and thinking about what speakers have been saying. Speakers like to know their audience is paying attention and is interested in what they are saying.
  - o Good questions can also provide a means to demonstrate your business smarts.
  - o *Don't be afraid to ask a "dumb" question that helps you understand what is being said* - as in "this might sound like a dumb question, but what does that mean, or, how does that apply to our work?" (refer back to page 143 for more comments about dumb questions). A dumb question speaks well of the person asking it. Smart business people recognize that these questions can cut to the heart of a matter and help a speaker clarify for his audience what he meant to communicate.
  - o Having prepared at least one question in advance is a good contingency plan for not being able to think up a question during the meeting.

After meetings, stick around and talk to influential managers who also have stayed in the room. Take advantage of valuable "face time" with these people. Say hello, shake hands, and introduce yourself to people who don't know you. Sell yourself, tactfully.

Develop a reputation for trying to "make lemonade out of lemons".
- Avoid getting dragged into co-worker gripe-fests. If you are in a conversation in which one or more people begin to gripe about a valid concern about a situation at work, try to

steer the conversation into a positive conversation aimed at developing suggestions for how to improve the situation, and how to implement those suggestions.

- And, don't you just gripe to co-workers about a situation that bothers you. Try to come up with constructive ideas about how to improve the situation, and then:
  - o You do something about it; and/or
  - o Share your ideas with people you think can do something about improving the situation.
- Employers don't like to hear about employees griping in the company lunchroom, or at social gatherings, or anywhere else. Typically, griping is not good for business. It contributes to negative employee attitudes, which in turn impair employee performance. Keep in mind who may be listening. You never know who knows who. Things have a way of getting back to people. "The walls have ears."

Volunteer: one highly effective self-marketing tactic I have observed many businesspeople use is volunteer service - as a committee chairperson, officer, coach, trustee, leader, teacher, etc.
- Company athletic teams, social clubs, or community service projects, especially those activities in which company managers participate or hold near and dear to their hearts.
- Industry trade associations.
- Local community service organizations.
- Helping to teach classes in local schools (e.g. Junior Achievement).

Volunteer activities can be used to demonstrate your brains, skills, and abilities in ways that are not perceived as brash attempts to sell yourself.

Learn how the military uses "psychological operations" to "win the hearts and minds" of a local population (target market audience) - often using covert tactics that are not perceived by the target market audience as direct attempts to influence their thinking and behavior. Many psychological operations tactics are excellent marketing tactics.

Write a resume that sells you. Writing a good resume and keeping it up to date can:
- Help you prepare for performance reviews and compensation negotiations by helping you:
  - o Identify the personal strengths you have to sell.
  - o Identify "holes" in your resume - qualifications or experience that you should seek to acquire in order to boost your marketability.
- Keep you prepared to capitalize on a desirable new job opportunity if such an opportunity should present itself, e.g. in a different division in your company or with a new employer.

Too many resumes read like bland, fill-in-the blank, formulaic copies of some generic resume model – blah, blah, blah.
- They don't attract the interest of smart employers.
- They don't distinguish the writer's resume from all the other resumes employers receive.
- *They don't sell the seller.*

Do some homework before you start to write.
- Write an inventory list of "sellable" things you can offer an employer:
  - o Expertise - specific skills and abilities.
  - o Experience - gained with past employers and in life in general.
  - o Accomplishments, awards, and honors that have demonstrated your experience in applying your expertise – either in the business world or in your personal life, e.g. captain or manager of an athletic team on which you play(ed), coaching a

youth athletic team, coordinating volunteers at a community service event, officer of a club, setting up a computer system for parents and mentoring them in how to use it.
- o Qualifications such as education, certifications, or licenses.
- Ask people on your business team for their thoughts about what you do well and your accomplishments in business and in life.

As you write, consider these suggestions:
- *Limit your resume to one or two pages.* A resume should be a brief summary, not a long autobiography. Busy people like brief and to the point; they tend to skip past long and wordy.
- Include items from your inventory list that you think would be of significant interest to an employer: expertise; experience; accomplishments, awards, and honors; qualifications.
- Use bullet points to highlight and separate key points.
- Avoid overused adjectives and clichés to describe yourself, e.g. "I am a smart and highly motivated professional".
- Have confidants on your business team read your resume and provide constructive critique to help make it as attention grabbing as possible.

If you send a resume to a prospective employer, attach a brief cover letter that personalizes your resume for that prospective employer, and for the specific person who will be reading it if you can find out who that person will be. Consider including in the letter:
- Name of person who referred you, if someone referred you.
- Reason(s) why you want to work for the employer, e.g. love for the work involved with a job, long-time fan of the company and its products, respect for their reputation.
- Reason(s) why you would be a good hire.

Never submit a hastily prepared resume, especially one that contains errors in spelling or grammar. Business people seek zero defects. First impressions count.

As you write your resume, prepare to answer interview questions about everything you write. If you write that you are good at doing something, be prepared to cite examples of experience and accomplishments that demonstrate how good you are.

Use social networking wisely. Learn all you can about effective ways to use social networking in a comprehensive business marketing plan.

Caution: keep in mind how your current employer, or a current customer, or a prospective future employer or customer might perceive everything you put up on social networking websites. Consider how someone of a different age group or different social background might perceive whatever you write or pictures you post. What would they think a posting on a social networking site says about you, your common sense, and your business smarts? This is especially critical for younger people who can't yet picture themselves in the job market.

Treat performance reviews as sales meetings. More on performance reviews next.

Use your performance reviews to your advantage

Prior to each performance review meeting, do your homework.

- *Evaluate your supervisor's likely receptivity to an open and honest discussion of your performance, your concerns, and planning how to achieve your career path objectives.* If you don't feel you can talk openly and honestly with your supervisor, take that as a warning that you might have:
  - o An internal issue of yours to resolve, e.g. lack of confidence, fear of handling a difference of opinion, your communication skills; or
  - o A communications problem you need to resolve with your supervisor (being as cautious, empathetic, and tactful as you possibly can be); or
  - o A need to consider planning for a new job in which you will feel free to talk openly and honestly with a new supervisor about your career path plan.
- Prepare to use the meeting to your advantage. This will be valuable time with your supervisor that is dedicated specifically to you and your career.
- Gather facts and figures to document the performance evaluation that you think you deserve.
- Get a copy of your company's performance review form and do a self-review of your performance. Be as objective and self-honest as you can. Try to put yourself in your supervisor's shoes and visualize how your supervisor might be evaluating your performance. If you think there is a possibility you two might be evaluating your performance differently, prepare to discuss any potential differences of opinion.
- If your company's performance review form provides space for employee comments, prepare written comments you would like to insert, e.g. training you would like, job enrichment you would like, a promotion you aspire to get. Make maximum use of this opportunity to provide your employer with career enhancement input.
- Prepare a list of things that you perceive have been impediments to your ability to achieve the objectives for which you are being held accountable and to your ability to exceed your employer's expectations of you.
- Get a copy of your job description to bring in with you. If there is not yet a written job description for your job, sit down with your supervisor and get a job description written.

Prepare a list of objectives to achieve during the meeting, such as:

- Get a clear understanding of your supervisor's evaluation of your past performance.
- Reach agreement on your objectives for the next performance review period.
- Determine the criteria that will be used for measuring achievement of your objectives.
- Reach agreement on what you can do during the next performance review period to get the best possible evaluation and optimize your total compensation package.
- Reach agreement on a plan to remove any impediments that you think might be obstacles you would need to overcome to achieve your objectives for the next performance period.
- Get your supervisor's thoughts and advice about your career path plan, e.g. maximum financial compensation you could earn in your current position, your potential for career path advancement within the organization, maximum financial compensation available in prospective future positions.

Prepare questions that help you gather information to use in planning your career path and your action plan to achieve your objectives. Consider putting into your own words questions such as:

- What do you see as my strengths? How do you recommend I capitalize on them?
- What do you see as my weaknesses? What do you suggest I do to strengthen them?

- What objectives will I be expected to achieve during the next performance review period?
- How will achievement of my objectives be measured? What "metrics" will be used?
- What can I do during the next performance review period that will help me exceed your expectations of a person in my position?
    - What should I work on learning?
    - What personality traits and behavior should I seek to demonstrate, e.g. initiative, enthusiasm can-do attitude, teamwork?
- How is financial compensation determined in our company? If there is a formal salary matrix or pay grade structure, may I have a copy?
- What career path do you envision for me?
    - What compensation package enhancements can I strive to earn?
    - What is the next promotion I can strive to earn?
- If you were me, what would you do?

During each performance review meeting:
- *"Read" your supervisor's receptivity to open and honest conversation - words he uses, tone of voice, body language, etc. Be careful as to your career path aspirations that you share until you are reasonably confident of his receptivity.*
- Based upon your "read", ask the questions you prepared prior to the meeting.
- As you seek to achieve your objectives during the meeting, have empathy for your supervisor's perspective. Try to see your objectives through your supervisor's eyes.
    - Be careful to not irritate a supervisor who may not be working his own career path planning process with as much diligence as you are working your plan, and may not have as much passion to succeed as you have.
    - Be careful not to be perceived as a threat to take over your supervisor's job before he is ready to give it up.
    - And keep in mind that your supervisor's compensation may not be as much as you think it is. The compensation you aspire to receive in the future might be more than his compensation today, and maybe even more than he has ever dreamed of earning.
- If you are surprised by your supervisor's opinion of your performance, talk it out.
- Performance reviews are a continuous process, not a series of one-off, isolated events. *Your next performance review starts the moment you walk into your current performance review meeting.* Lay the groundwork for your next performance review during this meeting. Don't assume you understand what your employer expects you to do. Make sure you have a clear understanding of your job description, job duties, performance objectives, and strategies you will be expected to use in achieving your objectives

Between performance review meetings, prepare for your next performance review meeting.
- Observe the work habits and behavior of people in your company who you perceive as being the most successful. Use them as role models.
- Monitor your progress toward achieving your objectives.
- To help avoid unpleasant surprises at your next formal performance review meeting, periodically ask your supervisor for informal evaluations and constructive critique of your performance, e.g. ask "how am I doing?" If your supervisor thinks you are doing well, ask for tips on how to do even better. If your supervisor doesn't think you are doing as well as you could, ask for advice on how you could do better. Most managers love this type of initiative. It gets them personally invested in helping their employees succeed.

Civility in business pays big dividends

Civility is what you were taught as a kid about getting along with people - be nice, polite, courteous, respectful, honest, and all the rest. *Rules of civil behavior evolve over the years for one practical reason – to enable people to live and work together in "civil society" over extended periods of time*, e.g. families, tribes, communities, countries, companies.

Civility plays a huge part in creating good luck in business.
- People tend to do their best for the people who treat them well.
- Civility attracts the type of good people who seek to help other people succeed.

Practice The Golden Rule - "Do unto others as you would have others do unto you." Think of "The Golden Rule" as an *Economic Law of Reciprocal Behavior* - treat other people well and they are likely to return the favor.

Say please. When you want someone to do something, ask politely "Will you please …"

Suggest, don't order. Most of us don't like to be ordered. We prefer to be asked. Most people respond better to polite suggestions to do something than they do to rude orders to "go do it, and do it my way." As Coach John Wooden said "the carrot is mightier than the stick".

Say thank you - often. *Saying thank you costs nothing, yet it can generate huge good will value* that will help motivate people to help you.
- *People like recognition for what they do.* A thank you, a pat on the back, a small token of appreciation, can generate greater satisfaction for some people than the money they get paid for doing their jobs.
- Be alert for opportunities to say thank you to people who help you, e.g. a co-worker going out of his way to help you with a specific task, or a manager coaching you on how to improve the way you do some aspect of your job.
- Good managers don't hear nearly enough "thank you's" from their employees. Thanking a manager for his help will help you "stand out from the crowd" of other employees.

Speak in terms of "we" not "I".
- "We" is a team building word. When people feel they are part of a team they are more likely to think they have a stake in what you would like done and be more likely to do it.
- "I" is a team dividing word. "I" puts a person out on an island alone.

Treat everyone with dignity and respect.
- Every person is an important person who deserves dignity and respect. We are all equals as human beings. "Everybody pulls their pants on one leg at a time."
- It feels good to treat other people well, and we tend to do our best work when we enjoy what we are doing.
- If your career path plan is to climb up the corporate ladder, it is extra important to treat everyone with dignity and respect. As you rise up to higher level management positions, the people you pass - the people who will then be below you on your employer's organization chart - will be providing the supporting foundation upon which you will need to build your future success. And, you never know who might be passing you tomorrow as they climb the corporate ladder higher and faster.

Smile.

- *There is great economic value in a smile.*
- A smile on your face will help your body generate the positive energy you need in order to do your best work.
- Smiles are magnets that attract the type of good people who can help you succeed.
- *Make your "game face" a smile.* "Check your personal problems at the door" when you walk into your workplace - along with the negative energy attached to personal problems.
- People like to work with happy, smiling people. If you work side-by-side with co-workers, your smile is likely to help motivate them to do their best work. And, the better the work of your co-workers, the greater the likelihood that their good work will contribute to helping you accomplish your objectives.
- If you have contact with customers, a smile is likely to make them think more favorably about whatever you do for them. Customers are then more likely to say good things about you to your managers, and good words from customers are strong influences on raises and promotions.

Be friendly.

- It pays to have as many friends as possible in your network of business contacts.
- As mentioned a few pages back, an old adage says "It's not so much what you know, it's who you know." Consider another corollary to that adage *"It's not so much who you know as who knows you and how much they like you"*. People tend to be the most motivated to help people they like – especially people they think of as friends.

Try real hard to be friendly, and try even harder to never make an enemy.

- Keep in mind that people change over time. People who had been unlikable when they were younger sometimes mature into much more likeable people as they get older.
- You don't have to like a person in order to be civil with him. And, given enough time, being nice to him can serve as a role model for his maturation into being more likeable.
- "It's a small world."
    - o We are all linked together in life.
    - o *"You never know who knows who"*. A person at work who you don't like very much just might be your boss' cousin, or work on a charitable organization committee with your boss, or have a daughter who marries your boss' son.
    - o *"Never burn a bridge"*. If you are ending a relationship try to end it as amicably as possible. You can't know if you will ever need to reconnect with that person in this rapidly changing world of corporate reorganizations, mergers, downsizing, and people changing jobs and employers.
    - o It's hard to predict which co-worker might get a promotion to a position in which he would have significant influence on your future compensation and career advancement – it just might be a co-worker you don't like too much (today).
- Enemies are not likely to help you, and they just might try to hurt you.

Compliment people.

- Give people sincere compliments about what you like, appreciate and/or respect about them. Polite compliments do wonders for improving human relationships. Compliments brighten people's days, and tend to make them friendlier and easier to work with.
- Just don't go overboard and become an insincere "suck-up". Most intelligent people recognize insincerity and they don't like it. In the old TV show "Leave It to Beaver", Eddie Haskell's over-the-top compliments to Mrs. Cleaver became a comedy classic based upon insincerity – a good life lesson for the Boomer Generation.

Be humbly assertive.
- Most people like to work with humbly assertive, quietly confident people and don't like to work with arrogantly pushy people.
- The more quiet and mild mannered you are, the more you might try to be more assertive.
- The more strongly assertive you are, the more you might try to tone it down.
- Find a happy medium between shy and show-off that best suits your personality.
- Humble assertiveness is a self-reinforcing behavior. The more you practice it, the better you are likely to get at using it to get good results from being humbly assertive.

Be humble enough to give credit to all the people who help you become recognized as a success, and assertive enough to stand up for yourself if a co-worker, supervisor, or anyone else tries to:
- Take credit for work you did yourself. Tell the person you know what he is doing, and you will let the appropriate people know the true story about who did what.
- Push you into doing something that you don't think is good for you to do, or "put you in your place", or take advantage of your good nature in any other way. Politely tell the person you understand the game he is playing – that being an attempt to assert authority over you (keep in mind that good leaders use their power of authority judiciously). You are likely to gain respect from good people, and flush out self-centered people. Based upon the person's reaction, you will learn where you stand in that person's eyes so that you can develop your career path plan accordingly.

If you should find yourself working with someone who you think brags too much, keep in mind the adage "*cream rises to the top.*"
- Over time, people who let their "actions speak louder than words" typically rise farther and faster than braggarts.
- If a "loud mouth" co-worker frequently brags about how great he is, be patient. This type person has a tendency to eventually "shoot himself in the foot" by doing something poorly that he bragged he could do well.

Be a good role model. As president of your own personal financial management company, act the way you would like your co-workers, supervisor, and senior managers to act.

Be careful about pointing a "finger of responsibility".
- There is an old saying that "whenever you point a finger at anybody else, you have three fingers pointing back at you."
- Heed the adage "people who live in glass houses shouldn't throw stones". Most people don't like tattletales who snitch on co-workers for every little thing they see done "wrong". Snitching has a way of making enemies – not a good thing in a work environment.
- That said, if you learn about a serious problem that could seriously endanger you, your co-workers, and/or your employer's business (and you have confirmed that the problem is real) being a "whistle blower" and reporting the problem is likely the right thing to do.

Don't take business too personally. Good businesspeople must learn to have "thick skins".
- REMEMBER - people are dealing with you in your role as an employee of your employer when you are in your work environment.
- In a business setting, some people might treat you in a way they would not treat you in a social setting "after hours". Such people might say things to you or about you while you are doing your job that they would never say in a social setting away from work.

More best practices for maximizing your compensation

Exceed expectations. Exceeding expectations is probably the single best way to maximize compensation and advance along a career path.

- To paraphrase an old adage *"You get out of a job what you put into it."*
- Do each of your job duties so well that you achieve all of your assigned objectives while exceeding your employer's expectations of a person in your job position.
- Seek to do "value added" things over and above the duties identified in your job description – things that help your employer operate more efficiently and profitably and help your supervisor and other senior managers achieve their objectives.
- The greater the value you supply to your employer (the more you exceed expectations), the more likely that your employer will be motivated to provide you the maximum compensation they can provide to a person in your job position, and promote you along your career path as opportunities arise for them to do so.

"Put first things first" - learn about "time management".

- There are only 24 hours in each day. Invest your time and energy so as to get the most bang for your time and energy bucks.
- Allocate your time and energy to job duties that will have the most impact on achieving your most important objectives and the most impact on your next performance review (you might ask your supervisor to help you prioritize your objectives and job duties).
- Allocate your remaining time and energy to objectives and job duties that will have lesser impact on your compensation and advancement along your career path.

Put in extra time as needed to get work completed on schedule. Managers love employees who go "the extra mile" to help them meet or beat their work schedules. Good managers typically will return the favor and try to help those employees. *BUT,* don't get sucked into "living at the office". If you begin to develop a habit of working longer hours than everybody else, step back and figure out why. Is it because you have been overburdened by being asked to do the work of employees who were laid off or retired, or to do things not contemplated by your job description? If you think you have more work to do than a reasonably capable person doing your job should be expected to do, speak up and say so.

Be a good teammate. As your time permits, pitch in to help cover for co-workers who are away from the office, and help co-workers who get swamped by an extraordinary crunch of new work. *BUT,* don't let helping co-workers impede your performance of your job. Manage the time you spend helping others so that you can continue to exceed expectations for doing your own work.

- If you think co-workers are overworked, speak up (using tact and common sense). Give your employer your well-reasoned analysis of the work situation. This could be an opportunity to shine in their eyes. A good employer will respect your business smarts.
- If you think a co-worker is slacking, it <u>might be</u> prudent to tell your employer. I strongly recommend you discuss such a situation with at least one trusted confidant whose business judgment you trust to help decide if you should say something, and if you do decide to say something, plan what to say and how to say it BEFORE saying anything.

Don't let yourself get:

- Sidetracked doing things that you mistakenly assumed you were being paid to do.
- <u>Over</u>-committed to activities that won't have significant impact on your performance review, e.g. company sponsored community service programs, charity events, athletic teams, etc. (prudent participation can be good self-marketing – just don't over-do it).

Ask for the best total compensation package that your employer can provide.
- With as much humbly assertive self-confidence as you can muster, ask for the best compensation your employer can provide. A good employer will respect your guts.
- Good employers are sensitive to the local cost of living, and the need that their employees have to pay for "reasonable living expenses" – "<u>reasonable</u>" being average expenses for people doing similar work in similar jobs in your local community; "<u>living expenses</u>" being housing, food, medical expenses, child care, commuting, parking, etc. *If your pay doesn't cover the <u>reasonable</u> <u>living expenses</u> in your budget, speak up and say so.* A good employer will understand that if you are having difficulty covering your reasonable living expenses, then your co-workers who have similar total compensation packages are likely to be having similar financial difficulties. If your employer values employees as human capital investments, you might be able to negotiate additional compensation.
- Objectively state your case for the total compensation package that you think would provide a fair return on your sweat equity (your valuable time and expertise).
- Employers sometimes make exceptions to their established compensation models for exceptional employees in exceptional circumstances. *You might never know if your employer would make an exception for you if you don't ask.*

Be trust worthy. The business world operates on trust. Employers don't like to have employees who can't be trusted to (a) do what they are expected to do and (b) do what they say they will do.

"Don't promise what you can't deliver."
- By all means have a self-confident, can-do attitude, but don't let that self-confident, can-do attitude snowball into the type of cocky over-confidence that causes some people to over-reach their capabilities.
- *The line of demarcation between self-confidence and self-delusion can get blurry* during the emotional excitement of a perceived business opportunity. Staying humble and surrounding yourself with smart people who have enough concern for you to tell you to calm down and think will help you avoid crossing that line into self-delusion.
- If you don't <u>yet</u> have the expertise or experience to handle a work opportunity or a promotion that is offered to you, be extremely careful about accepting it. Countless career ships have been wrecked on the shoals of The Peter Principle - rising to jobs that people have not prepared themselves to do well.
- When an employee lets down an employer who was counting on him to do what the employee had said he would do, the employee's trustworthiness gets questioned, and such a question in the employer's mind can limit the compensation increases the employee receives and the career path advancement opportunities he is offered.
- *Second chances are tough to come by* in business. Heed this axiom: *not getting enough new business orders from desirable customers is a big danger, but an even bigger danger is getting that work and then failing to do it well.* An unsatisfied customer (or employer) is much less likely to give a second chance to a company (or employee) whose failure to perform reliably in the past has given the customer (or employer) reasonable doubt about the likelihood of the company (or employee) to perform reliably in the future; and they may tell other people about why they have reasonable doubt – a reputation killer.

Don't try to "fake it". If you are asked to do something you don't know how to do, say you don't know how to do it but you will try to recruit people to help you who do know how to do it.

Be enthusiastic. You don't have to be gushing barrels of energy to be enthusiastic. Each person expresses enthusiasm in his own way. Smart employers know the *economic value of enthusiasm*:

- Enthusiasm is contagious. It spreads quickly from one employee to another.
- One reason good employers love enthusiasm - customers are drawn to companies that have enthusiastic employees. The more enthusiasm that employees display, the more customers are likely to do business with the employer, and the more money the employer will have available to share with employees. When you go to a store, do you like to discover employees who radiate enthusiasm for life, who seem to enjoy their jobs, and who are quick to offer a friendly "may I help you"? Will these people motivate you to come back to their store with your repeat business? Most likely they will.
- Another reason good employers love enthusiasm - enthusiasm typically is a sign that an employee is trying his hardest to do the best work he is capable of doing.

"Work hard" - bring your "A" game to work every day.
- Think of yourself as a professional athlete on a team. Pro athletes must bring their A games to work every day in order to demonstrate to team managers and owners that they deserve to hold on to their positions in team line-ups, and that they deserve salary increases when their contracts come up for renewal. Likewise, you need to bring your A game to work each day in order to demonstrate to your company managers and owners that you deserve to hold on to your position in the company, and that you deserve a salary increase and/or promotion at your next performance review.
- Best effort hooks into human nature. Fans love hustling, scrappy ball players who "bleed the team colors", "give 100% on every play" and "leave it all on the field". So too, employers love employees who give it all they've got for the company every day.
- Hard work will help generate the most profit for your employer, and the more profit your employer makes, the more money your employer will have available to pay to you.
- Keeping your "nose to the grindstone" maintains the competitively sharp edge you will need to cut through your job competition for future raises and promotions (in general I don't like negative analogies, but this one helps make an important point).

Never "mail it in". "Resting on laurels" earned for past performance ("easing up" or "coasting") usually has significant downsides, such as:
- Increasing the risk of sliding backward in a career instead of advancing. After an employee's level of effort starts to go down, managers typically see the quality of the employee's work sliding down. When good managers notice employees beginning to slack off, they typically begin taking steps to protect their profit, and those steps usually don't play out well for employees who continue to slack off.
- Generating complaints from co-workers. Individual employee work habits and overall work group performance evolve based upon each team member's performance. After a person has "set the bar high" with an excellent performance track record, co-workers typically expect his performance to continue at the same high level. Co-workers (and supervisors) notice when a workmate begins to ease up, even just a little, because when one person begins to carry less work load somebody else must step up to carry more workload. It is likely that at least one co-worker who has to do more work will complain, and such complaints can lead to problems for the person who eased up.
- Getting branded as a "slacker" in office gossip, which can be a career killer.
- Giving co-worker competitors for salary increases and promotions more opportunity to pass by the person who eased up. In sports, think about how often one team dominates another team during the first part of a game. Then the dominating team begins to get overly confident about winning the game, they start to ease up, momentum in the game shifts, and the competitor comes on to win the game.

"Work smart".
- Competition drives successful companies to continuously seek ways "do it better, faster, more profitably"; old ways of doing business are continuously reviewed and revised or replaced as needed. Smart people would be wise to learn from successful companies.
- *Try to work better, faster, more efficiently each day.* Challenge yourself to achieve a new "career best" each day.
- Seek to *"strengthen the weakest link in your chain"* – seek to improve how you do those things that you do least well.
- Professional musicians, athletes and craftspeople continuously seek to learn how to improve their skills, and they continuously practice hard to hone their skills. Learn from these good role models. Continuously seek ways to improve your performance, and practice your job skills to get as good as you can get at doing your work.
- Identify people who have the greatest expertise in skills pertinent to your job. Observe them and learn from them. Ask if they would be willing to share "tricks of their trade".

Get to the knowledge forefront in your industry and stay there.
- Read the "trade press" in your industry (e.g. trade association publications, websites) to learn what successful people are doing and how they are doing it. Stay up to date with current developments in industry practices, technology, and equipment.
- Get to know the people in your company responsible for employee training, e.g. training officers, training department. Ask for advice about:
    o Internal (company sponsored) classes and certification programs that will help you keep your job skills up to date with "best practices" in your industry.
    o External continuing education classes and programs, and how much of the cost of that education your employer will pay.
- Ask your supervisor, training officer, and others as appropriate, for advice and assistance in developing a continuing education plan that will help you advance along your career path. Seek to learn:
    o How you might improve your performance of your current job.
    o Skills that you are likely to need in future positions.
    o How your employer's organization works:
        ▪ How your job fits into the big picture of company operations.
        ▪ Work that is done in various work groups, departments, and divisions.
        ▪ Ways your employer's organization might operate more efficiently and profitably – ways that you might be able to suggest to management.
    o How people think your industry and your job are likely to be evolving, and how you might prepare to prosper as changes take place.
- Ask for advice about how to do your work as well as possible. Let common sense and sincerity guide you to ask in a manner that conveys your sincere desire to learn.
    o Avoid being perceived as a pain in the neck who asks too many questions.
    o Avoid embarrassing people who should know the answers to your questions, but don't. Remember, lots of people (including supervisors and managers) just do what they are told in the same old way they were taught to do it, without ever bothering to ask "why do we do it this way" (and learning from the answers they get), or thinking about ways to do things better, faster, or more profitably.

Avoid becoming an industry "dinosaur" who gets pushed into extinction by the next generation of employees who have skills you don't have, know industry best practices that you don't know, and are better adapted to living successfully in the evolving business world. The older you are the more important it becomes to proactively try to keep up to date

Treat your company as the group of living, breathing, imperfect people that it is, not as a thing.
- Some people get "behind the eight ball" in maximizing success in their careers because they think of their employers' organizations as "things" rather than groups of people.
  - o They think of managers in their direct "chain of command" as some abstract "they", in which "they don't understand me," or "they don't care about me," or "they are trying to take advantage of me".
  - o These people tend to think of senior management as a big, lifeless monolith – the "ivory tower" or "upstairs".
  - o They tend to think in terms of "putting in time" working for a corporate machine.
- Other people seem to think that they work in a fairy tale business world in which everyone and everything should be perfect.
  - o These folks need to "wake up and smell the coffee" and realize that they must deal with imperfect human beings in the imperfect real world of business.
  - o Each person in each position on each rung of the organization ladder leading up to and including the "ivory tower" has his own individual set of human imperfections e.g. emotions, feelings, biases, flaws, weaknesses.

Business is all about people, and your interactions with people. By accepting your position as an employee in your employer's organization you become a member of a group of people who have each decided to make his individual living by pooling his efforts with the efforts of other people in order to "make a living" together. Each person must do his job well enough to help his employer generate enough profit to pay everyone year after year.

Be a team player. Think of yourself as a professional athlete on a baseball team.
- Practice your job skills to get as good as you can get at playing your position.
- If you are not playing the job position you want to play, let your thoughts be known – tactfully. Ask your manager for his advice about how you can get to play the position you want to play.
- Do your best to help motivate co-worker teammates to play up to their fullest capabilities, and to facilitate the teamwork needed to work together smoothly and efficiently and win the business games you play together each day.
- Working together in close quarters inevitably leads to situations in which people's tolerance and patience get strained and tempers can flare.
  - o Do what you can to maintain "harmony in the locker room" and minimize friction among workplace teammates (minimize "dissension in the ranks").
  - o *If your emotions start to rise, it might be best to bite your lip and not say or do anything you might later regret having said or done.* Words said in the heat of the moment can't be pulled back, and the meaner and nastier the words, the longer they are likely to be remembered. Be guided by maxims such as "It takes two to tango", "Walk a mile in his shoes", and "Live to play another day".
- People perceived to be the best teammates tend to receive the best compensation.

Get people invested in your success by asking for their thoughts and their advice.
- Most people get satisfaction from being asked for their thoughts and their advice, and even more satisfaction from seeing people acting upon their advice.
- Through the act of providing their thoughts and advice, your success becomes their success; people are likely to become more motivated to help you succeed.
- *Be sure to say thank you for each piece of advice you receive.* Thank you's help "set the hook" of human interest in how "a little piece of them" is playing out in your success.

Play by the rules - behave ethically - as mothers say "play nice".
- People in every group must have a set of "rules to live by" – rules of generally accepted behavior that allow them to live and work together.
- Promotions and raises tend to come to those employees who both play by the rules AND are noticed by their managers as playing by the rules.
- Learn the rules of generally accepted behavior within your employer's organization, play by those rules, and use those rules to "*work the system*" to your benefit.
- *Don't "buck the system".* People who don't play by the rules (rebels, loners, and others who are perceived as having an "attitude") are more likely to be perceived by their managers as "sand in the gears of efficient operations". They tend to get flushed out of their companies by their managers as opportunities to do so present themselves.
- *If you ever get to thinking that you are right and the rules are wrong, work within the system to try to change the rules to what you think the rules should be.*
- Play by informal group rules too. It is likely that within your employer's formal organization there are informal groups such as cubicle neighbors, work groups, lunch groups, car pools (like cliques in a high school) whose members influence how well you can do your job. Each informal group has its own rules of behavior for people who want to be accepted as group members. Identify the informal groups in your workplace that influence your job performance, and learn to play by the rules of each group to which you currently belong and each group you think it would be helpful to join.

Play the game of "office politics".
- "Politics" are an essential fact of life in every social group, e.g. families, teams, clubs, and businesses. Every group must structure itself with a "political" hierarchy of leaders and doers in order to "govern" (manage) themselves and get things done.
- Practice the diplomacy of a good politician. Develop good working relationships with everyone with whom you have contact. You never know who may have the ability to help you now or in the future. Besides, it feels good to be liked.
- Try this mental game. Visualize yourself campaigning to get elected as "employee of the year". Try to gain the imaginary votes of as many supporters as possible throughout as many levels in your organization as possible.

Help other people succeed.
- Be vigilant to spot opportunities to help.
- Proactively seek ways to help co-workers and managers alike succeed in their jobs and get good performance reviews. Ask the simple question "how can I help"?
- Do what you can to make the jobs of everyone around you as easy for them as possible.
- Perform your job so well that your supervisor and other managers need to spend minimal time and effort supervising your performance. This will free up more of their time and talents to focus on their other management duties.
- Accumulate as many unspoken I.O.U's as you can, but never, ever, hold one of those I.O.U's over anyone's head. No one likes to feel that they "owe" somebody something.

"You get more back than you give."
- Give as much help as you can to as many people as you can.
- In return, most people are likely try to reciprocate by helping you when opportunities presents themselves. There is a pretty neat karma at work in the world.
- And, you will get back the "priceless" feeling good about helping people.

Seek win-win decision outcomes.
- Everybody likes to feel like a winner. Each time you help a person feel like a winner you will be helping to motivate that person to seek a win-win outcome the next time he makes a decision that impacts you.
- "Take the high road" when making decisions. *Answer the "higher calling" of seeking the "greatest good" for everyone impacted by your decisions.*
- The good feeling that typically comes from helping others will reinforce the positive attitude in you that is so important to success in business.

Demonstrate as much leadership potential as you can.
- The best compensation packages and career advancement opportunities (i.e. promotions) tend to go to people who managers perceive as having the most leadership potential.
- Be an exemplary employee who demonstrates good "leadership by example" in all that you say and do.
- Like a good quarterback or point guard, try to help your co-worker teammates play the game of business up to their full potential.
- Seek to become a leader within the informal work groups to which you belong, e.g. employer sponsored community service projects, employee clubs and teams.

View "problems" as "challenges" that present "opportunities" to demonstrate your leadership capability, business skills, analytical powers, creative thinking, and common sense.

Keep your wits about you when times get tough.
- Good business managers value highly employees who keep their wits about them under pressure - people who find ways to overcome obstacles and accomplish the job at hand. Conversely, managers don't appreciate employees who "crack under pressure".
- Decision makers who can influence your future may well be observing how well you handle your tough times. Show them how the best in you comes out in pressure situations. Think of each challenge you face at work as an opportunity to demonstrate why you should get whatever compensation increase or promotion you desire.
- *"When the going gets tough, the tough get going."*

"See every cloud with a silver lining".
- *The best time for you to shine is when your organization is going through its dark days.* During tough times, be a positive force around whom people can rally and from whom they can draw energy when their own energy is flagging - be a "rock" of stability.
- Tough times usually lead to some type of change. And, change frequently opens a door to opportunity for people who are looking for opportunity. Keep your mind clear and your eyes open so that you will recognize opportunity when it knocks.
- While negative thinking people are getting beaten down by what they perceive to be doom and gloom circumstances, positive thinking people are keeping their heads up, pressing on, and trying to see opportunities presented by those circumstances.
- *"Accentuate the positive".* No job is perfect. Nobody likes every single aspect of his job. Stay focused on all the good things that you like about your job, and work proactively to improve things you don't like so much. Be your own positive-spin doctor for your job.
- *"Eliminate the negative".* "Make lemonade out of lemons". Write a list of the things you like least about your job, whether that might be certain aspects of the work itself, certain people, your commute, whatever. Then put on your positive-thinking cap and come up with proactive ways you can work on improving those least favorite things.

Make suggestions for improvement of your company's operations. Think creatively about how your company could:
- Increase profit - increase revenue and/or decrease expenses.
- Increase efficiency and productivity - do things better, faster.
- Increase employee morale and job satisfaction thereby increasing employee retention.
- Improve interdepartmental coordination thereby increasing the synergy of operations.

Suggestions can do at least three things for you:
- Bring you to the attention of the people who make decisions about your future.
- Demonstrate your business smarts to those people.
- Possibly earn a financial reward for your suggestion.

Try to determine who would be most likely to make the decision about implementing your suggestion. Then try to find a way to get in front of that decision maker to pitch your idea.
- You could "read" the person to see if you need to clarify anything about your suggestion that you don't think is being understood in the way you want it understood.
- You would be right there to answer any "first thought" questions that pop into the person's mind, and mitigate the risk of a knee jerk "no" response.
- Getting in front of the decision maker would minimize the risk that an "intermediary" in charge of processing suggestions "through the system" wouldn't understand your suggestion and its full potential. An intermediary might "miss the point" and either:
  o Not pass your suggestion along to the person who would make a decision about adopting your suggestion if it had reached his desk; or
  o Pass along your suggestion with a negative recommendation that influenced the decision maker to decide against adopting your suggestion.
- If your company has a formal employee suggestion program, you could ask for the decision maker's advice about submitting your suggestion through that formal program. Submitting your suggestion through that formal program might help you earn greater recognition (and financial reward, if available).
- Follow up in writing to the decision maker to document discussion of your suggestion.

Make your ideas their ideas.
- When you have an idea you want to get implemented, or you want someone to do something, you might try taking an indirect approach.
- *If you talk about your idea in a subtle fashion enough times, your idea might gradually work its way into other people's heads so that over time those people come to think your idea is their idea.* If you are willing to trade-off some pride of authorship in an idea, you might improve the odds of getting done what you want done.
- The more your idea is a departure from "the way we have always done it", the more this subtle, non-threatening approach might be effective in getting things done your way.
- Also, think about how marketing and advertising professionals might advise using mental manipulation tricks of their trade to help convince people that your ideas are their ideas.

Check personal opinions about politics and religion at your employer's front door.
- Playing office politics does not mean bringing your government politics into the office.
- Political and religious beliefs typically are deeply rooted beliefs that form the foundation upon which people build their lives. Keep in mind that the personal beliefs of your co-workers and managers may differ from your beliefs. Don't risk irritating and possibly alienating people whose beliefs differ from yours.

- It is said that "it isn't polite to discuss politics or religion" in a social setting. Typically it isn't prudent in business settings either. Business meetings and relationships can take dramatically negative turns after differing political or religious beliefs are aired.
- If you get stuck in a business situation in which you have no alternative but to talk about government politics, be as tactful, tolerant and non-confrontational as possible.
- Before wearing a political button to work or putting a political or religious message bumper sticker on the car you drive to work, consider how the message will be received by people who make the decisions about your compensation and career advancement. If a person who can influence your future strongly disagrees with the message of that button or bumper sticker, it might have a negative influence on your future. If you want to consider wearing a political button to work or putting a bumper sticker on the car you drive to work, weigh the strength of your conviction to display your beliefs against the potential impact on your future income and your career.
- *"Practice, don't preach."*
  - o "Actions speak louder than words."
  - o Be a good role model for your political and religious beliefs, not a preacher.
    - If you are a social liberal, be as kind and helpful to others as you can.
    - If you are a fiscal conservative, be a model of prudent money management in your personal and business affairs.

"Dress for success."

Dressing for success is in the eye of the beholder.
- An old adage cautions "don't judge a book by its cover". But many (if not most) employers tend to make assumptions about an employee's performance capabilities based upon an employee's personal appearance "cover". They might be wrong in their assumptions, but they tend to make them anyway. Your employer might assume:
  - o Employees who look neat and clean are more likely to take better care of our business than people who look disheveled and unkempt.
  - o Trustworthy employees tend to adhere to our dress code and dress like team members, and less trustworthy people tend to rebel against our dress code.
- What assumptions might your employer make based upon your personal appearance?
- Make dressing for success an element of your personal marketing campaign.

A prudent degree of conformity can be profitable. It is said *"imitation is the sincerest form of flattery"*, and most people like to be flattered. Maintaining a personal appearance similar to that of the managers who will be making decisions about your future may well help increase the probability of achieving your career objectives.
- What does your supervisor wear to work?
- How do the senior managers in your employer's organization dress?
- How do your supervisor and your most successful co-workers wear their hair?
- Do successful people in your company have visible tattoos?
- Do successful men in your company have mustaches or beards?

If dressing for success sounds lame to you, think about what influences your personal appearance:
- Why do you wear the clothes you wear, and have the hairstyle you have?
- Do you dress more for yourself or more for your appearance to others?
- If you dress more for yourself, do you choose clothes that are comfortable to wear, that you like to look at, and that are affordable on your budget?

- Do you care what anybody else thinks about your appearance?
    - o If so, who - family, friends, co-workers, the opposite sex?
    - o What message might you be trying to send about yourself - stylish, conservative, member of a group, independent free spirit?
    - o If you care what anybody else thinks, consider what your employer thinks too.

Most of us tend to dress the same way as the people with whom we most closely identify.
- Check out the way that groups of friends tend to wear the same types of clothes, cut their hair in roughly the same way, and wear the same types of jewelry.
- Even non-conformists tend to conform to the dress code of their non-conformist friends, e.g. sandals in winter, tie dye, torn jeans, purple hair, lots of leather, or whatever the current "in" non-conformity is (rules of conformity among groups of non-conformists are another good reason to learn about sociology and small group dynamics).

Successful business people are often described with words such as neat, clean, trim, sharp, well dressed, and professional appearance. You may well improve the likelihood of your success in the business world if people use these words to describe you.

Be true to your heart in how you dress, but keep in mind how your heart may affect your wallet.

Be a futurist - don't cling to the past just because "that's the way we have always done it".
- Plan years ahead for how you can continue achieving your compensation and career path objectives in the workplace of the future.
    - o What changes can you reasonably project in your job, your company, your industry?
    - o Will people in the future still be doing the type of work you do? If so, how?
    - o Could technological innovations eventually cause your job, your company, or your industry to become obsolete?
- Project how current trends and cycles are likely to play out in the future. What opportunities might future change create for you?
- How might the continually increasing "global telecommunication connectedness" of activists for economic and social change around the world impact governments, economies, wealth redistribution both here at home and in countries around the world? How might economic and social change at home and abroad impact you?
- What can you do today to prepare yourself to achieve your long term objectives?

Learn about techniques successful companies have used to plan for future revenue and profit, and seek ways you might use these techniques to continue achieving your objectives.
- *Re-inventing themselves*: some companies that have been successful for generations have achieved their long term successes by periodically shedding old businesses and growing new businesses, e.g. GE and IBM.
- *Innovation*: finding new ways to do things better, faster, more efficiently.
- *Imagining what might be* - re-imagining current business operations. Learn about The Walt Disney Company's practice of "Imagineering".
- *Research and development*: to make discoveries and generate profitable new business ideas. Make habits of continuous continuing education and market intelligence research.
- *Brainstorming*: two or more people get together to bounce their individual ideas off each other in order to stimulate each other's thinking and come up with new ideas; "throw a bunch of ideas at the wall and see what sticks". Surround yourself with a business team of smart, creative people with whom you can brainstorm.

- *Hiring think tanks*: "think tanks" are organizations established for the purpose of "thinking up" ways to solve problems, meet challenges, and project how current events, trends and cycles are likely to play out in the future. Some companies hire think tanks to get advice about how to prosper in the future. You might use members of your business team as your personal think tank to help you plan how to achieve your career objectives.

Don't put limits on yourself.
- Some people get stuck in the rut of a job because they are afraid to step outside their comfort zone and stretch the limits of their current expertise and experience, or because they think they might not be as good at doing certain things as they might actually be.
- Seek business challenges that <u>gently stretch</u> the limits of what you have done successfully in the past. But, <u>avoid stretching your time and talents past their breaking points</u>.
- If you have the opportunity to consider a big career leap forward that would test the outermost limits of your current skills and abilities, maintain a self-confident, can-do attitude, but keep in mind The Peter Principle and be prudently careful. *The longer the leap, the greater the risk of failing to make the leap successfully.*
- Don't be afraid to "grab the bull by the horns", just grab the bull's horns with enough care to avoid getting gored.

Most of us can do most of what we commit ourselves to doing, provided we plan well enough, and work long enough and diligently enough on our action plans to do it.
- Use your planning process to guide your career path toward achievement of your career path objectives.
- On-the-job-training (OJT) after making a job change or receiving a promotion typically is an essential part of learning how to do that new job well. However, it would be wise to prepare yourself to succeed in each new job along your career path by learning as much of what you think you will need to know in the next job BEFORE you move into the job. <u>Gently stretching out the limits of your skills and abilities before accepting the responsibilities of a new job will maximize your probability of success, and minimize the probability of over-extending the limits of your skills and abilities</u>.
- Think of all the overweight or skinny little kids who weren't very good at a sport when they first started to play it, but wound up becoming pretty good at it because they committed themselves to getting good, created a plan to get good, and then diligently applied themselves to an action plan of diet and exercise, learning the fundamentals of the sport, and practicing the fundamentals as hard as they could.

Don't let yourself get "pigeon-holed" by limits that anyone might try to place upon you.
- To use an acting analogy, don't let yourself be typecast forever as the person you were <u>yesterday</u>. Apply yourself to an action plan that lets people see who you are <u>today</u>, and who you are on your way to becoming <u>tomorrow</u>.
- Don't let yourself get stuck in the rut of where you are today by a false perception that people might have of you, your skills and abilities, and your capabilities.
- For women especially, don't passively accept gender stereotypes. There is still too much stereotypical thinking in the business world along the lines of "it's a man's job". Seek to sharpen your skills enough and strengthen your resolve enough to break through any "glass ceiling" limits that certain men may have been trying to place upon your career path aspirations.

Chapter 15. Investment Management

Hire professional help!

Hire professional help! I can't make a stronger recommendation than to <u>hire an investment professional</u> to help you manage your investments, especially in generating passive revenue.
- Observations of many investors over many years tell me that most people who pay for professional help have better investment performance than people who don't.
- Most of us don't have the expertise, the experience, nor the time to manage our investment portfolios as well on our own as we could if we hired professional investment management help.
- *The less we do, the more we make*: for most of us, the less investment work we do for ourselves, the better our investment performance is likely to be.
- *Amateurs who dabble in investing often get burned.*

<u>Hiring professional help does NOT mean giving up management control of your investments</u>.
- As president of your company, hiring professional help means delegating specific responsibilities and authority to one or more financial professionals who have greater expertise and experience than you have in investing money.
- Your job as president of your company is to manage the performance of the financial professional(s) you hire.
- You retain the ultimate responsibility for the performance of your investment portfolio.

Two types of professional financial management help you might consider hiring:
- *Mutual fund company(s)*: a reputable mutual fund company will do virtually all the investment management work for you after you decide in which of their mutual funds you want to invest.
- *Financial advisor (a/k/a financial planner or investment advisor)*: to advise and assist in preparing a financial plan tailored to your unique situation, and advise you on specific investment decisions; also an advisor will typically buy, sell, and hold investment securities for you.

Why hire a professional financial advisor?
- <u>A good advisor can help you protect your money from yourself</u>. Being human, we are all prone to act based upon emotion rather than rational thinking – especially during times of rapid stock market increases and decreases. And, when we do act based upon rational thinking, we sometimes make mistakes. *Helping to protect our money from ourselves might be the single most valuable service that financial advisors can provide.*
- Expertise: professionals typically have greater financial management expertise than most of us amateurs. The older you get and the greater the role that you plan for investment income to play in your projected income statement budget, the more valuable the expertise of a financial advisor is likely to become – especially if you are planning to sell some investments each year as one component of your diversified stream of revenue.
- Experience: professionals typically have more experience than most of us amateurs - they manage investments all day, every day; they get to experience more things, and learn more about how to handle real life personal financial management situations, than most of us amateurs would ever get the opportunity to do in a full lifetime.
- A professional can save you precious time. A professional can devote more time to the business of financial management than most of us amateurs can devote.

- o It takes lots of time to be a successful investor.
- o Managing your own investments can lessen the quality of your life by using up precious time that might be better allocated to family, friends, recreation, and all the other things that could make your life richer and more satisfying.
- o Each person must decide for herself how much time in a well-planned, well-balanced life is prudent to spend managing her investments.
- It out-sources much of the stress and aggravation that can come with doing all the work needed to invest successfully, e.g. doing research; making purchase, sale, and investment income management decisions; maintaining records of purchase and sale transactions.
- It makes logical sense. Good CPA's, bankers, attorneys, insurance agents, surety agents, and other types of professionals have helped countless people achieve their objectives. It's logical to think that good professional financial advisors can help their clients achieve their business plan and budget objectives.
- *It's often the "best value" choice in terms of (a) annual return on investments, (b) lost opportunity cost of time, and (c) reduction of stress and aggravation.*

If you decide that hiring a financial advisor would be prudent, then "hire" a "<u>registered investment advisor</u>" who has a "<u>fiduciary duty</u>" to act in your best interest, not her best interest!

- *Registered investment advisors* must register with the United States Government Securities and Exchange Commission or a state's securities commission. They are regulated as to the advice they provide.
- *Fiduciary duty* means that a person has a legal obligation to offer you advice that is in your best interest, not hers.
  - o Not all professionals who offer financial advice have a fiduciary duty to offer advice that is in your best interest and not in their best interest.
  - o Research the term "fiduciary duty" to make sure you understand what it means, and the benefits of working with a person who has a legal duty to look out for your best interests rather than her own.

Focus on "<u>net investment return</u>", NOT cost (net investment return being the increase in your net worth from year to year AFTER paying for a professional financial advisor's services). Way too many people get hung up on the cost of professional investment management services.

- It is NOT about the cost of services.
- *It is all about how much more you could increase your net worth with professional help than you could without professional help.*
- Example: if your historical average annual investment return has been 6%, and you can hire a financial advisor who has a track record of helping clients earn an average annual return of 9%, and the cost of the advisor's services is only a 1% fee, hiring that professional advisor might help improve your investment return by 2%. A no brainer.

Many people make a big mistake when they think they could make more money by doing for themselves the job that <u>they think</u> professionals do.

- Most amateur investors don't understand all the research, analysis, and practical experience (as well as heartache and frustration) that underlies what they see on the surface as being such a simple and easy job for a professional to do.
- Much of the good work that good professionals do is "invisible"; we don't get to see all that they do "behind the scene". *Good professionals consciously try to make the investment process seem as simple and easy as possible for their clients.*

- The news media tell us attention grabbing stories about the few crooks and incompetents in the financial services industries, but rarely if ever do they tell us the "boring" mundane stories about the many, many financial advisors who do fine work helping clients earn reasonable investment returns and helping clients avoid doing themselves financial harm.

Good advisors typically pay for themselves in at least three ways:
- Helping clients earn better investment returns than they could have earned on their own.
- Helping clients prepare financial plans to achieve future financial security that clients might not have prepared on their own.
- Helping clients save money that clients might otherwise have lost by making investment mistakes or getting diverted from their financial plans.

The more you feel an urge to manage your investments on your own, the more you should think about all that it takes to be a successful investor:
- *Immense self-discipline.*
- *A rational thinking nature* that can resist emotional urges.
- *Expertise* in the different types of investments that you think would constitute a well-diversified portfolio of stocks, bonds, real estate, annuities, etc. appropriate for you at your age in your unique life circumstances.
- *The time it takes* to do all the research that is needed to make well-informed buy and sell decisions, and to manage the administrative burden of maintaining accounting records.

Two warnings
- Don't get seduced by news stories about people who "made big money in the market" in a short period of time. There are many cautionary reasons why there are so few of them.
- Be wary of advertising that urges you to buy and sell stocks on your own, and makes it sound easy to do so.
  - o If you hear "save money on each trade", remember <u>your objective</u> – is it to <u>minimize the cost of trading stocks</u> or <u>make money on your investments</u>?
  - o If you hear "we offer investment advice at a lower price" (a) decide if your objective is to buy cheaper advice or good advice, and (b) research the advertiser.
  - o It is NOT easy to get good investment returns by investing on your own.
    - *If successful investing was easy, there would be one heck of a lot more wealthy people today.*
    - "If it sounds too good to be true, it probably is."

DISCLAIMER: *I am NOT a professional financial advisor. I am NOT trained, NOR certified, NOR licensed to offer investment advice.* This book is simply meant to stimulate your thinking about managing your investment portfolio, and *offer ideas to discuss with someone who is a licensed professional financial advisor.*

This book does NOT provide any investment advice. It simply offers personal ideas about the subject of investment management from my perspective as:
- An amateur investor who has made some painful investment mistakes.
- A student of life offering my layman's interpretations of what I think I have understood professional financial advisors to say and write.
- An observer of many individual investors, some successful, some not so successful.
- A surety bond professional who has worked with many successful investors.

<u>Investment basics to study & discuss with a professional financial advisor</u>

Become an educated investor. The more that "Average Joe" investors like me learn about trying to invest successfully, the more likely we are to see the wisdom of hiring a professional financial advisor to help us. Below are a few suggestions of basics to learn about.

Meanings of "<u>registered investment advisor</u>" and "<u>fiduciary duty</u>":
- *Registered investment advisors* must register with the United States Government Securities and Exchange Commission or a state securities commission. They are regulated as to the advice they provide to their clients.
- *"Fiduciary duty"* is the legal duty that certain financial advisors have to look out for their clients' best interests, and put their clients' best interests ahead of their own.

Investment portfolio: all the investment assets you own lumped together as a group.

Classes of financial investment assets: the various types of assets that are typically thought of as investments can be grouped into *three broad classes based upon the roles they can play in a well- diversified investment portfolio*:
- *Preserve capital*: protect you from losing money.
- *Appreciate* (increase) in economic value so that they can be sold for more money than you paid for them.
- *Generate passive income*: generate a stream of predictable income (e.g. interest and dividends) - *your money working for you to make more money for you.*

Certain financial investment assets might be able to play all three roles: preserve capital, appreciate in value, and generate a steady stream of predictable dividend income, e.g. a "blue chip" stock or a prudent real estate investment.

A 4th class of investments – investments in yourself: investments that help you increase your capability to earn income and to manage your money. Some people say that *"the best investment a person can make is an investment in herself"*. Investments in yourself might include:
- Education and training.
- Tools and equipment such as a computer, craft work tools, or a musical instrument.
- A vehicle you need to get to a job or to classes.
- Expenses you must incur in order to turn a hobby into a paying job.

Types of investment assets
Cash
- Checking accounts
- Savings accounts
- Certificates of deposit (CD's)
- Treasury bills (T-bills)

Stock - individual securities
- Common stock: the type of stock you hear about most.
- Preferred stock: a typical role is to generate passive income in the form of dividends.

Stock - mutual funds and their close cousins exchange traded fund (ETF's), such as:
- Small cap
- Mid cap
- Large cap

- International
- Emerging markets (companies in countries with emerging [developing] economies)
- Balanced: a mix of stocks and bonds

Bonds - individual securities
- Municipal and state
- US Government
- Corporate (commercial)

Bonds - mutual funds
- Municipal and state bonds
- US Government bonds
- Corporate (commercial) bonds

Real estate
- Home (primary residence); vacation home (perhaps rented out at times to generate rental income)
- Real Estate Investment Trust (REIT)
- Rental property

Annuities: learn about the different types of annuity contracts, benefits and costs of each type of annuity; terms and conditions to seek and to beware of in each type of annuity.

Commodities, such as:
- Gold
- Silver
- Natural resource mutual funds and exchange traded funds

Collectibles: invest in what you know and love. Collectibles commonly owned as investments include:
- Stamps and coins
- Antique furniture and historic cars
- Fine art

Capital: money you might invest to start and grow your own company to pursue a dream to dsomething you love to do.

Venture capital
- Money you might invest in one or more small companies in which you would be one of a limited number of stockholders.
- Typically should comprise only a small percentage of a prudent investor's portfolio; probably should be considered "play" money that the investor could afford to lose

Pros and cons of actively managed and passively managed mutual funds
- Actively managed: a fund manager makes individually researched buy and sell decisions.
- Passively managed: "index" funds and exchange traded funds (ETF's) operate mostly on "autopilot" with the objective of mirroring the performance of various market indexes (e.g. S&P 500) or entire types of investments (e.g. financial institutions).

Three types of income, and how each type of income is taxed
- Ordinary income, e.g. salaries and wages, interest income from bank accounts, proceeds from the sale of investment assets that had appreciated (increased) in value and were owned for <u>less</u> than one year.
- Capital gain income, e.g. proceeds from the sale of investment assets that had appreciated in value and were owned for <u>more</u> than one year.
- Dividend income from:
  - o Stocks

  o Bonds issued by
    ▪ Companies
    ▪ Governments (may be free of certain state or federal income taxes).

Tax advantaged savings plans, e.g. IRA, 401(k), 403(b), health savings plan. Investments within tax advantaged accounts should be coordinated with investments outside of tax advantaged accounts. Different types of accounts have different terms and tax benefits that are too varied and complex to explain in a few words.
- Identify tax advantaged accounts for which you might be eligible.
- Research the benefits of each tax advantaged account for which you are eligible. If possible discuss the benefits of each account with a financial advisor.

Diversification means investing the money in an investment portfolio in a diversified mix of classes and types of investment assets. Diversification can provide benefits such as.
- Enabling different classes of investments and different types of investments within each class to play different roles in building net worth, e.g. cash to preserve capital, stocks to appreciate in value, bonds to generate income.
- "Spreading the risk" of losing money (a) on any single investment or any single class or type of investment (b) during any one planning period (c) during a recession.
- Helping to provide the steadiest possible increase in value of an investment portfolio from planning period to planning period; it helps smooth out the normal cycles of price increases and decreases that different classes and types of investment assets go through, e.g. typically (not always), as stocks are experiencing a cyclical decrease in value bonds are increasing in value.

Diversification strategy = asset allocation strategy
- "Asset allocation strategy" means establishing objectives for the percentage amount that each class and type of asset will comprise in a diversified investment portfolio, e.g. 60% stocks and 40% bonds.
- A person's asset allocation strategy should be "age appropriate" – that is the strategy should be tailored to her age and the number of years:
  o She can reasonably expect to continue working, saving part of her annual income, and adding money to her investment portfolio.
  o Until the time she plans to start using income from her investments as one component of a diversified stream of revenue in her annual projected financial statement budgets.

Value means different things to different people - <u>investments only have the value that people think they have</u>. Consider the following ideas about ways to think of value:

Economic value = dollar value
- Before you buy - the dollar price at which a seller would agree to sell you an asset.
- After you buy - the price at which a buyer would agree to buy that asset from you.
- Learn who and what "market forces" drive the economic value of investments, e.g. analysts, large institutional buyers and sellers, financial pundits, news media.
- In particular, learn about Benjamin Graham's idea of "Mr. Market".
- Economic value typically is a function of supply and demand. Typically, but not always:
  o The greater the supply of an asset and the lower the demand for that asset, the lower the economic value (dollar value).

o   Conversely, the greater the demand for an asset and the lower the supply of it, the greater the economic value.

Economic value in relation to time
- Historical market value: the price at which an asset was sold in the past.
- Current market value: the price at which you could buy or sell an asset today.
- Future market value: the price you could reasonably expect if you wanted to buy or sell an asset in the future. Future market value is key to investment management planning.

Personal value of an asset for you - can be more or less than its economic value for you.
- Utility value: the amount of use you could get from an asset.
- Sentimental value: a measure of how good an asset makes you feel. Your favorite childhood toy may have next to zero economic value for anybody else, but it is priceless to you – you wouldn't exchange it for any amount of money.

A few examples of differences in value people might think assets have:
- *Toy doll*: a toy doll can have great <u>sentimental</u> value to an eight year old girl who desperately wants it, and to her father who wants to buy it as a present for her. That doll also has an <u>economic</u> value for the father equal to the price he is willing to pay for it. That same doll might have zero sentimental or economic value to the girl's brother because he couldn't care less about it, but it might have <u>utility</u> value to him as a means to tease his sister.
- *Common stock*: some investors make decisions to buy and hold the stock of a company primarily because of the sentimental value of love they feel for the company or its products. These investors are prone to letting sentimental value blind them to the economic value that should be guiding their purchase and sale decisions.
- *Food and fresh water*: have huge utilitarian value to each and every person on Earth because we need food and water in order to survive. And, they are gaining rapidly in economic value as global demand is increasing while supply is not keeping up with demand in many places (especially in certain geographic areas where weather conditions and climate change are contributing to severe food and water supply shortages).

Long term investment strategy versus short term trading strategy

Long term investment strategy: buying and holding assets for longer terms rather than shorter terms - years more than months, months more than days.
- Most of the successful investors who I know, and know about, tend to buy and hold assets for longer terms rather than shorter terms.
- Price movements of sound investments tend to be more predictable over longer terms than over shorter terms.
- A long term investment strategy helps mitigate the risk of business and economic cycles. Stock values and economies tend to advance upward over the long term, but they get to those long term increases by going through a cycle of ups and downs over shorter terms.
- "A rising tide lifts all boats." Like a rising tide lifting all the boats in a harbor, the rising market value phase of the typical market value cycle of a particular class or type of stock tends to lift the market value of all the individual assets in that class or type (conversely, the market value of all those individual assets tends to recede during the ebb tide phase of the market cycle).

Short term trading strategy: buying and holding assets for shorter terms rather than longer terms – days more than months, months more than years (sometimes even seconds or minutes).
- To me, short term money "plays" such as "stock trading" and "real estate flipping" tend to be more about gambling than investing.
- Short term prices can move up or down with alarming speed based upon current events and daily news reports.
- If a person buys an asset with the hope of a short term gain, he is betting that another person will buy his asset at a higher price than he recently paid for it.
- People who want to feel a gamblers' thrill of action on short term bets on the future prices of specific stocks, commodities, etc. might be wise to carve out a small amount of money that they can afford to lose within their investment portfolios, perhaps no more than 5%, and treat that money as "play" money with which to "play the market".

My personal opinion as an investment amateur is that:
- Adopting a long term investment strategy is enlightened self-interest – it benefits all investors by helping to support viable stock markets.
- The higher the percentage of investors who hold their stock investments for longer periods of time, the more stable, more predictable, and more financial risk management friendly a stock market is likely to become.
- The higher the percentage of stockholders who hold their stock investments for shorter periods of time, the less predictable and less financial risk management friendly a stock market is likely to become.
- If too high a percentage of the stock available in a stock market was to be bought and sold by stock traders my thought is that prudent investors would tend to exit that "gambling house" stock market in search of investments that would provide more stable and predictable returns on their money, and then that stock market would not be able to survive as we know it.
- We should all learn about the history of stock markets and the roles stock markets are intended to play in a healthy capitalist economy.

Risks of a "new paradigm": w*hen you hear people say it's a "new paradigm" or "it's different this time" in regard to investments, most likely it is not really all that new or different.* Precious little ever comes along that is truly new in regard to the fundamentals of successful investing. Be extremely cautious about changing your investment strategy based solely upon a purported "new paradigm". Learn about past "new paradigms" that wound up costing a lot of people a lot of money. Ask some savvy older investors to tell you their stories about so called new paradigms in the past.

Investment bubbles are relatively short term "feeding frenzies" of people chasing past performance and buying investments while the prices of those investments are escalating rapidly.
- *Irrational exuberance* whips masses of people into buying certain assets at unjustifiably high prices. Irrationally exuberant buyers stop thinking rationally about the economic realities of supply and demand that inevitably drive future market value. They typically fail to consider all the factors that a prudent investor should consider.
- During an investment bubble, people act like lemmings and "follow the crowd" of other investors who are going over a financial cliff just because everybody else is doing it.
- *"What goes up must come down."* Investment bubbles always burst. Don't let "investment bubble gum" burst in your face.

It's never too late to start building an investment portfolio.

<u>Follow consensus advice offered by the financial services industries</u>

Most reputable financial service providers agree upon most of the fundamentals of prudent personal financial management for one overriding reason – these fundamentals have proven to work over many, many years!

Research the websites of reputable financial services companies and the written materials they publish. Notice the pieces of advice that you see over and over again. The same advice may be said a little differently by different companies, and some companies may omit certain pieces of advice for the sake of brevity and user friendliness, but you will notice that there is a great deal of agreement upon the fundamentals of prudent personal financial management. Research what financial planning professionals such as the following advise us to do:
- Mutual fund companies
- Members of the Financial Planning Association (FPA)
- Members of the National Association of Personal Financial Advisors (NAPFA)
- Members of the Personal Financial Planning section of the American Institute of Certified Public Accountants
- Banks

Include a "financial plan" as an integral part of your business plan and projected financial statement budget.
- Learn what professional financial advisors mean by the term "financial plan". Financial plans typically include things such as an investment management plan, a retirement (or "financial freedom") plan (see Chapter 17), and an "estate plan" for the inheritance you want to leave to your heirs (also see Chapter 17).
- Tailor your financial plan to your unique situation: age, family circumstances, current and future income levels, assets you currently own, risk tolerance, etc.
- *The advice of a professional financial advisor can be of immense value in preparing your financial plan - especially with planning how to generate revenue from your investments.*

In your personal business plan (the words part of your "financial plan):
- Describe the lifestyles you dream of living at various ages in your life (last year of each of your planning periods – e.g. 1 year, 3 year, 10 year, 30 year, last year of your life).
- In particular, think about how far into the future you want to continue working at a job to generate actively earned income as one part of a diversified stream of annual revenue.
- Describe the work you want your investment portfolio to be doing for you at each of those ages. These descriptions can serve as a guide in setting (a) dollar number budget objectives for increases in your net worth and (b) percentage number objectives for allocating those dollars to various classes and types of investments in a well-diversified portfolio (remember the farther out into the future you plan the more that objectives become aspirational more than practical). A few examples:
  - Provide cash to pay for future education or to provide a cash contingency reserve that could be used in times of emergency need.
  - Appreciate in value.
  - Generate income.
  - *Provide financial freedom* (e.g. build an investment portfolio that generates enough passive income to achieve the entire annual revenue objective in each projected income statement budget and eliminate a financial need to work).
- Define the investment strategies you want to use in building your investment portfolio and develop an investment management action plan to achieve your objectives.

In your projected financial statement budget for the last year of each planning period, plan for the money you will need in order to finance the lifestyle you are planning to live at that age.
- In each projected statement of income and expenses:
  - o Determine the annual revenue you can reasonably expect from sources such as:
    - ▪ Actively earned revenue from a job.
    - ▪ Passive revenue from sources such as:
      - • Social security
      - • Pension
  - o Determining projections of revenue from the above sources will guide you in determining the revenue your investment portfolio will need to generate each year in order to achieve your annual total revenue objectives.
  - o Set a net profit objective for cash savings to add to your investment portfolio during that year.
- In each projected balance sheet, plan for the evolution of an "age appropriate" diversification of your investment portfolio.

Investment strategies you might consider include:
- *"Don't lose money".*
- Set reasonably achievable financial objectives - don't try to "shoot for the moon".
  - o Be guided by the principle of risk-reward – the greater the potential reward of an investment, the greater the risk of losing money on that investment.
  - o Over an extended period of time, it's tough for an investor to pick individual stocks that beat the average performance of an entire class or type of stock.
  - o Learn about "reversion to the mean" (regression toward the mean): this theory says that over time the price of any given investment will eventually trend toward the average (mean) price of the class or type of assets to which it belongs.
  - o *Learn why some experts advise us to invest in a portfolio of index funds that seek to match the average investment returns of classes or types of assets.*
- *Seek reasonable growth at a steady pace in your investment portfolio.*
  - o Very few people "strike it rich quick" in the stock market.
  - o Heed Aesop's Fable about "The Tortoise and the Hare". Maintaining a slower and steadier pace toward increasing wealth over the long term tends to be more successful than attempts by amateur investors at relatively fast sprints to riches.
- Regarding interest and dividend income, seek a "reasonable" return - discuss the definition of a reasonable rate of return with an investment professional.

Maintain a "disciplined investment strategy" - stick to your well-reasoned strategy.
- Don't jump from a strategy that sounds good one day to another strategy that sounds better the next day - don't flip-flop from strategy to strategy.
- Carefully consider any change in your investment strategy – discuss with a professional.

All too often, the stuff swirling around us in our daily lives causes us to forget about the well-reasoned investment strategies we had planned to use. It's easy to get diverted from our financial plans by things such as:
- Pressure exerted by family members to change.
- Peer pressure to do what we perceive our friends are doing.
- Incessant reports of what the stock markets are doing every minute, hour, and day.
- Newscasters and financial pundits telling us what the "smart money" is doing. Keep in mind that newscasters and financial pundits get paid for attracting people's eyes and ears to their broadcasts, not for educating their audiences. "Tune out the noise".

Professional financial advisors I know tell me that the number of telephone calls they receive from their clients spikes each time there is a series of news stories about:

- Forecasts of bad economies - some clients succumb to doom and gloom stories and want to sell good investment assets.
- Reports of rapidly rising stock markets - some clients don't think the values of their portfolios have been increasing fast enough. They want to buy potentially over-priced assets in order keep pace with "the market".

These advisors say they must try to talk their clients down from "emotional ledges", and convince clients to stick to the prudent financial plans they had prepared together. Getting help in sticking to an investment plan is one of the huge benefits that a good financial advisor can provide.

Don't let advertising that seems at odds with generally accepted "best investment practices" advocated by the financial planning industry seduce you into deviating from your financial plan. Beware:

- Advertisements that try to be funny. Investing is not an inconsequential hobby to be taken lightly.
- Advertisements for cheap stock trading facilities (which seem to be aired during sports programming and seem to be targeted at people who advertising professionals think might be susceptible to the allure of the emotional thrills they could get from "playing" a stock trading game).
- Advertisements that tempt people with ideas about getting rich. Some advertisers try to make it seem easy to get rich by investing with them or using their system, but it is highly unlikely that most of us would get rich if we did business with such advertisers.
- Advertisements to buy gold, collectibles, or other commodities. Think about why such advertisements tend to be aired in low cost broadcast media time slots. Such advertisements typically do not point out the role that collectibles and commodities probably should play in a well-diversified investment portfolio.
- "Info-mercials" (commercials presented to look like informational / educational programs) selling the proprietary investment systems of financial gurus.

Maintain a diversified investment portfolio – *"don't put all your eggs in one basket"*. Factors to consider in planning an <u>asset allocation strategy</u> for diversification of your portfolio:

- Your age.
- Your risk tolerance: the amount of risk of losing money that you are willing to accept.
- Your investment objectives.
- Total amount of money you have available to divide up among various classes and types of investments; the more money you have available to invest, the broader the diversification you can plan to have in your investment portfolio.

As a general rule (with many exceptions, of course):

- The younger you are, the greater the percentage of assets in your portfolio might be allocated to investments that have a higher risk of losing money, but potential for higher return, e.g. stocks (dependent upon your tolerance for the risk of losing money).
- The older you are, the greater the percentage that lower risk investments probably should be in your portfolio (dependent upon your risk tolerance), e.g. cash and bonds.

Two frequently quoted rules of thumb for the percentage allocation of money in the stocks and bonds portion of an investment portfolio are:

- Percentage of bonds should equal a person's age, e.g. for a 35 year old that would be 35%

bonds and 65% stocks.
- Percentage of stocks should equal 110 minus a person's age, e.g. for that same 35 year old the allocation would be 75% stocks and 25% bonds).
- You might consider splitting the difference between these two rules of thumb, e.g. for that same 35 year old a prudent allocation might be 70% stocks and 30% bonds.

One financial advisor I know likes to talk to his clients in terms of having two separate diversification strategies for two different "buckets" of investments within their portfolios:
- Current lifestyle bucket:
  - Investments that might significantly impact the client's current lifestyle if value was to be lost (i.e. money splashed out of the bucket). For example:
    - Investments generating income that the client plans to use as one component of revenue in his annual projected income statement budget.
    - Investments that the client plans to use a contingency financial reserve in the event of an unplanned need for cash.
  - This bucket of money would be managed more conservatively than the second bucket so as to minimize the impact of the cyclical decreases in market value inherent in investment markets.
- Longer term investment bucket:
  - Investments that would not significantly impact the client's current lifestyle during a decreasing value phase of the investment market cycle.
  - This bucket of money could be managed less conservatively than the first bucket if the client's risk tolerance would allow her to sleep comfortably while "riding out" decreasing value phases of the investment market cycle.

Rebalance your investment portfolio periodically to maintain your asset allocation strategy percentage targets for diversification - perhaps quarterly, semi-annually, or annually.
- Within the various classes and types of investments in your portfolio, consider (a) selling some of the assets whose prices have gone up the most, and (b) buying more of the assets whose prices have not increased as much or that have decreased the most.
- Be sure to consider taxes: assets held in tax advantaged accounts might be rebalanced more frequently than assets held in accounts in which investment gains would be taxed.

There is a saying about drinking alcoholic beverages - *"know when to say when"*. The same can be said for investing - know when you have enough money invested in any given class or type of investment. "Enough is enough".

Food diets provide a good analogy for maintaining a well-diversified investment portfolio. Medical professionals advocate a well-balanced food diet to maintain physical health. So too financial professionals advocate a well-balanced investment diet to maintain fiscal health.
- A well balanced food diet of the different food groups (e.g. vegetables, fruits, whole grains, nuts, beans, fish, and lean meat) creates a nutritional synergy in your body to help maintain its physical health.
- So too, a well-balanced investment diet of different classes and types of investments creates fiscal synergy in your investment portfolio to help maintain its fiscal health.
- Consuming too much of one particular food group to the exclusion of other food groups can increase the chances of your body developing physical ailments.
- So too, investing too much money in one class or type of investment to the exclusion of other classes or types of investments can increase the chances of your portfolio developing fiscal ailments.

Gardening provides another good analogy for maintaining a well-diversified investment portfolio.
- A well-diversified and well-trimmed mix of plants typically yields the healthiest possible garden that has the lowest risk of damage caused by the usual hazards that gardens face, e.g. weather, pests, and disease. So too, a well-diversified and well-trimmed (rebalanced) mix of investments typically yields the healthiest possible portfolio that has the lowest risk of damage caused by the usual hazards that portfolios face, e.g. recession, inflation, and other hazards of an economy; market risks associated with investment markets in stocks, bonds, commodities, and real estate; business risks associated with specific individual investments, types of investment, or industries.
- Just as over time a gardener should carefully trim back and thin out old plants and occasionally add new plants in order maintain a healthy bio-diversity (diversification) in his garden, so too you should consider trimming back and thinning out old investment positions, and adding new investments in your portfolio as your financial position and life circumstances evolve.

Save first, spend later. When preparing your projected financial statement budgets, consider placing a higher priority on saving money for your future financial security than on spending money on discretionary purchases of things you don't "need". Heed the old advice *"pay yourself first"*. After receiving each paycheck from your employer, consider making a deposit into a savings or investment account before buying anything you don't absolutely need.

"Mutual funds make the most sense for the most people", say most of the professional financial advisors I have known. They say most people would achieve greater investment success by investing in mutual funds rather than individual securities.

Two things to consider when evaluating a decision about investing in mutual funds:
- Mutual funds typically can provide a well-diversified portfolio of stocks and bonds with less money than would be needed to invest in an equally well-diversified portfolio of individual stocks and bonds.
- A portfolio of mutual funds requires less time and less expertise to manage successfully than does a portfolio of individual stocks and bonds.

"Don't spend the "principal" - principal being the investments you have accumulated in your investment portfolio. Over the course of each budget "planning period" year try to pay all of your expenses with revenue you earn that year.

Harness the power of "compounding" – reinvesting interest and dividend income in order to earn more interest and dividend income on that money.
- Re-investing interest and dividend income speeds up the growth of an investment portfolio.
- Allowing interest and dividend earnings to compound amplifies the power of the money you have invested to make even more money for you.

"Buy low, sell high"
- Consider buying while other people are selling and prices are decreasing. Investment bargains can be found as demand is decreasing and the supply of assets being sold is increasing (learn about a "contrarian" investment strategy).
- Consider selling while other people are buying and prices are increasing.

- Two common pieces of advice regarding news stories:
    - "Buy on the bad news" when prices are being driven down by the bad news.
    - "Sell on the good news" when prices are being driven up by the good news.
- A good time to buy is often after an investment bubble has burst and some people are "dumping" valuable assets with the same irrational emotional intensity as they had been buying those assets during the pricing run-up that created the bubble. People often over-react when they see the value of their investment portfolio dropping. They sell really good investments at bargain prices - they "*throw the baby out with the bathwater*".

"Historical price charts" can be good tools to help people buy low and sell high. Historical price charts track the price patterns over time of classes of investments, types of investments, and individual investments. Learn how some sophisticated investors use price charts.

- Prices of good investments move upward over the long term, but they usually get there by going through a cycle of price increases and decreases (like a sine wave tilted upward).
- Price charts allow investors to see where the current price of an investment asset is in its historical pricing cycle, and where the current pricing of comparable investments are in their historical pricing cycles (or an entire class or type of asset).
- *Don't try to "time the market"*. Don't try to pick the highest price point during the upswing phase of a price cycle, nor the lowest price point during the downswing phase.

Learn about Benjamin Graham's idea of "Mister Market".

Don't "chase past performance". When people "chase past performance", they are buying an investment asset based largely upon a mistaken belief that the asset's market price will continue to rise in the future just because it had been rising in the past. Investment bubbles are born of large herds of people chasing past performance.

- *"Past performance is no guarantee of future results"* (or words to that effect) is a standard waiver required by the SEC in every mutual fund prospectus. This waiver is required for good reason - too many investors do NOT understand that an investment's past track record of price increases does not guarantee that the same price increase performance will continue in the future.
- *Buy investments based upon well-informed, well-reasoned <u>projections</u> of <u>future market value</u> and <u>future return</u> on money invested* – not based solely upon past performance.

Consider your "lost opportunity cost" as you make each investment decision. Consider what other things you might do with that money BEFORE you buy a prospective investment.

- Once you invest a dollar, you lose the opportunity to use that same dollar again to buy another investment that might generate a better future return (at least in the short term). For example, if you invest money in shares of a mutual fund that some research indicates might gain 10% over the next year, you lose the opportunity to invest that money in another mutual fund that other research indicates might gain 12% over the next year.
- People frequently chase past performance by investing in a new investment that has been increasing in value faster than the value of investments they already own. Typically they fear missing out on the opportunity to earn a better return on that new investment. The irony of this "grass is greener" fear of missing out on a lost opportunity for possibly greater gains is that all too often (a) investors sell a good investment that "hadn't been doing much lately" (b) in order to buy a high-flying stock that is just about to hit its peak price and begin sliding back down, and (c) the investment that was sold is just about ready to make its long expected move upward in price.

Consider putting your investment management on autopilot as much as possible. For instance you might consider:
- Electronic deposit of each paycheck into a bank account.
- Scheduling a withdrawal from each paycheck for deposit into tax advantaged investment accounts offered by your employer, e.g. 401(k) or health savings account - "pay yourself first".
- Regularly scheduled electronic transfers from your bank account into other investment accounts.
- Scheduling automatic rebalancing of investments in tax advantaged investment accounts - perhaps quarterly, semi-annually, or annually.

Plan for the impact of income taxes.
- Learn about:
  - Differences in taxation of interest income and dividend income.
  - Differences in taxation of ordinary income and capital gain income - when making a decision about selling an asset that has appreciated in value determine how the sale proceeds will be taxed - as ordinary income or as a capital gain.
- Set aside enough cash from investment income earned during each year to pay the income tax that will become due at the end of the year (unless you are generating enough income from your job or other sources to pay that tax).
- Be cautious about selling an asset solely for the purpose of taking a tax loss. Be sure you fully understand what you are doing. Consider getting advice from a tax expert.
- As your income and net worth increase, consider talking to a professional financial advisor about the estate planning pros and cons of a tax advantaged trust.

Revise your financial plan as your life evolves - as you age, as your financial position changes, and as you gain financial management expertise and experience.
- "Maintain a disciplined investment strategy" does not mean never revising your strategy. To maintain a disciplined investment strategy means:
  - Revising your strategy only as a well-informed, well- reasoned analysis indicates would be prudent.
  - Don't let the investment strategy you initially adopted become a calcified dogma that you continue to use year after year just because "that's the way I've always done it.
- Revise your long range and ultra-long range objectives to reflect the evolution of your dreams.
- Revise your short term and mid-term objectives based upon your success in achieving your short term milestone objectives.

Use history to help project future market value

"History repeats itself".
- Human behavior hasn't changed much from generation to generation throughout history. It blows me away how similar are the ways that people are described as thinking and acting in books written 2,400 years ago, 400 years ago, 40 years ago, and last year.
- Societies change as knowledge, wisdom, and wealth are passed down from generation to generation, but the behavior of individual people living in societies doesn't change much.
- Knowing how historical events played out in the past can help you project how current events are likely to play out in the future, which will in turn help you project future market values of investments.

Cycles: knowledge of cycles that typically play out over and over again through the years can be a valuable tool to help project the future market value of investments. Learn about:
- Historical "market price" cycles: prices of investments such as stocks, bonds, and real estate tend to go through cycles of increasing and decreasing prices.
- Economic cycles of expansion and recession; and inflation and deflation.
- Interest rate cycle of increasing and decreasing interest rates.
- Life cycles of companies and industries: birth, growth (evolution), and eventual rejuvenation or obsolescence and death.
- Life cycles of technologies: discovery, development, adoption into common usage, and revision or death by obsolescence.

Trends that have been developing tend to be better predictors of future market prices than isolated single events, especially when we can see how a current trend fits into an historical cycle. Seek to identify trends that are likely to drive future market values of your investments, such as current trends in supply (e.g. availability of the supply of raw materials, or new manufacturing plants coming on line) and demand (e.g. more consumers having more [or less] money to spend).

Study the history of investment bubbles as if you were preparing forensic "autopsy reports" to learn how those bubbles were blown up and what caused them to eventually burst. Learn how factors such as the following may have contributed to the bursting of historical bubbles:
- Demand: at some pricing level, demand for any desirable investment will start to diminish when new buyers cannot or will not pay the rapidly rising prices.
- Folly of playing the *"greater fool gamble"* - "I can buy something that I think may be over-priced today, but there will be a greater fool who will buy it from me at an even higher price tomorrow." Over time, prospective future fools wise up and stop buying.

A few famous bubbles to research:
- 1600's Dutch tulip bulbs (perhaps the most frequently referenced example).
- 1700's British South Sea Company Bubble (during which the term "bubble" was coined); and the French Mississippi Company bubble.
- 1800's American railroads.
- 1907 and 1929 American stock market crashes.
- 1980's Japanese stock market and real estate industry; American financial institutions.
- 1990's to early 2000's high tech "Dot Com" bubble.
- Late 2000's real estate in many countries.

Investment risk management

There is risk inherent in every investment - some investments have greater risk and some have less risk.
- *If investment management was a perfectly predictable science with negligible risk, then everybody on Wall Street would be a billionaire.*
    - o If investment professionals could use economic principles, formulas, and financial ratio analyses to make the right investment decision every single time, they would all be fabulously wealthy.
    - o They can't, so they aren't.
- A person must manage investment risk well enough over a long enough period of time in order to wind up having been a successful investor at the end of her game of life.

Peril, hazard, and risk: learn what these terms mean and develop your own working definitions in your own words to use in managing your risk of losing money on your investments, such as:
- Peril: something that could cause an investment to lose money.
- Risk: probability that a peril will cause an investment to lose money.
- Hazard: a condition that increases the probability of a peril causing an investment loss.

Learn about the fundamentals of risk management, and use them (see Chapter 18).
- *Risk identification*: what perils could cause you to lose money on an investment? Learn about the perils, risks, and hazards of an investment BEFORE investing your money.
- *Risk avoidance*: avoid making investments that you think have unacceptably high risk.
- *Risk transfer*: transfer risk to others, e.g. invest the cash component of your portfolio in bank accounts insured by the Federal Deposit Insurance Corporation (FDIC).
- *Risk management*: manage the risk you willingly decide to accept or have no alternative but to accept to minimize the probability of suffering harm. Two suggestions:
    - o Hire a professional financial advisor.
    - o Follow consensus advice offered by the financial services industries.

Risk tolerance is the amount of risk a person is willing to accept. Different people have different levels of tolerance for the amount of risk of losing money that they are willing to accept. It is important to be honest with yourself about the amount of risk of losing money that you are willing to accept - amount of risk with which you could live comfortably. Avoid investments that would cause you to worry so much about losing money that your worry might cause you to lose sleep or lessen your enjoyment of life.

Spread of risk = diversification
- Typically, the greater the "spread of risk" among different investments in different classes and types of investments, the lower the risk of your portfolio losing value.
- Beware "concentration of risk" – too much money invested in any one single investment, single class or type of investment, single investment, or single financial institution.
- A common diversification guideline is to not allow any single investment to exceed 5-10% of your total portfolio (except perhaps a home that you own).

Risk – reward
- Typically, the greater the risk of losing money, the greater the potential for reward must be in order motivate people to buy an investment.
- Typically, the lower the risk of losing money, the lower the rate of return investors should expect (e.g. dividend rate, stock price appreciation)

Risk premium - the higher rate of return that a higher risk investment asset typically offers over and above the rate of return on lower risk investments in order to entice investors to buy that higher risk investment.

"Market" risk - "market" being a group of similar investment assets.
- Prices for the entire market of a particular class or type of investment asset typically go through a cycle of increases and decreases that impacts the price of each individual investment asset comprising that market.
- The stock price of a good company typically gets pulled upward along with all the other stocks of the same class or type during the upswing phase of the price cycle of the market for those stocks, but then has the "market risk" of being pushed downward during the downswing phase of that market's price cycle

Business risk, in regard to the stock price of a publicly traded company: the risk that a company's stock price might drop if the company began to operate less profitably than "the market" (e.g. stock analysts, large institutional investors) expected it to operate. Perils that could pose a business risk to a company's stock price include:
- Retirement or death of one or more senior managers who had been instrumental in the company's profitability.
- New competitor(s) entering the market and driving down prices that the company can charge; or taking business away from the company.
- New technology that causes obsolescence of the company's products or services, the company itself, or the company's entire industry.
- Changes in the elected officials of a government that result in changes to the tax structure upon which the company's financial plan and budget had been predicated.
- Business interruption caused by a natural disaster (e.g. hurricane, flood, fire, earthquake) or a catastrophic event (e.g. oil well blowout or terrorist attack).

Credit risk, in regard to the value of bonds issued by government and corporate organizations: the risk that a bond issuer would not be able to pay dividends during the term of the bond or return the full bond amount at maturity. Learn how professional credit ratings firms determine the level of credit risk they think is posed by a bond issuer - credit ratings firms such as Standard & Poor's Financial Services, LLC; Moody's Investor Services, Inc.; and Fitch Ratings, Inc.

Economic risk
- Interest rate risk: learn how rising and falling interest rates can affect stock and bond investments. There are too many variables to cover in this limited space.
- Risk of economic recession.

Risk of human emotion: *beware the risk of becoming so emotionally enamored of an investment that you lose the ability to objectively evaluate how good the investment is for you.*
- People sometimes fall in love with a company. They start evaluating performance of the company's stock from the subjective perspective of how they want the investment to perform rather than from an objective perspective as to how it has actually performed in the past and how it is likely to perform in the future.
- People who fall in love with a company often see what they want to see instead of the reality of the facts that they need to see in order to make a prudent investment decision.
- Don't fall so in love with any investment that you couldn't end your relationship with it.
- Don't have a blind, unquestioning allegiance to it to any investment.

Time helps mitigate the risk of investment loss.

- The prices of even the best performing investments typically go through periodic cycles of ups and downs on their way to increases over the long term.
  - o As an example, investors who sold their mutual funds when the stock markets tanked during the "Great Recession" of the late 2000's lost huge amounts of money. But investors, who held on to their mutual funds through the recession saw the prices of most (if not all) of their investments rebound, and in many instances, increase in price.
  - o When enough big investors (e.g. financial institutions, pension funds, and colleges that have huge endowments) sell a sound investment over a short period of time, they typically drive down the price of that investment; and then over time if enough big investors think the price has bottomed and they start buying it again, they can drive back up the price of that investment.
- When the market price of a well-researched and well-reasoned investment falls, don't automatically sell it just because its price dropped. A more profitable course of action might be to re-evaluate the investment to determine if it is still fundamentally sound, and if it is, continue to hold it in your portfolio at least until its market price has recovered.
- By simply holding on to a fundamentally sound investment through periodic declines in price, investors typically improve their chances to realize a gain.
- *You won't incur a loss on an investment that has decreased in price until you sell it.*
- Patience can pay.
- One of the best reasons to hire a financial advisor is help protect an investor from selling an investment as an emotional knee jerk reaction to a drop in current market price.

Learn how to identify the risk that an investment bubble might be developing.

- Studying the history of prior investment bubbles will help you learn how to identify signals that a new bubble might be developing.
- Signals that a bubble might be developing include:
  - o The faster that prices of a class or type of investment asset are increasing, the greater the risk a bubble might be developing.
  - o The more frequently that news stories say positive things about a class or type of investment, and the more positive the tone of the stories, the greater the risk a bubble might be developing.
  - o The more you hear people saying things like "they <u>feel</u> they should buy now because prices just keep on going up and up", or "the way prices are rising so fast, if I don't buy now I won't be able to afford to buy in the future", or "everybody else is buying now, so I guess I should buy too", the greater the risk a bubble might be developing.
  - o The more you hear people talking about "getting into the market", the greater the risk a bubble might be developing.
  - o The more you hear "*it's a new paradigm*" or "*it's different this time*", the greater the risk a bubble might be developing.
    - It is true that times change, technologies change, and new discoveries change our lives, BUT human investment behavior doesn't change a whole lot over time.
    - Time after time (bubble after bubble) people get lured into believing that prices of certain investment assets will continue increasing forever because "it's different this time". They buy, and then sadly discover that, once again, it really was NOT different this time.

Beware the risk of anyone selling a proprietary investment system advertised along the lines of "my system".

- The further that the person's proprietary system (proprietary meaning a system the person developed) departs from the consensus advice offered by professional financial advisors, the more likely it would be prudent to avoid using that proprietary system.

- Even if the person had been using her proprietary system over a long enough period of time to prove that her system had actually worked for her (rather than being just a case of pure luck), it is likely that most of us amateur investors would not be able to use that person's proprietary system as successfully as she had used it. It is likely that we wouldn't have the same understanding of how to use the system, nor perhaps the same financial management expertise, experience, self-discipline, etc. that had enabled her to use her system successfully.

- People selling proprietary investment systems can claim that investors "just like you" have gotten rich using "my system", but they don't have to tell us exactly how many people actually used their systems successfully, and they don't have to tell us the other side of the story about how many other people "just like you" might have lost money using their systems. And, in order to back up their claims, just how would they know how much money how many people actually had made using their systems?

- Think about what's in it for the seller.
  - What would motivate someone to sell the right to learn her proprietary system for buying and selling a certain type of investment, e.g. stock or real estate?
  - Why would she want to sell her system to a large number of people and run the risk that too many people would use the system and mess up the market dynamics that had enabled her to use her system successfully?
  - Might she be trying to make more money from selling her system than she could make from using her system?

Investment Decision Making

GET ADVICE FROM A PROFESSIONAL FINANCIAL ADVISOR!
- *I am not a professional financial advisor.* I am only an amateur investor. I am NOT certified nor licensed to offer investment advice.
- *No book can offer a "one size fits all" plan that will work for ALL readers in building their investment portfolios.* This book certainly does not. Each of us is a unique person living a unique life, therefore each of us must develop a unique financial plan tailored to her unique lifestyle and her unique financial position.
- The ideas and suggestions in this chapter and in this entire book are intended to:
  - o Stimulate your independent thinking about how to build an investment portfolio that helps you achieve your objectives.
  - o Motivate you to discuss the ideas and suggestions with a financial advisor.

Each investment decision should advance you toward your projected financial statement budget objectives. During the process of making each investment decision ask yourself questions such as:
- What role do I expect this investment to play in my portfolio?
  - o Provide better liquidity (cash or assets that could be quickly converted to cash)?
  - o Preserve capital?
  - o Appreciate in price?
  - o Generate income?
  - o Provide better diversification?
- How will this investment complement the other investments in my portfolio?
- Would the decision option I choose help me balance or rebalance my portfolio to bring it in line with my asset allocation strategy?
- What would be the lost opportunity cost of other investment opportunities I would have to forgo if I invest in this asset?
- Would it be more prudent to "clean up" my balance sheet by paying off debt (e.g. credit card balances) rather than buying this investment asset?
- Could I concisely explain to a confidant how this decision would advance me toward my projected financial statement budget objectives?

Investment decisions should be based upon rational thinking - not emotion (see Chapter 7).
- Act prudently and methodically, not in haste.
- Maintain a rational thinking business mindset if people around you are beating the emotional drums of excessively exuberant buying or doom and gloom selling.

The best investment decisions typically are the best informed decisions.
- Gather as much decision making information as:
  - o Would be prudent based upon the amount of money involved - the greater the percentage of your investment portfolio that the investment would be, the better informed you should try to be.
  - o Your time and resources allow.
- *Consider getting advice from a professional financial advisor.*

Investment decisions are complicated by imperfect knowledge.
- No one can know everything that would be helpful to know in order to make the most accurate projection possible of the future market price of an investment.

- Estimates of future market prices can only be made with a reasonable degree of probability, not a 100% guarantee of accuracy.
- Sellers have been known to tell prospective buyers all the positive information that they want those buyers to know and either sugar coat or hide in "the fine print" potentially negative information that prospective buyers should know.

As an example, think about relevant information you might not know when making a decision about buying or selling a company's stock, such as:

- Competitors' plans and capabilities that might impact the company's future market share, revenues, or profit.
- Management's ability to adapt to evolutionary changes in their industry.
- Pending retirement or departure of good managers who might be succeeded by new managers who are not nearly so good at making profitable business decisions.
- A significant number of older employees who had been key contributors to the company's profits might be getting ready to retire, or quit because they have become dissatisfied with new managers and new management practices.
- Personal problems of one or more key managers might have a spillover effect that negatively impacts their job performance and the company's performance, e.g. addiction to alcohol, drugs or gambling; extra-marital affairs that lead to messy divorces.

Do not rely upon a single source of investment decision making information such as:

- A person who promotes herself as a "financial guru".
- Any one television show, radio program, or internet source
- A source that provides headline and sound bite business news that just scratches the surface of things you should know more about.

Maintain an age appropriate diversification of assets.

- The younger you are, the greater the percentage of your portfolio that might be allocated to "growth" assets (assets whose primary purpose is to appreciate in price) and higher "risk premium" assets (higher potential returns at a higher risk of loss), depending upon your risk tolerance for losing money.
- The older you are and the fewer the years you plan to continue working at a job to generate revenue, the greater the percentage of your portfolio that might be allocated to assets that will help preserve your capital (not lose money) and generate income.

To repeat what we said several pages back, you might consider two commonly used rules of thumb for allocation of the stock and bond components of investment portfolios:

- Percentage of bonds should equal your age (e.g. for a 35 year old that would be 35% bonds and 65% stocks).
- Percentage of stocks should equal 110 minus your age (e.g. for that 35 year old the allocation would be 75% stocks and 25% bonds).
- You might consider splitting the difference between these two rules of thumb, e.g. for that 35 year old a prudent allocation might be 70% stocks and 30% bonds.

Think evolution, not revolution, in order to maintain prudent diversification.

- Decisions that result in a series of gradual, evolutionary "tweaks" to investment portfolios tend to yield better long term performance results than "big move" decisions that cause sudden, massive, revolutionary changes, e.g. an investor deciding to sell all her bonds and use all of her cash to "go all in" and buy stocks during a "bull market" for

common stock (while stock market price indexes are going up).
- Think in terms of refinements to your portfolio rather than major overhauls.

Let your investment decisions be guided by the evolution of your life.
- Your age.
- Your current financial position.
- Investment management expertise and experience gained from prior investment decisions, i.e. lessons learned from your successes and mistakes.
- New insights gained from advisors and other business team members.
- Revisions you make to your business plan and projected financial statement budget.

A good first step in building your investment portfolio might be to build your cash reserves.
- Learn why the adage *"cash is king"* is used so often in the world of finance.
- Cash is the most liquid asset. It can be used immediately to pay any expense and buy any product or service.
- Cash can provide a contingency reserve to pay for unplanned expenses or an unexpected interruption in a person's stream of revenue.
- When held in interest bearing savings accounts and certificates of deposit, it provides a predictable stream of revenue.
- Cash is perhaps the safest investment to own in order to preserve capital - to not lose money (although, if the inflation rate exceeds the interest rate financial institutions are paying, inflation will erode the value of cash reserves).
- For risk management purposes, consider bank accounts that are insured by the FDIC (Federal Deposit Insurance Corporation).

Consider opening multiple accounts to create separate cash reserves to serve separate purposes, such as:
- Checking account to pay your living expenses.
- Emergency cash reserve savings account to cover such things as:
  - A sudden interruption in your stream of income, e.g. loss of your job or a long term disability.
  - Major car or home repair expenses.
  - Uninsured medical expenses.
- Income earning account(s), e.g. laddered certificates of deposit (CD's). Learn about "laddering" - having multiple CD's that have different expiry/renewal dates.
- Special purpose account to help pay for big ticket purchases such as a car, home, college, vocational training, vacation, or wedding.

You might ask your banker and/or your financial advisor for advice about the pros and cons of multiple accounts, such as:
- Pro: separate cash accounts can help reinforce your self-discipline to not "raid" one specific purpose account for another purpose.
- Con: after splitting cash among multiple accounts, one or more of the accounts might not meet a bank's minimum deposit threshold needed to earn the highest interest rate the bank has available for that type account.

Factors to consider in planning the cash component of your investment portfolio include:
- Your business plan, your projected financial statement budget, your asset allocation strategy, and your risk tolerance.

- Your current financial position – balance sheet assets owned, debt owed, predictability of annual income, etc.
- Your age and physical health.
- How quickly you could raise cash using other assets you own, e.g. stock investments you could sell quickly, second loan on a home.
- How quickly you could reduce monthly expenses.
- How quickly you could get a new job if you lost your current job; stability of your position within your employer's company; stability of your employer in your industry.
- Potential financial safety net support provided by a spouse, parents, grandparents or other person with whom you have a close relationship. It probably wouldn't be prudent to place too much weight on a financial safety net – stuff happens. Self-sufficiency is the best financial planning policy.

Common advice I have heard regarding a prudent amount of cash to have in an emergency cash reserve account:
- Cash equal to somewhere between three months and one year of annual income.
- Enough cash to make you feel comfortable that you have enough cash set aside.

If you have unpaid credit card balances that you have been carrying over from month to month:
- Some financial advisors might recommend using part of "income in excess of monthly expenses" to pay off credit card debt and part to build up an emergency cash fund.
- Other advisors might recommend paying off credit card balances in full prior to building cash reserves (perhaps because credit card interest rates are so high, and credit card debt might be re-used if a cash emergency popped up).
- *If possible, talk to a professional financial advisor about your specific situation.*

As you are building cash reserves appropriate to your business plan and budget, you might also consider funding income tax advantaged savings accounts available to you, such as:
- Individual retirement account (IRA) – learn about Roth IRA's and regular IRA's.
- Retirement account offered by your employer, e.g. 401(k) or 403(b) plan – especially if your employer will make "matching" contributions equal to a percentage of the money you contribute.
- Medical savings account.
- Education savings account.

Benefits of income tax advantaged accounts include:
- They help maximize the power of compounding because income earned inside these accounts accumulates tax free until that money is withdrawn.
- In certain types of tax advantaged accounts, the money invested each year can be deducted from income on your income tax return. Learn how tax regulations would apply to tax advantaged accounts available to you.

Most types of tax advantaged accounts have withdrawal restrictions. Be sure to learn about withdrawal restrictions in tax advantaged accounts available to you.

As with all financial planning matters, it might be wise to talk with a professional financial advisor about funding income tax advantaged savings accounts available to you.

Stock and bond investments outside income tax advantaged accounts: after you have built up a prudent cash reserve, and begun funding tax advantaged accounts available to you, you might consider building a well-diversified portfolio of stocks and bonds outside of your tax advantaged accounts.

It might be prudent for most of us amateur investors to invest in a diversified portfolio of mutual funds.
- Learn about the pros and cons of <u>actively managed</u> mutual funds and <u>passively managed</u> index funds that seek to match the performance of a segment of the investment market, e.g. S&P 500, Russell 2000, Wilshire 5000.
- Learn also about exchange traded funds (ETF's), the cousins of mutual funds.

Most people probably would be better off if they didn't get caught up in the game of investing in individual stocks. But, if you do want to explore investing in individual stocks, it probably would be prudent to begin by practicing with an imaginary investment portfolio. If you couldn't beat the returns of market averages and index mutual funds during your practice with an imaginary portfolio, it wouldn't make good sense to think you could do better with an actual portfolio.

Home: you might consider buying a home after (a) you reach a stage in life where your business plan, (b) your current financial position, and (c) your projected financial statement budget for the next year indicate it might be prudent to do so.
- *However, buy a home primarily for shelter and secondarily for investment.* The potential investment value of home ownership probably should be secondary to the satisfaction a home can provide as shelter and as a comfortable place in which to live.
- Home buying tends to be an emotional experience. If you decide to consider the purchase of a home:
  o Use your formal decision making process (see Chapter 7).
  o Use your emotional control system to help defend yourself against emotional urges to buy a home that your budget couldn't afford.
  o Consider discussing your thinking with at least one business team member who has a reasonable level of real estate expertise and experience. Ask for her critique of your thinking and any advice or recommendations she might offer.
- Learn about the pros and the cons of home ownership. In particular learn about the financial risks of home ownership.
  o Learn why the phrase "money pit" came into being – some homes require such a seemingly endless chain of maintenance and repair work that homeowners come think they are throwing their money into a bottomless money pit.
  o Learn about the many types of unplanned expenses that homeowners might incur.
  o Learn about the historical cycle of home price increases and decreases.
    ▪ Home prices typically increase over the long term, but not always.
    ▪ There is no guarantee that a home could be sold for more than the purchase price paid.
    ▪ Learn how the real estate market crash during the Great Recession of the late 2000's hurt so many homeowners.
- Research real estate purchase advice available online and at your local library.

- BEFORE you begin home shopping, determine financial guidelines for your decision:
  o Maximum monthly mortgage payment your projected income statement budget for the next one year planning period could reasonably afford.

- o Maximum cash down payment your balance sheet indicates would be prudent to pay. Keep in mind the principle of investment diversification – decide how much of your cash and other liquid assets would be prudent to tie up in a home.
  - o Interest rates and closing costs for various types of mortgages currently available.
- Equipped with the above three pieces of information, compute the maximum purchase price it would be prudent to pay for a home.
- Tax deductibility of mortgage interest payments and real estate taxes probably should be a secondary financial consideration in a home purchase decision.
- Whereas home prices typically get to long term price increases by going through a cycle of price increases and decreases over time, it would be wise to make well-informed, well-reasoned projections of when you might want to sell the home. Consider how a home purchase would fit into your personal business plan and your career path plan, e.g. where you plan to be living in the future and when you plan to be living there.
- Research the types of homes and desirability of locations your budget could afford.
  - o Learn as much as you can about what to look for in a home: type, size, number and type of rooms, floor plan, maintenance and utility expenses, etc.
  - o Visit prospective neighborhoods to research the types and sizes of homes available, and the potential pros and cons of living in each neighborhood.
  - o Ask residents of each prospective neighborhood what they like and dislike about living in the neighborhood.
- After you have done all of your homework, then hire a professional realtor.
  - o Ask your business team members for recommendations of realtors.
  - o Interview the recommended realtors.
  - o Hire a realtor who is on the same wavelength of thinking as you are. To help make sure you two are on the same wavelength, ask each prospective realtor to parrot back to you exactly how you described the home you want to buy, e.g. *maximum purchase price,* type and size of home, location.
- Then go shopping for a home.

A professional financial advisor can be especially helpful in building and managing the income generating component of your investment portfolio! A few suggested topics you might discuss with a professional financial advisor:

- What would constitute an appropriately diversified mix of income generating assets for you in your unique position:
  - o Cash: savings accounts that pay interest; certificates of deposit?
  - o Money market funds?
  - o Treasury bills?
  - o Stocks that pay dividends?
  - o Bonds and bond funds?
  - o Balanced funds (funds that include stocks and bonds)?
  - o Equity income funds (funds that focus on stocks that pay dividends)?
  - o Annuity(s)?
  - o Real estate to serve as a rental property?
- "Laddering" income generating investments that are designed to be held for specific periods of time, such as certificates of deposit (CD's), Treasury bills, and bonds. To "ladder" means to arrange staggered expiry dates of these investments – such as 6 months, 1 year, 3 years, 5 years, or longer. Learn about the benefits of laddering.
- Reinvesting interest and dividend income to maximize the power of compound earnings.

Monitor your performance

Monitor your investment management performance on a regular basis to determine if you are on track to achieve your projected financial statement budget objectives for things such as increasing your net worth and generating passive income each year.
- Research what the websites of various financial service providers have to say about how to monitor investment performance and how often to monitor performance.
- Ask people who you think have been successful investors what they would advise about how to monitor investment performance and how often to monitor performance.
- Consider asking a professional financial advisor for advice.
- Just don't drive yourself nuts by checking the value of your investments too often - like some people who have worried themselves sick by checking their portfolio way too often during a downswing phase of a stock market pricing cycle.

Measure the performance of the components of your investment portfolio versus benchmarks such as:
- Dow Jones Industrial Average
- S&P 500 Stock Index
- Russell 2000 Index
- Wilshire 5000 Index
- Indices published for various commodities
- Lipper averages of performance of actively traded mutual funds
- Results of passively managed index funds that seek to match the returns of various and stock and bond indices.
- Performance of comparable mutual funds
  - o Learn about various research tools available.
  - o Use the quarterly reports published by various mutual fund companies.

Develop a system of investment management reports that works well for you.
- Reports provided by your financial advisor, mutual funds, banks, and other financial institutions with which you invest money.
- Financial statements to track your actual performance versus your projected financial statement budget objectives (perhaps quarterly and yearly).
- Management reports you create for yourself.

Consider revising your financial plan:
- Based upon how well your investment strategy and investment action plans have been working to help you achieve your projected financial statement budget objectives.
- Based upon advice and recommendations you receive from:
  - o A professional financial advisor.
  - o People on your business team who have proven to be successful investors.
- As you gain investment expertise and experience.
- As your life evolves.

Chapter 16. Money, Love & Family

Money, love and family

Husbands and wives take marriage vows to live together as a "couple", not to live as two individuals under one roof.
- *If you are married, the idea of "couplehood" complicates the idea of thinking that "your money is your business".*
    - <u>As one half of a couple, you need to think of treating "your" money as "our" money.</u>
    - <u>When you marry, you establish a "joint venture" business that combines your personal financial management business with your spouse's personal financial management business to form a family financial management business.</u>
    - Your spouse becomes your joint venture business partner.
- The above said, and following along with this book's theme of individual responsibility, this chapter is addressed to each person in a couple as an individual person responsible for the money in his or her life. Each person should apply the ideas contained in this book to managing his or her money as he or she thinks is the good and proper thing to do.
- Each person in a couple should exercise the highest degree of care, concern, and respect for the other person as an equal partner in order to have a financially successful spousal business team (especially important for certain men raised in social environments in which women were not perceived as equals of men).
- If one partner in a couple is the sole income earning "breadwinner" that person should avoid trying to "rule the roost".
    - A breadwinner should practice the most enlightened, benevolent, inclusive, team oriented management style possible.
    - Management of money in a family should be geared to positively influencing family member behavior, not dictating behavior.
    - There is a big difference between being an enlightened president and a dictator.

Love requires us to mix strong emotional feelings with the rational thinking needed to make financially prudent decisions – we must mix love and money.
- It takes a gentle "loving" touch to mix strong emotional feelings of love with the rational thinking mindset that is needed to make financially prudent decisions.
- Keep in mind that the strong emotion of love can:
    - Easily morph into excessive emotion that interferes with rational thinking.
    - Cause a great deal of conflict within a rational mind that is trying to make financially prudent decisions that will impact loved family members – especially if "tough love" is involved - tough love being a decision that the decision maker thinks is best for a family member over the long run, but causes some degree of discomfort, suffering, or anger for that family member in the short run.
- Living together under the same roof complicates financial decision making because physical proximity can make it harder to get into the rational thinking business mindset needed to make prudent decisions – we can't get away from each other to think clearly.

In order to optimize marital harmony and happiness:
- Family counselors tell us that it is important for spouses to talk openly and honestly about their thoughts, their feelings, their beliefs, and the lives they each desire to live.
- Financial advisors tell us that it is important for spouses to talk openly and honestly about their plans for managing the money in their lives both as individuals and as a couple.

Things that might be good to place near the top of an agenda of items to talk about include:
- Beliefs about money management - spending, saving, and investing.
- The enormous power of disagreements about money management to cause divisive problems in a loving relationship.
- Thoughts about careers, having children, and education of children.
- "Division of labor" within the family - who will do what in regard to earning income, child care, paying bills, managing investments, household chores (e.g. cooking, cleaning), etc.
- *Owning certain assets jointly* (for estate planning and financial risk management), perhaps the home you share, a bank account to pay household expenses, and one or more "cash reserve" savings accounts for emergency needs and big ticket asset purchases; and
- *Owning certain assets individually*, perhaps individual bank accounts, individual investment accounts, and individual retirement accounts.
- Each person's thoughts about this chapter.
- *Working with a professional who has family financial planning expertise.*

Keep in mind today's high rate of divorce and the fact that money is one of the leading causes of divorce.
- Few if any lovebirds can conceive of getting a divorce at the time they get married.
- But, all sorts of unforeseen stuff has broken up marriages, such as:
    - People didn't really know each other well before they got married and then discovered stuff they didn't like after marriage.
    - People changed as time went by. Personalities and behavior often change as we age and life circumstances change. Please re-read Chapter 6 that cautions readers about the nasty powers that money could have to bring out the worst in good people as "family" income and net worth increased.
    - And, maybe more than any other single cause, disagreements and disputes over money – how money should be spent, who is entitled to how much of "family" money, etc.
- In states having "community property" laws, a divorced spouse might become entitled to up to 50% of your net worth and possibly a part of your future income as alimony.
- *As part of the risk management component of your business plan, plan to minimize the risk of divorce. Place a heavy emphasis on what the insurance industry calls "loss control" – do all that you can do to keep your marriage bonds strong.*

Please read this chapter with the understandings that:
- The generally accepted "best practices" of good management apply to some extent to all groups of people, including families.
- Judicious use of the best practices of good management can help you manage your money in a happy family IF you understand that there is a difference in the ways a person should try to manage the behavior of:
    - Family members who share his home.
    - Employees he supervises in his workplace.
    - Professional service providers he hires.
- The book might be most effective as a family financial management tool if you and your partner read it together, and discuss how you might use ideas and suggestions that you both agree have potential to help you have a long, happy, and financially prosperous marriage.

Develop a family business culture

As president of your family business:
- It is your job to lead family members toward achieving family financial objectives (refer to the leadership techniques discussed in Chapters 3 and 9).
- Seek to develop "partner" relationships and avoid "provider/dependent" relationships.
- Seek to <u>blend</u> <u>prudent control of your money</u> <u>with</u> <u>providing family members as much freedom as they can handle</u> to act as managers on your family business team.
- Don't let the "power of position" as a "breadwinner" take you on a "power trip".
  - o Beware the capability of money and the power of position as a breadwinner to lead people to hurt the ones they love. Money and attempts by one spouse to exert what is perceived as excessive control over the other are said to be two of the primary causes of divorce.
  - o Make sure each family member knows in his rational thinking mind and feels in his emotion feeling heart that you have his best interest in mind each time you make a decision that will impact him.
  - o Avoid "bossing" family members about money (especially important for men raised in families or communities where women were treated as subservient).
- If your partner has proven to be a better money manager than you have been up to this point in life, a wise management decision might be to delegate to your partner the role of chief financial officer in your family business.

Promote the ideas that:
- Family members are all your partners in the family's business.
- *"We are all in it together".*
  - o Each family member is responsible for managing "our family's money".
  - o Each individual family member has a personal responsibility for the entire family's financial prosperity.
  - o Whatever one person does with "our" money will affect us all.

Help family members become the best business and financial managers they can become by:
- Educating, coaching, counseling, and motivating each person to:
  - o Become the best business and financial manager that he has the potential to become as early in his life as possible.
  - o Think and behave as a highly valued family business partner.
  - o Understand that the greater the contribution he makes to helping the family achieve the family's budget objectives, the greater the financial resources the family is likely to have available to help him finance realization of his dreams.
  - o Understand how the old adage "if you are not part of the solution, you are part of the problem" applies to each family member in regard to his efforts to help the family achieve financial prosperity.
- *Asking each family member to read this book* and discuss with you how he thinks ideas and suggestions in it might be applied to managing the money in the family's business.

Help family members learn economic facts of life such as:
- "Money doesn't grow on trees." Somebody must work to earn each dollar that family members spend.
- The family has a limited amount of money available to spend each year.
- Lost opportunity cost: once a dollar is spent, it isn't available to spend on anything else.
- Buying things just because "everybody else is getting one" is not a good reason to spend

"our family's" money.

- If one person overspends the family budget, and he can't make enough future spending cuts in his share of the family budget to pull the family back on budget (or go out and earn enough money to do it), then other family members will have to "pay the price" by not being able to spend money that they had planned to spend.
- It is important to save "our" money and use "our" savings to invest for "our" future financial security, and to pay for big ticket items "we" want to buy, e.g. a house, car, vacation, or someone's education.

Consider guidelines such as the following for making your decisions:

- The closer a decision is to mentoring and motivating a family member to make prudent money management decisions on his own, the better. To paraphrase ancient wisdom *"teach family members how to catch fish so that they can feed themselves rather than just giving them fish to eat"*.
- The more that prudent reasoning indicates you could avoid making a decision for a family member, the better his learning opportunity is likely to be.
- The more detail you think is prudent to share with a family member about a decision to be made, the better his learning opportunity is likely to be.
- The more that a decision helps a family member develop a sense of self-worth and personal responsibility for his actions, the better.
- *A compromise is often the optimal decision option, especially regarding family members.*
- Two acid tests of a good decision involving family members:
  - Sleep test: will you be able sleep well at night?
  - Mirror test: will you be able to look at yourself in the mirror in the morning knowing that you made the most prudent decision you could with the information you had at the time?

Keep in mind that you can't fire family for poor performance. The more you do to help family members become good financial managers, the more successful the family business will be.

Take the time needed to develop a family business plan and a family budget that support your personal business plan and your budget. <u>No matter how busy you and your spouse think you are, it would be smart to make time to do some financial planning</u>.

- *Develop a family business plan* for living the lifestyle you two dream of living together as a marital joint venture, e.g. individually satisfying working careers balanced with mutually satisfying personal lives, to have kids or not, where to live, type of housing, activities to do alone and activities to do as a couple, how long each person will work.
- *Develop a projected financial statement budget* for financing the life you two dream of living together.

Before beginning discussions with your spouse about a family business plan and budget:

- It would be helpful if each of you individually referred back to Chapter 4 and prepared a written business plan and projected financial statement budget for living life together as a marital joint venture the way you each visualize living it. Be guided by answers to questions such as:
  - What are my long term and ultra-long term objectives for things I dream of achieving:
    - By myself during my lifetime?
    - Together as a couple during our lifetime together?
  - How much annual revenue and net worth will we need to finance the lifestyle I

dream of us living in 30 years? During the last years of our lives?
- As you each write your own budget, be sensitive to how much of your combined family income your partner might desire to manage as if that money was his own business.
- Having individual written plans and budgets in hand will give you two a good foundation for discussing how to combine your individual plans and budgets into a mutually agreeable family business plan and projected financial statement budget.

Keep in mind that you and your spouse are likely to have some differences in your dreams about the life you would like to live together.
- *It is likely that each of you will need to <u>compromise</u>* – that is, each of you will need to give up a little of what you would have planned to do if you were living alone as a single person in order to reach agreement on a plan and budget for living together as a couple.
  - o As so many of our mothers told so many of us "you can't always have it your way".
  - o As sociologists tell us, members of a social group typically must make compromises in order to maintain social harmony, govern themselves, and achieve group objectives.
- Each person having his own ideas for a family business plan and budget written down will help you work together to reach compromises on a family plan and budget that provides each of you with the best opportunity to make each person's dreams come true.
- The more dominant the personality of your partner, the more important it will be for you to have your dreams for both (a) your life and (b) your life together as a couple, written down and fixed firmly in your mind in order to prevent regrets years in the future that you passively went along with everything your spouse wanted to do rather than working out compromises on a family plan and budget that factored in realizing your dreams.
- If you and your spouse have any significant differences in your dreams about the life you would like to live together, a professional in family counseling might be of great help in reaching mutually agreeable compromises on your differences.

If you have children old enough to understand the concepts of planning and budgeting, consider meeting with each child individually to discuss the basics of planning and budgeting.
- Explain the big picture purpose of planning and budgeting. Help each child understand:
  - o Every family has a limited annual revenue which puts a limit on how much money is available to allocate to buying and doing all the things that everyone in the family would like to buy and do each year.
  - o Each decision about spending money should take into account potential future spending decisions and how much money would remain available to spend during the remainder of each year.
- As appropriate for each child's age, maturity level, and understanding of the basics, encourage each child to write down his dreams, and work with him to prepare a plan and budget (in an age appropriate level of detail) that guides him toward making his dreams come true.
- Let each child know that to the extent of your ability to do so you will try to integrate his business plan and budget into the family business plan and budget. Discuss how seeking to integrate each family member's individual dreams into a family plan and budget can benefit each person:
  - o A family plan and budget that incorporates each child's objectives as much as possible will enable the family to provide each child with as much help as possible to realize his dream objectives.
  - o Everyone can work together as a team to achieve family objectives that everyone

would love to achieve, e.g. going on fun vacations, buying a boat.
- o "The more we all pull together in the same direction as a team, the easier it is likely to be for each one of us to get where we want to go individually".
- Commensurate with each child's age, maturity level, behavior you expect of him, and demonstrated ability to maintain family confidences, consider providing each child with excerpts from the family plan and budget in an appropriate level of detail.
  - o A 12 year old typically would receive less detail than an 18 year old.
  - o It might be best to start with:
    - Prudent strategies for living a happy, satisfying, financially prosperous life.
    - Generalities about certain family business plan and budget objectives, and specifics about action plan items directly relevant to him that he could use to guide his own planning.
- Establish mutually agreed upon:
  - o *Job descriptions* for each child, e.g. daily and weekly "duties" such as making his bed, keeping his room neat, and doing household chores. A job description could be as simple as a "to do" list.
  - o *Expectations of performance*: behavior you expect while each child is living "under your roof" (how many times have parents said "not while you're living under my roof").
  - o Compensation in the form of an allowance he might receive for doing his job in a satisfactory manner - if you believe in providing children with an allowance.

Have family business meetings on a regular basis, perhaps quarterly. Keep them short and lively so that people look forward to getting together. Include children as soon as they have a level of maturity to participate intelligently. Regular meetings will provide you opportunities to:
- Keep each person focused on the family business plan and projected financial statement budget.
- If there are any negative variances from the family budget (e.g. utility expenses), discuss how to work together to get back on track toward achieving budget objectives.
- Provide children an appropriate level of detail about progress toward achieving those family business plan and budget objectives that you have shared with them.
- Encourage each family member to:
  - o Resist peer pressure to make budget busting spending decisions.
  - o Share any valuable lessons he has learned since the last family meeting that he thinks other family members might find useful
- Build team spirit, and reinforce each person's sense of personal responsibility for the family's well-being. Emphasize that by virtue of living under the same roof:
  - o Each person's individual life becomes interwoven with everyone else's individual life to create a tapestry of family life.
  - o Family members can't live in their own "silos" oblivious to each other (as some people have trouble grasping, such as teens going through a "rebellious teen" phase).
- Coach and counsel family members on financial literacy.

Between family meetings:
- Review monthly bills and statements with your spouse (e.g. utility bills, joint bank accounts, joint investment accounts, and credit card accounts in which you both agree that you have a joint interest) and discuss variances from budget objectives.
- To help keep the idea of treating money management as a business percolating through

people's minds, include a "business take" in conversations about things going on in their lives (as opportunities present themselves). Point out how some aspect of budget management might be involved, e.g. where will the money come from to pay for an upcoming event, why does it cost what it costs. Seek "teachable moments".

- o Discuss how money is intertwined with specific events, e.g. how much it might cost a high school to field a football team and play a game, and how the school generates the revenue to pay the expenses.
- o Talk about how current events in the local, national and global economy are likely to impact their money in the near future and more distant future.
- o Point out examples of behavioral control systems at work in the world to manage organizations, such as checks and balances systems in business and government.
  - ▪ Discuss how elements of checks and balances systems might be incorporated in the checks and balances system of the family business.
  - ▪ Discuss how each person might help other family members resist temptations to spend unbudgeted money.
- • Seek ways to motivate each person to learn about business and financial management.
- • As it feels comfortable and prudent to do, have informal discussions with each child.
  - o Discuss his individual performance as a member of the family business team.
  - o If he has prepared his own plan and budget, ask if he would like to discuss his progress toward achieving his personal objectives.
  - o Use these conversations as coaching and counseling opportunities.
- • Use this book as a tool to stimulate discussions about money management. Leave the book out in a conspicuous spot that encourages people to pick it up and read it. Make it a family reference book from which people can springboard into the universe of other financial management educational resources available to them.

If you deem it appropriate, pay each child a weekly or monthly salary in the form of an allowance. Encourage each child to treat that money as revenue he has earned for his own personal financial management company. Then coach each child in how to:
- • Use a projected financial statement budget to help manage his money.
- • Generate a profit each year – i.e. save money.
- • Invest his annual profit in a savings or investment account in order to save up a cash reserve account to pay for expensive things he wants, or to build his net worth.

Nurture good lines of communication that help make family members feel comfortable talking with you about their thoughts and feelings about the money in their lives (and hopefully the other parts of their lives too). Good lines of communication help a family work together as a team.

Discourage manipulation games. Family member attempts to manipulate each other's behavior can be especially effective (and disconcerting) because people living together under the same roof can't get away from each other.

Cultivate a "just say no" attitude to playing manipulation games such as.
- • *Crying*: when we were babies we all learned how effective crying could be to manipulate our parents. Most little kids, and some adults, will continue to use crying as a manipulation technique as long as it works to help them get what they want. "Calculated" crying (crying as a means to achieve an objective) can be such an effective manipulative technique because it is so easy to do and it grates on listeners' senses like few other things. Listeners often cave in just to stop the crying. (I say calculated crying to differentiate it from the "autonomic" biological reaction of crying after a person has been

truly hurt or emotionally moved; more times than I can count I have observed calculated crying stop almost instantly after a person gets what he wants).
- *Whining* - a close cousin of calculated crying: the sound of protracted whining can push just about anyone out of a rational thinking business mindset.
- *Guilt trips*, e.g. "if you really loved me you would …"
- *Peer pressure*, e.g. "but everybody else is getting one, or doing it": this type manipulation attempt is closely related to, and often used as a part of, guilt trips.
- *Playing one against another*: children are famous for trying to lead Mom or Dad to think that the other parent had said it was OK to buy something or do something when in fact the other parent had said no such thing or had not even been asked.

Ways to deal with manipulation games include:
- As calmly and kindly as you can, describe to the manipulator the game you think he is playing - "call out" the person and "get it up on the table".
- Try to talk out what the person is trying to achieve in a calm, rational manner.
  - o Try to dig down to the underlying reasons why he wants what he is manipulating to get.
  - o If it is an expense matter, and you have begun to include the manipulative person in the family business planning and budgeting process, discuss how an unplanned expense would impact the family's plan and budget. You might try asking the person to develop a plan for revising the family's budget in such a way that the money he wants spent could be fit into the budget (e.g. how could he help generate additional revenue or what expenses could he contribute to trimming?).
- Don't cave in and do what the person wants you to do. Caving in sets a precedent that encourages future manipulation games. Make sure the person understands that his manipulation game won't work now, and that his behavior is steeling your resolve to be even more resistant to manipulation if he tries to play the same game again in the future.
- Manipulative behavior is likely to diminish after a person realizes that you are "on to his game", and that his manipulation games won't work.
- *The best defense against manipulation games is a good offense.* To help prevent as many manipulation games as possible, you might consider encouraging family members to use:
  - o The family's business planning and financial budgeting process as their preferred, and most effective, means to get what they want.
  - o A decision making process to make well-informed, well-reasoned decisions about what they want you to do or what they want you to buy for them, which will in turn enable them to present "business like" proposals to you for what they want.

Keep in mind that the longer a manipulation game has been going on, the tougher it will be to end the game. Keep your wits about you and be patient.

Promote the importance of preventative care and maintenance to minimize repair and replacement expenses. Explain how taking good care of family assets can minimize repair and replacement expenses, maximize the useful life span of each asset, and help free up money to do other things with family budget money. You might try parental classics such as:
- "Don't jump on the furniture" and "don't play ball in the house" – and explain why not to do it.
- "*A place for everything, and everything in its place*": don't leave bikes, sports gear and toys outside where they can be damaged by the weather, lost, or stolen.
- "Tell me when you see …" that something is broken or needs to be fixed so that we can

prevent small problems from growing into big expensive problems.
- "When you get out of the car make sure all the windows are closed and the doors are locked" so that rain doesn't come in and thieves are discouraged.

Also, promote preventive personal healthcare, e.g. healthy diet, exercise, enough sleep, brushing and flossing teeth. By means of taking good care of their bodies, family members will help minimize the family's medical and dental expenses.

Create and play family games that promote a business mindset. A few ideas to spur your imagination:
- *Dream vacation*:
  - Have each person prepare a plan and budget for a dream vacation and try to sell everybody else on his idea.
  - Work together to prepare a plan and budget for the next family vacation.
- *Money farmer*: have each person start with the same imaginary amount of "seed capital" money and see who can grow the biggest, healthiest crop of investments - an optimum combination of investment portfolio amount and age appropriate investment risk management over a specific period of time - a "growing season" (see Chapter 15 for more on investment management). Perhaps have each person defend his return on his seed capital with an oral presentation of his age appropriate investment portfolio and investment risk management strategy.
- *Economic Rorschach test: what do you see in these two adages*, "You get what you pay for" and "You can't get something for nothing"?
  - You might play this game in two ways.
    - Individually - ask each person to write an answer and then discuss each person's answer together. Encourage people to be as creative as they can be.
    - As a group - make it a debate with two teams. The two sides might debate true versus false, or, material (relative to things that cost money) versus spiritual (relative to things that don't cost any money).
  - Two teaching points to make in this game:
    - Understand the concept of best value.
    - Business should be enjoyable.
- *Business news reporter*
  - Have each family member pick a news story about financial or operations management of a company, sports team or league, government entity or government program, etc.
  - Have each person analyze the facts in the story he picks:
    - Identify what might be accurate information or inaccurate information, misleading statements, selective use of statistics/numbers, etc.
    - Do his own "fact checking" research – confirm accuracy of the facts with at least one other source (within reasonable limits of time and effort).
  - Then prepare a short presentation on lessons he thinks family members can learn about business and/or financial management from the story.
  - Then as a family group critique (NOT criticize) each person's analysis, and discuss lesson(s) to learn.

For people who are not yet married

Marriage is a legally binding contract.
- Marriage legally binds two individual lives together in a joint venture of partners in a couple.
- The legal rights and responsibilities of marriage play a huge part in the financial affairs of each partner.
- When partners are starting out in any new business there are smiles and happy handshakes all around. Everybody "loves" each other. They "feel" good at the outset. There is a "honeymoon" period.
- All too often it is AFTER a business has been operating for a while that partners discover things about each other that they hadn't known before they "got in bed together". The truth comes out as they try to resolve differences of opinion about decisions to make regarding business plans, budget management, investment management, etc. Then the practical realities of the legally binding business relationship sink in.
- Partners in a business relationship going bad often feel trapped because there would be so many legal and financial ramifications if they tried to get out of the relationship. Don't let that be you in your love relationship.

Love can be awfully expensive. As cold and callous as that sounds, for the sake of your financial well-being you would be well advised to think about how your love life might impact your financial position immediately after a marriage and years out in the future.

Talk about money as soon as prudently possible after you feel your relationship has evolved into the serious stage. Polite dating etiquette says you aren't supposed to talk about money. OK. But, after you begin to consider a decision about "tying the knot" with someone, you have moved past dating etiquette territory. You have moved into serious life altering decision making territory. You need to talk about money. Financial compatibility is a crucial factor in a happy, healthy, long term relationship.

Don't rush into marriage. Take enough time to _use your decision making process to make a well-informed, well-reasoned decision_.
- Marriages entered into in haste in the emotional heat of the moment tend to end in divorce at a higher rate than marriages in which the partners have taken enough time to get to know each other.
- As an age old adage says _"love is blind"_.
  - o The emotion of love can put blinders on the ability of two love birds to see how different they may be in many practical aspects of day to day living, including money management.
  - o Give yourself enough time to let the temporary blindness induced by a new love run its course so that you can see your future life together as clearly as possible.
- _Get past the infatuation stage so that you will be able to evaluate the person as a prospective joint venture partner with a rational thinking business mindset._
  - o Get past "she's so beautiful and sweet", or "he's so handsome and strong".
  - o Get past the human biology of sexual attraction.

Gather enough information to make a well-informed decision about marriage.
- Each person's visions for the future, e.g. lifestyle, career path aspirations, children?
- Are you psychologically independent equals in your current relationship?
- Could one person be playing a rescuer role and the other a rescued role?

- Could one person be playing a provider role and the other a dependent role?
- How empathetic have you each been in your lives to date? Will you each be trying to understand the other's dreams, plans, needs, wants, likes, and dislikes?
- Are you both good at the art of compromise?
- Is either person prone to take hard line stands that "I'm right and you're wrong"?
- What do you each believe about money? Is there more to life than money and the material things it can buy? Is money a tool to do good in the world or a tool of the devil?
- What do you each know about the fundamentals of financial management?
- Family lifestyle to which you each became accustomed while growing up?
- Money management behavior of parents and siblings (as role models and potential sources of future pressure on the way family money is managed)?
- Each person's financial management track record?
  - o Each person's current financial position?
    - ▪ Balance sheet: cash reserve account(s), investment portfolio, debt, etc.
    - ▪ Statement of income and expenses for the prior 1 year.
  - o Where would each of you place on a "frugal saver - free spender" continuum?
  - o Do you each live below your means – living a less expensive lifestyle than your income would allow you to live?
  - o Self-discipline: to stick to a budget; to withstand peer pressure to spend money?
  - o Personal credit score (learn how credit scores have been used as an indicator of future behavior)?

If you are on the younger side of life, you might talk to older married people who have successfully maintained a happy, healthy, long term relationship.
- Pick their brains about how they have managed the money in their marriage.
- Learn what they think they did right – behavior to consider emulating.
- Learn what they think they did wrong – mistakes to avoid making yourselves.

To help you each avoid mistaken impressions and assumptions it might be wise to discuss points of disagreement that couples have frequently experienced after they got married.
- Will each person have an equal say in decisions that will have significant impact on family finances?
- How will you settle differences of opinion about money management and other matters of significance?
- Career plans?
  - o A two income earner family in which both spouses work?
  - o A family in which you agree that one person will stay at home while the other person works at a job to generate the family's income, such as a "stay at home parent" family?
- Children – to have them or not? If children are planned:
  - o Number of kids desired? Be sure to research and discuss the financial expenses of a child, e.g. medical care, food, clothing, education. This sounds brutally cold and calculating, I know, but, the hard fact is that kids are expensive.
  - o How to provide for their education - public school, private school, home school?
- *If one or both of you already has children, research and discuss the issues related to creating a blended family (put the children first or years later you will regret you didn't).*
- Where you will live?
- Type and size of home?
- Division of household labor, e.g. cooking, cleaning, childcare, home maintenance?

- How will spending decisions be made about typical family expense items, e.g. eating out at restaurants versus cooking at home, expensive resort vacations versus camping, financing a new car purchase with a loan versus continuing to drive an old car for a longer period of time while saving up cash to buy the new car?

Seek classes, podcasts, books, articles – whatever materials you can find – that are intended to (a) help couples research potential points of disagreement in a marriage and (b) facilitate a healthy discussion of these potential points of disagreement.

<u>An objective third party such as a professional family counselor or pastoral counselor might be of great help to</u>:
- Facilitate a calm, rational discussion about money and marriage compatibility.
- Minimize the risk that an open and honest discussion of potential points of disagreement could flare up into emotional arguments.

After gathering enough information to make a well-informed decision, carefully evaluate your compatibility in areas such as:
- Love – however you define love.
- Companionship - feelings of comfort and joy in each other's company.
- Ability to provide each other emotional support through life's highs and lows.
- Ability and willingness to take care of each other in times of need, especially as you age.
- Children.
- Money management.

Don't plan on changing your partner's behavior after you marry.
- All too often one person thinks he can get the other person to "see the light" - to come around to his way of thinking and acting. But, nobody can change anybody else's behavior. Each person is the only person who can change his own behavior.
- If you don't think you can live with your prospective partner exactly as he is today, you might be better off not entering into a legally binding marriage.

Consider a "prenuptial agreement" – an agreement as to what would happen to each person's net worth and future income if the marriage ended in divorce,
- A fairly worded prenuptial agreement can help minimize the risk of financial harm that a divorce could cause.
  - Many people have lost up to one half of their net worth as the result of a divorce, and many others have been saddled with alimony payments that continue to drain their future annual income.
  - Many people's dreams about life in their senior years have been shattered because divorces cost them so much money.
- It might be money well spent to get some professional advice, perhaps from a professional family counselor, or an attorney who has developed a good reputation as a "counselor" (an attorney who specializes in advising people how to avoid legal problems) rather than as a "litigator" (an attorney who specializes in winning cases in court after legal problems have arisen, e.g. a "divorce lawyer").

For parents

Your role as a parent:
- Learn what various professional family counselors and psychologists think the role of parents should be in the lives of their children.
- One aspect of the parental role should be to prepare children to live happy, healthy lives as financially self-sufficient adults. A few suggestions to consider:
    o Be a good role model for money management and all other aspects of living a good and satisfying life - lead by example.
    o Educate - be the best teacher, coach, and counselor you can be.
        ▪ Begin each child's financial management education as early in life as he can understand what you are talking about.
        ▪ Follow the lead of schools. Expose each child to a progressively more complex "grade level" education in the fundamentals of good money management as he grows up and matures.

Learn also what professional family counselors and child psychologists think about:
- How a disciplined family environment might help children learn.
- How having structured routines might help free a child's mind to think more creatively.
- Practicing "tough love" as needed:
    o Saying "no" and "depriving" your child of what he wants, and then using those experiences as teaching moments to explain the reason(s) why you decided to say no (thereby minimizing use of the parental classic "because I said so").
    o And then after having said no, having the mental toughness to not cave in to the subsequent crying, whining, and other manipulation games that children often try to play in follow-up attempts to get what they want.

Treating family money as a business can provide a framework for teaching your children how to become financially self-sufficient adults.
- *Think of your children as trainees in your family business.*
    o Develop "job descriptions" – perhaps including things such as:
        ▪ Performance of designated household duties / chores.
        ▪ Marketing - helping to build a good "brand name" for the family in the local community.
        ▪ Learning how to become a happy, healthy, financially independent adult.
    o Empower each child with a sense of authority and responsibility to participate in the family business planning and budgeting process to an extent appropriate to each child's age, maturity level, and ability to keep confidences confidential.
    o Provide them with "career path" opportunities to work their way up the family business management ladder from trainee to senior manager running their own "divisions" within the company (as they gain ever greater maturity and financial management expertise and experience).
    o Prepare them to "spin off" their divisions as independent companies - to move out of the house and become self-sufficient adults.
- Consider providing a salary in the form of an allowance and performance bonuses in the form of tickets to movies and events they want to see, going out for ice cream, etc.
- Consider encouraging children to earn their own money doing part time jobs outside the family after they become of legal age to do so.

Encourage each child to use a business planning and budgeting process to help make his dreams come true (in a level of detail appropriate for each child's age and level of maturity).
- Just as your money is your business, so too each child's money is his business.
- Begin talking to each child about planning and budgeting as early in life as you think he will understand the concepts.
- Encourage, but don't push, each child to begin using his own business planning and budgeting process, and a formal decision making process, after he has reached a level of maturity at which you think these life management tools would help him make decisions about what he does in his life - school, sports, career, money, etc.
- *Regarding a business plan*, encourage each child to dream big about what he wants to do in life (keep in mind that as kids grow up and get exposed to more and more of life, they frequently change their minds about what they want to do in life).
  - o You might suggest, and perhaps nudge, your child toward doing what you think is best for him to do, but consider the wisdom of not pushing a child too hard to do what you want him to do.
  - o *Remember, it's his life, not a do-over for you of your life.*
- *Regarding a projected financial statement budget*, help each child prepare a budget having an age appropriate level of detail. Then you could help each child add more detail each year as he progresses through school grades, gains progressively greater understanding of the budgeting process, and eventually begins to earn money from jobs outside the family.

Consider sharing excerpts from your family budget with your children in an age appropriate level of detail (e.g. utility expenses, school expenses, family entertainment expenses, auto insurance expenses as they near driving age) as a means to help them learn how to manage their own budgets – a level of detail that (a) you think each child could understand at his age and maturity level, (b) you think he would keep confidential, and (c) you would feel comfortable sharing. *Each parent who decides to share some level of detail about the family budget will need to find the right balance between sharing too much information and not giving children enough information with which to learn how to manage their own budgets.*

Encourage your children to defend themselves against the peer pressure of friends by thinking and acting as presidents of their own personal financial management companies.
- Encourage them to think independently and make well-informed, well-reasoned decisions about what they do (e.g. in school, at home with friends) and how they spend money.
- As early in life as they can understand the concept of peer pressure, help them learn to manage the peer pressure they are likely to feel from friends and schoolmates to conform, especially in regard to buying things and doing things that cost money:
  - o Wearing the same clothes that "everybody else wears".
  - o Doing the same things that "everybody else does".
  - o Buying the same things that "everybody else has".

Consider encouraging your children to do some research with you on the peer pressure that all of us are prone to feel as we seek acceptance by friends, neighbors, co-workers, schoolmates, etc.
- Research what psychologists and family counselors have to say about the impact of peer pressure on the thinking and behavior of all people, and young people in particular.
- Research what sociologists and anthropologists have to say about peer group pressure that most of us humans feel to be accepted as members of all sorts of groups.
- Research the physiological development of the human brain as we age; particularly the idea that the prefrontal cortex (which is primarily responsible for reasoning, complex

decision making, and inhibiting behavior driven by emotion) typically isn't fully developed until we reach our early twenties.

- You might try telling your children about peer pressure you can remember feeling from your friends and schoolmates when you were their age (unless you were an extremely rare breed of kid who felt no peer pressure to conform and "be one of the gang").
- You might also try doing some "field research" when you are out of the house together:
  o Observe how young people in a group tend to dress and talk in the same ways.
  o Notice that even groups of people who appear to be rebelling against society as "non-conformists" tend to conform in the ways that they dress, talk, and behave. *Talk about why rebels typically conform so much in the ways they rebel.*
  o Encourage your children to actively observe what people are doing and actively listen to what they hear people saying, and discuss whether those people are thinking and acting independently or "just going along with a crowd".
- And you might try watching some of your children's favorite television shows and online entertainment with them with an intent to spot <u>occasional</u> opportunities to discuss how peer pressure seems to be influencing what characters are wearing, saying, and doing.
- CAUTION: don't go overboard with this idea of doing research together. If you try it, be subtle. Try to avoid the classic teenage reaction of "just leave me alone". *Seek inclusion in your children's lives - avoid exclusion.*

Help your children learn to think about why things cost what they cost, and about value received for money spent.

- When shopping together, encourage your children to try to determine the "best value" among comparable items - best value being the optimum combination of price, quality, and the practical utility and personal enjoyment likely to come from using the product.
- When grocery shopping, discuss the many factors that go into determining the price of various food and beverage items, and how to make best value choices that fit within the family's monthly food and drink budget to get the nutrition each family member needs.
- When dining out at restaurants, discuss the many factors that go into determining the price of menu items (e.g. food costs, compensation of kitchen staff and servers, rent, utilities, profit acceptable to restaurant owners) Also, discuss the meaning of the word "tip" (<u>t</u>o <u>i</u>nsure <u>p</u>rompt <u>s</u>ervice), the services you are paying for with your tip money, and the amount of tip to leave.
- If a child breaks a lamp while playing or loses a bike or toy, discuss the cost of fixing or replacing the broken or lost item, and how that cost impacts the family budget as a <u>lost opportunity cost</u> – the ability to spend that money on something else.
- When children are mature enough to maintain family confidences, consider discussing utility bills with them, e.g. phone, internet, television, electricity, gas, water.
  o Help them learn about the costs of the utilities they use, and think about ways they could help minimize those costs.
  o A good learning experience might be to have them research best value choices of phone, internet, and television service providers.
- As each child is learning to drive, review your auto insurance policy with him. Discuss how much insuring him will cost, and how much an accident or a speeding ticket would increase that cost. Consider making him pay for some or all of the gas he uses.

Consider helping each child open a bank account, and perhaps get a debit or credit card, after he is legally old enough to do so and mature enough to learn how to use these financial management tools responsibly.

- Teach each child how to use these tools prudently before getting any of them.

- *Ask your banker and financial advisor for advice and recommendations* about:
    - o When and how to help children secure a bank account and a debit or credit card.
    - o Financial literacy education materials they have available to help young people learn how to use these financial management tools responsibly.
    - o Ways that parents might monitor their child's use of these financial management tools and how parents might help protect their children from using these tools irresponsibly.

Thoughts on securing a best value return on money you invest in your children's education.
- Encourage your children to:
    - o Think about how important a good education is likely to be as a qualification they will need in order to get jobs they desire and advance along the career path they desire to take toward their dream jobs and dream income.
    - o Do the best they can in their studies in order to prepare for the job-seeker competition they are likely to face for jobs they desire.
- Encourage your children to take classes offered in their schools on subjects such as:
    - o Personal financial literacy: if such a class is not yet offered in your children's school become an advocate to get a class offered.
    - o Economics, finance, and business management, such as classes offered in association with Junior Achievement.
- Research the vast amount of information available regarding the management of education expenses. As your children become old enough to think critically about their education, have them do their own research into <u>all</u> the costs of their education, and ways they might help pay those costs and minimize the need for a student loan, e.g. earning a scholarship, saving up their own money, getting a job(s) while in school.
- If you are thinking about sending your children to private schools instead of public schools, make sure of your reasons. Would you be sending them to private schools because you made a well-informed, well-reasoned decision that it would be in their best interests or because of social pressure you feel from family or friends?
- Unburden yourself of any internal pressure you might put on yourself to send your children to college, and any external pressure you might feel from family or friends. Many young people might be better off in the long run if instead of going to college immediately after high school they pursued opportunities such as:
    - o An apprenticeship program offered by an employer. In an apprenticeship program an employer hires a person as an apprentice employee and pays the person while he is learning job skills through on-the-job training. Research:
        - ▪ The historical role of the master-apprentice system as the primary means of "knowledge transfer" - passing down job skills from one generation to the next.
        - ▪ The success of apprenticeship programs in Germany and other countries.
        - ▪ Information about apprenticeship programs available on the United States Department of Labor website.
        - ▪ Apprenticeship programs available in your state and your community.
    - o Attending a trade school to get training and/or certification that would enable them to get well-paying jobs.
    - o Getting a job for a year or two in order gain real world and business experience while they are trying to figure out what they want to do in life; perhaps a job away from home that would provide an opportunity to expand their horizons and "see the world".
    - o Joining the Armed Forces to explore as a career, to gain career training and

experience while in service, and to qualify for education reimbursement benefits offered while in service and after service.
- If a child is planning to go to college, discuss the economic and utility value of that educational experience. Encourage him to:
  - o Plan ways to minimize college expenses, e.g. take pre-requisite classes at a lower cost, local community college, and then transfer to a college of choice to get a bachelor's degree; attend a public, in-state college instead of a private school.
  - o If he will need to take out a student loan to help finance his college expenses:
    - ▪ Prepare a projected statement of income and expenses budget that factors in repayment of the loan while also paying all his other expenses during the term of the loan.
    - ▪ Develop a career path plan for getting a job(s) that has reasonable potential to generate the annual revenue that would be needed to repay the loan as well as pay all his other expenses during the term of the loan.
  - o Do a cost-benefit analysis to determine if the knowledge he gains and his "college experience" will generate enough benefit in his life to justify the cost.

Give your children enough opportunity to learn invaluable "street smarts" – how to manage their lives and their money "out in the real world" away from the protective nest of the family.
- Research what various child psychologists, public safety professionals, and experts in other fields advise parents about protecting their children.
- Don't be "overly protective" - overly protective being a highly relative term that means different things to different people. Each parent must decide for himself what an appropriate level of protection is for his children, and what would be overly protective.
- *Raise your children with prudent caution, but don't "baby" them.* Treat them as intelligent young people. Consider giving them "as much rope" (as much freedom and responsibility) as they can handle as early in life as you think they can handle it.
- *Bite your lip and let your children make small money management mistakes* (but NOT big mistakes that could cause serious financial harm). If a child wants to blow his own money (e.g. allowance or job income) on things that you don't think make good business sense, you might let him do that. That would help him learn about the lost opportunity costs of spending money - living without money until he generates additional revenue.
- Consider encouraging each child to get a job outside the family as early in life as prudently reasonable. A job can provide an invaluable opportunity to learn street smarts. The process of finding a job also will help him learn about career path planning.
- *Children who have grown up in overly protective families (i.e. lived "sheltered" lives) without much opportunity to learn street smarts are at a competitive disadvantage when they get out into the business world.*

After your adult children have become old enough to have their own jobs, encourage them to become as financially self-sufficient as possible as soon as possible.
- The longer that you continue to provide financial support for adult children, the less money you will be able to save for your future financial security and your financial freedom.
- If an adult child expresses a desire to continue living with you, and you make a well-informed, well-reasoned decision that it would be best for your adult child to do so:
  - o Think long and hard about how much financial support to continue providing, e.g. room, board, clothing expenses, wireless electronic services.
  - o Work with him on his career path planning to become financially self-sufficient.

For sons and daughters who are financially dependent upon their parents

Think of yourself as a <u>trainee</u> in your family's business <u>and</u> the <u>president</u> of your own personal financial management business (read Chapter 14).
- You have two financial management roles to play within your family:
    - Trainee in your parents' family business: scripted by your parents family business plan and projected financial statement budget for their lives.
    - President of your own company: scripted by your personal business plan and projected financial statement budget for your life.
- Think of your parents as the founders and senior partners of your family's business. Their positions give them the authority to make the final decisions about the family's money.
- Plan a "career path" that moves you up the organization ladder of your family's business from entry level trainee, to junior partner, to senior partner; and then eventually "spin off" on your own as the president of your own personal financial management company.
- If your parents give you an allowance, think of that allowance as a salary. The more "work" that you do to "earn" your "salary" (e.g. household chores such as making your bed, washing dishes, taking out the garbage, cutting the lawn) the stronger your case will be to negotiate an increase in your compensation for your work (see Chapter 14).

To earn promotions in your family's business and gain more control of the money in your life (e.g. to increase the allowance you are paid, and increase the weight your opinion carries in family money management decision making):
- Exceed your parents' expectations of you (see Chapter 14).
- Play by the rules of expected behavior within your family (a good reason to study sociology and learn about "norms" of acceptable behavior within small groups).
- Demonstrate mature control of your emotions.
- Demonstrate good common sense in what you say and do.
- Demonstrate the use of a decision making process (see Chapter 7) in making well-informed, well-reasoned decisions about things such as:
    - Behavior with your parents and brothers or sisters.
    - Friends you choose.
    - Personal hygiene habits.
    - Clothing you wear.
- Demonstrate good effort to learn in school.
- Demonstrate diligence in practicing sports, playing a musical instrument, etc.
- Build a good performance track record doing household chores and performance of any jobs you get outside the family.
- Demonstrate responsible use and care of furniture, toys, sports equipment, electronic equipment, family car, etc.
- Demonstrate a good working knowledge of the fundamentals of financial management in conversations with your parents. *The smarter you sound about financial management, the more your parents are likely to listen to you about money matters.* Learn about:
    - Prudent use of a bank checking account.
    - Prudent use of credit and debit cards.
    - Benefits of accumulating a cash reserve and a diversified investment portfolio.
- Demonstrate prudent financial management behavior, e.g. prudent spending and saving habits, and accumulation of a cash savings reserve.
- Prepare a business plan for the life you dream about living and a projected financial statement budget to finance your efforts to achieve your business plan objectives (see

Chapter 4). This would likely impress the heck out of your parents.
- *The more that you can demonstrate you know about financial management, and the more that you demonstrate use of that knowledge to guide your own prudent financial management behavior, the faster you are likely to earn promotions in the family business.*

NOT doing certain things can also help you earn promotions in your family's business:
- Avoid "childish" behavior.
- Don't whine, pout, pitch fits, throw tantrums, try to play one parent off against the other, or ceaselessly beg for things that your friends have or that you see advertised.
- Don't display an immature attitude of "I know better than you".
- Don't display "teen angst" nor an attitude of "nobody understands me".
- Don't rebel against authority. Work "within the system" in your family and in school.

Learn and practice good communication skills. The more effectively that you can communicate your well-reasoned thoughts to your parents, the more likely you are to:
- Obtain the money you want for entertainment, clothes, social events, etc.
- Influence your parents' decisions on family financial matters such as vacations, new electronic equipment, and cars.

Effective communication requires that:
- You clearly communicate your message in both verbal and body language.
- You listen attentively to what your parents are saying (and not saying) in reply.
- You confirm you have the correct understanding of the messages your parents intend to communicate to you - minimize the number of times you tell your parents that you misunderstood what they said.

A few thoughts on developing your communication skills:
- Practice – by having intelligent discussions with your parents, teachers, etc.
- Learn to actively listen to what your parents are saying, and to ask follow-up questions that clarify what they meant to say or that give you deeper insight into what they said.
- Identify people who speak well. Pay close attention to the ways they "frame their ideas" and use their vocabulary. Use them as role models.
- Study public speaking and debate. Learning these skills will enhance your ability to organize your thoughts and communicate them effectively. If your school doesn't offer these subjects, seek an organization in your community that does offer opportunities to learn and practice these skills, e.g. Toastmasters, community center, religious institution.
- Take writing classes: English composition, business letter writing, creative writing, etc. Learning how to organize your thoughts and effectively communicate those thoughts in writing will have a carry-over impact on your oral communication skills.
- Practice, practice, practice.
- Two bonuses:
  o Developing and practicing good <u>oral</u> communication skills will have great economic value for you in the future with college admissions personnel, employers, co-workers, customers, sales people, and service providers.
  o Developing and practicing good <u>written</u> communication skills will impress older people in the business world who think that too many younger people are lacking in their ability to write effective business emails, letters, reports, and proposals.

Try to understand how tough it is to be a good parent.

- *Most parents try to be the best parents they can be, but no parent is perfect - just as no child is perfect.* We are all loaded with human weaknesses and we all make mistakes.
- Parents go through continuous "on the job training" (OJT) in their jobs as parents. From generation to generation, OJT is how we parents have learned to become the best parents we can become.
- Most parents know that they don't know all there is to know about being a parent, and they often suffer mental anguish when they make parental mistakes (whether or not they admit their mistakes to their children). But good parents try to learn from their mistakes to become better parents.

Try to understand how tough it is for parents to walk the line between:

- Making "the right" decisions for you <u>and</u> allowing you to make your own decisions; even decisions that may not turn out so well in the short run, but allow you to learn valuable street smarts "in the school of hard knocks".
- Letting you go so you can grow <u>and</u> holding you back to protect you.
- Giving you the freedom to experience the joy of going off on your own outside the house to do whatever you want to do <u>and</u> keeping a close eye on you outside or keeping you indoors in order to keep you safe. PHYSICAL DANGER is a fact of life for young people today. It is brutally tough on parents to cope with the dangers they know are out there.

Based upon my own first-hand experience learning to be a parent, and observations of friends learning to be parents, I can tell you that parenting can be incredibly tough at times, particularly when telling a child something he doesn't want to hear.

- The parent's perception might be "I am doing this because I think it is in my child's best interest, be that the child's health, safety, learning to become a good person, etc."
- While the child's perception might be "my parent doesn't understand me. He is just being mean, jealous, etc."

Appreciate the lost opportunity costs in time and money that your parents incur because of you.

- <u>Try to grasp the full scope of *"parental sacrifice"*.</u>
- Understand that (a) your parents will never be young again and (b) they can't spend the same dollar twice. Ask yourself:
    - o What opportunities do they give up to do things they would like to do?
    - o What do they give up buying for themselves so that they will be able to afford to buy things for you, or give you money, or spend family money the way you want it spent.
- Money they spend on you today is money they can't save and invest to help provide for their future financial security and their future financial freedom.
- Appreciate the mental stress that children can cause their parents when children beg, whine, or otherwise pressure parents to spend money that would strain the family budget.
- Be thankful for whatever financial support your parents provide you. Don't take it for granted. *If you want to score huge maturity points with your parents, say "thank you", and tell them you understand and appreciate all the financial support they provide for you and the sacrifices that they make for you.*

To get a better appreciation of your parents, talk to other adults you know well enough to ask how their perceptions of their parents evolved as they aged, e.g. grandparents, aunts, uncles, religious leaders, teachers, coaches. *Parents tend to get smarter in our minds as we age.*

Also understand that no child can fully appreciate what it is like to be a parent until he becomes a parent himself. Countless parents have said these immortal words:
- "Just you wait. You'll see what it's like to be your mother after you have children".
- "I hope you have a child just like you. Then you'll see."

Talk to your parents about what it is like for them to be your parents.
- If you and your parents haven't talked much in the past about things that are important to you, be especially tactful so as to avoid hurting, offending, or angering them.
  - o Observe how level headed and understanding your parents have been in prior conversations with you, other family members, their friends, and neighbors.
  - o "Read" how your parents are reacting to each conversation you begin with them, and guide the conversation accordingly.
- Ask them what they think their roles are as your parents.
- Ask what their parents and grandparents were like as parental role models for them.
- Discuss parental control over the way you live your life.
  - o Discuss the difficulty your parents face in making decisions about how to protect you from harm.
  - o Discuss the life experiences it takes for young people to learn the street smarts that are needed to lead happy, healthy, prosperous lives as financially self-sufficient adults.
  - o Discuss the term *"helicopter parents"* - parents who are said to "hover" over their children and try to exert too much control over their children's behavior, thereby limiting their children's opportunities to learn how to live out on their own as independent, financially self-sufficient adults.
- After your parents realize that you are actually trying to understand their perspectives on being your parents, their respect for your growing maturity is likely to rise. Empathy (trying to see a situation through the eyes of another) is a strong signal of maturity. Learn about the power of empathy to connect people.

Talk about what life was like for them as they were growing up. All of us go through stages of life as we grow up physically and mature mentally. It's never all peaches and cream for any kid. Your parents may well have suffered through some (maybe many) of the same emotional highs and lows you have felt or are feeling - insecurities, fears, anger, young love, expectations that got crushed, unrealized dreams, ... Since you have to live with the results of their life experiences when they were young, you might as well learn all that they are comfortable sharing with you about what they went through on their way to becoming your parents. This will help you gain perspective on why they do what they do as your parents, and help you gain greater empathy for them while you are living with their decisions and the way they treat you.

Talk to your parents about what it is like for you to be their child.
- Talking to your parents about your life might seem monumentally tough at first, but it is likely to get a lot easier after you "break the ice" the first time, and it is likely to generate significant benefits for you.
- Your ability to talk about the emotionally loaded issues with which you grapple will demonstrate to your parents that you have been gaining a high level of maturity.
- When you think your parents are making a parental mistake, try discussing your thoughts with them in a calm, mature manner. Try offering them a well-reasoned, businesslike "constructive critique" of their parental behavior. *Learn about the big difference between constructive critique of performance and criticizing performance, and how to effectively present a well-reasoned critique – a very mature, and very valuable, life skill to possess.*

- Understand that when many (if not most) of us older people were young and learning about ourselves and the world in which we lived, we found it tough to open up and talk with our parents about what we truly thought and felt. Many of us just didn't even try, and we lost out on an opportunity to learn some things and get some help that might have made our lives a lot easier. Try your hardest to "open up" to your parents.
  - o Many parents lament that they don't know what their children are thinking and feeling.
  - o Most parents would love to have their children open up and talk about what is going on in their lives.

Most young people struggle with all sorts of emotionally loaded issues, and many feel like they are the only person who has ever felt like they do. As we said above, you may well discover that when your parents were your age they struggled with some of the same issues with which you are now struggling. They might be able to share with you how they dealt with issues such as:
- Feelings of insecurity about personal appearance, clothes, athletic ability, etc.
- Peer pressure to join cliques and do things that "everyone else is doing".
- Not having had the same things that "everyone else had".
- Young love / puppy love / raging hormones.
- Feelings of rebellion against being told what to do.

Ask for your parents' advice, and listen to it. *After they recover from fainting in shock the first time you ask for their advice, the respect they have for your maturing mind is likely to skyrocket.*

Study biology to learn about the biological challenges that all young people (not just you) must deal with while growing up. The ways in which each young person deals with the biological challenges of being a human animal influences the way his parents deal with him.
- Learn how hormones and emotions can overpower rational thinking in all of us, especially young people. Parents were kids. Your parents are likely to remember how raging hormones and youthful emotions drove them to say and do things that they later regretted and/or laugh about today.
- Learn about the physical maturation process that our bodies go through as we age from infancy to fully grown adult. In particular, learn about the development of the human brain.
  - o Science tells us that the brains of most humans aren't fully developed until people reach their early to mid-20's.
  - o Learn about the development of the brain's prefrontal cortex, the part of the brain that is primarily responsible for our ability to reason, plan, and control our moods – the brain functions that are most critical for managing our lives and our money. It is human biology why we can't reason with most three year olds, and why teenagers can have such tough times with mood swings.
  - o The more you understand about the biological development of your brain the more likely it is that you will want to develop and use a formal decision making process (see Chapter 7) to help you make good decisions about what you do and minimize the "youthful" impulsive behavior mistakes you make.
- To gain a broader perspective on what you are going through as the human child of human parents, study the growth and maturation process of the young in other species of mammals - particularly at what stage in life they begin to learn survival skills, how they learn those skills, how early in life they must begin using those skills to take care of themselves, and how early in life they typically start to live their lives as adults.

Study psychology to learn about the mental maturation process.
- Learn how we humans gradually develop the mental skills and abilities that it takes to become successful business people and money managers.
- Learn about the "stages of life" we humans pass through as we age.
- Keep in mind that parents continue to grow in mental maturity throughout their lives.
  - Many (most?) parents do a lot of growing up after they have had their first child and begin bearing the burden of responsibility of caring for a child.
  - It might be just as tough for your parents to learn to talk with you about what they truly think and feel as it is for you to learn to open up to them.

Study sociology to learn how the society in which your parents were raised and the community in which your family now lives influence the varying ways people treat you as you age.
- *Child*: The communities in which you live sets out societal expectations as to how your parents should treat you at various ages as you "grow up" into being considered an adult.
- *Minor*
  - The law says you are the ward of your parents until you reach "legal age". They are legally responsible for your well-being and your actions, e.g. if you break a window with a ball, they are responsible for the financial damages.
  - Laws set minimum age requirements for younger people to have certain jobs and sign legal contracts.
- *Dependent*: the Internal Revenue Service (IRS) considers you to be a dependent while you are dependent upon your parents for financial support.

Learn about generational differences - typical differences in thinking and behavior of people born in different generations, e.g. Greatest Generation, Baby Boom, Generation X, Millennial, and Post-Millennial (a/k/a Generation Z or the iGeneration).

Study history to gain perspective on your life as a young person today. Learn how the roles of young people in society, and adult expectations of young people, have evolved through the years.
- The concept of being a "teenager" didn't come about until the early to mid-1900's. Learn how the concept came into being.
- Learn how children worked in family businesses as soon as they were physically able to do so in order to help their families survive, e.g. farming, herding livestock, and helping in small family owned businesses (artisan manufacturers, merchants, etc.). Parents needed their children to help them do the daily work that was necessary to keep family members fed, clothed, and housed; and to continue running family businesses as parents aged and could no longer do all the work that was required.
- Learn the history of child labor laws, and how prior to those laws being instituted many children had to do hard work in factories and the military in order to help their families survive. Learn about jobs in which children's smaller bodies and hands allowed them to do certain jobs that the physical size of adults precluded them from doing as well, e.g. boys who worked as "powder monkey's" handling gunpowder on old warships, and girls who worked in textile and clothing factories.
- Learn how mechanical inventions in agriculture, transportation, manufacturing, and communications contributed to changes in the ways children have been treated in their societies through the years. In particular learn how the industrial revolution impacted the lives of children.
- Learn why summer vacations from school came into being (in large part so that children were available to work on family farms).
- Get a good appreciation for how many things that we take for granted today would have

seemed like luxuries to young people in the past (if they could have even conceived of such things): availability of higher education, free time to just hang out, indoor toilets and water faucets, cars in which to get around, hand held electronic devices, etc.

- The more privileged you have been in your upbringing, the more important it is to gain an appreciation for how children around the world today still must work in family businesses, on family farms, and as employees in "sweat shop" manufacturing facilities in order to earn money that their impoverished families desperately need.

Develop your "street smarts". Get out of your house and into the world as much as your parents agree makes good sense for you. Interact with as many different types of people as you can in as many different social settings as is practical for you. Learn how "the real world" works and how to manage real world situations you encounter. Gain as much life experience as you can as soon you can. Consider:

- Joining clubs and teams, getting active on committees, and seeking leadership positions.
- Joining scouting programs.
- Volunteering to work with a local community service group, charitable organization, religious institution, hospital, or your school.

Get a job as soon as your parents agree it would be prudent for you to do so. A job can help you:

- Learn about the business world and money management through on-the-job training experiences (OJT).
- Develop and practice business skills, e.g. specific job skills, how to build a network of business contacts, negotiation and compromise.
- Develop your self-confidence - so important for so many young people.
- Begin your journey toward becoming financially self-sufficient. As you earn money, consider saving some of your earnings rather than spending all that money, and start building up a cash reserve and perhaps an investment portfolio (which would provide a golden opportunity to develop investment management expertise and experience).

A few thoughts about seeking a job:

- The process of seeking a job can help you:
  - o Learn about planning a career path toward a job you would love;
  - o Gain experience in how to work the hiring process to your advantage.
- You might try to find a job in an industry in which you think good and satisfying work is being done, and explore jobs you think might lead to good career path opportunities.
- You might try to get a fun job that would provide good life experience, e.g. lifeguard, work in a camp or resort, assistant or apprentice of a local craftsman/musician, coach of a team of younger children.
- Historically, all sorts of jobs have been available to young people of a legal age in restaurants, construction, etc.
- If you aren't old enough to get a job working for an employer, consider creating your own job working for yourself as an entrepreneur in your neighborhood shoveling snow, mowing lawns, babysitting, pet-sitting, etc.
- If you can't find a job that pays money, you might try to get an unpaid position as an "intern". If there aren't any unpaid intern positions to be had, you might try being creative and think up an unpaid position that a prospective employer hadn't thought about and try to sell that employer on how you could help them.

Learn all you can about the budgets and financial management of organizations in which you participate, e.g. sports teams and leagues, clubs, scouting program, religious institution.

Seek to learn whatever information people are willing to share with you about the organization's budget, financial reports, and financial management.

- Learn what the term "financially solvent" means. Determine if each organization is financially solvent - are they generating enough revenue to pay all their expenses and save some money each year; do their assets exceed their debts?
- Ask if you can see the organization's most recent year end financial statement, and what this report "tells" each person who reads it about the organization's financial position.
- Ask if you can see the organization's projected financial statement budget for the current year. Ask who prepares each year's budget and what is involved with preparing budgets.
- Ask how the organization's revenue is generated and expenses are managed.

If you are thinking about taking on student loan debt to pay for college:
- Identify the reasons why you want to go to college, such as:
  - Earn a degree that will help you achieve your career path, business plan, and projected financial statement budget objectives?
  - Experience the joy and satisfaction of studying a subject you love?
  - Enjoy the once-in-a-lifetime college experience?
  - Defer the need to go out into the world and earn your own living?
- Plan ways you could minimize your expenses thereby minimizing the amount of money you would need to borrow. A few ideas to consider:
  - Take pre-requisite classes at a lower cost, local community college, and then transfer to your college of choice to get the degree you want.
  - Attend an in-state public college instead of an out-of-state or private college.
  - Continue to live at home while going to school.
- Prepare a projected statement of income and expenses budget that factors in repayment of the loan while also paying all your other expenses during the term of the loan.
- Develop a career path plan to secure jobs that have reasonable potential to generate the annual revenue that would be needed to achieve your budget objectives during the term of the loan.
  - If you plan to earn a degree in a subject you love, but in which relatively few well-paying jobs are available, consider planning a career path that begins with one or more jobs that would be likely to pay you enough money to achieve your projected statement of income and expenses budget objectives.
  - Then, after your loan is repaid you could plan to segue into a job you love using the college education you purchased.

Understand that "the world doesn't owe you a living".
- Use your youth wisely to prepare for living the evolving lifestyle you dream of living as you age, and earn the money you dream about having to finance your dream lifestyle.
- Avoid the sense of entitlement that is creeping into the minds of too many people today.

The less experience you have had earning money without help from your parents, the more important it will be to:
- Develop a business mindset - an entrepreneurial "can do" mindset that you can do whatever you plan to do.
- Not believe any mass media commentator who says that the younger generation may not be able to do as well financially as their parents' generation. Such a prophecy could become true only if enough young people believed it, and didn't try hard enough to make their dreams come true.

Regarding parents, siblings and other close relatives

There will be times when some people will feel a need to make a decision about providing financial support to a parent, brother, sister, or other close relative.
- Parent(s) facing financial challenges presented by issues such as having spent all of their financial nest egg, the aging process, medical expenses, or the passing of a spouse.
- Brother, sister, or other close relative who:
  - Lost a job through no fault of his own because an employer went out of business or reorganized and eliminated his job.
  - Suffered a debilitating disease or accident that prevented him from working.
  - Had his home and possessions destroyed by a fire or a weather disaster.
  - "Needs to be rescued" because he dug himself into a deep financial hole.

There is no simple answer to the question of how much financial assistance to provide to a family member. This is a question people have wrestled with through the ages. The answer for you in your unique situation should be decided based upon factors such as:
- Practical limits of financial assistance your budget could afford.
- Your personal beliefs - what you believe is the right thing to do. How would you live with yourself over the long years ahead?
- Family pressure - what the rest of your family would think is the right thing to do. You would have to live with them after making the decision. What impact would your decision have on your family life?
- Social norms - what your friends, neighbors, and community in general would think is the right thing to do.

"An ounce of prevention is worth a pound of cure."
- Making a decision about how deep a person should dig into his pocket to provide financial support to a loved one can be so loaded with emotion that it becomes incredibly hard to make a well-reasoned, financially prudent decision.
- To help minimize the risk of having to make such an emotionally agonizing decision:
  - *Do all you can do as early in your life as you can do it to motivate family members to:*
    - *Use a business planning and financial budgeting process* to plan how to achieve financial well-being, and diligently work toward achieving their plan and budget objectives.
    - *Use a formal decision making process* to make financially prudent decisions throughout their lives.
  - Share this book with family members. Encourage them to use it to help manage the money in their lives.
- Knowing that you had done all you could do over the years to help family members avoid financial difficulty could help ease your conscience if you ever had to make a gut wrenching decision to provide less financial assistance than a loved one wanted or needed because your budget just couldn't afford it.
- You might include a contingency plan in your business plan and projected financial statement budget for providing financial support to loved ones, such as how you might provide room in your home for loved ones who needed housing, and building an emergency cash reserve fund to provide financial support.

<u>Consider the benefits of a professional financial advisor and/or family counselor</u>

A variety of professionals might be able offer you advice and counseling regarding various family financial matters, such as a:
- Financial advisor.
- CPA or accountant.
- Marriage counselor, family counselor, or pastoral counselor who has a reasonable level of expertise and experience in family financial matters.
- Attorney who specializes in family practice, e.g. prenuptial agreements, estate plans.

A financial advisor and an attorney familiar with estate planning and income tax codes can be valuable people to have on your business team to provide advice on matters such as:
- Which family members should own which assets.
- Estate planning: gifting of money, trusts, wills, etc.

If a serious disagreement, dispute, or financial problem were to arise within your family, a professional advisor / counselor might be able to help you defuse an emotion laden financial time bomb before it blew up your loving relationship.

An objective third party professional can help family members:
- Cut through the emotional part of family life in order to identify the root causes of money management disagreements, disputes or problems.
- Identify and discuss decision options to resolve disagreements, disputes or problems in a rational, unemotional way.
- Make prudent decisions that work out as well as possible for everyone involved.

Business people hire professional mediators and arbitrators as needed to help resolve their disagreements and disputes. Follow their lead and consider hiring a professional financial advisor or a family counselor as needed to help resolve any serious financial disagreement, dispute or problem that might arise with a family member.

There are thorns on beautiful rose bushes that require us to use care to avoid hurting ourselves when we are in rose gardens. So too, *money can put thorns on marriages that require us to use care to avoid hurting ourselves when we are in marriages.* An objective third party can help guide a couple in working their way through thorny money management issues without hurting each other.

Chapter 17. Plan for Financial Freedom, Not Retirement

Plan for Financial Freedom, Not Retirement

Adopt a mindset of pursuing "financial freedom" rather than "retirement".
- Thinking in terms of "financial freedom" contributes to a positive mindset - to continue living a life full of joy in pursuit of making dreams come true.
- Thinking in terms of "retirement" contributes to a negative mindset - to stop doing; to begin pulling away from active involvement in life; to consciously begin the process of dying.
- Financial freedom can be defined in different ways by different people. One definition might be *"financial freedom is the freedom a person would have to do whatever she dreams of doing without any limitation imposed by a lack of money"*.
- Financial freedom requires different amounts of money for different people. The amount of annual revenue and net worth that you think you will need to live in financial freedom is likely to be different than the annual revenue and net worth I think I will need.
- Having all the money you will need in order to do whatever you dream of doing in life will be a function of the cost of whatever it is that you dream of doing.
  - o There are hugely significant things that would cost very little money.
  - o There are frivolously fun things that would cost a small fortune.
- *An aspirational long term objective for financial freedom* might be along the lines of "generate enough passive income each year to pay all the expenses of the lifestyle I dream of living" (see pages 5 and 6 of this chapter for more on passive income).
- Many of us will not have enough time in life to achieve the complete financial freedom we aspire to achieve, but if we plan well and work diligently to achieve our projected financial statement budget objectives, it is likely we will:
  - o Achieve a lot more financial flexibility than we would have had if we had just let our lives unfold without actively using a planning and budgeting process.
  - o Live a happier, more comfortable lifestyle than we would otherwise have lived.

Plan for the next chapter in life, not the last chapter.
- *Don't plan to "retire"*. Plan for the "next chapter" in your life".
- *The sooner you begin planning for the later years in your life, the more financial freedom you are likely have to do whatever you want to do during the next chapter in your life.*

Think of a job as a "fountain of youth" – be that job as a paid employee or unpaid volunteer.
- Our brains, like our muscles, require exercise in order to maintain peak performance capability and avoid atrophy. Meeting the daily challenges that a job presents can provide one of the best forms of brain exercise to help keep our minds sharp. *"Use it, or lose it."*
- Jobs increase our opportunities to:
  - o Keep up to date with all that is new in this world - new technologies, new gadgets, new ways to do things, new discoveries, etc.
  - o Interact with people of all ages - especially younger people. Such interaction can help prevent our thinking from getting stale and dated by freshening it up with a steady stream of new ideas from a variety of people who have a variety of perspectives on current events and the way the world around us is evolving.
- Getting up each morning to go to work helps provide structure for people's lives. It can help older people avoid the mental drift I have seen in some retirees – some of whom admit to having a tough time keeping track of what day of the week it is.

- Follow the role model of successful companies that re-invent themselves as needed to keep up to date with the world in which they do business and to continue prospering.
- "If you aren't growing, you are dying."

In addition to providing fountain of youth benefits, a job that pays money can provide significant financial benefits:
- A predictable stream of revenue.
- Employee benefits such as medical insurance.
- A hedge against inflation - as inflation increases the costs of things, financial compensation might also increase.

Use a career path planning process to get to a job you love so much that you wouldn't want to "retire" from it - or at least like the work so much that you would be enthusiastic about doing it each day. *"If you love what you do, you will never work a day in your life."*

If the idea of having a job as either a paid employee or unpaid volunteer doesn't fit into your plan for the next chapter in your life:
- Plan to do things that help keep your mind sharp and your body strong.
- Plan to stay connected with younger people as a means to help you:
  o Stay young at heart.
  o Keep up to date with the exciting new things in life.
  o Avoid a slow, steady evolution into becoming "a grumpy old codger".
- Plan to get out of your home and into the world as much as possible.
- In the objectives section of your personal business plan, write a "bucket list" of things that you have always wanted to do, and action plans to do as many of them as possible.

If *you are not planning to continue working at a job as a paid employee in order to generate one part of a diversified stream of annual revenue, plan extra conservative long term and ultra-long term projected financial statement budget objectives*:
- Plan for the lowest range of investment income that professional financial advisors recommend we factor into our long range planning (e.g. lowest interest rates and lowest dividend yields).
- Plan for the highest range of expense increases that professional financial advisors recommend we factor into our long range planning (e.g. highest rate of inflation, typical medical expenses of older people).
- Plan for an extra-large liquid asset financial contingency reserve.
- Plan to spend as little of your investment nest egg as possible. Don't plan to "spend every penny". Plan to let your nest egg continue serving as a financial contingency reserve:
  o That continues to earn money for you as a component of a diversified stream of annual revenue, and protect you from unexpectedly lower revenue generated by the other revenue sources you had included in your budget.
  o That can be tapped if needed for unexpectedly higher expenses and emergencies.

"Life is long" and it keeps getting longer.
- My understanding is that the average human life expectancy in 1900 was about 47 years, and in 2000 it was about 78 years (slightly longer for women and slightly less for men). That's an increase of about 60% in 100 years.
- If the average life expectancy continued to increase at the same rate, the average life span would be about 101 years in 2050 and 125 years in 2100. Many of us would live longer.

Learn about research being done that is likely to contribute to increasing life expectancy, retention of mental acuity, and maintenance of an enjoyable quality of life in our older years:
- Prevention and cure of disease.
- Identification of genetic markers that provide early warnings of potential health problems that we can work at preventing.
- Surgical replacement of worn out body parts.
- Control of the cellular aging process.
- Use of mental exercise to keep minds sharp.

Learn about and practice preventive healthcare habits that doctors say can help us maximize life expectancy and mental vibrancy, such as:
- Healthy food and beverage choices.
- Regular exercise.
- A good night's sleep each night.
- Avoidance or moderate consumption of beer, wine, and alcohol.
- Avoidance of tobacco products.

Plan for a life longer than the current average life expectancy.
- It probably would be prudent to plan to live at least 10 to 20 % longer than the current average human life expectancy.
- The younger you are, the longer the life you should plan on living.
- Even if your family's genetic history is such that most family members haven't made it to the average life expectancy, it would be prudent to plan for a life longer than the current longest average life expectancy. "Better safe than sorry".

To stimulate your thinking about financial planning for the later years in your life, learn about the history of the concepts of "retirement" and "pension plans".
- Learn about the impact of the Industrial Revolution (IR) and the invention of machines on the way people earned their livings as the IR progressed through the 1700's and 1800's, and especially as the IR kicked into a higher gear of evolution in the 1900's.
- Prior to the IR people typically continued to work for themselves as farmers, craftsmen, shopkeepers, etc. for as long as they were physically able to work.
- During the IR increasing numbers of people shifted from working for themselves to working for industrial company employers.
- My research indicated that the concept of retirement from a job didn't come into being until the late 1800's - early 1900's. Not being an expert on the subject, I think reasons that the concepts of "retirement" and "pensions" came about may have included:
  o "Depersonalization" of employees on assembly lines – many employers thought of employees as replaceable cogs in the machinery of production - a commodity.
  o "Muckraker" journalists and authors wrote stories that raised public awareness about atrocious working conditions and corrupt politicians.
  o Populist and Progressive social movements emerged and sought improvements in working conditions and worker compensation, and political reform, e.g. The People's Party and Theodore Roosevelt's "Bull Moose" Progressive Party.
  o Labor unions were formed to advocate for workers' rights, fair compensation, and government regulation of employment practices.
  o Retirement with a pension is likely to have come about in large part as a defensive measure in response to the efforts of progressive social movements and labor unions. Adopting the practice of retirement is likely to have helped enable employers to replace older, theoretically less productive workers with younger,

theoretically more productive workers without looking like villains to journalists, progressives, labor unions, and government officials.

- Factors that likely contributed to enactment of The Social Security Act in 1935:
  - o Response to the number of older people who were losing their jobs and their incomes because of:
    - ▪ The Great Depression.
    - ▪ Machines doing work that people had previously done by hand.
    - ▪ Increasing numbers of industrial companies adopting mandatory retirement practices.
  - o In1935 the average life expectancy for men and women combined was only 62. Full Social Security benefits were set at age 65. The percentage of the population collecting benefits was affordably low relative to the working population who would be paying Social Security taxes.
  - o To gain perspective on just how "old" people in their 60's were considered to be back in 1935, watch some films made in the 1930's and early 1940's in which scripts had actors talk about how "old" they were while still only in their 50's.

Advertising has played a role in manipulating our thinking about retirement.
- All sorts of companies that seek to sell their products and services to older people use the idea of retirement in their marketing.
  - o Advertisers try to create the image of happy retirees "living the good life" in a "life of leisure" using the advertisers' products and services.
  - o To get some perspective on how advertisers can shape our thinking, learn how advertising for Coca Cola contributed to shaping our image of Santa Claus today.
- Advertising never touches on the idea that too much leisure can get pretty boring. Have you ever been on a vacation and begun looking forward to going back home?
- Keep in mind that the cute little grandchildren we see with their grandparents in so many commercials will eventually grow up. They won't stay frozen in time as eternal five year olds. (Speaking of grandchildren, they are in a continuous process of learning and intellectual growth as they age. So too should adults as we age. Retiring from the paid or volunteer workforce lessens the opportunities that older people have to live a life of continuous continuing education that stimulates our intellectual growth as we age.)

Learn about factors that are likely to shape the evolution of the concepts of retirement and pensions in the future.
- Learn how experts in various fields think technology and demographics will shape the future of work, retirement, and pension plans in the future.
- Likelihood that the average life expectancy will continue to increase and that on average people will be able to retain their physical fitness and mental acuity longer than today.
- Economic sustainability of employer funded defined benefit pension plans and Social Security (as we know it today) - the number of retirees is increasing and retirees are living longer which is requiring increasingly greater amounts of funding.
- Impact of an increasingly global economy on employer practices and decisions:
  - o Employer compensation practices in the United States must remain competitive with employee compensation in other countries where compensation is lower.
  - o Employer decisions to switch from employer funded defined benefit pension plans to employee funded retirement plans such as 401(k) plans as a means to help manage expenses and remain competitive in the global marketplace.

Prepare an ultra-long range projected financial statement budget

Prepare an ultra-long range projected financial statement budget for financing the lifestyle you dream of living during the last year of your life.
- Plan conservatively. Be a pragmatic pessimist regarding your future revenue and expenses:
    - *Plan for less annual revenue than you can reasonably expect to generate.*
    - *Plan for more annual expenses than you can reasonably expect to incur.*
- Develop a reasonably conservative Plan A projected statement of income and expense budget AND an even more conservative Plan B budget for what you could do if:
    - Your actual annual revenue decreased below your projected revenue; or
    - Your actual expenses increased above your projected expenses.
    - You needed to get a Plan B job that paid less than the Plan A job you had planned to be doing in your later years because physical or mental impairments diminished your ability to do the Plan A job.

Plan to generate a predictable, diversified stream of revenue from sources such as:
- Passive revenue:
    - Social security (consider waiting to file until the age at which your annual benefit payments would reach the maximum amount for which you would be eligible).
    - A pension.
    - Investments (stocks, bonds, annuity(s), real estate, etc.)
- Actively earned revenue from a job.

The farther out into the future we try to plan:
- The tougher it becomes to project (a) how current events will play out and impact our revenue, (b) economic conditions, and (c) how our life circumstances will change.
- The more conservative we should be in planning for annual revenue.
- The more secure we are likely to feel if we plan for income from multiple sources.

If you plan to continue working at a job to generate part of your diversified stream of revenue:
- Develop a career path plan that advances you toward your dream job. The sooner you begin planning how to get to a job you love, the more time you will have to get there.
- It would be great if this job could pay you as much money as you were earning during your "peak earnings" years, but the job satisfaction and free time parts of a total compensation package might become more valuable than money to you as you get older.
- Think about creating a job for yourself as an entrepreneur doing something you love to do, e.g. turning your favorite hobby into a job. You might consider teaming up with one or more friends who share your love of whatever it is you dream about doing.
- Keep in mind that our human bodies grow older each day.
    - As time passes many of us will become physically or mentally unable to continue doing the work we currently do and earning as much money as we currently earn.
    - As you revise your career path plan over the years, develop a Plan B to segue into a job that you could continue do if and when the need ever arose.

A few thoughts on planning for passive revenue from your investments:
- <u>A professional financial advisor can be of great help in planning for investment income</u>.
- *Projections of revenue from other sources such as a job, social security, a pension, etc. will help you determine the amount of investment income you will need in order to achieve the total revenue objective in your projected income statement budget.*

- There are two general ways to generate revenue from an investment portfolio:
  - o Collect dividends, interest, and/or rent from assets you continue to hold.
  - o Sell investments such as stocks, precious metals, collectibles, etc.
- *If you plan to sell some of your investment assets or spend some of your cash savings in order to achieve your projected income statement revenue objective each year, take great care in planning what percentage of your investment portfolio you might be able to sell or withdraw each year without depleting your investment portfolio.*
  - o Research the advice in materials published by reputable professional financial service companies regarding the percentage of an investment portfolio that might be sold or withdrawn each year without depleting the portfolio.
  - o Then consult with a professional financial advisor (as your budget allows).
  - o Lean toward using the most conservative advice.
  - o *A personal plea* - please plan to sell as few of your nest egg investments as possible. It breaks my heart to hear so many stories of older people who chewed through their savings too fast and now remorsefully think of themselves as being broke, especially when better financial planning, started earlier in life, could have helped prevent many of them from thinking they are broke.
- *Revenue from investments could be lower than planned for extended periods of years.*
  - o Dividend and interest rates go through cycles of ups and downs, and some of the down phases of the cycles last a lot longer than others.
  - o During the periodic recessions and depressions that we must plan for in our budget projections, prices of individual stocks that we had planned on appreciating in value are likely to get driven down.
- <u>While you are physically able to do so, plan to build the largest possible investment portfolio.</u>

When planning to generate revenue from "fixed income" sources, learn about, and factor in, the risks associated with receiving a continuing stream of revenue from sources such as:
- Social Security
  - o We are going through a demographic shift in population. There may be too many older people drawing benefits, and not enough younger workers paying taxes, to keep the Social Security program as it exists today fully funded in the future.
  - o Benefit payments might need to be cut back, perhaps by "means tests" such that people who have higher incomes from other sources get lower benefit payments.
- Pensions - learn all you can about:
  - o Impact an employer's bankruptcy can have on a retiree's pension. Companies and government entities that offered pensions have gone bankrupt in the past.
  - o Risk of insolvency of a pension plan - not enough assets to pay benefits.
  - o Risk of restructuring pension benefit payments: increasing life expectancy is likely to increase the number of future pensioners, which could possibly strain the ability of an employer to pay future retirees the same pension benefits that they pay to retirees today.
  - o The Pension Benefit Guaranty Corporation and the benefits that might be available in the event of a bankruptcy or insolvency years out into the future.
- Annuities
  - o Insurance companies can fail. If you decide to invest money in an annuity, choose an annuity issued by a financially strong insurance company (as rated by A.M. Best Company).
  - o Remember diversification. If you are considering investing a significant portion of your investable money in annuities, be careful about investing too much of

your investment portfolio with any one insurance company. It might be prudent to invest money in two or more annuities issued by two or more highly rated insurance companies.

Plan for increases in your expenses, such as:
- Regarding things you buy regularly (e.g. food), consider the impact of:
    - <u>Increasing demand</u> from an increasing global population, particularly in developing countries in which the annual income of the average household is increasing at a fairly rapid rate.
    - <u>Decreasing supply</u> over the long term as the result of causes such as natural resources being depleted, oceans being over-fished, and desertification of arable land.
- Transportation: cars (purchase price, fuel and maintenance); public transportation (planes, trains, buses, subways); requirement of alternate forms of transportation when many of us are no longer able (or allowed) to drive a car.
- Housing: utility prices (electricity, gas, water, telephone/television/internet); real estate taxes; hired help that may be required to maintain our homes as we age and experience a decline in physical abilities; assisted living or nursing home facilities.
- Taxes (income taxes, sales taxes, gasoline taxes, etc.) and public facility user fees.

In particular plan for the likelihood of significantly increased medical and personal care expenses.
- The older we get, the more physical and mental ailments we are likely to experience.
- The younger that people are the harder it is to grasp the idea of what happens to human bodies as we age - our bodies wear out. They don't last forever.
    - As time passes our bodies typically need more medical and dental "maintenance and repair work" to keep them functioning well.
    - Genetics give some of us better odds of having lower medical expenses for longer periods of time, but eventually "time catches up" with most of us.
- Things we did when we were younger often come back to haunt us with expensive physical and mental ailments: sports injuries, use of alcohol, use of tobacco, sunburns and sun tans, over-eating, not getting enough sleep (chronic sleep deficit), etc.
    - People can minimize their medical expenses as they get older if they give more thought to the "price they will be paying in the future" (in the form of aches, pains, disabilities, and lots of dollars) for things they do when they are younger.
    - In particular, people in their teens and early twenties need to think about the price they may have to pay in the future for doing some of the famously risky things that young people are prone to do.
- *Insurance*: learn about the types and costs of insurance that might be available to help you transfer some of the risk of rising medical and personal care expenses, such as:
    - Medicare, Medicaid, and other government programs.
    - Medicare supplements insurance.
    - Short term disability.
    - Long term disability.
    - Long term care.

Keep in mind that inflation has spiked rapidly at times in the past. It might do so again at times in the future. It would be prudent to take this into account as you decide just how conservative you should be in preparing your long term and ultra-long term projected statement of income and expense budgets.

Develop a business continuity plan

Develop a business continuity plan for management of your money during times when you are not able to carry out your money management duties as president of your company. Consider the following elements in your business continuity planning:

- Management succession planning
- Legacy planning
- Exit planning

Management succession planning
- Management succession planning involves preparing one or more people on your business team (e.g. family member, financial advisor, professional trust company, CPA, attorney) to be ready, willing, and able to succeed you in managing your financial affairs for you during times you are not able to manage them yourself, such as if:
    o You suffer a physical or mental impairment that reduces or completely takes away your ability to manage your money on your own.
    o You want to back away from your business for an extended period of time, e.g. take an extended dream vacation, volunteer to help with a charitable organization's work in a remote location, get away from it all on a long spiritual retreat.
- One key element in your management succession planning might be to create a family business culture that helps each family member gain as much financial management expertise and experience as possible.
- Another key element might be to develop the capabilities of your business team to the point that you can "manage by exception" – which means (a) delegating to team members as many of your routine financial management duties as possible, (b) stepping back and letting them do their assigned duties, and (c) getting involved with their performance of their duties only to the extent that exceptional circumstances dictated your involvement.
    o The idea of management by exception is to "work yourself out of your job" to the greatest extent possible.
    o Delegate, motivate and empower team members to manage as many aspects of household budget management, home maintenance, investment management, etc. as you think would be prudent.
- Let each professional service provider (e.g. financial advisor, accountant, attorney) on your business team know who else is on your team. Encourage these team members to communicate and coordinate their work on your behalf as much as possible BEFORE you might need or want them to act on your behalf. The better they get to know each other, the better they will be prepared to coordinate their efforts to handle your financial affairs for you when you need them or want them to do so.

Choose one person to serve as a successor Chief Executive Officer who could step in to perform your CEO duties for you. This is important for managing the risk that you might become physically or mentally impaired to perform your CEO duties (by medical condition, serious injury in an accident, aging, etc.). A few ideas to research and discuss with one or more close confidants and perhaps an appropriate professional service provider:
- Pros and cons of choosing prospective CEO candidates such as a:
    o Family member (e.g. spouse, parent, adult child, or other close relative) perhaps the person who has the most financial management expertise and experience, has managed her life most prudently, and has the best ability to manage your other business team members.

- o Professional service provider who specializes in managing people's financial affairs when they need such help, such as a professional trust company, financial advisor, CPA.
- If you choose a family member, when and how to tell the person she is your choice.
  - o Explain the duties she would assume, and get her consent to accept the position.
  - o After the person accepts the responsibility of being your successor CEO, educate her as to your financial affairs, and work together to put in place the legal powers she will need in order to start performing CEO duties after a need arises.
- If and how to tell family members you didn't choose about your choice.
  - o This might be emotionally loaded news for people who thought of themselves as the logical candidate to be your successor CEO.
  - o People who are not the "chosen one" might have their feelings hurt, and some might even go so far as to become vindictive. Personally telling family members in advance might help prevent family strife after you are gone.
  - o Be sure to have well thought reasons for your decision that would be hard for anyone to refute.

There are different ways to legally delegate authority to someone to act as your successor CEO. A few options to discuss with your spouse (if you are married) and one or more professional service providers trained in such matters (e.g. family attorney, CPA, or professional trust company):

- *Revocable living trust* in which to hold specific assets, with a trustee you appoint to manage those assets should you become unable to manage them yourself.
- *Durable power of attorney* that gives a person legal authority to act on your behalf to manage the assets you do not place in a trust, as well as your other financial affairs should you become physically or mentally impaired (often the same person who is trustee of a revocable living trust).
- *Will* in which you give an executor authority to distribute your assets according to your written instructions (often the same person who is trustee of a revocable living trust).

Plan for the risk of disability as much or more than you plan for death.

- Based upon my years in the surety industry, I can tell you that many business owners don't give as much thought as they should to how their businesses would carry on without them if they were to become physically or mentally impaired to manage their businesses for an extended period of time.
- Your death will be important for your heirs, but not for you. You won't be here.
- *Planning for disability* IS critically important for you. You will still be here.
- Plan how to maintain your financial and physical well-being if you should suffer a long term impairment of your capability to generate actively earned income, to manage your financial affairs, or to advise medical professionals about your medical care. Consider:
  - o *Long term disability insurance* to provide a continuing stream of revenue if your ability to work should be impaired by serious illness or accident.
  - o *Long term care insurance* to help pay the expenses of home care assistance or an assisted living facility or nursing home if you should become unable to perform all the basic activities of living on your own, e.g. preparing and eating meals, bathing, dressing, walking.
  - o A revocable living trust and a durable power of attorney to provide for management of your financial affairs.
  - o *Living will (advance directive)* to provide medical professionals with guidance as to what to do for you if you could no longer instruct them yourself.

Legacy planning

Legacy planning involves planning what you want to leave behind after you're gone. Following are some ideas to stimulate your thinking as you plan what you might want to leave behind:

- Material asset legacies:
  - o Financial inheritance - investment portfolio, personal residence, personal possessions that have sentimental value to specific people, etc.
  - o Gifts to charities, religious institutions, causes in which you believe.
  - o A non-profit trust or foundation that you establish and fund.
  - o A body of creative work (e.g. photographs, writings, paintings, music) that can serve two purposes:
    - Give your heirs "something of you" that will last their lifetimes.
    - Inspire your heirs to use their creative talents.
- Non-material / non-financial legacies:
  - o A role model for a life well lived.
  - o Wonderful memories for people to cherish.
  - o A body of good deeds done - seeds of good sown so that those who follow you might grow those seeds into greater crops of good.
  - o Helping people prepare to lead happy, satisfying, financially prosperous lives by means of providing them opportunities to:
    - Acquire a well-rounded education that includes the liberal arts, business management, and financial management.
    - Practice their life management, business management, and financial management skills and abilities.
    - Gain "street smarts" through experience.

Working to create a non-material legacy can also provide you with significant rewards while you are still "alive and kicking":

- An invaluable good feeling in your heart that emanates out to those around you as "good vibrations" that light up your life as they brighten their lives.
- Acting as a magnet to help passively attract good luck into your life.

Develop a wealth transfer plan (a/k/a estate plan). Ask yourself questions such as:

- How might I "invest" money in my heirs to help them become financially self-sufficient before I die, thereby minimizing their need for a financial inheritance?
- Should I "gift" assets to people or non-profit organizations while I am still alive?
- How can I help my heirs gain the financial management expertise and experience they would need in order to manage a financial inheritance prudently?
- How might money that I bequeath to my heirs affect their behavior and impact the quality of their lives after I am gone?

Research and consider the use of two written documents in your wealth transfer plan:

- *Revocable family trust*
- A legal *will* that:
  - o Appoints an executor to manage the distribution of your assets.
  - o Instructs your executor as to which of your assets you want distributed to whom.

Professionals such as a financial advisor, trust company, and attorney can be of invaluable help in preparing a wealth transfer plan and preparing the appropriate legal documents.

"Exit" planning

"Exit" planning means planning for your death – decidedly not fun, but important.

Thinking about one's own death can be such an emotionally loaded subject that I will just suggest a few topics below for you to think about and discuss with your spouse and/or other close confidants on your business team, *and with professional service providers who specialize in the subjects mentioned.*
- Plan how you would like to manage:
  o The terms of the process of your dying that are within your control.
  o The cost of the terms of the process of dying that you choose.
- Legal documents that can help you control the terms and the cost of the process of your dying:
  o *Living will*: to advise your family and doctors about your preferences for end-of-life medical care in case you become incapacitated and can't tell them yourself what you would like them to do, such as:
    ▪ Just let me die naturally at home surrounded by my loved ones; or
    ▪ Take me to a hospital and do everything you can to keep me alive as long as you can, e.g. artificial life support systems, intravenous hydration and nutrition, pain management medication.
  o *Durable power of attorney*: to authorize a person to make decisions for you and manage your affairs for you if you could not do so yourself, such as if you became incapacitated for a period of time prior to your death.
    ▪ Manage your financial affairs for you.
    ▪ Make decisions about the medical care you receive, and tell medical service providers what they think you would want done, in situations which were not specifically addressed in your living will.
- Arrangements for:
  o Funeral services, a wake, and perhaps a reception after the wake (e.g. an "Irish wake"), if you so desire them.
  o Disposition of your body, e.g. burial, cremation, "anatomical gift" of body parts for transplant or your entire corpse for medical research.
- Life insurance:
  o To help cover expenses that your family might have to pay after your death, e.g. repayment of debt, taxes, uninsured medical expenses, funeral, wake, disposition of your body.
  o To provide financial support to your family if such financial support makes good financial planning sense in light of their current financial positions and the financial inheritance you will be leaving to them.

A few personal thoughts about life insurance:
- A number of variables should be considered when making a decision about buying life insurance, among them:
  o Current financial positions of your heirs.
  o How much would your heirs "need" life insurance proceeds in light of their current financial positions, and money and other material assets you will be leaving to them?
  o How significant would the dollar amount of life insurance proceeds be relative to the dollar value of money and material assets that heirs will be inheriting – relatively insignificant or a real big deal?

- o Debt that family members would be obligated to repay after you die, e.g. mortgage on the home they share with you, loan on a car they will continue to need.
  - o Number of people dependent upon you for financial support, and the likelihood that after you die those financial dependents would be able to get jobs that would pay them enough money to replace the financial support you had been providing them.
  - o Your lost opportunity cost on the money you would need to pay for the insurance? Could you invest that money in other ways that would generate greater economic utility, joy, and satisfaction while you are still alive?
  - o Your age. The cost of life insurance increases as a person ages.
- Minimize the need your heirs would have for life insurance proceeds by helping them become as financially self-sufficient as possible while you are still alive.
- *Discuss the subject of life insurance with financially savvy business team confidants before talking to a life insurance agent about a prospective purchase.* Get the opinions of different people from their different perspectives as to what they think you should do about life insurance.

Again, a DISCLAIMER:
- I am neither licensed nor certified to offer you advice about estate planning, medical insurance, long term care insurance, life insurance, or any of the other topics mentioned in this chapter and this book.
- *The intent of this chapter and this book is simply to motivate you to think about the ideas mentioned, and to then talk to licensed and certified professionals who specialize in the various subjects mentioned, such as*:
  - o *Professional financial advisor.*
  - o *Attorney who specializes in estate planning.*
  - o *Professional trust company.*

Chapter 18. Risk Management

Build risk management into your business plan and financial budget

Whereas some measure of risk is involved with pretty much every facet of human life, risk management should be built into pretty much every facet of our business plans and projected financial statement budgets, and incorporated into our decision making processes.

- *The purpose of risk management planning* is to identify the perils we face in our lives and use our planning and decision making processes to minimize the risk of those perils causing us harm. Learn how the insurance industry defines the terms peril, risk, and hazard, and then develop your own "working definitions" to help guide your risk management planning. Suggestions for working definitions to consider are:
  - o Peril: something that could cause you harm.
  - o Risk: probability that a peril will cause you harm.
  - o Hazard: condition that increases the risk that a peril will cause you harm.
- Planning to manage the risks we face in life requires that we think about things that could hurt us. Not fun.
- And, because thinking about things that could hurt us is not fun, many people avoid planning how to minimize the risks they face. Big mistake. Risk is inherent in living. If we close our eyes and pretend risk isn't there, risk isn't going to go away.
- Don't let thinking about what might possibly cause you harm suck you down into a mental funk of negative thinking. Rather, get yourself into a rational thinking business mindset and plan how to manage the risks you identify in your life so that you can go about living a joyful, satisfying, and financially prosperous life.

Learn about the following basics of <u>risk management</u>:
- *Risk identification*
  - o Identify the significant perils and hazards in the lifestyle you are living today and in the investments you currently own, and in the lifestyle you plan to live in the future and the investments you plan to own in the future.
  - o Then evaluate the risk (probability) that each peril might cause you harm.
- *Risk avoidance:* seek to avoid whatever risk you think would be prudent to avoid in your life.
- *Risk transfer:* seek to transfer risk that you think would be prudent to transfer to others through vehicles such as insurance and contracts.
- *Risk management*: manage the risk you willingly decide to accept or have no alternative but to accept in order to minimize the probability of suffering harm.

Learn about "enterprise risk management" as practiced by corporate risk managers – a "holistic" approach to identifying and managing the risk of every conceivable peril that might cause a company a loss. Use your knowledge of enterprise risk management to guide you in managing the risk in your life – your personal financial management company.

Learn what the insurance industry means by the term "loss control program", and incorporate a loss control program in your business plan and projected financial statement budget.

Ask for risk management advice from the professionals on your business team.
- *Insurance agent*: risk management is THE business of insurance professionals.

- o *The less you know about risk management, the more beneficial it would be to work with an insurance professional who has earned a good reputation as a risk management advisor.*
  - o A good insurance professional can advise you about risks to consider avoiding, risks that might make good economic sense to transfer through insurance, and ways to manage risks you decide to accept or have no alternative but to accept.
  - o Seek an insurance agent or a direct writing insurance company whose business model and marketing materials feature providing risk management advice.
  - o Seek a best value package of advice and price. Don't shop for insurance so much as you seek to hire a good risk management advisor.
- *Financial advisor*: financial risk management is a key element of the business of good financial advisors.
  - o *The less you know about investing and financial risk management, the more beneficial it would be to hire a good financial advisor.*
  - o When deciding about where and how to invest your money, seek a financial advisor (e.g. mutual fund company) whose business model and marketing materials feature providing financial risk management advice.
- *Banker*: financial risk management is a key element of the business of good bankers.
- *Attorney*: consider talking to an attorney who has earned a good reputation as a "counselor" advising clients how to manage the risks of legal perils in their lives. If you are planning to get married, consider talking to an attorney who has expertise and experience in (a) counseling people who are planning to get married about prenuptial agreements and (b) preparing prenuptial agreements that minimize the financial risk of the peril of divorce but "don't wreck a marriage before it gets started".

Identify your "risk tolerance" level.
- Everybody has a different tolerance for risk – amount of risk a person is willing to accept.
- Identify how much risk you are willing to accept (tolerate) in your life.
- Your risk tolerance level should guide your planning, budgeting, and decision making.

Think of lifestyle risk as being on a continuum.
- On one end of the continuum is the lowest risk lifestyle you could possibly choose to live and still go out of your house to work and maintain human relationships. Characteristics might include being ultra-cautious and conservative, spending as little money as prudently possible, and investing only in FDIC insured bank accounts and treasury bills.
- On the other end is the highest risk lifestyle you could choose to live and remain alive. Characteristics might include spending all your income on a daring, carefree, freewheeling, "devil may care" lifestyle while letting the future take care of itself, and investing all of your money as venture capital in start-up companies.
- Somewhere in the middle is where each of us is likely to find a lifestyle that provides a satisfying level of joy and financial prosperity at a risk level we can tolerate comfortably.

Are you risk tolerant or risk averse? Don't try to kid yourself. It is likely that you will save yourself regret and heartache in the future if you are honest with yourself today. Ask yourself:
- Regarding investment planning: would you rather accept less risk of losing money by investing in assets that have the potential to earn less return, or accept greater risk of losing money by investing in assets that have the potential to earn a greater return?
- Regarding career path planning: would you rather take a longer, less risky career path toward your dream job in a mature industry, or take a faster, more risky shot at "hitting the big time" in a high tech start-up company?

- Regarding marriage: would you rather elope in the heat of the moment after meeting "the woman of your dreams", or date her long enough to get to know what she is really like before making a legal commitment in marriage?

This book reflects my bias toward low to moderate risk strategies. My bias is based upon:
- Observation of many successful people over many years who have used low to moderate risk strategies to achieve success in their lives.
- A career in the insurance industry surrounded by people whose business it is to help clients manage the risk in their lives.
- All the mistakes I have made in my life (and hopefully learned from).
- All the mistakes I have observed or heard about other people making after they chose to take greater risk than a prudent person would have taken – at least in the eyes of professionals whose business model includes providing risk management advice, e.g. surety agent, insurance agent, banker, financial advisor, accountant, attorney.
- A belief that low to moderate risk strategies can guide people on a more predictable, more "plan-able", more successful journey through life toward achieving their objectives and realizing their dreams - a less "wild ride" through life.

Consider adopting some of the low to moderate risk strategies mentioned in this book, such as:
- Use the "prudent person" rule of thumb - do what a prudent person would do and avoid doing what a prudent person would avoid doing.
- Surround yourself with good people who use low to moderate risk strategies in living their lives.
- Hire professionals to do things that would be "risky" for you to do yourself.
- Plan a series of small step "milestone" objectives that lead toward achieving your long term objectives. "The longer the leap, the greater the risk of not being able to make it successfully."
- Don't "stretch yourself too thin." Don't overextend your resources:
  - o Financial resources: live below your means; don't take on more debt than your current financial statement and project financial statement budget would deem prudent.
  - o Time: don't commit yourself to doing things that you don't think you have enough time to do well enough.
  - o Skills and abilities: try to avoid doing things that common sense tells you that you don't yet have the skills, ability, or experience to do at that point in time.
- Plan for change. Try to anticipate change and proactively manage the risks of change.
- Seek a career path with an employer who values employees as an investment in "human capital".
- Treat wealth building as a long term marathon not a short term sprint. Seek a reasonable rate of return on investments over a longer period of time rather than trying to "make a killing in the market" in a short period of time.
- Plan for a good "spread of risk": "don't put all your eggs in one basket"; diversify your investment portfolio; don't concentrate too much risk in any one financial institution.
- Buy best value, not lowest price.
- Read purchase agreements, professional service agreements, and other forms of contracts before signing them in order to minimize the risk of getting stuck with onerous terms.
- Have a Plan B ready to implement just in case Plan A isn't working. Practice the motto of the Boy Scouts of America "Be prepared".

Identify, avoid, transfer, manage

Identify the risks of the perils in the lifestyle you are living today and the risks of perils you can reasonably expect to encounter in the lifestyle you plan to live tomorrow. You might start by writing a list of specific risks that immediately come to mind, perhaps:

- Risk of losing your job and the income you get from it.
- Risk that your good job might take a significant turn for the worse to being not such a good job if a change in management was to occur, e.g. good supervisor being replaced by a not so good supervisor, or significant change in a good senior management team.
- Risk of not saving enough money and accumulating enough net worth to help finance the lifestyle you want to live in your later years.
- Risk of losing money on your investments.
- Risk of not being able to repay debt you accumulated, e.g. credit card, school loan, mortgage.
- Risk of an expensive medical condition.
- Risk of a long term impairment of your ability to do your job.
- Risk of losing your home and personal possessions in a house fire or catastrophic weather event.
- Risks associated with the location of your current home, and any location where you might plan to live in the future.
  - Catastrophic weather events - learn about and plan for 100 year weather events and the impact of evolving global weather patterns.
  - Flood.
  - Earthquake.
  - Wild fire.
  - Changing climate conditions and ocean water levels.
  - Catastrophes caused by man, e.g. pollution of water or land caused by a leak from a nearby trash dump or waste storage facility.
  - Changes in real estate zoning or public rights of way plans that could hurt your property value, e.g. new roads, public transportation lines, utility transmission lines.
  - Significant increase in property taxes, e.g. gentrification.

Then you might list some of the general risks inherent in life, such as:

- The world as "we used to know it" is continually changing (evolving).
- Nothing in life is perfectly predictable.
  - If experts could always predict exactly what would happen in the future, there would be no need to run races or play ball games, and every financial advisor would be a billionaire.
  - "Nothing in life is guaranteed but death and taxes." There are precious few "sure things" in life and in financial management. Be real skeptical if anyone tells you that anything involving business or an investment is a sure thing.
  - Murphy's Law "if it can go wrong, it will go wrong." Murphy's Law came into being (and has been stated in various ways for so long) because it has proven so true to so many people for so long.
  - Unintended consequences: things that we had no intention to make happen sometimes do happen as the result of things we say and do. Whereas everything in life is connected either directly or indirectly, everything that we do will lead to other stuff happening. We can make the best-informed, best-reasoned decisions about what to do, but after we take action we can never know for sure what chain

of future events our actions might be setting in motion.
- o Unforeseen and unknowable events occur - curve balls get thrown at us.
- We can't have perfect decision making information.
  - o *We don't know what we don't know*, therefore we can't know for sure what information we should have tried to get prior to making a decision.
  - o We can't have perfect knowledge of every single piece of information that might impact a decision outcome. Almost always there is something we don't know that creates some measure of risk in whatever we decide do.
- Human behavior is not perfectly predictable.
  - o There isn't a single perfect person on this planet. We each have our own set of imperfections – our own human weaknesses – that cause us to do unpredictable things on occasion.
  - o People cooperate at certain times to get what they need or want and compete at other times in order to get what they need or want.
    - ▪ Friends and colleagues might cooperate to get something that they all want when there is enough supply of that thing for everybody to get all that they want of that thing, but then they might switch to competing with each other if supply decreases or demand increases to the point that there isn't enough supply for everyone to get all that they want.
    - ▪ It can be tough to predict exactly when people will cooperate and when they will compete.
  - o People act irrationally at times. Even the most level headed, rational thinking people get overwhelmed by their emotions or hormones on occasion and begin to act irrationally.
  - o Some people can't actually do what they say they can do.
  - o Some good people make mistakes.
  - o Some people are just bad people who would seek to profit at your expense.
- *No company is perfect.*
  - o Companies are just groups of imperfect people.
  - o As much as marketing professionals would like us to think otherwise, companies do not operate with perfect efficiency without ever making mistakes.
  - o A company may seem to be pretty perfect during the course of one business transaction or even over the course of a number of years, but eventually it is likely that at least one employee within a company will do or not do something that could cause you harm.

Then try to calculate the degree of harm that that each risk could cause you, and prioritize that degree of risk in your mind.
- *Risks that pose significant danger* to you and your money should be addressed in your business plan and financial budget, and specifically factored into your decisions.
- *Risks that pose <u>insignificant</u> danger* to you and your money (e.g. the risk that an ice cream cone may drip down onto your shirt versus the relative drip free risk of a cup of ice cream) would be better to tuck away in the back of your mind for recall at the time you make your next ice cream purchase decision.

Avoid risk
- As you make significant lifestyle choices and routine daily decisions, *avoid risk that the proverbial "prudent person" would try to avoid.* As parents often say, "stay away from trouble."
- Deciding to not expose yourself to certain perils is one way to help avoid risk:

- o Not making certain types of high risk investments.
- o Not developing relationships with certain high risk people.
- o Not putting yourself in certain high risk locations or situations.
- o Not buying or using things known to have a high risk of causing harm.
- "Stick to your knitting." Do what you know how to do well, and avoid doing risky things that you don't do as well as experts in their fields could do for you.

Don't accept unnecessary risk in contracts you are asked to sign.
- *Read contracts before signing them.*
  - o You are responsible for reading and understanding all the terms and conditions of legal documents before you sign them.
  - o After you sign a contract, professional services agreement, or a bill of sale for a product, you are legally bound by the terms and conditions of that document.
  - o Buyers beware - *"caveat emptor"*. If you hadn't bothered to read the fine print and tried to understand terms and conditions before signing, and then after signing you discovered terms or conditions that you didn't like, typically you would be stuck.
- Don't accept an unfair request to waive legal liability that should be borne by another party in a contract.
- Have an attorney review legal documents of significance such as an employment contract.

Transfer risk that the proverbial "prudent person" would try to transfer by means of:
- Buying insurance
- Hiring people who have greater expertise and experience than you have in doing things that pose significant risk, such as a financial advisor, electrician, or plumber. For example, if you are "all thumbs" with home improvements, hire a professional electrician or plumber as needed so you don't burn down your house or flood it.

Regarding insurance: consider buying insurance to transfer financial risks that are reasonably transferable.
- Ask your insurance professional to explain the following types of policies:
  - o Homeowner's or renter's policy to cover damage or loss of your property (building and contents) and your legal liability under "tort law".
  - o Flood insurance (and the National Flood Insurance Program)
  - o Automobile
  - o Excess personal liability ("umbrella")
  - o Healthcare: medical, dental, eye care
  - o Long term disability
  - o Life
- Ask your insurance professional to explain:
  - o Exactly what coverage is available in each policy he recommends.
  - o Meanings of deductibles, exclusions, and warranty clauses in each policy you decide to consider.
- Regarding the selection of an insurance professional with whom to work, learn about the following two business models:
  - o *American Agency System*: independent insurance agents represent a variety of insurance companies from which they can select an insurance company(s) that they think provides the best match for each client's insurance needs in terms of the financial strength and stability of the company, the company's

reputation for paying claims, insurance coverages offered, and pricing, etc. In full disclosure, I am an independent agent.
- o *Direct writing insurance companies*: insurance is sold by insurance company employees who represent only the insurance company for which they work.
- Regarding the purchase price of insurance - seek to buy best value.
  - o "You get what you pay for." Cheapest price typically is not the best value.
    - Research the business practices of insurance companies who advertise that their prices are lower than their competitors' prices.
    - Ask low priced insurers how they can afford to provide the same coverage and the same level of policyholder services at their lower prices.
  - o Prices you will be charged by an insurance company are a function of things such as:
    - Your "loss history" – claims made by you in the past and losses for which insurance companies have reimbursed you.
    - Historical claims paid in the past to members of demographic groups into which the insurance company would place you.
    - The "law of large numbers" – learn about it.
    - Projections made by the insurance company's actuaries of future claims that the company is likely to pay to members of the above mentioned demographic groups (ask your insurance professional to explain the roles of actuaries and actuarial projections in the insurance business).
    - The probability they think they will have to pay a claim made by you.
    - The insurance company's <u>loss ratio</u> and <u>combined ratio</u> (learn about these ratios) for the type of policy being sold ("line of business").
    - Deductible, exclusion, and policyholder warranty clauses included in the policy being sold. Learn how insurance companies use these tools in pricing their products.
    - Investment income the insurance company projects that it will be able to earn on the aggregate premium dollars they collect each year from all policyholders.
    - Prices being charged by their competitor insurance companies.
- Buy insurance from insurance companies that have:
  - o Good A. M. Best Company ratings - a measure of an insurance company's financial strength and the likelihood that will be around in the future to pay claims. Ask your insurance professional for the A. M. Best rating of each prospective insurance company, and ask for an explanation of what the rating means (you might also check out the A. M. Best Company website).
  - o Reputations for good policyholder service and claim payments.
- Ask prospective insurance professionals what "loss control" suggestions they can offer you. Good insurance professionals like to suggest ways their clients can minimize their risk of future loss, thereby minimizing their "out of pocket costs" and premium expenses – a win-win scenario for insurer (insurance company) and insured (you).

If you volunteer as a director or officer of a non-profit organization:
- Tell your insurance professional about your volunteer position(s), and ask for advice about:
  - o Insurance you should buy for yourself.
  - o Insurance the organization should buy to protect you from a lawsuit.

- Ask to see a copy of the directors and officers liability policy (D&O policy) the organization has purchased to protect you from legal liability.

Regarding hiring people who have greater expertise and experience than you have in doing things that pose significant risk:
- Ask your insurance professional for advice about insurance that people you hire should have in order to protect you from financial harm you might suffer as a result of their work.
- Ask for a "certificate of insurance" from people you consider hiring. A certificate of insurance will tell you the type and amount of insurance that they have. You might also ask your insurance professional for his opinion about the insurance (e.g. amount and coverage available to protect you and the quality of the insurance company).

Manage risk that you can't avoid or transfer. A few ideas to stimulate your thinking:
- *Loss of your job*
    o Try to exceed your employer's expectations of you (see Chapter 14).
    o Develop a Plan B for another job you could go to just in case:
        ▪ Injury or illness rendered you unable to do your current job.
        ▪ Your employer eliminated your job position, or reduced your compensation to an unacceptable level.
        ▪ You made a big mistake and got fired.
        ▪ A weather disaster destroyed your workplace.
        ▪ Your company went out of business.
- *Loss of money on your investments*:
    o Hire a professional financial advisor!
    o "Spread your risk"
        ▪ Adopt an age appropriate diversification strategy to diversify the assets in your investment portfolio.
        ▪ Depending upon the amount of money you have available to invest, consider splitting your invested money among two or more financial institutions or financial advisors.
    o Ask one or more confidants on your business team who have proven to be successful investors to critique your investment strategy and the diversification of assets in your portfolio.
- *Crime* (burglary, theft, fraud, scam artists, embezzlement, etc.)
    o Maintain an awareness that the greater your annual income and the greater the wealth that you accumulate, the greater the risk that others will be motivated to try to take some of your money away from you.
        ▪ Don't let the world know how much money you have; "play your cards close to your vest" in regard to your annual revenue and net worth.
        ▪ Beware conspicuous consumption.
        ▪ Don't advertise how much money you might have by wearing expensive looking jewelry and clothes "out on the street".
        ▪ Think about how an expensive car might attract car-jackers and robbers.
    o Identity theft
        ▪ Ask your insurance professional and appropriate business team members for advice about how to manage this risk.
        ▪ Research the vast amount of information online.

- Damage to your home that would require you to move out for some period of time. Develop a "business continuity plan" for living arrangements and management of your financial affairs.
  - o A place in which to live and continue managing your business efficiently while your home is being repaired or replaced.
  - o Secure your valuable papers in a fireproof box at home or "off-site" in a bank safe deposit box, e.g. birth certificate, social security card, home mortgage and loan papers, marriage license, employment records, military records, will.
  - o Maintain electronic copies of paper documents.
  - o Take an inventory of the assets in your home and valuables you have stored off premises.
- *Risk of legal liability*
  - o Plan to do what society says you should do.
    - Statutory laws.
    - Norms of proper behavior.
    - "Common law".
    - The prudent person rule.
  - o Learn about, and prudently protect yourself against, three types of "feasance" (a legal word for action or inaction). Following are my best shot at working definitions:
    - Nonfeasance: failure to do something a person should have done.
    - Misfeasance: intentionally doing something incorrectly (e.g. cutting corners to save money), but without intent to cause anyone harm.
    - Malfeasance: doing something with an intent to cause harm (illegal act).
  - o "Contract" lawsuits arising from specific contracts you sign. Be sure you understand and abide by the terms to which you obligate yourself in contracts such as:
    - Employment contract with an employer.
    - Confidentiality / non-compete agreement.
  - o "Tort law" lawsuits: lawsuits that can be brought against you by someone with whom you don't have any specific contract obligations. Take proper precautions to protect yourself against lawsuits that arise as the result of things such as:
    - "Attractive nuisances" on your property, e.g. swimming pool, swing set.
    - Keeping your home and property in good shape so as to prevent injury to others.
    - Acts of your children and pets.
    - Driving a car, boat, wave runner, or all-terrain vehicle.
    - Being a volunteer leader in a non-profit organization.
  - o Learn about "contributory negligence".
  - o Plan how you would defend yourself if you were wrongly accused of some crime, such as sexual harassment.
- If your career path plan is leading you toward starting your own commercial business as an entrepreneur, consider setting up a limited liability company or corporation to "shield" yourself from legal liability. Learn about the "corporate veil", and how "gross negligence" (severe negligence) can pierce the corporate veil.

About the Author

A 40 year career in the surety bond industry gave Steve the opportunity to work with, and learn from, a wide variety of successful business people – company presidents, financial officers, CPA's, attorneys, business consultants, financial advisors, and surety industry colleagues. His work provided 40 years of continuous continuing education in business and financial management through analyzing and evaluating the business plans, financial budgets, cash flow projections, management practices, and performance track records of all sorts of successful businesses.

Experience in varied work and volunteer positions enabled him to learn about business and financial management from different perspectives:
- Military: officer in the United States Army.
- Non-profit organization paid employee: District Executive of the Boy Scouts of America.
- Non-profit organization volunteer: officer and director positions in a number of trade associations; church board of trustees; officer of homeowners' associations; coach of recreation league and youth sports teams.
- Business: surety bond underwriter; surety company branch manager; partner in an insurance agency; officer of M&T Insurance Agency, Inc., a subsidiary of M&T Bank.

Experience as a parent helped him learn and re-learn valuable money management lessons, and how to talk about business and financial matters in terms young people understand.

Experience as a teacher of Junior Achievement classes and career related classes on business management and business finance gave him the opportunity to learn from preparing lesson plans and class presentations, students' comments, information shared by students in class, and trying to answer students' insightful questions.

Formal education
- Bachelor of Science, Business Administration, University of New Hampshire
- Master of Science, University of Baltimore
- United States Army: Infantry Officers Basic Class and Psychological Operations School
- Boy Scouts of America: District Executive Training School
- Aetna Casualty and Surety Company: Bond Trainee Program
- Continuous continuing education classes and seminars

Printed in the United States
by Baker & Taylor Publisher Services